NORTH VIETNAM

DMZ

QUANG
PRO...

Hue
(1)

Da Nang

LAOS

THAILAND

Mekong River

Central Highlands

CAMBODIA

Kontum

Pleiku

(1)

(7B)

Tuy Hoa

S O U T H

Ban Me Thuot

Mekong River

PHUOC LONG
PROVINCE

QUANG DUC
PROVINCE

Phuoc
Binh

V I E T N A M

Nha Trang

Dalat

Cam Ranh Bay

Boa Loc

Phnom Penh

CHAU DOC
PROVINCE

(1) Bien Hoa

Xuan Loc

(1)

Saigon

Vung Tau

*Phu Quoc
Island*

Can Tho

Vi Thanh

Bassac River

Mekong Delta

South China Sea

Con Son Island

| 0 Miles | | 100 |
| 0 Kilometers | | 100 |

FOAL

Honorable Exit

Also by Thurston Clarke

JFK's Last Hundred Days
The Last Campaign
Ask Not
Searching for Crusoe
California Fault
Pearl Harbor Ghosts
Equator
Thirteen O'Clock
Lost Hero
By Blood and Fire
The Last Caravan
Dirty Money

Honorable Exit

HOW A FEW BRAVE AMERICANS
RISKED ALL
TO SAVE OUR VIETNAMESE ALLIES
AT THE END OF THE WAR

Thurston Clarke

Doubleday

New York

Book design by Maria Carella
Endpaper map designed by Jeffrey L. Ward
Jacket design by Emily Mahon
Jacket photograph © Dirck Halstead/The LIFE Images Collection/Getty Images

Library of Congress Cataloging-in-Publication Data
Names: Clarke, Thurston, author.
Title: Honorable exit : how a few brave Americans risked all to save our
Vietnamese allies at the end of the war / Thurston Clarke.
Other titles: How a few brave Americans risked all to save our Vietnamese
allies at the end of the war
Description: First edition. | New York : Doubleday, [2019] | Includes
bibliographical references and index.
Identifiers: LCCN 2018029232 (print) | LCCN 2018042953 (ebook) |
ISBN 9780385539654 (ebook) | ISBN 9780385539647 (hardcover)
Subjects: LCSH: Vietnam War, 1961–1975—Evacuation of civilians—Vietnam
(Republic) | Vietnam War, 1961–1975—Campaigns. | Vietnam War,
1961–1975—Diplomatic history. | Vietnam (Republic)—Foreign
relations—United States. | United States—Foreign relations—
Vietnam (Republic)
Classification: LCC DS557.7 (ebook) | LCC DS557.7 .C53 2019 (print) |
DDC 959.704/31—dc23
LC record available at https://lccn.loc.gov/2018029232

MANUFACTURED IN THE UNITED STATES OF AMERICA

1 3 5 7 9 10 8 6 4 2

First Edition

FOR TOM GILLILAND AND BEN WEIR

Contents

CONTENTS

Principal Characters

WASHINGTON, D.C.

PRESIDENT GERALD FORD

HENRY KISSINGER: secretary of state and national security adviser

JAMES SCHLESINGER: secretary of defense

BRENT SCOWCROFT: National Security Council deputy adviser

DAVID KENNERLY: President Ford's personal photographer

KENNETH QUINN: National Security Council staff member

CRAIG JOHNSTONE and LIONEL ROSENBLATT: Foreign Service officers who
   return to Saigon to rescue their Vietnamese friends

SOUTH VIETNAM

State Department

GRAHAM MARTIN: U.S. ambassador to South Vietnam

WOLFGANG LEHMANN: deputy chief of mission

DON HAYS: Foreign Service officer whom Martin expels from South
   Vietnam

JOE MCBRIDE: Foreign Service officer

FRANCIS TERRY MCNAMARA: consul general in Can Tho

WALTER MARTINDALE: Foreign Service officer in Quang Duc province

KEN MOOREFIELD: Foreign Service officer, former special assistant to
   Ambassador Martin

THERESA TULL: acting consul general in Da Nang

Defense Attaché Office

MAJOR GENERAL HOMER SMITH: U.S. defense attaché

BRIGADIER GENERAL RICHARD BAUGHN: deputy defense attaché

ANDREW GEMBARA: plainclothes military intelligence officer at Defense Attaché Office

Department of Defense and U.S. Military

ERICH VON MARBOD: deputy assistant secretary of defense

RICHARD ARMITAGE: former naval officer with extensive experience in South Vietnam

COLONEL AL GRAY: Marine Corps officer in charge of the ground security force at Tan Son Nhut on April 29

LIEUTENANT GENERAL RICHARD CAREY: commander of the Ninth Marine Amphibious Brigade

U.S. Delegation to the Four-Party Joint Military Team

COLONEL JOHN MADISON: head of U.S. delegation

LIEUTENANT COLONEL HARRY SUMMERS

CAPTAIN STUART HERRINGTON

SPECIALIST 7 GARRETT "BILL" BELL

Central Intelligence Agency

THOMAS POLGAR: Saigon chief of station

JAMES DELANEY: base chief in Can Tho

O. B. HARNAGE: U.S. embassy deputy air operations officer

JAMES PARKER: CIA agent in the Mekong delta

National Security Agency

TOM GLENN: senior NSA official in South Vietnam

Civilians

MARIUS BURKE: pilot who helps prepare rooftop helipads in Saigon

ED DALY: president of World Airways

BRIAN ELLIS: CBS Saigon bureau chief

ROSS MEADOR: program director for Friends of the Children of Vietnam

BILL RYDER: deputy chief of the U.S. Military Sealift Command

AL TOPPING: Pan Am station manager

Honorable Exit

Prologue:
The Man in the White Shirt

———┤├———

On the afternoon of April 29, 1975, Dutch photojournalist Hubert "Hugh" Van Es looked out the window at the United Press International (UPI) office in downtown Saigon and saw a helicopter landing on an elevator shaft rising from the roof of 22 Gia Long Street. Van Es grabbed his camera and a 300 mm lens and hurried onto the balcony. As a man in a white shirt was reaching down to help a person at the top of a staircase board the helicopter, Van Es took the last great iconic photograph of the Vietnam War. A UPI editor in Tokyo misidentified the building as the American embassy, and despite later corrections the mistake has survived in books, in articles, and on the internet, perhaps because placing the helicopter on the roof of the embassy makes the photograph a more potent symbol for America's first lost war.

Compare the Van Es photograph with the even more iconic one that Associated Press (AP) reporter Joe Rosenthal shot of six U.S. servicemen raising an American flag on the summit of Mount Suribachi during the World War II battle for Iwo Jima. Both were taken near the end of a war, and both show Americans framed against an open sky—reaching up to plant a flag or down to grab a refugee. Otherwise, they seem to have nothing in common. One symbolizes victory in a war Americans have spent decades celebrating; the other, defeat in a war they have spent decades trying to forget. One represents courage and sacrifice; the other, catastrophe and disgrace. But the more one learns about the staircase on the roof of 22 Gia Long Street, the people standing on it, the pilots of that helicopter, and the man in the white shirt, the more apparent it becomes that Van Es had also memorialized a moment of stirring heroism.

He later described the 22 Gia Long Street stairway as a "makeshift wooden ladder." But zoom in from a different angle and with a stronger lens, as French photojournalist Philippe Buffon did that same afternoon, and it becomes a sturdy staircase wide enough to be climbed by four people abreast. Zoom in some more and the helicopter becomes a Bell Huey 205 painted in the blue and white livery of Air America, one of the CIA's proprietary airlines, and you can see that the man in the white shirt has a seven-day beard, a black patch over his left eye, and a cigar clenched in his teeth and that his shirt is ripped and filthy. Patrons of Saigon's rowdier bars would recognize him as Oren Bartholomew "O. B." Harnage, the U.S. embassy's deputy air operations officer and a middle-aged roustabout described by one friend as "a gregarious, macho good old boy, a bull-shitter of the first order . . . [and] suds-sipper of renown." The cigar was one of the seven that Harnage smoked daily, perhaps as an homage to his father, a Tampa cigar roller who had abandoned him at birth, in either 1925 or 1926—he was uncertain which. He had volunteered for the navy at seventeen (or eighteen) and been wounded on Okinawa. A sliver of old shrapnel had worked its way into his left eye the previous month, explaining the patch. He had joined the air force after the war, moved to the CIA as a contract employee, and after seven years in Laos and Vietnam had concluded that America had been "naïve" to involve itself in the Vietnam War.

Earlier that afternoon CIA chief of station Thomas Polgar had asked him to commandeer one of the Air America helicopters that had been landing on the embassy roof and direct its pilots to 22 Gia Long Street to evacuate a group of Polgar's personal friends and senior South Vietnamese officials. Risking his life to rescue some dignitaries rubbed Harnage the wrong way. He decided instead to board everyone, he explained later, "first come, first served . . . ladies and infants being the exception." After landing on the Gia Long Street roof, he punched out a burly Korean diplomat (a Polgar VIP) who had elbowed the other evacuees aside, and threw large suitcases—some heavy with gold bars—off the roof. Parents handed him their children before climbing back down the stairs in tears. Notes pinned to the children's shirts read, "My son wants to be a doctor," and "My daughter is very musical."

Van Es photographed Harnage as he was leaning down to grab Dr. Thiet-Tan Nguyen, a young military doctor who would become an anesthesiologist in Southern California. Next he grabbed Dr. Tong Huyhn, who would practice family medicine in a suburb of Atlanta. Next came Tuyet-Dong Bui, a slender teenage girl who will call herself Janet at the California university where she will earn a degree in microbiology before becoming a biotech researcher. Hours before, a stray bullet had killed one of her high school classmates, and her mother had urged her to leave. Her brother, who stood a rung below her, had traded his motorbike to the chauffeur of a high-ranking military officer in exchange for being led here. Standing below him was a Polgar VIP, Minister of Defense Tran Van Don, who had recently told South Vietnamese troops, "In the coming hours, in the coming days, I will be by your side."

Elevator shafts like the one at 22 Gia Long Street usually have a rudimentary iron or wood ladder so mechanics can climb up and service their machinery. Yet no one seeing the Van Es photograph appears to have asked why such a large and sturdy staircase happened to be leading to the top of the elevator shaft—in effect, leading nowhere. It was there because on April 6 Marine Corps colonel Al Gray had flown over downtown Saigon in a helicopter, surveying the roofs of buildings leased by U.S. government agencies. Air America pilots Marius Burke and Nikki Fillipi had then inspected the roofs that Gray believed capable of supporting a helicopter, gauging their strength and checking for obstructions. After choosing the thirteen most promising ones, they had supervised a crew of American contractors who rerouted electrical and telephone cables and removed flagpoles and washing lines. The contractors custom built two staircases for 22 Gia Long Street: a short one leading from the main roof to an intermediate platform, and a longer one connecting that platform to the top of the elevator shaft. Their staircases had handrails and short steps so that children and the disabled could climb them.

Major General Homer Smith, the U.S. defense attaché and senior military officer in South Vietnam, approved Burke and Fillipi's preparations, but Ambassador Graham Martin was furious when he learned about their makeshift helipads. He believed that any indication that the United States was preparing an evacuation would demoralize South Vietnam's military, undermine the government of President Nguyen Van Thieu, and lead to revenge attacks on American civilians. He refused Burke's request to pre-position barrels of fuel on the roofs, park helicopters on them overnight, and paint an *H* in green Day-Glo paint on them that matched the dimensions of a Huey's skids so that Air America pilots could see which ones had been converted to helipads and where to align their skids to ensure a 360-degree clearance. Martin argued that the *H* might alarm the Vietnamese washerwomen who dried laundry on the roofs. On his own building's roof, Burke painted the outline of an *H* in green dots that he later connected. Other Air America pilots ignored Martin and painted a green *H* on other helipads.

Bob Caron and Jack Hunter piloted the helicopter that landed on 22 Gia Long Street. They were among the thirty-one middle-aged Air America pilots who had volunteered to make these hazardous flights. Before Harnage recruited them to rescue Polgar's VIPs, they had been setting down wherever they saw people standing on a roof with an *H*. Caron was a West Point graduate and Vietnam War veteran who, like Harnage, did not give a hoot if the people he collected from these roofs were high or low priority, government ministers or their chauffeurs. He was rescuing them, he said, "to preserve America's honor." By the time Van Es took his iconic photograph, Caron and Hunter had made three pickups from Gia Long Street. Each time they lifted off, Caron shouted to the people being left behind on the stairs, "We'll make as many runs as we can!"

A Huey could carry twelve combat-loaded American soldiers, but because Vietnamese are smaller and many of the evacuees were women and children, Harnage packed twenty people onto every flight. To make more room, he rode outside, standing on a skid while holding a Swedish machine gun in one hand. A passenger gripped his other arm to prevent him from falling to his death in case he was hit by ground fire from North Vietnamese troops or disgruntled South Vietnamese soldiers. (Earlier that day, while stopping at Tan Son Nhut to transfer his passengers onto one of the larger Marine Corps helicopters that were shuttling out to the U.S. fleet, Caron had noticed a bullet hole in his drive shaft.) Harnage had suffered wounds on Okinawa while fighting for his country and his comrades; on April 29, he was risking his life to turn a few more Vietnamese strangers into American citizens.

Van Es had captured Caron's last pickup from Gia Long Street. Caron was almost out of gas and would have to fly half an hour out to the U.S. Navy fleet to refuel. As he lifted off for the last time, he met the eyes of those he was leaving behind—people who were unlikely to become doctors, musicians, biotech researchers, or anything else in the United States and might instead be among the hundreds of thousands of "class enemies" that the Communists would send to a gulag of "reeducation" camps. Some would be incarcerated for as long as seventeen years, unless they died first from malnutrition, disease, hard labor, and mistreatment. It was in their eyes, Caron thought, that "you could see they knew we were never coming back." Harnage never forgot their "pleading eyes" and would remember his last flight from Gia Long Street as a "nightmare" of people "waiting on a ladder for a helicopter that does not return." All across Saigon on April 29, Americans avoided Vietnamese eyes. As a group walked down a boulevard toward an evacuation bus, passing Vietnamese watching silently from the doorways of their homes and shops, one man kept saying, "Don't look in their eyes. . . . Don't look in their eyes. . . . Don't look in their eyes." A reporter who had refused to help her Vietnamese translator and his family escape, telling herself they would be "better off" in Saigon, never forgot "the look of supplication in the eyes of his wife and children." Decades later, an American diplomat remained haunted by "the look in the eyes of those I had to leave behind."

As Caron's helicopter lifted off, a passenger noticed her teenage son standing on the stairs and burst into tears. Tuyet-Dong "Janet" Bui had been excited to take her first helicopter ride, but as Saigon slipped away, she thought, "Oh my God, I don't know where I'm going. I don't know anybody. Where are my parents?" and began weeping. She and the other passengers were, in their way, as courageous as Caron and Harnage. They were leaving behind friends, family, country, and culture to become exiles in a nation where, according to a recent poll, two-thirds of its citizens did not want them. On the same day that Harnage's evacuees were flying over Saigon, U.S. senator George McGovern, who had run for president in 1972 on an antiwar platform, was telling reporters in Ohio, "I am opposed to large numbers of Vietnamese coming, not only because I think it is not in our interests. I don't think it is in their interest. I think the Vietnamese are better off in Vietnam, including the orphans."

Harnage looked down from the skids of Caron's helicopter and saw smoke: puffs of smoke rising from backyards where South Vietnamese were burning photographs, documents, and anything else connecting them to the United States or the Thieu government; plumes of it spiraling from the American embassy as diplomats fed files into a rooftop incinerator; black clouds of it billowing from oil tanks and warehouses along the docks; and more smoke marking the bridges and boulevards where some South Vietnamese soldiers were mounting a brave resistance so that politicians like Tran Van Don could escape on helicopters like this one.

Caron's helicopter joined dozens of others stitching a patchwork of contrails across the sky. Helicopters had become symbolic of the Vietnam War, and their whomp-whomp-whomping was its descant. They flew troops into battle, rescued the wounded, retrieved the dead, and brought journalists and generals back to Saigon for clean sheets and French restaurants. Before Senator Robert F. Kennedy opposed the Vietnam War, he had told a reporter that the United States would win it because it had helicopters. "We have them," he said, "the French did not." Instead, America's first helicopter war would become its first lost war, one ending with the largest helicopter evacuation in military history.

The passengers on Harnage's last run were among the 1,000 evacuees whom Air America pilots extracted from rooftops and paddies on April 29. Between noon and 5:00 a.m. the next day, U.S. military and civilian helicopters airlifted 1,373 Americans and 5,595 South Vietnamese and third-country nationals to the U.S. fleet. Add them to the 45,000 South Vietnamese and third-country nationals that U.S. Air Force transports had evacuated during the month of April, the 73,000 South Vietnamese that the U.S. Navy rescued at sea, the 2,000 Vietnamese airmen and their families who escaped to Thailand, and the others who had already left on Air America fixed-wing planes and so-called black flights, and you have more than 130,000 South Vietnamese refugees whom the U.S. government and military would process through transit camps in the Philippines, Wake Island, and Guam before flying them to relocation camps on the U.S. mainland. It would be the greatest evacuation under wartime conditions since Dunkirk and the largest humanitarian operation in American history, although at the time few Americans recognized or celebrated it as such. It occurred largely because U.S. military personnel, government employees, and private citizens staged a spontaneous, uncoordinated, and clandestine mutiny against the policies and inaction of senior U.S. officials in Saigon and Washington, and against the wishes and prejudices of a majority of Americans and their elected representatives in Congress, risking their careers and lives to evacuate South Vietnamese who they believed were facing years of incarceration or worse under a Communist regime.

Jackie Bong, the widow of a South Vietnamese politician assassinated by the Vietcong, later compared the Americans who spirited her out of Saigon to the Righteous Gentiles of the Holocaust, men like Raoul Wallenberg and Oskar Schindler. The wife of a U.S. Foreign Service officer arranged to have Bong and her children collected in a car with diplomatic plates. As they neared the airport, their chauffeur pulled in to a villa that American diplomats were using as a safe house for stashing their Vietnamese evacuees. Bong and her children were hustled into a large black sedan flying an American flag from one bumper and a South Vietnamese flag from the other. Jim Eckes, a longtime American resident of Saigon who managed a charter airline, sat in front next to the driver. Bong and her children climbed into the backseat to join Pat Barnett, an American in his late thirties whom Eckes introduced as "your husband." President Thieu had ordered the MPs and national police manning the gate at Tan Son Nhut airport to arrest South Vietnamese attempting to leave without passports and exit visas. Eckes explained that they would bluff their way through by having her pretend to be the Vietnamese wife of a senior U.S. official. "I was being shipped out clandestinely with the help of Americans," she wrote later. "It reminded me of the stories of Jews being helped to flee Europe during World War II."

Others made the same comparison. Teenager Linh Duy Vo escaped from Saigon on an American helicopter on April 29. He settled in California, where he raised a family and became a poet. He credited the U.S. defense attaché in South Vietnam, Major General Homer Smith, with saving his life, writing in a poem, "The general issued an order, / His soldier put my name on the list . . . / I will never forget my American Schindler." He established the General Homer Smith Prize, awarded annually to "a U.S. citizen's distinguished contribution which makes one proud to be an American." In 2011 he traveled eighty-seven hours round trip on Greyhound buses to attend Smith's funeral in San Antonio, writing in a tribute, "You had saved thousands of lives, a repeat of the Schindler's List. I was among them."

Many among the approximately seven thousand Americans residing in South Vietnam at the beginning of April 1975 had fallen in love with the country and its people. Two decades earlier, author Graham Greene had written of falling in love with Indochina "by chance," seduced by the "tall elegant girls in white silk trousers," "the pewter evening light on flat paddy fields," and "that feeling of exhilaration which a measure of danger brings to a visitor with a return ticket." General Marcel Bigeard, the commander of the French paratroopers who had suffered a catastrophic defeat at Dien Bien Phu in 1954, claimed to have "left half his heart" in Vietnam and later asked to have his ashes scattered over the battlefield. White House press secretary and former war correspondent Ron Nessen thought there was something "seductive about Vietnam and its people." During Nessen's first posting to Saigon, the noted French journalist Bernard Fall warned him that he had contracted "the yellow sickness," an incurable affection for Asia and Asians. But the two most powerful Americans in South Vietnam in 1975 were resistant to its charms. Ambassador Graham Martin admitted never developing "any great attachment to the Vietnamese, North or South," adding, "I don't particularly like any of them. I love the Thai." And CIA station chief Thomas Polgar confessed to being "not one of the people who was wedded to Vietnam," saying he lacked "a great emotional attachment to it like some of my colleagues who really fell in love with the country."

There had always been romantics and idealists among Americans posted to South Vietnam: diplomats who believed in winning hearts and minds, soldiers risking their lives to protect noncombatants, generals skeptical of the Pentagon's body-count mentality, members of John F. Kennedy's "ask not" generation who still considered government service an honorable calling, and others who had crossed the tracks—making close Vietnamese friends, fighting with Vietnamese units, and falling in love with Vietnamese women. After the 1973 treaty and ceasefire reduced the size of the U.S. civilian and military community, they became a larger percentage of the remaining Americans, and many of the Righteous Americans came from their ranks. Many believed that their country's political and military leaders had mismanaged the war, that Americans had a moral duty to evacuate their South Vietnamese allies, that a nation built by immigrants had room for more, and that they were saving Vietnamese from years of imprisonment in a Communist gulag, or a bloodbath like that occurring in neighboring Cambodia. And so they cobbled together underground railroads of safe houses, black flights, disguises, and fake flag vehicles, and smuggled friends, co-workers, and strangers past the police checkpoints at Tan Son Nhut airport in ambulances, metal shipping crates, and refrigerator trucks with airholes drilled in their floors. They impersonated chauffeurs, generals, and hospital patients, and they embossed documents with counterfeit consular stamps and signed affidavits stating that they would be financially responsible for the Vietnamese adults whom they claimed to have "adopted."

An American who had served with the CIA and the U.S. Agency for International Development (AID) in South Vietnam and had flown back to rescue his friends wrote afterward that many of his fellow countrymen in Saigon were "determined to protest [U.S. government inaction] in their own way by getting out as many people as possible." He believed that their mutiny had ultimately forced the U.S. government to relax its immigration restrictions and increase its evacuation flights, and concluded, "When one considers that these Americans had to accept responsibility—financial or otherwise—for these Vietnamese for an indefinite period, it becomes apparent that this impulse to save the Vietnamese was an act of conscience as well as a gesture of contempt for Capitol Hill."

The Righteous Americans faced anguishing decisions. Many began by evacuating co-workers and friends but were soon including friends of friends, and strangers. Some favored those whom the Communists seemed most likely to punish; others wanted to rescue the bravest South Vietnamese or those who had sacrificed the most or were most likely to flourish in the United States. Some, like O. B. Harnage, followed a first-come, first-served policy. Others were like U.S. marine colonel Al Gray, who commanded the ground security force of marines who flew into Tan Son Nhut on the afternoon of April 29. Although the Pentagon was pressuring the marines to evacuate Americans as quickly as possible, and although two marines had been killed by a Communist rocket earlier that day, and North Vietnamese units had reached the northern perimeter of the airfield—despite all this, Gray told his officers and men, "We're not going to play God. We're taking everyone who wants to go. And we'll stay here until we're finished."

Many Righteous Americans believed that evacuating Vietnamese who faced retribution under a Communist government represented a last chance to accomplish something noble at the end of an ignoble war—to replace President Nixon's discredited peace with honor with an honorable exit. While Harnage was rescuing twenty Vietnamese at a time from the roof of 22 Gia Long Street, several blocks away at the U.S. embassy Lieutenant Colonel Harry Summers climbed onto the roof of a soft drink stand in the recreation center and, shouting through a bullhorn, told the several thousand Vietnamese who had taken refuge there, "Every one of you folks is going to get out of here. Let me repeat that: all of you people here with us today are going to be flown to safety and freedom. None of you will be left behind. I will only go after the last of you has left. And the United States ambassador has assured me he will leave right at the end, after you and me. On that we give you our solemn word." Then he climbed down and walked through the crowd saying, "Don't you worry," and "Sure, you'll get a job in the States." A journalist who witnessed Summers's performance called him "a man of honor and of compassion," writing that he had "taken it upon himself to sweep up some of the dust of America's honor in Vietnam."

CHAPTER 1

Omens

—⊣⊢—

I t was said that swarms of bees drowned themselves in the South China Sea and a dragon streaked across the sky above the port of Vung Tau. An American diplomat transplanted a black orchid from the Central Highlands to a tree outside the embassy, and his staff accused him of cursing South Vietnam. During a state dinner for a delegation of American congressmen at Independence Palace, a gust of wind blew through the banquet hall, extinguishing candles and flapping the white curtains like flags of surrender. A cabinet minister whispered to an American that it was "a bad sign."

A more palpable bad sign appeared on January 6, 1975, when white flags fluttered as North Vietnamese troops entered Phuoc Binh, the ramshackle capital of mountainous and thinly populated Phuoc Long province. The town was only sixty-six miles north of Saigon, but with its large population of Montagnards, a catchall term for Vietnam's tribal peoples, and with its main boulevard doubling as a landing strip for the cargo planes that had become its lifeline after Communist troops cut its surrounding highways, it felt more like an outpost on a distant frontier. Twenty thousand seasoned North Vietnamese Army (NVA) regulars easily overwhelmed its defenders, a ragtag collection of militiamen and regular troops. President Nguyen Van Thieu flew in eight hundred elite South Vietnamese Army (ARVN) rangers and ordered them to hold the town "at all costs." A hundred survived, and according to the official government account, "The few province, village, and hamlet officials who were captured were summarily executed."

Phuoc Long had little strategic or economic value, but losing an entire province was a psychological catastrophe for South Vietnam. Thieu closed cinemas and nightclubs, declared three days of national mourning, and ordered "Phuoc Long Will Be Retaken" banners hung over boulevards. North Vietnam's chief of staff, General Van Tien Dung, wrote that the battle had demonstrated that the United States lacked the political will to reenter the war. South Vietnamese chief of staff General Cao Van Vien called it the Communists' "first big step toward total military conquest, boldly taken yet apparently without fear of any reaction from the United States," and asked, "What more encouragement could the Communists have asked for?"

Soon after Phuoc Long fell, two of Washington's foremost Vietnam experts, Sandy Berger and Douglas Pike, were walking down the Mall after judging a doctoral thesis titled "Is the South Vietnamese Defense Viable Without the Americans?" Its author claimed that it was. They disagreed. "It's all over, isn't it?" Berger asked. Pike took a few steps before saying, "Yeah, it is." Meanwhile, the State Department and the Pentagon were telling some personnel who had been on home leave over the holidays not to return to South Vietnam. Nelson Kieff, a military intelligence officer operating undercover as a civilian in the Central Highlands, received orders to recruit "stay-behind" agents.

President Gerald Ford issued a statement condemning Communist aggression but several days later neglected to mention Vietnam during his State of the Union address and told reporters that he could not foresee any set of circumstances leading him to order U.S. military units back to Vietnam. In fact, there was little he *could* do without outraging Congress and the American people. The U.S. Senate had passed an amendment in June 1973 named for Senators Clifford Case (R-N.J.) and Frank Church (D-Idaho) that prohibited the Pentagon from funding U.S. military operations in Vietnam, Cambodia, and Laos without the approval of Congress. This was followed five months later by the War Powers Resolution, a bill barring a president from sending the military into combat anywhere in the world for more than sixty days without congressional authorization or a declaration of war. The circumstances elevating Ford to the presidency also constrained him. President Nixon had appointed him vice president in 1973, after Vice President Spiro Agnew resigned in disgrace for accepting bribes. He had become president eight months later after Nixon resigned in disgrace due to the Watergate scandal. His unpopular decision to pardon Nixon was courageous but further weakened his accidental presidency.

Ford's tepid response to Phuoc Long unnerved General Alexander Haig, Nixon's former chief of staff. Haig flew to Washington from his post in Brussels as NATO commander hoping to persuade him to defy Congress and retaliate militarily. "Roll up your sleeves like Harry Truman did and take a principled stand," he said, warning that otherwise Ford might not be reelected. "Al, I can't," Ford replied. "The American people have no stomach for it." Haig rose to his feet and said, "I think you'll be a one term president."

There was no evidence that Phuoc Long had fallen because its defenders lacked weapons or munitions. Henry Kissinger, who was serving as Ford's secretary of state as well as his national security adviser, nevertheless blamed its loss on Congress's refusal to increase military assistance to South Vietnam. He told a meeting of the administration's interdepartmental Washington Special Actions Group (WSAG) on Vietnam and Cambodia, "The cuts they [Congress] have made last year have resulted in a deterioration of the situation and that is their god-damn fault," adding that Congress should "take responsibility for the fact that 50,000 men [the United States had lost 58,220 troops in the Vietnam War] died in vain."

While author and Vietnam War critic Frances FitzGerald was visiting Hanoi that winter, the editor of the Communist Party newspaper informed her that some in North Vietnam's Politburo subscribed to the "decent interval" theory. The editor explained that the theory posited that Kissinger would accept a two-year interval between the withdrawal of U.S. forces and a Communist victory in South Vietnam, and added, "The two years are over."

Kissinger had used the term "decent interval" while preparing for his secret trip to Beijing in 1971. His briefing book included this talking point: "We are ready to withdraw all our forces [from South Vietnam] by a fixed date and let objective realities shape the political future." Next to this he had written in the margin, "We want a decent interval. You have our assurance." When he accompanied Nixon to China the following year, he told Premier Zhou Enlai, "If we can live with a communist government in China, we ought to be able to accept it in Indochina." He also said that the United States considered the Hanoi government a "permanent factor" and had "no intention of destroying or even defeating it."

Kissinger provided more evidence that he had resigned himself to a Communist victory during an Oval Office conversation on August 2, 1972. When Nixon said that he worried about being judged harshly if the Communists took South Vietnam soon after the United States had signed a peace treaty, Kissinger replied, "If a year or two years from now North Vietnam gobbles up South Vietnam we can still have a viable foreign policy if it looks as if it's the result of South Vietnamese incompetence." Later in their conversation, he said, "So we've got to find some formula that holds the thing together a year or two, after which, after a year, Mr. President, Vietnam will be a backwater. If we settle it, say, this October [1972], by January '74 no one will give a damn."

The United States, South and North Vietnam, and the Vietcong's political organization in South Vietnam, the Provisional Revolutionary Government (PRG), signed the Paris Peace Accords in January 1973. By the time Phuoc Long fell in 1975, most Americans no longer gave a damn about Vietnam, except those who were there serving out the final days of Kissinger's decent interval. One of them likened their situation to that of the rear-guard troops who had protected the British army's 1940 evacuation from Dunkirk. But at least those soldiers had been sacrificed to protect an evacuation that would contribute to their nation's victory. The rear-guard Americans in South Vietnam had no D-day or V-E day in their futures. Instead, they would be condemned to witness, compressed into these last days, the nobility and perfidy, compassion and brutality, irrational optimism and mendacity marking their nation's intervention in the Vietnam War.

The decent interval would be the last chapter of America's three-decade-long participation in the Vietnam conflict. From 1945 to 1954, Presidents Truman and Eisenhower had supported France's war against a Communist-dominated insurgency in its Indochina colonies. They and subsequent presidents had subscribed to the domino theory: the assumption that if Vietnam fell to the Communists, other Southeast Asian nations would follow. After the Communists defeated the French colonial army at Dien Bien Phu in 1954, the two parties signed the Geneva Accords, a treaty dividing Vietnam at the 17th parallel and mandating elections within two years to choose a national government. Ho Chi Minh led a Communist state in the North, and Ngo Dinh Diem headed a republic in the South. The United States supported Diem, who was a genuine nationalist but had the disadvantage of being a Catholic in a largely Buddhist nation. Communist cadres in the South known as the Vietminh (later the Vietcong) rebelled against the Diem government, prompting Eisenhower to increase military assistance to Diem. President Kennedy increased the number of American military advisers from Eisenhower's nine hundred to sixteen thousand, and President Johnson sent U.S. combat units to South Vietnam in 1965, an escalation that Kennedy had resisted. During the next several years, Johnson and his secretary of defense Robert McNamara and his national security adviser McGeorge Bundy pursued a strategy of sending more troops, dropping more bombs, and killing more Communists in the belief that North Vietnam would find the price of the war unsupportable and capitulate. They failed to appreciate that North Vietnam was motivated by political ideology, not a cost-benefit analysis, and underestimated its willingness to suffer appalling casualties to reunify the country under a Communist government. When Johnson left office in 1969, the United States had 540,000 troops in South Vietnam, victory remained elusive, and the "light at the end of the tunnel" that a French general had once promised was fainter and more distant.

President Nixon pursued a "Vietnamization" strategy of reducing U.S. ground forces and transferring their combat responsibilities to South Vietnamese troops. This meant replacing half a million well-equipped American soldiers with a smaller number of poorly paid, trained, and led South Vietnamese ones. Nixon also directed Kissinger to negotiate a treaty that would deliver the "peace with honor" that he had promised during his 1968 campaign. Following an intense December 1972 U.S. bombing campaign, North Vietnam dropped its insistence that President Thieu's resignation precede any treaty, and Nixon pressured South Vietnam to accept the presence of North Vietnamese troops south of the 17th parallel. In exchange, he promised Thieu continued U.S. military and economic assistance, and military retaliation should North Vietnam violate the treaty.

On January 27, 1973, the representatives of all four parties—the United States, North and South Vietnam, and the PRG—signed the Agreement on Ending the War and Restoring Peace in Vietnam, commonly known as the Paris Peace Accords. The accords stipulated that the United States must remove its military forces from South Vietnam within sixty days, except for fifty officers and men assigned to the Defense Attaché Office (DAO) at the U.S. embassy in Saigon. Yet the accords also permitted North Vietnamese troops to remain in place throughout the South in de facto sanctuaries. The accords mandated a cease-fire, the repatriation of prisoners of war, an accounting of soldiers missing in action, the National Council of National Reconciliation and Concord, and "free and democratic elections" to determine South Vietnam's future. The United States promised to contribute economic aid to North Vietnam to heal "the wounds of war" and promote "postwar reconstruction."

Most of the 100,000 North Vietnamese Army troops remaining in South Vietnam occupied a swath of territory running from the 17th parallel south along the Laotian and Cambodian borders through South Vietnam's mountainous and lightly populated highlands. Communist troops also held territories scattered across the South known as "leopard spots" because of their appearance on military maps. North Vietnam resupplied its troops in the South via the Ho Chi Minh Trail, no longer a network of narrow jungle paths but now a wide all-weather highway, asphalted for miles, running alongside oil pipelines, and reaching to within sixty miles of Saigon. The trail enabled North

Vietnam to mass its army and attack where it chose, while South Vietnam had to disperse its armed forces to defend each of its forty-four provinces. Phuoc Long had been the result of this strategic imbalance.

The accords gave Americans the peace they wanted, with their troops home and their POWs freed, but failed to settle the question of who would rule South Vietnam. Veteran war correspondent Keyes Beech thought the treaty proved that "all the U.S. cared about was getting its prisoners back" and did not "give a damn about anything else." He found it telling that even the young antiwar correspondents condemned the treaty as a sellout. When Kissinger and his North Vietnamese negotiating counterpart, Le Duc Tho, won the 1973 Nobel Peace Prize, two members of the Nobel committee resigned in protest and Tho refused the honor. Kissinger later considered returning it, telling Ford on April 3, 1975, after South Vietnam had suffered a string of calamitous defeats, "I am returning the Nobel Peace Prize, but the money is in a trust so I will have to borrow to return the money." Later, he changed his mind.

Marshal Ferdinand Foch, the commander of Allied forces during World War I, said of the 1919 Versailles Treaty, "This is not peace. It is an armistice for twenty years." The same could be said of the Paris Peace Accords, although they lasted two years instead of twenty and did not provide the semblance of an armistice. They called for a "cease-fire in place" to begin at midnight on January 27, 1973, but failed to stipulate what "place" opposing troops were supposed to be occupying. During the next two years, South Vietnam lost fifty-one thousand soldiers, almost as many as America lost during its entire participation in the war. There would be no Council of National Reconciliation, free and democratic elections, U.S. funds for reconstructing North Vietnam, accounting of the missing, or end to the mortar barrages and civilian casualties. Instead, the accords created the International Commission of Control and Supervision (ICCS), a multinational organization charged with overseeing elections that never occurred and investigating violations of a cease-fire that neither side respected. Throughout the decent interval, the ICCS remained deadlocked between its two Communist members, Hungary and Poland, and its pro-Western members, Iran and Indonesia. (Former member Canada had resigned in frustration and been replaced by Indonesia.) Because the ICCS could act only if it was unanimous, it seldom acted. Its 1,160 inspectors flew across South Vietnam investigating cease-fire violations and otherwise passed the time at swimming pools and nightclubs, arguing over their rights and privileges while trying to recruit one another into the intelligence services of their respective nations. Had the ICCS been impartial, it would have ruled that North and South Vietnam had been more or less equally responsible for cease-fire violations during the initial months of the truce but that by the time Phuoc Long fell, the North had become the principal offender. By then, Saigon wags were calling the ICCS "I Can't Control Shit," and one of its inspectors compared the accords to "a dictionary for a language that nobody speaks."

The signatories of the accords also pledged to exchange information about military personnel missing in action and to repatriate remains. To accomplish this, they created the Four-Party Joint Military Team (JMT), an organization that comprised delegations from the United States, South Vietnam, North Vietnam, and the PRG. Most of the ten officers and five enlisted men on the U.S. delegation had served in Vietnam during the war and had volunteered because they believed that a flawed peace was better than the war they had fought, and considered recovering the remains of fallen comrades a noble enterprise.

The JMT enjoyed the privileges and immunities of a diplomatic mission, including its own flags, vehicles, and armbands marked with a "4" inside an orange circle. The two hundred members of the Communist delegations were quartered at Camp Davis, a group of Quonset huts adjoining the U.S. embassy's Defense Attaché Office's compound at Tan Son Nhut airport. The huts had formerly housed U.S. Army code breakers and had been named in honor of James T. Davis, the first American serviceman killed in action in South Vietnam. The JMT sponsored weekly liaison flights between Saigon and Hanoi so that the U.S. and South Vietnamese delegations could confer with senior North Vietnamese officials, and the Communist delegations could resupply their headquarters at Fort Davis and rotate their staffs. During biweekly meetings at Camp Davis, the American delegation handed the Communist delegations MIA dossiers, and the Communists promised to investigate each case but never did so. The Communists encircled Camp Davis with barbed wire and security personnel; the South Vietnamese encircled the Communists with lip-readers, telescopes, and their own security agents. The Communists flew in their food from Hanoi to prevent the Thieu regime from poisoning them; South Vietnamese military police ran their hands through the food, spilling it on the tarmac. Every Saturday morning the Communist spokesman gave a press conference during which he called for the overthrow of the Thieu government. The sound of South Vietnamese jets taking off to bomb Communist positions sometimes drowned him out.

The United States had pledged in the accords to "contribute to healing the wounds of war and to postwar reconstruction of the Democratic Republic of Vietnam," and President Nixon had promised a sum of $3.25 billion. The North considered the money a quid pro quo for providing information on American MIAs. Having recently exchanged six hundred American POWs for the withdrawal of all U.S. troops in South Vietnam, Hanoi was in no hurry to hand over MIA remains for free. During a coffee break at one of the JMT's fruitless meetings, Captain To, a senior member of North Vietnam's delegation, told Captain Stuart Herrington of the American delegation, "Of course we have information on many of your MIA personnel and in some cases even the remains of your pilots. . . . But why should we give them to you for nothing? Your government has done so much damage to our people and our land that it must pay."

Herrington was one of several Vietnamese speakers on the U.S. JMT delegation. Like many in his generation, he had been, he said, "swept along on a wave of idealism" by President Kennedy and, like many, had become skeptical that Vietnam had been the right war to fight, or a winnable one. Soon after Phuoc Long fell, he began hearing from South Vietnamese Army officers who knew him from his earlier tour as an intelligence officer. Their pretexts for contacting him were flimsy, and he recognized that they were looking for an American to help them escape.

He noticed other omens. An American contractor working at the South Vietnamese Air Force (VNAF) base at Bien Hoa reported that morale was so low that pilots schemed to avoid missions. An intelligence analyst based at the Defense Attaché Office reported filing a pessimistic memorandum, only to have the embassy's deputy chief of mission, Wolfgang Lehmann, return it with "CRAP!" and "Where did you get this?" scrawled across the top in red ink. One evening a posse of inebriated South Vietnamese soldiers pulled an American contractor from his car a block from Herrington's building and pummeled him. They told the policeman who intervened that he deserved it because he was an American. Herrington told his brother in the United States that the South Vietnamese Army was "a demoralized force," "completely convinced that we've . . . betrayed them," "irate and increasingly ill-disciplined," and a greater danger to Americans than the North Vietnamese. He began shipping his possessions home and told his parents to expect him by August.

Army specialist 7 Bill Bell was the best Vietnamese linguist on the U.S. JMT delegation. His superior officer had been on home leave when Phuoc Long fell and had remained in the United States, leaving Bell to assume his position as head liaison officer to the other three JMT delegations. After Phuoc Long fell, Bell decided that the crucial question was not *when* the Communists would strike next but *where*. He received an answer while lunching in Saigon on February 25 with members of the Santilli family, who owned a coffee plantation outside Ban Me Thuot, a provincial capital in the Central Highlands. The family patriarch was an Italian who had fought with the French Foreign Legion and had married a Rhade, one of the tribal peoples native to the region. Bell had met Santilli several years earlier while serving with the Twenty-Fifth U.S. Infantry Division and providing security for his plantation. He was stunned when Santilli revealed over lunch that his family was selling its plantation and moving to Italy. Santilli explained that his Rhade friends had warned him that North

Vietnamese troops were massing on the Cambodian border west of Ban Me Thuot and had been observed logging near his plantation. On closer inspection, the Rhade had discovered that the Communists had sawed the trees only halfway through, making it easier for the lead tanks in an armored unit to push them over as they headed for Ban Me Thuot.

Regulations prohibited members of JMT delegations from collecting human intelligence, so Bell shared Santilli's warning with Andy Gembara, a burly Ukrainian American plainclothes military intelligence operative with a no-bullshit swagger acquired while growing up on New York's Lower East Side. Gembara served under Colonel William LeGro, who headed the military intelligence unit at the DAO. After hearing Gembara's report, LeGro warned the embassy and the Pentagon that Ban Me Thuot might be North Vietnam's next target. When they ignored LeGro's warning, Bill Bell invited officials of South Vietnam's Central Intelligence Organization and a delegation of U.S. intelligence operatives to meet at his home. The Vietnamese officials said that they were shocked that the Santillis were leaving but insisted that Ban Me Thuot was an unlikely target. Their intelligence indicated a Communist offensive in the Mekong delta. Bell saw some of them next on April 29, while helping them board a helicopter leaving from the roof of the U.S. embassy.

Soon after Phuoc Long fell, Colonel LeGro ordered his files microfilmed and a copy flown to Guam. In February, he asked Gembara to represent their office at a meeting at the embassy called to discuss an evacuation. Gembara was surprised that the only people attending it were a lone CIA agent and the three military attachés. None of them knew how many Americans lived in South Vietnam or how many Vietnamese worked for the various agencies of the U.S. mission in South Vietnam—people who Gembara believed had a "moral right" to evacuation. The only plan under discussion involved loading Vietnamese onto landing craft and taking them down the Saigon River. He reported this to LeGro, adding, "I think they're smoking something."

"Let's ignore the embassy and organize our own evacuation," LeGro said, launching what would become the first American underground railroad.

The army had taught Gembara Vietnamese, made him an officer, and assigned him to a Special Forces psychological operations unit that he considered "worse than useless" because it was alienating the same people he was fighting to protect. He was wounded in 1968, and at a time when most officers were running the other way, he volunteered to return as an intelligence officer because he had "fallen for these people." The Paris Peace Accords limited the United States to fifty uniformed military personnel in South Vietnam, so he traded his uniform for civvies and a Department of Defense civilian identification card. After receiving the go-ahead from LeGro, he began compiling lists of potential evacuees among the Vietnamese working for the DAO, giving priority to anyone who might rank high on Communist execution lists. He added to his list former members of ARVN military intelligence, interpreters, and his counterparts in South Vietnam's Military Security Service. U.S. military intelligence was based in the DAO compound inside the Tan Son Nhut airport, giving it easy access to the U.S. Air Force transport planes that were arriving daily with military supplies before returning empty to Clark Air Base in the Philippines. Thanks to Gembara and others, during the second half of March, the transports began landing at Clark with small groups of Vietnamese passengers.

The faded red banners flapping over Saigon's boulevards proclaimed President Thieu's threadbare political philosophy, his "Four No's"—"No Coalition Government!" "No Negotiating with the Enemy!" "No Communist Activity in the South!" "No Square Inch of the National Territory Is to Be Abandoned to the Communists!" The first three contradicted the spirit and provisions of the Paris Peace Accords, and Thieu had now violated the fourth by failing to retake Phuoc Long. After he struggled to explain this during a rambling three-hour televised speech, it fell to Joe McBride, one of the more cynical of the embassy's junior diplomats, to draft a cable to Washington summarizing it. (McBride: "As if anyone *cared* what Thieu said.") After sending his cable, McBride walked past the embassy recreation center, where a raucous Hawaiian-themed party was under way. Americans wore leis, and the Vietnamese waitresses had wrapped themselves in sarongs. Tiki torch flames reflected in the swimming pool. "There's something wrong here," he thought. "South Vietnam has just lost its first province, Thieu has delivered a three-hour speech, and it's Luau Night at the embassy. This can't last."

He had reached a similar conclusion in October, when he and Sergeant Thong, his former interpreter, had traveled to the province in the delta where he had served with the U.S. Agency for International Development during 1971. Passengers on their bus were shocked to see an American traveling unarmed, and the bus stopped at roadblocks that had not existed in 1971. The headman at McBride's former town was so uncomfortable having him and Thong stay overnight that they continued on to a "showcase hamlet" that McBride had formerly shown to visiting dignitaries. The village headman offered them his hut but refused to join them. The Communists were everywhere, he warned, waiting to take over. He handed McBride some flash grenades and said, "If they come for you, throw them and run." In a report describing his trip, McBride wrote that a district deemed 80 percent secure in 1971 had become "a hollow eggshell waiting to be cracked." His report moved through the ranks of the embassy's political officers, and he assumed that Ambassador Martin read it. ("He read everything to learn what we were saying rather than what the Vietnamese were saying.") Before McBride had left Washington for Saigon, the State Department's South Vietnam desk officer had warned him that Ambassador Martin regarded pessimistic reporting as disloyal and defeatist and routinely censored it. But the good news, he said, was that Washington knew Martin was peddling a fantasy—of a thriving South Vietnam deserving American assistance—so McBride should avoid sticking out his neck to challenge him. As the desk officer had predicted, McBride's report never made it past Martin's desk. He had stuck out his neck for nothing.

While McBride was revisiting his former province and warning of the deteriorating security situation, and while North Vietnam was preparing its Phuoc Long blitzkrieg, diplomat Ken Moorefield, a West Point graduate and Vietnam War veteran, was serving as military reports officer at the U.S. consulate in Nha Trang, a pleasant seaside town 250 miles northeast of Saigon. His job involved gathering reports from South Vietnamese sources and U.S. provincial representatives stationed throughout the Central Highlands and the coastal strip constituting Military Region II, and condensing them into a summary for the embassy. In the fall of 1974, he had warned that the Communists' network of all-weather roads along the border with Laos and Cambodia meant that North Vietnam could quickly concentrate its forces, threatening ARVN bases at Kontum, Pleiku, and Ban Me Thuot, a strategic crossroads in the Central Highlands whose capture could provide a launching pad for a drive to the coast that would cut South Vietnam in two. He also reported that a North Vietnamese POW had identified Ban Me Thuot as a likely target. He returned to Saigon in December convinced that the North was preparing a major offensive in the Central Highlands, commencing with an attack on Ban Me Thuot.

Several months after Moorefield sounded the alarm, and a month after Phuoc Long fell, CIA chief of station Thomas Polgar visited the CIA base at Bien Hoa, a small city fifteen miles northeast of Saigon. Polgar had been an undercover agent in Nazi-occupied Europe and a legendary spymaster at the CIA's famed Berlin Station in the 1950s. Instead of the suave, swashbuckling James Bond that his résumé promised, he was a rotund middle-aged Hungarian émigré with thick black-rimmed glasses who spoke in a Central European accent thicker than Henry Kissinger's. He had recently sent Ambassador Martin a memorandum predicting that "the Vietnamese Communists are not going to risk that which they have in an 'all or nothing' gamble of another general offensive." His briefing to the agents gathered in the recreation room at the CIA's Bien Hoa base hewed to that line. "I want you to know that everything is going OK," he told them. "We don't see any major problems in 1975. Our reading is that the situation is under control." The agents stared at him in disbelief. All winter they had been warning Saigon and Washington that a Communist offensive was imminent. They had reported that North Vietnamese soldiers were removing camouflage from tanks in a nearby rubber plantation, Russian SAM anti-aircraft missiles were coming down the Ho Chi Minh Trail, and their three most trustworthy double agents—Goldmother, Grandpa, and Duc Hue Tiger—were saying that three additional North Vietnamese Army divisions had arrived in the region. According to one agent, they found Polgar's pep talk "incredibly demoralizing."

In February, Polgar sent his chief analyst "Terry Balls" (an alias) to Can Tho to brief the thirty CIA agents stationed in the Mekong delta. After hanging maps and charts in a conference room at the consulate, Balls told the agents that despite losing Phuoc Long, South Vietnam had a bright future and would hold elections in October. An agent interrupted and said, "If you attend elections in October you're going to be the only American here, because we're on the way out." Another added, "That may be what's going on in the rest of the country, but it sure as hell isn't what's going on down here."

Balls assured them that there would be work in the delta for "generations of case officers" and that there were factors at work not apparent to field agents that involved tacit understandings between North and South Vietnam. When he described a recent Communist attack as insignificant, an agent retorted that he had just flown over the battlefield and seen plenty of corpses. Others protested that they had been reporting Communist infiltration for over a year but Saigon had buried their accounts. When he insisted that there was "no question" that South Vietnam would survive, the deputy base commander shouted, "That's bullshit!"

Balls shrugged and said, "Guys, I'm just quoting the party line."

CIA agent James Parker was the only American official stationed in a province where the Communists controlled most of the countryside.

He thought that Balls's claim that North and South Vietnam could coexist was a fantasy and that no reasonable person could believe that North Vietnam would stop short of a complete victory. When he ran into Balls at the bar of the CIA club afterward, he told him that there was no way that the North would negotiate. Balls gave him a strange look and turned away.

CHAPTER 2

Walter Martindale's Convoy

———┤├———

Consular officer Walter Martindale was the only U.S. government official remaining in Quang Duc, a remote province in the Central Highlands bordering Cambodia to the west and Phuoc Long to the south. He became concerned for the future of what he had taken to calling "my country" during the winter of 1975 as the skirmishing in Quang Duc became more frequent and ferocious. After hearing that the government's intelligence services had lost an entire North Vietnamese division, he flew over a river near Gia Nghia, the provincial capital, and saw North Vietnamese Army engineers moving large rocks into the water to create a bridge for armored vehicles and heavy equipment. Fearing an all-out attack, he urged the province's civilian and military leaders to respond forcefully to Communist incursions, telling them, "If we don't show we can fight, we'll lose our whole country overnight." After his Montagnard agents reported a well-equipped NVA division moving into the Central Highlands, he evacuated schoolchildren, pregnant women, hospital patients, and selected members of his Vietnamese staff south to Bao Loc, a town just over the border in Lam Dong province. He described the ominous developments in Quang Duc in reports that he sent by courier to the embassy, where they were ignored.

The fighting in Quang Duc province concerned U.S. consul general Moncrieff Spear, and on March 9 he ordered Martindale to report to the consulate in Nha Trang. Martindale refused, saying that as the last American official in Gia Nghia he was being closely watched and his departure would trigger a panic. The next day the North Vietnamese Army attacked Ban Me Thuot, the strategic provincial capital a hundred miles north of Gia Nghia that Ken Moorefield and Bill Bell had identified as a likely target.

Tom Glenn, who headed the National Security Agency (NSA) detachment in South Vietnam, had also predicted an attack on Ban Me Thuot. He was only thirty-six but looked younger. He supervised forty-three American cryptologists and provided advice and assistance to General "Tran" (a pseudonym), his South Vietnamese counterpart who commanded South Vietnam's twenty-seven-hundred-man cryptology unit, the Directorate General for Technical Security (DGTS). A hard-knocks childhood that had included his attorney father being jailed for embezzlement and leaving the family destitute, a paper route in a dodgy Oakland neighborhood, and paying his way through Berkeley by pumping gas had toughened and matured Glenn. After he graduated first in his class in Vietnamese at army language school, the army had seconded him to the NSA, and he had spent most of the next thirteen years in South Vietnam, becoming so fluent that Vietnamese speaking to him on the telephone assumed he was a native. His civil service ranking made him the equivalent of an army general, placing him on equal footing with CIA station chief Polgar. But despite his seniority, skills, and experience, the embassy and the South Vietnamese Army undervalued or dismissed his warnings. At the beginning of March his signals intelligence (SIGINT) indicated a Communist strike on Ban Me Thuot.

On March 9 he and General Tran made an inspection tour of DGTS cryptology units in the north of the country. While stopping at Pleiku in the Central Highlands, they warned the commander of Military Region II, Major General Pham Van Phu, that their SIGINT indicated an impending Communist attack on Ban Me Thuot. Only a million of South Vietnam's twenty million inhabitants lived in the Central Highlands. Half were Montagnards, and their loyalty to the Thieu government was tenuous. The region's steep valleys, dense forests, and thick fogs favored attackers over defenders, and Thieu's insistence that his armed forces defend every province had spread them thin. Phu needed to anticipate a Communist attack and send reinforcements to a probable target, a strategy requiring accurate intelligence on enemy troop movements. He nevertheless dismissed Glenn's SIGINT as the result of clever Communist diversionary tactics and argued that Pleiku was a more important prize than Ban Me Thuot because it was his headquarters and *he* was there.

Glenn and Tran continued to Ban Me Thuot, where they landed on a ridge overlooking the town. North Vietnamese Army units had already started attacking ARVN outposts on its periphery. As Tran was inspecting his troops, Glenn watched Communist shells hit an ARVN position in the valley. The next day, twenty-four hours after General Phu had dismissed Glenn's warning, and only days after Bill Bell had alerted South Vietnamese and American intelligence operatives to the half-sawed-through trees near the Santilli plantation, North Vietnamese tanks knocked those trees over while spearheading a blitzkrieg that hurled twenty-five thousand troops against Ban Me Thuot's twelve hundred defenders.

For South Vietnam, the battle was the full catastrophe. Its pilots dropped bombs from ten thousand feet to avoid anti-aircraft batteries and hit the ARVN command post. Some Montagnard troops switched sides, and some ARVN soldiers deserted after their officers fled the battlefield in helicopters. General Phu airlifted in reinforcements who discarded their uniforms and scattered to find their families. Within two days most of Ban Me Thuot's defenders had been killed, wounded, or taken prisoner or had deserted. The Communists also captured U.S. provincial representative Paul Struharik and the twenty Americans and third-country nationals who had taken refuge in his compound.

For days the U.S. embassy and Washington remained unaware of what had happened at Ban Me Thuot and what it meant. As South Vietnamese resistance was collapsing, Kissinger sent President Ford a memorandum from British counterinsurgency expert Sir Robert Thompson without comment, an indication that he subscribed to its conclusions or at least considered them worthy of the president's eye. On the strength of having devised the strategy that had enabled Britain to defeat Communist guerrillas in Malaya during the 1950s, Thompson had become Washington's favorite counterinsurgency expert. Nixon had named him a special adviser on Vietnam, and Kissinger had praised him as "one of the leading experts on Southeast Asia."

Thompson had just returned from a twelve-day tour through Vietnam and Cambodia. He wrote in his memorandum that "Hanoi's intention is probably more directed at the collapse of South Vietnam, not its conquest. . . . There will be no major offensive on the 1972 scale during 1975." (In his memoir, *Our Great Spring Victory,* North Vietnamese general Van Tien Dung stated that in October 1974 the Politburo had decided to launch a major offensive during the 1975 dry season aimed at total victory.) Thompson declared, "There is no alternative to Thieu and no sign that his political position is crumbling." (Thieu would resign six weeks later.) Thompson insisted that "the ARVN soldier is superior to and is still fighting better than the enemy" and that "South Vietnam has played its part in a manner unsurpassed in history" and was "ready to continue fighting" even in the absence of further support from the United States. (Before the end of the month, South Vietnam's forces would have surrendered all of their nation's northern provinces without mounting a significant defensive battle.)

U.S. secretary of defense James Schlesinger was as clueless as Thompson. During a cabinet meeting on March 12, he reported that ARVN troops in the Central Highlands were "holding fairly well" and called the military situation "basically a stalemate." It was almost midnight in Saigon when he said this, and the battle for Ban Me Thuot was finished, as was South Vietnam. At least that was the conclusion of Parker Borg and Al Adams, experienced Vietnam hands who were special assistants to Henry Kissinger and to his executive secretary Lawrence Eagleburger, respectively. After hearing about the battle, they looked at each other and said, "That's it. That's the end. If [South] Vietnam is going to let a city like Ban Me Thuot fall, the rest can't be far behind."

In September 1973, Kissinger had told the Senate Foreign Relations Committee, "The Vietnam War is behind us." By March 10, 1975, it was apparently behind him. He had not visited South Vietnam since 1972 and was focused on settling the Arab-Israeli conflict. Ban Me Thuot fell as he was shuttling between Middle Eastern capitals. A March 12 memorandum from National Security Council staffer William Stearman titled "Ominous Developments in Vietnam" must have been an unwelcome distraction. Stearman predicted that although the coming Communist offensive promised to be "extremely intense," intelligence sources believed it would be "a prelude to a new round of negotiations designed to achieve an implementation of the Paris Accords on North Vietnamese terms," and that North Vietnam would "make its gains in the spring and early summer and then offer a cease-fire."

President Thieu was under no illusions about what the Communists wanted, or what Ban Me Thuot meant. On March 11, he summoned his chief of staff, General Cao Van Vien, Prime Minister Tran Thien Khiem, and his national security adviser, Lieutenant General Dang Van Quang, to the only conference room in Independence Palace believed free from CIA bugs. He announced that he was adopting the "light at the top, heavy at the bottom" strategy recommended by Brigadier General Ted Serong, the retired Australian officer who had become his unofficial military adviser. Serong's plan called for withdrawing South Vietnam's armed forces from its northern provinces while holding coastal enclaves at Hue, the nation's spiritual and intellectual capital, and Da Nang, its second-largest city. Abandoning half of South Vietnam to save its richer southern provinces assumed an army with the tactical skills to execute a retreat under fire, a challenging maneuver for even the best armed forces. Although adopting Serong's strategy would be the most important decision Thieu would make during his eight-year presidency, he made it without consulting the United States. The CIA claimed to have "access" to Prime Minister Khiem and General Quang, but neither told Polgar about a decision that would jeopardize the lives of CIA agents and other Americans in the provinces that Thieu intended to abandon.

On March 14, Thieu flew to the former U.S. base at Cam Ranh Bay to inform General Phu of his decision. Thieu often spoke elliptically and appeared to issue Phu two contradictory orders: retake Ban Me Thuot with the troops at hand (an impossibility), and withdraw his forces to the coast from Pleiku and elsewhere in the Central Highlands without notifying civilians, local defense forces, or the Americans. Thieu was sufficiently vague that everyone left the meeting unsure which territories he wanted Phu to abandon. Phu and his staff believed that he had ordered them to withdraw to the coast, an impression furthered by General Vien, who had suggested that Phu surprise the Communists by retreating down Route 7B, an abandoned logging road snaking through 135 miles of rough terrain. During the flight back to Pleiku, Phu told his staff that his career was over and South Vietnam was lost. Then he burst into tears. He had fought in the French colonial army, and after almost dying of tuberculosis in a Communist POW camp, he had vowed never to be taken prisoner again. To minimize the chance of this occurring, he persuaded Thieu to promote Colonel Pham Van Tat to brigadier general so he could lead the retreat down Route 7B while Phu and his staff flew to Nha Trang.

The next day, March 15, Thieu met with U.S. deputy chief of mission Wolfgang Lehmann, the senior American diplomat in South Vietnam while Ambassador Martin was on home leave. Instead of informing Lehmann that Phu was withdrawing, Thieu told him that the battle to retake Ban Me Thuot would be "hard" and "last a long time." Lehmann cabled Deputy National Security Adviser Brent Scowcroft that he believed that Thieu would "use the Ban Me Thuot battlefield as an occasion to destroy major enemy units" and a lengthy battle could be expected. General Vien also neglected to mention Phu's withdrawal during a meeting with Major General Homer Smith, the defense attaché and senior U.S. military officer in South Vietnam.

After a CIA agent in Pleiku noticed fewer planes than usual parked at the airfield, he went to Phu's headquarters and found his staff packing. An officer admitted that they were retreating and that Thieu had told them not to alert the Americans. Phu also followed Thieu's order not to alert Pleiku's civil servants, local defense forces, or Montagnard irregulars. "Let them [the Montagnards] find out about it later," he told his staff. "They're Moi [savages]. Let them return to their mountains." Instead, some stayed and joined the Communists.

South Korean troops, who had been allied with U.S. forces in South Vietnam, had mined the shoulders of Route 7B. Logging trucks had carved deep crevices into its surface, and five of its seventeen bridges lay in ruins. On the morning of March 15, an advance convoy of military engineers under orders to repair the road rumbled through Pleiku as helicopters began ferrying General Phu's staff to the local airfield. Panic ensued. Soldiers deserted to find their families, and businessmen abandoned stores and workshops, expecting that the Communists would confiscate them anyway. In its haste to retreat, the air force left behind sixty planes, and the army failed to destroy large stores of arms, ammunition, and fuel. When the main body of Phu's troops left the following morning, thousands of panicky civilians followed. They knew that the Communists had executed several thousand South Vietnamese after capturing Hue in 1968 and that after the Communists took Pleiku, the South Vietnamese Air Force was certain to bomb it.

U.S. provincial representative Earl Thieme and Nelson Kieff, the intelligence operative working under civilian cover who had been ordered to recruit Vietnamese stay-behind agents, threw together a convoy of jeeps and vans and sped through Pleiku collecting the Vietnamese employees of U.S. agencies. They drove them to the airport, bribed the MPs, and put them onto Air America planes and helicopters. Kieff also evacuated his stay-behind agent, Sergeant "Minh," a member of an elite ARVN Special Operations unit. Kieff and Thieme returned on a helicopter the next day to pick up more Vietnamese employees, and several days later the indefatigable Thieme flew over the refugee columns in a helicopter, searching for vehicles belonging to U.S. agencies in Pleiku and zooming down to rescue their occupants.

Cars, trucks, bikes, motorbikes, and oxcarts became entangled with military vehicles on Route 7B. By March 21, the retreat had become a death march. Thousands of soldiers and civilians drowned while fording rivers under Communist fire or succumbed to thirst and hunger. Communist mortars and artillery killed tens of thousands more. Those leaving the road risked triggering mines; those walking on it risked being flattened by armored cars and tanks. Corpses littered the shoulders, and rivulets of blood flowed into ditches. Horrific accounts appeared in Saigon's newspapers. Reporter Nguyen Tu called the retreat "The Convoy of Tears" and wrote of shells hitting trucks packed with civilians and the "roaring artillery, crackling small arms, screams of the dying and crying of the children," merging into "a single voice from hell." Never before during this brutal war had so many people died in such a short period of time. Estimates of military and civilian casualties ranged from 50,000 to 100,000, a staggering number for a country of 20 million. General Phu would lose three-quarters of his 20,000 troops, and all but 900 of the 7,000 elite rangers who had left Pleiku. The debacle delivered six provinces into Communist hands and sixty thousand starving people to the coastal town of Tuy Hoa.

While this tragedy was unfolding, Ambassador Graham Martin was recovering from dental surgery at his home in North Carolina. Secretary of Defense James Schlesinger and his logistics expert Erich von Marbod called to brief him on the retreat. "Why, I know all about that," Martin drawled. "Phu has long been planning to withdraw part of his headquarters from the highlands. That's all it is." Schlesinger urged him to come to Washington, but Martin refused to interrupt his leave to address what he called "a minor problem."

After the Communists captured U.S. provincial representative Paul Struharik in Ban Me Thuot (Struharik would spend months in captivity), the U.S. consul general in Nha Trang, Moncrieff Spear, strapped a large revolver to his waist and ordered Walter Martindale and other official Americans in the Central Highlands to report to Nha Trang. Unlike several days before, this time Martindale obeyed Spear. After he arrived, Spear said that he could not risk losing another American to the Communists and ordered him not to return to Gia Nghia.

Martindale said he had to go back because he had promised to evacuate his Vietnamese employees. Spear accused him of having "a John Wayne complex"—of wanting to play the hero and be last man out.

"Mr. Spear," Martindale replied in an icy voice. "The United States made certain commitments to these people, and we must try to fulfill them." He was furious at Spear, furious that the United States was abandoning "his country," furious at Kissinger for writing off South Vietnam, furious at Congress for refusing to increase military aid, and furious at cowardly and corrupt Vietnamese generals. He defied Spear and persuaded an Air America pilot to return him to Gia Nghia.

He had put roots down in Gia Nghia. In February, he had adopted two Amerasian children, five-year-old Luc and his three-year-old sister, Van. Their mother was a Franco-Vietnamese Catholic from the North, and their father had been an American contractor who had returned to California and broken his promise to send for her and the children. She spoke of a church wedding, but Martindale could find no evidence of it, and while on home leave he had failed to track down her husband. He returned to find that in his absence her two-year-old daughter had died of neglect. He adopted her siblings, and this thirty-two-year-old bachelor who had lived in South Vietnam for five of his last seven years, and who was engaged to marry a Franco-Vietnamese woman whose family owned a nearby coffee plantation, suddenly had two more reasons to care about what happened to "his" country.

He had chosen this country sight unseen, joining the U.S. Navy Reserve in college and volunteering for South Vietnam after graduation. His father was a career naval officer and had pulled strings at the Pentagon to stop the posting, writing to him afterward, "Your brother is a Marine, your sister is an Air Force nurse and I've served my country throughout my life, but we're not going to win this war because they [the politicians] won't let us." Martindale belonged to a proud southern military family whose members had served in every branch of the armed services and in every American war. He persisted, and in 1968 the navy finally sent him to South Vietnam. He joined a civic action team, advised a South Vietnamese regiment, counseled ARVN widows and orphans, raced around the highlands in a vintage jeep, and joined Chinese mercenaries on cloak-and-dagger missions.

He returned as an AID development officer in 1971 and never left. He entered the Foreign Service, served as a consular representative and a province senior adviser, advised the national police and the People's Self-Defense Force, and took on more jobs and responsibilities as the embassy withdrew other official Americans from Quang Duc after the fall of Phuoc Long.

His pleasant demeanor concealed a steely interior. According to a Vietnamese woman who admired him, he was "brave, but sometimes too adventurous." He was also, at least by the standards of the Central Highlands, a bon vivant. He lived in a French villa with a commanding view of a curving river and jungly mountains, employed a renowned cook and a faithful housekeeper, Mr. Tua and Ba Duc, served meals on fine china, handed out printed calling cards, and had instructed his gardeners to cut "Welcome" into his hedge. His friends gave him a sign for his villa that said "Chez Walt."

Soon after he arrived back in Gia Nghia to evacuate his employees, Spear called him and said, "Get your ass out of there and come to Nha Trang."

Martindale ignored Spear and evacuated his friends and employees down unpaved back roads to Bao Lac, the border town in Lam Dong province. He evacuated everyone who had worked for him, even the two boys who cleaned his compound and had carved "Welcome" in his hedge. After sending out five hundred people, he joined them, bringing along his two devoted Montagnard bodyguards, Kulie Kasor and Nay Ri. Before leading his evacuees overland to Dalat, Lam Dong's provincial capital, he returned to Chez Walt to collect his Burmese cat, Ralph. He had outfitted Ralph with a collar announcing in English and Vietnamese, "Ralph. Property of U.S. Senior Advisor. Do Not Eat," but feared this might not protect him from the Communists. He was also returning to rescue his friend Ly Quyen, a slight man with thick glasses who headed Quang Duc's Provincial Reconnaissance Unit, a military group that tracked and identified Communist infiltrators and agents. Martindale considered Quyen the bravest soldier he had ever met. An Air America helicopter pilot who also admired Quyen agreed to fly Martindale back to Gia Nghia to rescue him.

While they were in the air, a friend of Martindale's in the Gia Nghia police force radioed to say, "The tiger has left the cage," a prearranged code meaning that the province chief had departed. As Martindale's helicopter was about to land, South Vietnamese troops guarding the Gia Nghia airport began shelling Chez Walt. The province chief had ordered the barrage to prevent Martindale from landing. He feared that if he allowed the American provincial representative to set foot in Gia Nghia after he had left, he would also have to return or lose face. The shells unnerved the policeman who had collected Ralph, and he dropped the cage and the cat escaped. The Air America pilot landed several hundred yards from Chez Walt, and Martindale disembarked to collect Quyen and other members of his Provincial Reconnaissance Unit. As they were boarding the helicopter, a deserter with pinwheeling eyes leveled his rifle at Martindale and demanded to be included. Quyen jumped between them and disarmed the soldier.

After returning to Bao Lac, Martindale scrounged up a convoy of vans, pickup trucks, and dump trucks so he could transport his evacuees sixty miles east to Dalat. Some of his people had already made it there, but three hundred remained, too many for his vehicles. He made decisions that still haunt him, and one woman was so grateful to be included that she renamed her baby Walter.

He led his convoy in an International Harvester Scout pickup truck. A dozen of his armed Montagnards brought up the rear in a vehicle he grandiloquently dubbed his "gun truck." They left early on a red laterite highway winding through tree farms and coffee plantations. Lines of dispirited South Vietnamese soldiers, deserters, and stragglers trudged along its shoulders. As Martindale's convoy slowed for a turn, several jumped into the road and stopped one of the vans. They yanked open its rear door and began pulling people out.

Martindale ran back and grabbed one of the soldiers. Another deserter pointed his rifle at Martindale and yelled for his comrade to duck. Martindale unholstered his .38 and fired off several rounds. The soldiers shot back, missing Martindale but wounding an elderly man in one of the trucks. Martindale emptied his revolver, and the deserters scattered into the bush. As they were regrouping to mount another attack, the Montagnards in the gun truck arrived like the cavalry, firing their weapons and sending the hijackers fleeing. Martindale believed that if they had been farther away, the deserters would have massacred everyone.

Soon after he arrived in Dalat, the young deputy chief of his Montagnard guard units approached him and said, "My men respectfully ask the permission of the American senior adviser [Martindale] to allow them to keep two of the trucks and weapons and fade into the mountains with their families." He reminded Martindale that the Communists had been known to massacre Montagnards allied with Americans, adding, "We are mountain people, and if we have our backs to the sea, the Communists will kill us for sure." Martindale's throat tightened, and tears welled in his eyes. Turning away to conceal his emotions, he asked himself, "What in the hell have we done to these wonderful, loyal, brave people?" He composed himself and said that he understood that the mountains were the Montagnards' home and urged them to take whatever they needed. The guards lined up and saluted. Martindale shook their hands and thought, "These people have risked their lives to protect me and other Americans. I have a moral responsibility to protect them. Instead, I'm abandoning them." He would call this moment the most "gut wrenching" of his life and speak of his heart "breaking into a million pieces."

As his convoy entered the coastal town of Phan Rang, groups of soldiers cheered him and clapped. They claimed to be happy that he had escaped Quang Duc and the Communists. But he noticed that they belonged to the same unit that had attacked him earlier. He told his bodyguards to ready their weapons and shouted that anyone approaching his vehicle would be shot.

If President Thieu was going to accept advice from any of his generals after the Ban Me Thuot debacle, he should have listened to General Ngo Quang Truong, who commanded Military Region I, the northernmost of South Vietnam's four military districts. Truong was an unprepossessing man in his mid-forties, so quiet and emaciated that out of uniform he could be mistaken for a peasant or day laborer. His soldiers revered him for his honesty and courage, and he often joined them on the front lines. American generals had praised him as a "tough, seasoned, fighting leader" and "probably the best field commander in South Vietnam." Norman Schwarzkopf, who would command U.S. troops during the Persian Gulf War and had fought alongside him in Vietnam, thought he was "the most brilliant tactical commander" he had ever met.

Truong commanded the First Division, the finest of the regular ARVN divisions, and the Airborne Division, the best trained and led military formation in South Vietnam. After deciding on his "light at the top" strategy, Thieu had ordered him to transfer the Airborne Division to Saigon. It can be said in Thieu's defense that because he was planning to surrender most of Military Region I to the North, the other units under Truong's command should have proven sufficient to hold enclaves around Hue and Da Nang and that bolstering Saigon's defenses with the Airborne Division was prudent. Cynics have suggested that Thieu feared a coup and trusted his airborne troops to thwart it. Truong flew to Saigon and begged Thieu to change his mind. Thieu agreed to postpone the transfer until the end of March but reversed himself after Truong left.

Truong had forged a close friendship with Theresa "Terry" Tull, a handsome, large-boned, thirty-nine-year-old Foreign Service officer who was second-in-command of the U.S. consulate in Da Nang, South Vietnam's second-largest city. She had grown up in New Jersey as the youngest of seven children and had been working as a secretary to help support her mother and earning night school credits when she read an article in *Good Housekeeping* that made the life of a female diplomat sound daring and glamorous. She arrived in Saigon in January 1968 as a newly minted political officer, witnessed the Tet attack, saw Vietcong bodies in the embassy's front yard, learned Vietnamese, and befriended the president of the National Assembly, giving him English lessons while he volunteered confidential information that she included in her reports. Back in Washington she served on the State Department's Vietnam Working Group and was studying for a graduate degree in Southeast Asian studies when she returned to South Vietnam in 1973 as deputy principal officer in Da Nang.

As a female Foreign Service officer, she was accustomed to being marginalized, and Secretary of State William Rogers had mistaken her for a secretary when she arrived at his office to brief him about South Vietnamese politics. After Consul General Paul Popple asked her to represent the Da Nang consulate at General Truong's daily staff briefing, she approached the assignment cautiously, wearing a long skirt and taking care not to appear too pushy or aggressive. Truong sat her on his right, a signal to his staff to treat her with respect. Both were gentle yet capable people, and they established an immediate rapport. He invited her to join his inspection tours, another signal that he held her in high esteem, and she invited him and his generals to dinner, always including their wives. Because of their friendship, she probably understood the military situation in Military Region I better than any American in South Vietnam.

In January 1974, Popple asked her to write a *tour d'horizon* of their consular district. She synthesized reports from American advisers in outlying districts into a gloomy memorandum that concluded "all the parameters are negative." She had spent the last six years in South Vietnam or focused on Vietnamese affairs at the State Department. She knew more about the country and had closer relationships with its people than Martin or Polgar, and her pessimistic report should have rung alarm bells in Saigon and Washington. Popple praised it as a "fine job" but said that he doubted Martin would send it to Washington because he wanted to avoid providing the administration or Congress with any excuse for reducing military assistance to Thieu.

Popple's term ended later that year, and Martin replaced him with Al Francis, one of Martin's most loyal subordinates. In February 1975, the State Department evacuated Francis to the United States for treatment of a thyroid condition, leaving Tull acting consul general. After General Truong reported that Thieu was withdrawing the Airborne Division from Military Region I, she began planning for the evacuation of her consular district's American and Vietnamese employees. She was appalled when she read the emergency evacuation plan for the first time. It called for the U.S. military to execute a countrywide evacuation restricted to Americans and made no provision for the kind of incremental collapse occurring in the Central Highlands, or for evacuating South Vietnamese working for the U.S. government, no matter how loyal and endangered. After finishing it, she thought, "We can't do this to the people who have worked for us."

She called a meeting of the heads of the consular sections and U.S. agencies in Da Nang and briefed them on the official plan. They agreed that the consulate should ditch it and evacuate its Vietnamese employees. One called their evacuation "a matter of conscience." They decided to limit the evacuees to employees and their spouses and children, leaving behind siblings and parents. It was harsh, but they could not imagine finding transportation for extended Vietnamese families. Tull returned to her office and drafted a cable to acting ambassador Wolfgang Lehmann requesting permission to begin a phased evacuation. She looked out her window and saw the sun sparkling on the river and a city at peace. Yet she was about to inform Saigon and Washington that the greatest U.S. foreign policy and military adventure since World War II was about to end in ignominy and defeat. She had no illusions about the possible consequences to her career of being the first U.S. diplomat in South Vietnam to deliver this unwelcome news, nor would it help that the person delivering it was a woman.

She cabled Lehmann that if Thieu withdrew the Airborne Division, the Communists would seize South Vietnam's northernmost provinces. She proposed bringing official Americans stationed in outlying provinces into Da Nang by car or helicopter every evening and returning them to their posts every morning to avoid panicking the Vietnamese. She asked for aircraft to fly American dependents and the consular district's Vietnamese employees and their families to Saigon. When she showed a draft to her section chiefs, CIA base chief Bob Grealy asked her to add a sentence saying, "The Base Chief concurs."

She included Grealy's line and decided that if she was going to wreck her career, she might as well go whole hog. She added another line saying that a massive evacuation from all of South Vietnam was inevitable and imminent and recommended that the U.S. Navy reposition elements of the Seventh Fleet off the coast. Her secretary typed up a final draft. As Tull signed off on it, she said, "Okay, here we go. Either they give me what I'm asking for or there's going to be a demand that I leave the post immediately and I'll be back in Washington with my career in shambles." At that moment, Al Francis's wife came into her office with coffee and a plate of fortune cookies. Tull's fortune read, "You've come a long way, baby."

Tull thought that if Ambassador Martin had been in Saigon, he would have dismissed her cable as panicky and premature. Instead, Lehmann called several hours later to say that he had approved her request and that Air America planes would begin arriving the next morning. She informed General Truong and promised that the evacuation would be discreet and done in stages to avoid upsetting the public. She added that some Americans had asked if Vietnamese military personnel such as translators could be included. They feared that the Communists would punish them harshly because of their close working relationships with Americans. Truong approved their departure and called her evacuation "a wise move," a reaction confirming her impression that with the Airborne Division gone, he despaired of defending Hue and Da Nang.

Her slow-motion evacuation ran smoothly. Americans stationed in the provinces brought out a contingent of Vietnamese for evacuation every evening and slept in Da Nang before returning to their posts. Martin learned about what she was doing while on leave and complained to the State Department. He accused her of overreacting and promised to square things away when he returned. Al Francis was also critical when he came back from medical leave. She had already been scheduled to leave for Washington in February, and Francis encouraged her to depart as soon as possible. On March 24, two days before she left for Saigon, General Truong held a dinner in her honor. As she was heading into the dining room, his wife pulled her aside and asked in Vietnamese, "If our country is about to fall to the Communists will you take three of our children?"

Tull recalled the atrocities that the Communists had committed after taking Hue in 1968 and thought, "Oh, this makes perfect sense."

If they captured Truong, he was sure to be executed or spend years in a concentration camp, and his family would face punishment and discrimination. She agreed to take the couple's three middle children, aged nine, eleven, and fifteen. Mrs. Truong could not bear to part with her toddler, and her seventeen-year-old son was almost draft age. Tull doubted that Truong or his wife would escape and assumed that she would be raising their children as her own.

Truong seated her next to him at dinner. CIA base chief Grealy sat on the other side. Speaking to Truong in Vietnamese so Grealy would not understand them, she said, "You know, your wife has asked me to take your children to the United States if the Communists take the country." As Truong turned to face her, she added, "I have told her that I will."

Speaking slowly and pausing between each word, Truong said, "Thank . . . you . . . very . . . much." She took his reply as more evidence that the war was lost and she had been right to risk her career to launch an evacuation.

CHAPTER 3

Who Lost Vietnam?

——⊣⊢——

The photograph that White House photographer David Kennerly took of the March 25 Oval Office meeting called to brief army chief of staff General Frederick Weyand before he led a mission to South Vietnam reveals little about the complicated relationships between some of those in attendance. President Ford sits behind his desk, hands crossed and leaning back in his chair. Ambassador Graham Martin is directly opposite him, and General Weyand and Henry Kissinger are on Martin's left, staring at him intently as he makes the kinds of statements that sixteen days later will prompt Kissinger to tell *Washington Post* editor Ben Bradlee, "Between you and me, we've got an Ambassador there [in Saigon] who is maybe losing his cool."

Weyand had agreed to lead what would prove to be the last and most futile of the multiple fact-finding missions that American presidents had sent to Vietnam. Ford had charged him with determining how much U.S. military aid was necessary to replace South Vietnam's recent losses in arms and equipment and to restore the morale of its armed forces. Before resigning the previous August, President Nixon had requested $1.45 billion in military and economic aid for South Vietnam. Congress had authorized $1 billion but had appropriated only $700 million. Despite Phuoc Long, Ford had been unable to persuade Congress to release the unappropriated $300 million. Now that the situation had worsened, he planned to request the $300 million again, in addition to whatever sum Weyand recommended.

The conversation between Ford, Weyand, Kissinger, and Martin was largely untethered from reality—from what Theresa Tull had reported, Walter Martindale had experienced, Bill Bell had heard, Stuart Herrington had observed, and Tom Glenn's intelligence had revealed. This was not surprising because the premise of the Weyand mission—that additional American aid could alter the outcome of the war—was at best wishful thinking and at worst a fantasy postponing the moment when Kissinger and Ford would have to face the task of evacuating Americans and South Vietnamese. In fact, as Ford, Kissinger, and Weyand knew, Congress was unlikely to authorize whatever sum Weyand suggested, and even if it did, no amount of aid could arrive in time to save South Vietnam. Weyand's mission amounted to political theater, a way for Ford to appear to do *something*. The only person at the Oval Office meeting who apparently did not recognize this was Graham Martin.

The night before leaving Saigon for home leave on March 1, Martin had informed *Los Angeles Times* correspondent George McArthur, the only member of the Saigon press corps whom he professed to like and trust, that there was "no way" that North Vietnam could win militarily. "I told him he was full of shit," McArthur recalled, "although I phrased it more politely." He and Martin had a complicated relationship that McArthur likened to that between "friendly enemies." McArthur had cut his teeth on the Korean War and had been covering Vietnam since 1965. He admired Martin's patriotism ("he's a patriot all right") but believed that pumping more money and arms into South Vietnam was sinful because it would result only in more killing and destruction, given that the final outcome was bound to be a North Vietnamese victory. Among their other disagreements was Martin's unwavering support for Thieu, who he claimed possessed a "boldness of vision" making him "like Napoleon."

By the time of the March 25 Oval Office meeting, Martin had been away from South Vietnam for almost a month. Despite Ban Me Thuot and the Convoy of Tears, at a State Department meeting the day before he had told Kissinger that the situation was not "in any way hopeless" and suggested that the secretary persuade Americans that by surrendering the Central Highlands to the Communists, Thieu had made a "wise consolidation." On this day, he told Ford that South Vietnam's armed forces would give the Communists "a helluva scrap."

As the meeting was ending, Ford turned to Weyand and said, "This is one of the most significant missions you have ever had. You are not going over to lose, but to be tough and see what we can do. . . . We want your recommendations for the things which can be tough and shocking to the North." He added, "I regret I don't have authority to do some of the things President Nixon could do."

Weyand's mission would instead be fruitless and insignificant, and the only "tough and shocking" thing that Ford could have done would have been to order B-52 bombers back to attack North Vietnamese positions, a move that would violate the Case-Church amendment and infuriate Congress and the American people. Martin knew this, but as if channeling Richard Nixon, he said, "If we are not legalistic, there are things we can do."

"Like what?" Kissinger asked.

Martin was silent.

Weyand promised to give the South Vietnamese "a shot in the arm." The day before, Secretary of Defense James Schlesinger had warned him that it was too late for that, telling him, "Fred, be careful. Don't overpromise. Don't get caught up on the notion that you are going to reverse the tide. It is all going down."

Ford and Kissinger disliked and distrusted Schlesinger and had not included him in this meeting. (In November, Ford would fire him.) But despite Ford's talk of doing something "tough and shocking," he and Kissinger privately agreed with Schlesinger's pessimism. Kissinger would later claim that by the time Weyand went to Saigon, "President Ford and I had no illusions about the outcome of the tragedy" and had sent Weyand to reassure America's allies because "we thought cutting off aid to an ally *in extremis* was shameful and could have a disastrous impact on nations relying on America for their security." He failed to mention their other motive: shifting the blame for losing South Vietnam to Congress when it refused to appropriate whatever sum Weyand had recommended. Kissinger would also claim that Ford had requested additional aid for South Vietnam "for largely symbolic reasons," that "those of us who favored going through the motions of giving aid knew it would never get there before the collapse," and that those opposing it knew that "the end was imminent no matter what the fate of the aid bill."

Years later, Kissinger would write that he and Ford had also sent Weyand to South Vietnam and requested that Congress approve supplemental aid to buy time to organize an evacuation. Had they not asked for more aid, he argued, Thieu's government would have panicked, and Americans residing in South Vietnam might have faced retribution from an enraged populace and military. "Above all," he wrote, "we were fully determined to save as many Vietnamese who had cooperated with America as we could. All this imposed a need for gaining time." Because of this, he said, Ford had sent Weyand to South Vietnam, even though "the $300 million supplemental had become largely irrelevant." But if he and Ford had been so concerned with evacuating Vietnamese, he never explained why neither of them had raised the issue with Weyand on March 25.

Before the meeting ended, Kissinger had some fun at Martin's expense, telling him, "I'm glad you're going back out there. When it all goes down and the American people ask, 'Who lost Vietnam?' Philip Habib will have someone to point to."

Assistant Secretary of State for East Asia and Pacific Affairs Philip Habib was a long-standing Martin enemy. He considered Martin "wrong about a lot of things," "a strange, strange man," and "a cold, calculating man with a very keen mind," whom Vietnam had "destroyed physically and somewhat mentally." He had formed some of these opinions while accompanying a congressional fact-finding delegation to South Vietnam in February during which Martin had asserted that his analysis of the situation in Vietnam was correct because "I've been in this business for forty years and I've never been wrong."

There had been a testy exchange between Habib and Martin at the previous day's State Department meeting. After Martin asserted that it was "quite possible" that South Vietnam could hold Da Nang, Habib had shot back that it was not "a possibility," adding, "The situation is so grave that they will be lucky to hold on to the heartland right now."

Martin took offense at Kissinger's joke about Habib blaming him for losing South Vietnam and retorted, "Remember, the one thing you've got going out there is the fact I am the only guy involved in this whole business who has absolutely no pressure to make some god-damned fool decision to avoid criticism. There is absolutely no way I am going to be held responsible for the fall of Saigon. . . . So I am not interested in doing anything except what makes sense right now to get the Americans out alive and as many of our Vietnamese friends, to whom we have committed ourselves, as we can. And I'm going to do that, and I'm not going to be pushed unless you relieve me."

Kissinger's joke had been particularly unkind if you knew, as he did, how much Martin claimed to admire him. Earlier that year, Martin had seized the opportunity of standing next to him at a State Department urinal to praise him as "a genius." Kissinger had replied coolly, "Well, Graham, you're a genius in your own way."

The joke was unkinder still if you knew, as Kissinger did, how reluctant Martin had been to accept the Saigon post because he dreaded being known as the ambassador who had lost South Vietnam. When Nixon offered him the job in 1973, he had been preparing to retire as ambassador to Rome and move to his Tuscan hill farm, where, he liked to say, his greatest ambition was to graft an olive tree onto a juniper so he could put the olive in a martini and get instant gin. (He also told friends and family that he would have liked "to have written, to have explored, just to have lived.") He told his daughter Janet that he would refuse Saigon, "because if anything happens they'll have to make a scapegoat out of somebody." But over the course of several months Kissinger's deputy Alexander Haig bullied him into accepting the position by implying that to refuse it would be dishonorable, on one occasion saying, "If the President [Nixon] says he needs you to go, you go. You cannot spend eight years in Paris, four in Rome, and then turn down a tough job."

Three weeks after Phuoc Long fell, Martin tried to escape his sacrificial goat tether by suggesting that Kissinger name him deputy secretary of state. He made the request in a January 27 cable headed "Personal and Absolutely Eyes Only via Martin Channel." He opened with a blast of flattery, telling Kissinger, "That was one hell of a speech you made in Los Angeles. Historians may compare its long range effect with [Secretary of State] Marshall's Harvard speech which led to European recovery." Marshall's speech had provided "a rallying point, a blueprint," he said, but it had taken "a great many dedicated and intelligent people . . . working under the direction of Under Secretary [Dean] Acheson to effect the historic reversal in American attitudes and preserve Western Europe for the Free World."

Without mentioning Deputy Secretary of State Robert Ingersoll by name (yet), Martin compared him to Dean Acheson and found him wanting, telling Kissinger, "It should, by now, be quite clear to you that you do not have the comparable mechanism to provide for you the indispensable backstopping which Acheson provided for Marshall. With it, under your leadership, the U.S. could really embark on a series of breakthroughs which would make the Marshall period, and even your own remarkable record to date, look like a kindergarten exercise. Without it, your individual genius can provide only such gains where you have time to personally supervise the follow-through of your initiatives." He then volunteered to become Kissinger's Dean Acheson, saying, "I have absolutely no doubt of my ability to organize and marshall the intellectual resources of the Department to provide you the kind of backstopping you need." And if Kissinger decided to make him deputy secretary of state, he added, "Now would be the most appropriate time to do so."

He suggested that Kissinger appoint Ingersoll ambassador to West Germany, giving him "a graceful exit." To discourage Kissinger from thinking that he was trying to escape South Vietnam, he said that if Congress provided the necessary appropriations, "there is no way for Saigon to lose." He reminded him that he had promised to serve in Saigon for only a year and was now into his second and planning to leave in the spring. He closed, "It's been fun working with you."

His pitch was crude: Kissinger could become the century's greatest secretary of state and make Marshall's State Department look like "a kindergarten exercise," but only if Martin was around to "backstop" him. There is no evidence that Kissinger responded, and their first face-to-face meeting since Martin's cable had probably been at the State Department on March 24.

It must have been galling for Martin to have Kissinger brush aside his offer, not least because some of the great American diplomatic luminaries of the twentieth century—Averell Harriman, David Bruce, Douglas Dillon, and George Marshall—had mentored and promoted him and praised his brilliance, leaving him with a Kissinger-sized ego, one even less well disguised than Kissinger's.

Martin was a man who could tell a congressional committee, "For more than 40 years I have [had] a record of totally and unquestioned integrity so secure it needs no defense," claim that "nothing happened in Vietnam, or any other place that I served, that I didn't know about it," and write to Senator William Fulbright (D-Ark.), chairman of the Senate Committee on Foreign Relations, "The one asset I have prized most highly is a reputation for complete and total integrity. . . . This fact is too widely known to be open to serious question and will be completely evident to historians when the archives containing all my reports are finally open." He also informed Fulbright that his experience as a journalist (as a young man, he had briefly reported from Washington for several North Carolina newspapers) governed his policy in dealing with the press, adding, "I was regarded as a good reporter. I often wondered what would have happened had I accepted the invitation to do a column for the *Washington Post*. Perhaps today it might be my byline rather than Scotty Reston's [the noted *New York Times* columnist] to which you would turn over your morning coffee."

Martin's silver hair, elegant suits, patrician bearing, and penetrating pale gray eyes—eyes that an aide said could "open an oyster"—encouraged the assumption that he was a member of the southern gentleman division of the same eastern establishment that had molded Averell Harriman and Douglas Dillon, although, had that been true, he might not have praised his own rectitude and intelligence quite so lavishly. NBC correspondent Garrick Utley noted in a diary that he fit "the familiar profile of a particular generation of American diplomats, those in their fifties or sixties, who rise to positions of influence in the Cold War. Their dress, voice, and demeanor are cut from the same cloth and in the style of privileged backgrounds in the Old South or Boston . . . [and] their eyes are steady and hard."

But instead of a silver spoon, Martin had been born with a tobacco leaf in his mouth. He had grown up as the son of an itinerant Baptist minister in rural North Carolina, walking to school barefoot and stopping to pick tobacco leaves and roll his own cigarettes. His father sold some land during the Depression that was the family's only valuable possession to send him to Wake Forest, where he majored in Latin and Greek. He graduated at twenty, moved to Washington, and married a nurse whose childhood had also been impecunious. They used milk crates as tables and chairs, practicing a frugality that became so ingrained that while serving as ambassador to Rome, he had refused to use government cars for family errands, leaving his wife, Dottie, to drive around in a clapped-out station wagon.

His first break had come when Averell Harriman hired him as his assistant in the National Recovery Administration, one of President Franklin Roosevelt's New Deal agencies. He impressed Harriman, as he would his other mentors, with his intelligence, loyalty, and diligence. With Harriman's backing, he rose quickly through the ranks of the New Deal's bright young men. He opened the first regional office of the Social Security Administration in New York City, where he became a drinking companion of author and fellow North Carolinian Thomas Wolfe, and a close enough friend to serve as a pallbearer at Wolfe's funeral in 1938. He joined the U.S. Army Reserve in 1936 and served during World War II as an intelligence officer in the U.S. Army Air Corps transport command, sometimes briefing army chief of staff General George Marshall. Marshall thought so highly of Martin that when he became secretary of state, he arranged for him to enter the Foreign Service without taking the examinations. Martin served in Paris for eight years, becoming deputy chief of mission under Ambassador Douglas Dillon, the heir to an investment banking fortune. After President Eisenhower appointed Dillon deputy secretary of state, Dillon brought Martin with him to Washington as his special assistant. After President Kennedy appointed Dillon secretary of the Treasury, Martin filled several important New Frontier positions before Kennedy named him ambassador to Thailand.

During his four years in Bangkok, Martin resisted attempts by Secretary of State Dean Rusk and Secretary of Defense Robert McNamara to send U.S. ground troops to Thailand to help its army fight a Communist insurgency. He argued that young American soldiers were finding it difficult to distinguish between friendly and enemy Vietnamese and would find it no easier in Thailand. He pointed out that he "did not see any white faces" on the Communist side in Vietnam and that introducing American soldiers into the Thai conflict risked adding a dangerous racial element. He forbade American advisers in Thailand to carry sidearms, mocked the "narrow military mind" of his opponents in the Pentagon, and expelled an American general who crossed him.

He also became a strident opponent of President Johnson's escalation in Vietnam, later telling a congressional committee, "I felt then, and I still feel now, that it would have been far better if we had chosen, as a matter of national policy, to have confined ourselves to the provision of military and economic assistance, and perhaps some training, but not direct military involvement." His cables to Rusk became more forceful after November 1965, when his beloved adopted son, Glenn Mann, a Marine Corps helicopter pilot, was killed while turning back a Vietcong attack on a South Vietnamese outpost. Mann was Dorothy Martin's nephew, and the Martins had adopted him at an early age after his father had been murdered while witnessing a service station robbery in Georgia. The government of South Vietnam awarded Mann its Gallantry Cross with Palm, and Martin flew to the battlefield where he had fallen to attend a memorial service and receive his decoration from Colonel Pham Van Phu, the officer whose troops would be decimated during the Convoy of Tears. It was believed in Vietnam that French commander General Jean de Lattre de Tassigny had become even more determined to defeat the Vietminh after they killed his son in battle, chopped off his head, and tied his corpse to a water buffalo that they sent back to French lines. It was similarly believed that, like de Tassigny, Graham Martin could not accept that Glenn Mann might have died in vain. Mann's death had been even more devastating because it followed that of Martin's oldest son, who had been killed in an automobile accident during his senior year at the University of Virginia. The boy had missed a curve in the English sports car that Martin and his wife had given him as an early graduation present, driving it down an embankment and into a tree. Martin's hair had turned white overnight.

Rusk finally lost patience with Martin's opposition to transforming the Thai insurgency into the kind of war that had killed his son and recalled him to Washington. Martin would acknowledge that his temperament might have been partly to blame, admitting that he might have erred by "expressing those opinions within the privacy of private channels, but with some pungency of expression that was perhaps too tart." He told friends that he was proud of having taken a stand, remarking wryly that while others had been losing their heads over the Vietnam War, he had already been carrying his own head under his arm. He would also remind friends that the Thai army had defeated its nation's Communist insurgency without help from U.S. combat troops and that Thailand never had a My Lai massacre.

Rusk made him a special assistant for refugee affairs, a demotion probably meant to show him the door. But the same integrity and irascible temperament that had poisoned Martin's relationships with Rusk and McNamara had impressed Richard Nixon when he visited Bangkok as a private attorney on a trade mission that included Vice President Hubert Humphrey. As Humphrey was preparing to offer a toast to the Thai king, Martin had restrained him and said that as President Johnson's personal representative in Thailand he outranked Humphrey and that protocol demanded that he deliver the toast. Nixon overheard him telling Humphrey afterward, "If you become President yourself someday, Mr. Vice-President, you can be sure that I will guard your interests as closely as I did President Johnson's tonight." Instead, it was Nixon who became president. After his election a member of his transition team called Martin to say that the president-elect wanted to offer him an embassy and would like to know where he wanted to serve. Without hesitation Martin said, "Rome," a post usually reserved for a major donor or close friend. The aide urged him to be more realistic and name some other capitals. Martin said "Rome!" again, and got it.

While serving there, he funneled millions from a covert embassy fund to anti-Communist parties, including a payment of almost $1 million that he sent over the objection of the CIA to an Italian general who would be accused of plotting to overthrow the government. Martin was such a private man that it is difficult to know whether he had become an increasingly hard-line cold warrior because Communists had killed his son or because it put him more in tune with the Nixon administration, but his politics had always been idiosyncratic. During World War II the army had threatened him with a court-martial for making scathing attacks on the policy of incarcerating Japanese Americans in concentration camps. His liberal convictions were also evident in the two men he lionized as his heroes: David Bruce, the moderate southern Democrat who had preceded Dillon as ambassador to Paris, and Adlai Stevenson, a favorite of left-wing Democrats despite his two failed presidential candidacies. In a letter to the secretary-general of Amnesty International, Martin would describe himself as "a hopelessly old-fashioned liberal humanitarian."

Rome had capped a brilliant diplomatic career for a barefoot boy from North Carolina. In mid-twentieth-century America it was harder to be a self-made diplomat than a self-made businessman, and few ambassadors of Martin's rank had come from such modest beginnings. He had proven himself smart and diligent and had hitched his wagon to some of the century's brightest diplomatic stars. His detractors, however, would accuse him of being "a born conspirator" and "a skilled bureaucratic knife-fighter." *Los Angeles Times* correspondent George McArthur believed that his courtly manner concealed "the most Machiavellian mind" he had ever encountered. Kissinger has described him as a paranoid who "tended to consider anything less than 100 percent support as betrayal." An anonymous subordinate told a reporter that he was "a man with a mission different from the rest of us," adding, "He was going to save Vietnam all by himself. He thought he was one of the Caesars." Martin compared himself to a honey badger, a ferocious weasel-like beast known for sinking its sharp teeth into an opponent's balls.

Still, he was the only one at the March 25 Oval Office meeting to express any concern over what might happen to America's South Vietnamese allies and to pledge to evacuate "as many of our Vietnamese friends" as possible. His concern might have been motivated more by his belief that abandoning them, like incarcerating the Japanese Americans, was morally wrong and could only tarnish America's honor than by any great affection for the Vietnamese people.

White House photographer David Kennerly was also concerned about America's South Vietnamese allies. He had failed to raise the issue at the Oval Office meeting because he had made it a rule not to speak while he was shooting. Once Martin, Weyand, and Kissinger had left the Oval Office, he plopped into a chair and said, "Mr. President, I really want to go on that mission." He argued that his friends in the Saigon press corps and among the younger diplomats at the embassy would speak more openly with him than with Weyand, telling Ford, "Vietnam is falling to pieces. I've spent two and a half years there . . . and I've just got to go back. I've got to see for myself." He did not add that he wanted to help his Vietnamese friends escape and hoped that his photographs and eyewitness account might influence how Ford handled the fall of South Vietnam.

He also wanted to witness the final days of a war that had been the defining experience of his life. He had joined the UPI as a staff photographer at twenty-one and lobbied to be sent to Vietnam because he knew that the war would be the biggest story of his generation. He had taken daring combat photographs, won a 1972 Pulitzer Prize, covered the release of American POWs from Hanoi, and returned to the United States to work for *Time* and shoot the photograph of Gerald Ford appearing on the magazine's cover. Their photo session had led to an intergenerational friendship between Ford, the straight-arrow midwestern politician, and Kennerly, the bearded and blue-jean-wearing West Coast hipster. Ford found Kennerly's iconoclastic humor and high spirits refreshing; Kennerly admired Ford's lack of guile and vanity. After Nixon resigned, Ford appointed Kennerly White House photographer and gave him unrivaled access to him and his family.

After considering his request to accompany Weyand, Ford said, "Sure, David, I understand. And I'll be interested to hear your views of what's going on when you get back."

Kennerly slapped a sign on his office door announcing, "Gone to Vietnam, back in a week or so," and went upstairs to the family quarters to say good-bye. Ford asked if he could do anything for him before he left. Kennerly said the banks were closed and he was out of cash. Ford emptied his wallet and handed him $47. As he was leaving, Ford flipped him a quarter and said, "You might as well clean me out." Then he threw an arm around his shoulder and said, "Take care of yourself over there."

The Weyand mission flew to Saigon on a U.S. Air Force Lockheed C-141 transport outfitted with "comfort pallet" modules containing bedrooms and conference rooms. Kennerly's black-and-white photographs of the flight have a film noir quality. Men with tight expressions stand in shadows or sit under weak cones of light. Weyand stares up at a large map of Vietnam pinned to a curtain. Martin leans against a wall, head down, his profile a dark silhouette. Martin and Weyand speak in the corridor, and although Martin is over six feet, Weyand, a raw-boned man with a receding hairline who bears a resemblance to John Wayne, stands hands on hips, towering over him.

During much of the flight Martin sat alone, his head wreathed in smoke as he chain-smoked his way across the Pacific while reading the reports and cables that had piled up during his leave. He was a chronic insomniac, and sleepless nights and cigarettes had carved deep lines into his face, making him appear a decade older than sixty-two. His pallor and habit of working late into the night had led to his nickname, the Gray Ghost.

The CIA had sent George Carver and Ted Shackley, men who, according to Kennerly, "worked in the deep shadows." Shackley had an archetypal Cold War résumé: West Berlin in the 1950s, Miami during the Bay of Pigs and Cuban missile crisis, chief of station in Saigon from 1968 to 1972. His light blond hair, pale complexion, and reluctance to be photographed had led colleagues to call him the "Blond Ghost." During the flight, the Blond and Gray Ghosts joined General Weyand around a table covered by a map of South Vietnam. Weyand and Shackley took turns briefing Martin on the retreats and defeats of South Vietnam's armed forces. Martin pointed to a place on the map and asked incredulously, "You mean that division is no longer here?"

"That division is nowhere, Graham," Weyand said. "It no longer exists."

"But that doesn't happen!"

"It does; it has," Shackley said.

Weyand decided that Martin could not accept the dimensions of the catastrophe and signaled for Shackley to end the briefing.

Since arriving in Saigon in 1973, Martin had insisted that Thieu was popular and competent and that his armed forces could defeat the Communists and his country would prosper if Congress increased U.S. aid to its government and if the press and the antiwar Left—opponents he called the "worldwide community of alienated intellectuals"—stopped criticizing and undermining him. Ban Me Thuot and the Convoy of Tears had not shaken Martin's faith in Thieu nor his belief that he knew Vietnam better than anyone. Nor had they convinced him that the war that had killed his adopted son might be lost.

The Vietnam War had channeled the careers of Shackley, Weyand, and others on the mission, and they had in turn contributed to the catastrophe they were flying to Saigon to assess. Weyand had arrived in South Vietnam in 1966 in command of the famed Twenty-Fifth "Tropic Lightning" Infantry Division. Two years later he was commanding U.S. forces in the southern third of South Vietnam and reporting directly to General William Westmoreland. He had next served as the chief military adviser to the U.S. delegation at the Paris Peace Talks before becoming the last U.S. commander in South Vietnam. In that role, he had presided over the flag-lowering ceremony at the U.S. military headquarters at Tan Son Nhut on March 29, 1973, declaring in English and Vietnamese, "Our mission has been accomplished," and saying that he was departing "with a strong feeling of pride in what we have achieved." He concluded, "It is our sincere hope that the peace with honor that has been our goal will last forever."

Kissinger, Ford, and Martin probably assumed that because of this Weyand would make a strong case for additional aid. They might have been less confident had they known that in 1967 he had drawn aside CBS correspondent Murray Fromson at a Saigon cocktail party and said, "Westy [Westmoreland] just doesn't get it. The war is unwinnable. We've reached a stalemate, and we should find a dignified way out." Several days later he had repeated his pessimistic assessment to *New York Times* reporter R. W. Apple, adding, "Unless a more positive and more simple theme than simple anti-Communism can be found, the war appears likely to go on until someone gets tired and quits, which could take generations." In a front-page *New York Times* article titled "Vietnam: The Signs of Stalemate," Apple repeated Weyand's scathing assessment of the war, identifying him as "a senior American general." Neither President Johnson nor Westmoreland ever learned his identity, and at Weyand's request it remained secret until Westmoreland died in 2005.

While the Weyand mission was airborne, the shadings and arrows on its maps identifying the movements of North and South Vietnamese troops became obsolete. Deputy Chief of Mission Wolfgang Lehmann cabled Washington that the situation in the North had "deteriorated considerably in the past 24 hours," and Ford and Kissinger received a March 28 National Intelligence Estimate (NIE) reporting that government forces in Military Region I had abandoned "large quantities of ammunition and fuel" and did not "appear capable of standing up to the communists" and that South Vietnam's leadership was reacting with "dismay and depression." The NIE predicted that the government would soon control "little more than the delta and Saigon and surrounding populated areas," and concluded, "The communists will keep up their military pressure to topple the GVN [government of South Vietnam] by outright defeat unless there have been political changes in Saigon that open the way to a new settlement on near-surrender terms." Its only note of optimism was a forecast that there was "likely to be defeat by early 1976." Three days before Ford and Kissinger received this assessment, North Vietnam's Politburo had ordered General Dung to "liberate Saigon" before the dry season ended in May.

And while Weyand was in the air, CIA director William Colby predicted at a meeting of the National Security Council (NSC) that government forces in Da Nang might hold out for two weeks (the city fell a day and a half later), and Secretary of Defense James Schlesinger, who was more realistic about Thieu's prospects, ordered the U.S. military to prepare to execute an evacuation. Kissinger meanwhile told reporters that South Vietnam's fate lay in the hands of the U.S. Congress and that the Paris Peace Accords had been "negotiated on the assumption that the United States would continue economic and military aid to South Vietnam." He framed the issue as "an elementary question of what kind of a people we are," and of whether Americans would "deliberately destroy an ally by withholding aid from it in its moment of extremity," declaring, "We cannot abandon friends in one part of the world without jeopardizing the security of friends everywhere." He was offering the same rationale for U.S. involvement in the war that Kennedy, Johnson, and Nixon had—that the United States had to support South Vietnam to prove itself a reliable Cold War ally.

Before landing at Tan Son Nhut, Martin invited David Kennerly, Foreign Service officer Ken Quinn, and Principal Deputy Assistant Secretary of Defense for International Security Affairs Erich von Marbod to stay at his residence. He knew that Kennerly was close to Ford and had to assume that his verbal report to the president might be more influential than Weyand's written one. Quinn was currently serving on the staff of Kissinger's National Security Council, and Martin also assumed (correctly, as it turned out) that he would be writing his own report for Kissinger. Martin had shown little interest in Quinn while he was serving as vice-consul in a provincial capital in the Mekong delta, but that had changed once he learned that Quinn was leaving to join the staff of the NSC. He had attended Quinn's wedding to his Vietnamese fiancée and had invited him to a private meeting at the embassy during which he had leaned back in his chair and while staring at the ceiling had delivered a rambling soliloquy about the war and the "mattress mice" at the State Department who were undermining him. After several minutes he lost his train of thought and drifted off. Quinn left unnerved.

Shortly before leaving on the Weyand mission, Quinn had joined a clandestine group of young Foreign Service officers who had started meeting over lunch in the State Department cafeteria or in empty offices. They had all served tours in Vietnam and made Vietnamese friends. They believed that South Vietnam was doomed and that the embassy's evacuation planning was inadequate. Quinn had lobbied to be included on the Weyand mission so he could help to organize the evacuation of his wife's relatives and encourage diplomats at the embassy to form a similar group that could coordinate its operations with the State Department cafeteria cabal.

Martin's third houseguest, Erich von Marbod, was the Pentagon's logistics expert for Vietnam, a legendary figure known as Mr. Military Assistance who enjoyed the confidence of Secretary of Defense Schlesinger and was skilled at moving equipment rapidly to trouble spots. The previous summer, Senator John Stennis, the powerful head of the Armed Services Committee, had asked Schlesinger to dispatch a trusted subordinate to South Vietnam to estimate how much assistance the Thieu government really needed. Schlesinger had sent von Marbod, who had concluded that the $1.4 billion that Martin and other Thieu supporters were requesting was excessive. Despite disagreeing on this issue, von Marbod liked Martin, saying later, "He was a friend of mine. I was a guest in his home. I drank his liquor. I held Nit Noy [his poodle]; I knew his wife, Dottie, and his daughter Janet. And I thought we were good friends, but obviously at the very end our relationship changed." This end was now five weeks away.

CHAPTER 4

Designated Fall Guy

———┤├———

When the Weyand mission landed at Tan Son Nhut at 3:00 a.m. on March 28, the runways of this once busy military and civilian airfield were deserted and its buildings dark. As passengers lined up to disembark, Martin pushed ahead of Weyand, explaining that because he was President Ford's representative to South Vietnam, protocol demanded that he disembark first. Deputy Chief of Mission Wolfgang Lehmann and CIA chief of station Thomas Polgar met him at the foot of the stairs. The week before, Polgar had cabled CIA headquarters complaining that the embassy had become "a rudderless ship" in Martin's absence and that Lehmann and other senior personnel had not grasped the implications of losing the Central Highlands and were wasting time debating improvements to the recreation center and overtime pay for Vietnamese employees.

When Polgar informed Martin that the situation in Da Nang was ominous, Martin brushed him off, saying that in his experience people always exaggerated how bad things were in Vietnam and were always proved wrong. Polgar pulled Quinn aside and urged him to persuade Martin that this time the situation really *was* ominous.

Lehmann accompanied Martin to his residence and briefed him for an hour. He reported that Thieu had lost the Central Highlands, South Vietnamese armed forces in Military Region I had disintegrated, and the Communists were poised to take Da Nang. Martin said he would catch a few hours' sleep before flying to Da Nang to assess the situation. Lehmann told him that would be impossible. Mobs had run amok at the airport there the day before, pummeling Consul General Al Francis and ending the U.S. airlift.

Several hours later Martin arrived at the embassy. He was jet-lagged and sleepless, but his optimism remained undiminished. He told a CIA officer who had just escaped from Da Nang that he planned to fly there that afternoon. According to a CIA report of their conversation, "Only strenuous argument persuaded him [Martin] that he could not land at an airfield controlled by the NVA [North Vietnamese Army]." Another CIA agent overheard one embassy employee telling another, "He [Martin] thinks Da Nang will be retaken. He's insane."

Theresa Tull had been sleeping on the couch in Martin's office while monitoring developments in Da Nang. She thought that Martin was in "Never, Never Land" and arranged to meet with Joe Bennett, who headed the political section. Bennett was a Martin acolyte but had struck her as realistic and comfortable working with a female officer. Gathering up her courage, she said, "Joe, it's over. This place can't last. . . . South Vietnam can't hold with I Corps [General Truong's command] gone. . . . I don't give it thirty days."

He replied, "I'm afraid you're right," but she wondered if he had the courage to tell Martin that.

She ran into David Kennerly, who announced he was flying to Da Nang that afternoon and said Martin had promised him a plane.

"You can't go there," she said quickly. "It's finished."

NSA chief Tom Glenn, who had predicted the attack on Ban Me Thuot and had almost been trapped there, came to Martin's office to brief him on the SIGINT intercepts indicating that North Vietnamese units were heading toward Saigon. He explained that the Communists would soon be in position to attack the city and requested Martin's approval to begin evacuating his forty-three American employees and their dependents. He added that he was also concerned for the safety of the twenty-seven hundred South Vietnamese working for the Directorate General for Technical Security (DGTS), South Vietnam's equivalent of the American National Security Agency.

Martin dismissed Glenn's intelligence as "gloom and doom" and Communist deception. He said that the NSA employees were "mission-essential" and that their departure would demoralize the DGTS. Glenn replied that the situation in Saigon could deteriorate faster than anyone anticipated, trapping his cryptologists. He offered to stay until the end with two communications specialists if Martin would permit the others to leave. "Calm down," Martin said, as if dealing with an excitable child. "I've got things under control. Let me handle it."

Glenn alerted the director of the NSA, General Lew Allen Jr., that because of Martin's intransigence the American cryptologists risked becoming Communist prisoners. Allen cabled back, "Close down the operation and get everyone out before someone gets killed." Glenn sent forty-one of his American employees and their dependents out of the country on bogus vacations, unmerited home leave, and sham business trips. He lent his Tan Son Nhut base pass to his Vietnamese driver so that the man could put his family on a flight. He filled the trunk of his black Ford sedan with Vietnamese friends and drove it through to Tan Son Nhut without being stopped because it had diplomatic plates. He tried to persuade a close friend in the army to evacuate his family, but the man's wife refused to leave without him, and he refused to desert his men. When Glenn asked him what he would do when Communist tanks rolled into Saigon, he said, "I will shoot my three children and I will shoot my wife, then I will shoot myself." He did not escape, and for decades Glenn has wondered if he carried out his threat.

Fred Thomas was serving as embassy duty officer during the week Martin returned. He read all the incoming and outgoing cables, including those from the consulate in Da Nang, and thought that Martin was "paying no attention to reality" and "off in his own dream world." On March 28, Martin's first day back, Thomas attended a meeting of the embassy evacuation committee called by its chairman, air attaché Gavin McCurdy. He had expected to find McCurdy's office jammed, but the CIA, AID, USIS, and the embassy's administrative and security departments had not sent representatives, leaving Thomas, McCurdy, and army attaché Chuck Wahle the only ones in attendance. After McCurdy reported that Martin had refused to meet with them to discuss the committee's plans, Thomas suggested enlisting Major General Homer Smith and the military. Wahle called Smith, and the three saw him at the DAO that afternoon. After listening to their criticisms of Martin, Smith proposed evacuating non-official Americans and their dependents on the air force transports that were delivering military supplies to Tan Son Nhut. Thomas later called it "the beginning of the evacuation of Vietnam." Two days later at Easter lunch, Wahle took Thomas aside and said, "Get your wife and children out of here as fast as you can. This thing is not going to last much longer."

But many in Washington thought it would. During a meeting of the National Security Council on March 28, CIA director William Colby predicted that Thieu would hold Saigon and the delta until 1976. Kissinger defended Thieu, calling his army's retreats "strategic" and arguing that he had ordered them "because he was not getting enough support from the United States" and needed to conserve his military's dwindling supplies. Deputy Secretary of Defense William Clements shot back that if that had been Thieu's goal, it had been a spectacular failure because his army was about to abandon $200 million in arms and equipment in Da Nang. Kissinger responded by praising Thieu, the architect of the war's greatest debacle, as "far and away the most capable of all Vietnamese leaders" and someone who "holds things together."

That same afternoon Martin summoned Foreign Service officer Don Hays and two Americans serving in the DAO and CIA to his office and accused them of evacuating South Vietnamese to Clark Air Base in the Philippines on U.S. Air Force transport planes, thereby violating the laws of the United States, South Vietnam, and the Philippines. Their shenanigans had come to his attention when President Ferdinand Marcos complained to U.S. ambassador to the Philippines William Sullivan about illegal Vietnamese immigrants arriving in his country. Martin told the three they were "fired" and must immediately leave South Vietnam. The DAO and CIA employees complied, but Hays simply returned to his office in the embassy's finance department and went back to work.

Hays was a physically imposing man, a rugby player and former paratrooper who stood out in any gathering, but because he was also the youngest, lowest-paid, and most junior Foreign Service officer in the largest U.S. mission in the world, he thought that he could fade into the woodwork. He had decided to defy Martin because he was afraid of what might happen to his driver and household staff and the fifty-two Vietnamese employees in his department if he left. Who else would evacuate them? he asked himself. Who else would tell his maid, who had two sons in the military and refused to leave without them, "Steal everything in this house, and tell the VC that you worked for a pig and had to lick his boots"? Who else would help the crotchety old Vietnamese man in the budget section who had told Hays when he signed pay vouchers for the clandestine DAO evacuation, "Don, you do what you've got to do and I'll cover for you."

Hays had always been something of a rebel, and joining the Foreign Service had not changed that. His father was on the West Point faculty, and they had had the customary generation gap arguments: Hays had his doubts about the war, and his father supported it. Hays had enlisted in the army anyway and had gone to Vietnam as a combat infantryman. Meanwhile, his father had changed his mind and wrote to him saying, "This war is a lost cause. I don't want to lose you so make sure you don't put yourself in harm's way." Hays replied that he had just transferred to the 101st Airborne so that advice had come a little late. He had the usual late-1960s Vietnam experience: fragging, racial tension, and soldiers refusing to join risky patrols who told him, "Sarge, I'm just not going to go." He thought that his men were bait, sent out in small groups to draw out the enemy so they could be bombed. By the time he returned to the United States, he had become, he said, "very cynical, very upset, and very angry," but also very much in love with his wife, whom he had met in New Zealand during his first R&R (rest and recuperation) trip. He volunteered for a second tour so he could return on another R&R and marry her. He attended college in Santa Barbara and graduate school at Georgetown

University, where he met Ken Moorefield. After entering the Foreign Service, he asked for Seville but got Saigon and arrived during the summer of 1974.

His job as embassy paymaster had ensnared him in the evacuation scheme. After Ban Me Thuot fell, embassy security officer Marvin Garrett had invited him to a late-night barbecue at the recreation center along with representatives from other U.S. agencies. They were all concerned that unless they began evacuating their Vietnamese employees, the embassy might suddenly pull out Americans and leave the Vietnamese behind. Garrett said they could not count on Martin doing anything and proposed sending some of the embassy's Vietnamese employees and their families to the Philippines on the underground railroad that Andy Gembara and Colonel LeGro were running through the DAO. Garrett asked Hays to sign vouchers so that Vietnamese evacuees could receive their severance pay before flying there. Hays understood that he was participating in a conspiracy to violate the immigration regulations of three nations, including his own, but agreed anyway. Martin did not suspect Garrett of being involved in the scheme and later complained to him about Hays and the others usurping his authority. When Garrett admitted having known about the operation, Martin asked why he had not alerted him. "Sir, I'm ready to follow any orders you give," Garrett replied. "But why don't you give any?" It was a cheeky response but one that the brash and larger-than-life Garrett could pull off.

Deputy Chief of Mission Wolfgang Lehmann's remarks to the American Chamber of Commerce in Saigon on March 28 bore no resemblance to the pessimistic briefing that he had given Martin earlier that morning. He told chamber members that Thieu's "light at the top" strategy was "wise," ARVN resistance was "stiffening," the retreats were over, the government would mount an "aggressive defense" of Saigon, and a successful assault on the city was "inconceivable." He implored them not to demoralize the South Vietnamese by evacuating their American staff and dependents and called the loss of the northern provinces "a blessing in disguise" because it had resulted in a more easily defendable and economically viable South Vietnam. There was stifled laughter when he insisted that there had never been a better time to invest in the next Asian economic powerhouse and suggested that they increase their investments in South Vietnam and urge their friends and associates to do likewise. Martin would later call remarks like Lehmann's part of a calculated "theater" aimed at preventing panic and boosting morale. But some embassy officials must have believed in their own "theater"; why else would they spend hours discussing the construction of a 550-room Hyatt Regency hotel and conference center?

While Lehmann was lecturing the American Chamber of Commerce, a fireplug-shaped middle-aged man wearing a Panama hat modeled on the one Clark Gable had worn in *Gone with the Wind* burst into Martin's office demanding to know why Martin was refusing to see him, shouting, "I can get in to see popes, heads of state, generals!"

This was Martin's introduction to Ed Daly, the perpetually inebriated, publicity-mad multimillionaire who had turned two World War II surplus transport planes into World Airways, a successful charter airline based in Oakland, California. He was a genuine, albeit erratic, humanitarian with a fondness for enterprises involving children, servicemen, refugees, and Vietnam. He supported half a dozen South Vietnamese orphanages, had launched a scheme to bring twenty-five thousand servicemen home from Vietnam for furloughs, donated several million of his $200 million fortune to programs for disadvantaged youths in Oakland, and had airlifted ten thousand Hungarian refugees to the United States after their nation's failed 1956 anti-Communist revolution. He described himself as "Wyatt Earp with airplanes."

After the U.S. government chartered three of his World Airways 727s to evacuate American and Vietnamese refugees from Da Nang, he had come to oversee the operation. During the previous three days, his planes had flown out two thousand evacuees, mostly women and children. The day before, the embassy had suspended his airlift after refugees and undisciplined soldiers mobbed one of his planes at the

Da Nang airport. Outraged at having his good works sidelined, he had blustered and cursed his way into Martin's office. A marine guard had noticed a shoulder holster under his Hawaiian shirt and arrived close on his heels.

When Martin became angry, his courtly southern gentleman manner became even courtlier, and he lowered his voice to make an adversary strain to hear him. "Give the gun to the Marine if you want to talk to me," he said, his voice low and calm.

Daly shouted that Saigon would fall within two weeks and accused him of concealing the truth and being "nothing but a used-car salesman," whatever that meant.

Martin politely informed him that he no longer had clearance to fly into Da Nang.

"What are those bastards at Tan Son Nhut going to do if I take off without their goddamned clearance?" he demanded.

"I imagine they'll shoot you down."

"And then what will you do?"

"Applaud," Martin said. "And who the hell do you think you are?" he demanded. "I mean you don't know your ass from a hole in the ground, you don't know what this whole thing is about."

As Daly left Martin's office, he told the World Airways executive accompanying him, "We're going anyway."

Martin gave the job of managing Daly to George "Jake" Jacobson, a retired army colonel in his early sixties with the vague title of "Special Assistant for Field Operations." Over the years he had become the embassy's jack-of-all-trades, filling a range of military and civilian positions, becoming an expert in rural pacification, establishing friendships with many senior South Vietnamese government and military officials, and working under four ambassadors. His greatest moment had come during the Tet Offensive when a Vietcong squad fought its way onto the embassy grounds, trapping him in his office on the second floor of a small villa. An American MP noticed a Communist soldier entering the villa building and had tossed Jacobson a pistol through an open window. The soldier emptied his AK-47 up the stairway, and Jacobson leaned down and shot him dead. He had the AK-47 silver plated and mounted on his wall with an engraving that said, "The Viet Cong fired this and missed. The Colonel fired back and didn't." Jacobson had been a professional magician and remained something of a showman. Kissinger was lukewarm about him, but Martin had kept him on, guaranteeing his loyalty.

Despite Martin's and Jacobson's admonitions, Daly flew to Da Nang the next morning. Jacobson would later condemn him as an "unhousebroken, miserable man" and "one of the most despicable human beings" he had ever met. Still, like Walter Martindale, Daly was one of the first Americans to risk his life to evacuate Vietnamese civilians. His plan was straightforward and noble. He would shuttle three World Airways 727s between Da Nang and Tan Son Nhut and rescue several thousand women and children, freeing their husbands and fathers to return to the battlefield. He joined the first flight and was in the cockpit when an air traffic controller at Tan Son Nhut ordered pilot Ken Healy to abort the flight and return to the terminal because he lacked clearance. Daly ordered Healy to "experience radio failure," and the 727 lifted off as the controller was shouting, "Abort! Abort!"

Da Nang's airport appeared peaceful from the air, but the moment Daly's plane touched down, crowds of civilians and soldiers burst from its hangars and terminal. They raced toward the jet in jeeps, cars, and armored vehicles, on bikes and motorbikes, and on foot. Healy tried to taxi to a distant corner of the runway but had to jam on the brakes when a military policeman drew his pistol and jumped in front of the plane.

Daly and the crew lowered a narrow metal stairway from the tail and were immediately besieged. Soldiers and civilians punched, tripped, and kicked one another in a mad scramble to get aboard. Soldiers trampled children and elbowed women. One shot a family of five and leaped over their bodies to reach the stairs. As the cabin filled with soldiers, a flight attendant screamed, "Where are the women and children? Where are the women and children!" Daly stood on the stairway, grabbing at the women and children who had made it this far, punching soldiers (he was a former Golden Gloves boxer), and smashing them with the butt of his pistol. He staggered down the aisle covered in scratches and blood. His clothes were shredded, and his trousers had been yanked below his knees.

The crew could pull the stairway up only halfway. Some refugees clung to it, while others climbed into the cargo hold and wheel compartment. As Healy began taxiing, a soldier lobbed a grenade and others opened fire. Abandoned vehicles, angry soldiers, and the bodies of people killed in the stampede blocked the main runway. Healy took off from the middle of the taxiway as North Vietnamese rockets slammed into the airfield. He detoured onto the grass verge to avoid an abandoned vehicle and ran off the pavement, smashing through some flimsy buildings before becoming airborne. Stowaways plummeted to their deaths from the stairs and wheel compartment. Blood covered the aisle and 268 passengers, twice the plane's capacity, sat two to a seat. Only five women and two children had made it aboard. Instead of rescuing the soldiers' families, Daly had rescued the soldiers, leaving the corpses of women and children behind on the runway. After watching news film of the fiasco, President Ford turned to a friend and said, "That's it. It's time to pull the plug. Vietnam is gone."

While Daly was barely escaping from Da Nang with his life, General Truong, who had entrusted his children to Theresa Tull, returned to his headquarters and found it abandoned. He drove to the beach at Hoi An, where small boats were ferrying his marines out to Vietnamese Navy vessels. He waded into the surf and swam toward one of these boats. On March 10, he had been the most respected general in South Vietnam; nineteen days later, he was swimming for his life. Some marines jumped into the water and grabbed him. As they were hoisting him aboard, he began sobbing.

His principal contribution to the catastrophe had been to obey conflicting and constantly changing orders from Thieu and the chiefs of staff. When he and Thieu had met in Saigon on March 13, Thieu had ordered him to prepare to abandon all of Military Region I except for Da Nang. He had complied and started withdrawing from the northernmost provinces. During a meeting on March 19, Thieu had ordered him to stop withdrawing from Hue and defend it "at all costs." That same afternoon, he had received a message from South Vietnam's chiefs of staff warning that his forces were insufficient to hold both Hue and Da Nang and ordering him to leave Hue. He obeyed and his marines began retreating toward Da Nang. North Vietnamese artillery pounded highways already jammed with refugees, and their retreat turned into a rout. The navy attempted to evacuate troops from the beaches, but artillery fire hit some ships and waves swamped others. When Hue fell on March 26, five marine battalion commanders shot themselves.

By March 29, half a million panicky civilians and angry soldiers had doubled Da Nang's population. Military officers and government officials fled, policemen shed their uniforms, and leaderless soldiers filled the streets, halting traffic and robbing pedestrians. Refugees searched for family members, wounded soldiers died before reaching hospitals, and bodies lay sprawled on sidewalks. Famished children begged; stores were looted and women raped. Instead of defending Da Nang, its garrison mutinied and shot their officers. The marines were the most terrifying. They had long hair and tiger-striped fatigues and had emulated the U.S. soldiers who had trained them, decorating their bodies with homemade "Love" and "Peace" tattoos. UPI reporter Paul Vogle wrote that "their skin seemed taut, like there was something high-powered behind their eyes."

A mob screaming anti-American curses besieged the U.S. consulate. Inside, phones rang unanswered and papers blew through empty corridors. A rear guard of diplomats leaped over the back fence as the mob pushed down the gate. Two nights before, consulate officials had attempted to evacuate three hundred Vietnamese toward whom, according to a CIA report, they "felt a specific obligation." The *Osceola*, an Australian tugboat under charter to the U.S. Military Sealift Command (MSC), a civilian branch of the navy, towed a barge to the dock opposite the consulate. The plan had been to load evacuees onto the barge at night and ferry them across the harbor to MSC freighters anchored offshore. Instead, thousands mobbed the barge. People tumbled into the water and drowned or were crushed against the dock.

One of the consulate's marine guards, despite having extensive combat experience, recalled the scene being "one of the most tragic things" he had seen while serving in South Vietnam.

On March 29, the remaining American consulate employees left on the *Osceola,* taking as many Vietnamese as they could fit aboard. The tug crossed the harbor, passing corpses and capsized boats. Sampans, rowboats, and fishing boats were so overloaded and low in the water that passengers tumbled overboard whenever they hit a wave or crossed a wake. The *Osceola* delivered its evacuees to the *Pioneer Contender,* an American-flagged freighter chartered by the MSC. Its American crewmen had barricaded themselves on the bridge, while deserters terrorized the civilians jammed onto its decks, executing anyone who resisted or whom they suspected of being a Communist.

On March 30, Easter Sunday, a lightly armed advance guard of Communist troops rolled into Da Nang and restored order. The most heavily defended city in South Vietnam, its warehouses filled with food and ammunition sufficient for a sixty-day siege, had capitulated without a fight. In nineteen days Thieu had lost five of his eleven divisions and over a billion dollars' worth of military equipment, and Communist forces had eviscerated an army that the United States had spent a decade training, financing, supplying, and advising.

The news reports, photographs, and films of Da Nang, the Convoy of Tears, and Ed Daly's flight received wide coverage in the United States. Instead of unleashing Americans' charitable impulses, the news convinced them that the United States should avoid becoming re-involved in the war, even on a humanitarian basis, and opinion polls showed a majority of Americans opposed to accepting Vietnamese refugees. After years of being misled and lied to, of mistakes and horrors, and billions spent and fifty-eight thousand U.S. servicemen killed, many American hearts had become so hardened toward South Vietnam and its people that even the Da Nang and Convoy of Tears horrors could not soften them.

Vietnamese in Saigon feared a similar debacle would occur in their city and that the Thieu government and its American allies would be unable to protect or evacuate them. Americans in Saigon heard about

Consul General Francis's narrow escape from Da Nang, the sudden collapse of civil authority, and refugees and deserters running amok, and they feared a repetition in Saigon. Da Nang convinced some in Congress and the Ford administration that the time had come to evacuate U.S. citizens from South Vietnam, even if that meant abandoning America's South Vietnamese allies. Ambassador Martin believed that the anarchy in Da Nang proved the importance of avoiding anything that might panic Saigon's civilians and military. But neither he nor anyone else in senior positions at the embassy, the White House, or the State Department seemed to understand why Da Nang's final days would not be replicated in Saigon: namely that in Da Nang, refugees had fought to the death for places on planes and ships because there was still a South Vietnam for them to escape to. In Saigon, however, people would face a different decision: whether to live in a Communist Vietnam or become exiles in the United States.

During a State Department staff meeting on March 31, Kissinger asked Deputy Secretary of State Philip Habib, "Why don't they [the South Vietnamese military] fight any place?"

Habib explained that a phased withdrawal had "turned into a rout, psychologically and militarily."

Kissinger criticized General Truong for being "on a goddam barge in the harbor" and pressed Habib to explain *why* the Communists had routed Truong's forces, even though they were "not being attacked very much."

"Because they were told to withdraw," Habib said, repeating that their retreat had "turned into a rout."

Kissinger blamed the Communists for violating the Paris Peace Accords and the U.S. Congress for demoralizing South Vietnam's government and military by slashing aid. He asked Habib, "But do you have any question in your mind that we triggered them into this rout?"

Habib did not "buy that line," he said. But neither he nor anyone else at the staff meeting told Kissinger the truth: that the fundamental reason that Generals Truong and Phu's armies "would not fight anywhere" was that the Nixon-Kissinger policy of Vietnamization had been a failure and that once the United States withdrew its firepower, warplanes, and advice, the South Vietnamese Army had been revealed to be a rickety structure, and so weakened by corruption, nepotism, and feckless leadership that it had collapsed in the first strong wind.

Dottie Martin had not yet returned from North Carolina and Ken Quinn was visiting his in-laws, so David Kennerly and Martin dined together alone at the embassy residence on the evening of March 28. They talked late into the night. Martin delivered a series of soliloquies about his career, Vietnam, and his sons that impressed Kennerly as anguished and sincere. Perhaps fatigue, jet lag, and the dispiriting reports from Da Nang had left Martin more open and vulnerable, or he might have felt more comfortable unburdening himself to Kennerly because the photographer was no longer a working journalist. He described the automobile accident that had killed his eldest son, and the battle that had claimed the life of his adopted son. He admitted being doubtful that South Vietnam could survive but said he had a duty to feign optimism and "keep the flag flying," because if the word got out that the embassy was planning an evacuation "the wheels are going to come off here even faster than you can believe." He called himself "the designated fall guy," adding bitterly, "They're going to blame me for this."

Kennerly's Vietnamese and American friends echoed Martin's pessimism. One acquaintance begged him to smuggle his children onto Weyand's plane. A veteran war correspondent said, "This fucker is unraveling," and none of the other journalists at the Caravelle Hotel bar disagreed. NBC bureau chief Art Lord asked him to arrange a meeting with Martin so he could plead for the evacuation of his Vietnamese employees. Martin agreed to see Lord as a favor to Kennerly but warned that Lord would be wasting his time. If he evacuated Lord's Vietnamese, he said, "everyone will assume I'm pulling the plug."

Even meeting Lord represented a concession for Martin, who blamed the press for turning Congress and the American people against Thieu. After *New York Times* correspondent David Shipler had written an article cataloging U.S. and South Vietnamese violations of the Paris Peace Accords, Martin had fired off a cable to the State Department calling him "a tool of Hanoi" and charging that the *Times* had "a deep emotional involvement in the success of North Vietnam's attempts to take over South Vietnam by force of arms." He condemned a negative article about the Thieu government in the *Times* as part of a "massive deception campaign" and slammed the newspaper for being a "witting vehicle in this carefully coordinated effort." Leaks to the press triggered in Martin a Nixonian paranoia. A series of articles by George McArthur challenging his rosy assessment of the war contained information that he believed came from within his embassy. He suspected his secretary, Eva Kim, who was dating McArthur, and asked U.S. military intelligence operatives at the DAO to tap her phone, break into her house, and rifle her purse to check for classified documents. When they came up empty, he arranged for an intelligence agent to join a golf foursome that included McArthur and diplomat Dick Peters. The agent carried a microphone in his golf bag and recorded a casual exchange during which Peters provided McArthur with information contradicting Martin's optimistic line. Martin exiled Peters to the consulate at Bien Hoa.

Martin's meeting with Art Lord was brief. He refused Lord's request to evacuate his Vietnamese employees and accused him of hypocrisy for even making it. "You guys [the press] have been saying all along that there isn't going to be a bloodbath, so what are you concerned about all of a sudden?" he asked sarcastically. "Why do you want to evacuate your Vietnamese when all of your news reports are saying that nothing will happen to the population [of South Vietnam] in the event of a North Vietnamese takeover?" Martin's charge that "all" of the news reports dismissed the likelihood of the Communists meting out a harsh justice to their former enemies was an exaggeration, but there was a general skepticism among some reporters of claims that Communist victories in Cambodia and Vietnam would be followed by a bloodbath.

Lord left the embassy empty-handed, but Kennerly was encouraged that Martin had hinted he would not interfere with any private and clandestine evacuation that Lord might care to organize.

Martin was more guarded with Ken Quinn when they dined alone several days later. The atmosphere in the residence struck Quinn as tense, and members of the household staff sidled up to him and asked, "What will become of us?" and "Who will protect us?" Some were trembling and had tears in their eyes. They had posed the same questions to Dorothy Martin after she returned from the States. She told Quinn, "I don't know what to tell the servants."

Quinn had visited his in-laws before dining with Martin. Their news was grim. His wife's eldest brother was an army pharmacist who had been on the Convoy of Tears, and he and his family had vanished. Her next-oldest brother, an officer in an elite ranger unit, had been seen lying in a ditch and bleeding profusely. Everyone assumed he was dead. Her youngest brother was seventeen, but the government had lowered the draft age and he would soon be conscripted. Quinn considered packing the boy into a crate, drilling airholes, and smuggling him onto Weyand's plane. One of Quinn's in-laws, a foreign policy adviser to Thieu, said, "Look, I'll only say this to you because you're a relative, but Thieu is frozen. He doesn't know what to do, and he can't make decisions. All is lost!"

Quinn's Vietnamese friends begged him to evacuate their children. Strangers approached him on the street with the same request. Friends at the embassy asked him to carry their valuables back to Washington, and he agreed to take Eva Kim's jewelry and her fur coat. One young diplomat said, "The jig is up!" Another said, "We've probably got until August." He visited the Defense Intelligence Agency analysts at the DAO who had impressed him with their realistic and reliable reports. They rolled out maps tracking the progress of North Vietnamese units and told him that the Communists enjoyed an almost two-to-one advantage in main force divisions and if the current offensive continued, their superior numbers promised a quick victory. The removal of U.S. airpower had given the North insurmountable advantages. Because the Communists no longer feared B-52s hitting their artillery batteries, they could fire their 130 mm guns with impunity, while South Vietnamese units lacked similar long-range guns to respond.

Quinn telephoned frequent reports to Bill Stearman, his superior on the National Security Council. Stearman said that the cables from Martin and others on the mission had been optimistic, along the lines of "It's not looking good, but we think they can hold on."

"Here's what's going to happen," Quinn said. "It's over!"

Stearman shared Quinn's assessment with the Washington Special Actions Group, the interagency organization chaired by Kissinger that was monitoring the crisis. Its reaction amounted to "Who the hell is Ken Quinn, this junior guy, to be insisting that we don't have more time?"

Quinn was only thirty-two, but he spoke better Vietnamese and had lived in South Vietnam longer than anyone on the Weyand mission. He had joined the Foreign Service to become a Western Europe expert but like most new officers entering in 1968 had been assigned to South Vietnam. The Tet Offensive had recently claimed the lives of several Foreign Service officers, and some of his classmates at the Vietnam Training Center questioned whether the war was worth their lives. After a few resigned or requested reassignment, the center's director had urged anyone with doubts about the war to speak with him privately. Quinn imagined joining a long line at his door, but he was the only one bold enough to discuss his misgivings. The director shouted that he could not fathom why any red-blooded American boy would not risk his life for his country and recommended his expulsion. The State Department was so desperate for bodies that it sent him to Vietnam anyway. He began as a district senior adviser, becoming one of the few American diplomats to command a joint civilian and U.S. military team advising South Vietnamese troops. He drank with his Vietnamese soldiers, met their families, accompanied them on night ambushes, and joined their victory celebrations, hugging them and throwing them into the canals. He participated in so many helicopter missions that he would be the only civilian ever awarded the U.S. Army Air Medal. When Ambassador Ellsworth Bunker invited him and several other field officers to dinner at the embassy, the others offered upbeat reports, but he said that South Vietnam's pervasive corruption was sabotaging the war. Bunker snapped, "That's not what I hear from others." Their exchange added to Quinn's reputation for being "a rather forward Irishman."

He had been preparing to leave to pursue graduate studies at Harvard before taking a post in Western Europe when he gave a *Life* magazine reporter a tour of his district. The reporter was incredulous that he was leaving. The Vietnam War was the epic event of their generation, he said, and Quinn spoke the language, had stepped through the cultural veil, and was making a difference in these villages. Why trade all that for Harvard and Europe? Quinn changed his mind and stayed four more years, meeting his wife. In 1972 he had climbed a small mountain outside his post at Chau Doc, looked into Cambodia, and seen that every village for miles was in flames. Refugees told him that a secretive group of Communist rebels, the Khmer Rouge, had marched their inhabitants into the countryside, conscripted them into labor battalions, and burned their homes to prevent them from returning. Quinn wrote the first report describing the Khmer Rouge's genocidal policies, but intelligence analysts in Saigon, Phnom Penh, and Washington discounted it because he had asserted that Hanoi did not control the Khmer Rouge, a position contrary to the consensus of the intelligence community. The U.S. embassy in Phnom Penh even asked the State Department to order him to stop following events in Cambodia. Twenty-five years later, after he had finished his tour as U.S. ambassador in Phnom Penh, Kissinger took him aside, squeezed his arm, and praised his Cambodian report as "brilliant." But at the time his memorandum had only furthered his reputation for being a forward Irishman.

He continued living up to his name while serving on the Weyand mission. He told Weyand that South Vietnamese had lost confidence in Thieu, and insisted that during the next three weeks Saigon would fall to the Communists. In response, Weyand uttered a loud and despairing sigh.

Quinn went from briefing Weyand to dinner with Martin. He hoped to persuade him to formulate a plan for the evacuation of the entire U.S. mission, including its Vietnamese employees, but knew that if he was too pessimistic, Martin would tune him out. He spoke carefully at first, but the moment he uttered the word "evacuation," Martin leaned back in his chair, templed his fingers, stared at the ceiling, and began drifting off, just as he had the previous April. This time Quinn found his performance even more unsettling because his decisions could mean life or death for thousands of Vietnamese, including his in-laws. He looked around at Martin's furniture, paintings, and antique French maps and thought, "What's going to happen to these wonderful things? They're going to be looted, taken by the Communists. He's going to lose them all!"

Before leaving Saigon, Quinn met in an empty office at the embassy with CIA agent Frank Snepp, Shep Lowman, a political officer married to a Vietnamese, and Lacy Wright, a slight, soft-spoken young diplomat who covered Vietnamese politics and had been in South Vietnam for several years. Quinn proposed that because Martin was refusing to plan an evacuation, they should do it themselves. Snepp said he was overloaded with responsibilities and would help out but would have to take a backseat. Wright agreed to come on board and would become the group's mainstay. He had bounced around in the 1960s, considering the priesthood, studying in Rome, teaching high school in Chicago, and joining the Foreign Service despite opposing the war. He promised to help collect the addresses and telephone numbers of prospective evacuees and establish a phone tree and network of safe houses where they could stash their people before sending them to Tan Son Nhut. He volunteered his own house and promised to recruit other young diplomats. Quinn gave him the names and addresses of his Vietnamese in-laws and, after returning to Washington, forwarded him the names of the Vietnamese relatives and friends of State Department and AID officers stationed in the United States. Because Quinn worked at the White House, his calls to Wright had a "flash preference" and were immediately connected. During the next several weeks, Wright and Lowman encouraged Americans working at USAID, the U.S. Information Agency (USIA), and the embassy to send them lists of South Vietnamese who merited evacuation. The lists poured in. Those on them ranged from prominent intellectuals and politicians to embassy file clerks and drivers and household staff.

In early April, soon after Da Nang fell, Lowman became involved in a complementary evacuation scheme when he and political-military counselor Jim Devine set up an evacuation control center in the embassy's fourth-floor communications room. He and Devine recruited two AID officers from the Da Nang consulate, Mel Chatman and Russell Mott, and told them to plan an embassy evacuation. Chatman and Mott recruited a contact person in each of the U.S. agencies, scouted Saigon for American-owned villas and offices with high walls that could serve as safe houses, drew up routes from these houses to Tan Son Nhut, and persuaded the DAO to provide some of its olive-green buses when the time came. But without Ambassador Martin's approval, none of these buses could head to Tan Son Nhut carrying evacuees from the lists that Wright and Lowman were compiling.

Martin's third houseguest was "Mr. Military Assistance," the swashbuckling Defense Department bureaucrat Erich von Marbod. Von Marbod knew that American advisers in uniforms impressed South Vietnamese troops, so he had packed the camouflage fatigues that South Vietnamese airborne troops had given him during one of his earlier inspection trips (in part because U.S. advisers in civilian clothes stood out and drew sniper fire). He wore the fatigues and the red beret of an airborne trooper when he helicoptered out to the front lines at Tay Ninh to count artillery shells. After interviewing frontline troops and inventorying their ammunition, he concluded that no government positions had fallen because their defenders lacked munitions.

His friend Nguyen Hung, an American-trained economist who was a special assistant to President Thieu, showed him a sandbag shelter that he had built in his kitchen and told him that South Vietnam was doomed unless President Ford ordered the U.S. Air Force to bomb North Vietnamese troops. On March 27, Hung had persuaded President Thieu to show Weyand the letters that he had received from

Nixon promising swift retaliation if Hanoi violated the Paris Peace Accords. Hung and Thieu hoped that Weyand would pass the letters along to Ford and that Nixon's unequivocal promises to Thieu would shame him into intervening. After asking von Marbod to act as an intermediary, Hung pulled three of Nixon's letters from a burgundy leather attaché case one by one, reading them out loud and sliding them across his dining room table. On October 16, 1972, Nixon had promised Thieu that any breach of a treaty by Hanoi would have "the most serious consequences." On November 14, 1972, he had written, "But far more important than what we say in the agreement on this issue [North Vietnam violating a treaty] is what we do in the event the enemy renews its aggression. You have my absolute assurance that if Hanoi fails to abide by the terms of this agreement it is my intention to take swift and severe retaliatory action."

Von Marbod was stunned and asked for copies to show Weyand. Hung copied some excerpts by hand. Von Marbod returned several days later and told Hung that Weyand had agreed to show the letters to Ford. Hung handed von Marbod copies of the initial three letters before pulling a fourth from his attaché case. It was Thieu's ace in the hole, the letter he believed would bring back the B-52 bombers. On January 5, 1973, several weeks before Thieu signed the Paris Peace Accords, Nixon had written, "You have my assurance of continued assistance in the post settlement period and that we will respond with full force should the settlement be violated by North Vietnam." Astonished that Nixon would have made such an unequivocal promise, von Marbod exclaimed, "Well, I'll be damned!"

CHAPTER 5

"*I'd* Tell the President That!"

———┤├———

O n March 29, one day after consular officer Walter Martindale
had arrived in Nha Trang after leading his convoy of refugees
there from Lam Dong province, a marine guard appeared at the house
he was sharing with his adopted Vietnamese son and daughter and
announced that Consul General Spear wanted to see him at once.
"What's he going to do if I don't come?" Martindale snapped. "Shave
my head and send me to Vietnam?"

After he reported to the consulate—and he had taken his time—
Spear ordered him to pick up David Kennerly at the airport. Martindale knew that Kennerly was a friend of President Ford's and had
won a Pulitzer Prize, but after having seen Chez Walt shelled, battling
ARVN deserters, losing Ralph, and watching his province fall to the
Communists, his Irish Cherokee blood was boiling, and he was in no
mood to chauffeur Kennerly around. He drove home from the consulate, leaving Kennerly stranded at the airport and Spear screaming,
"That damned Martindale!"

He ran into Kennerly at the American club that evening. "I was
supposed to meet you, Mr. Kennerly," he said, "and now I'm in trouble
with my boss."

"You can call me David," Kennerly replied.

"Very well, Mr. Kennerly."

He agreed to drive Kennerly to the former U.S. Navy base at Cam

Ranh Bay the next day so that Kennerly could photograph refugees from Da Nang disembarking. He also hoped to persuade him to urge President Ford to order back the B-52s.

The highway from Nha Trang to Cam Ranh Bay reminded both men of World War II newsreels showing refugees fleeing the Nazis. Martindale leaned on his horn and wove around motorbikes, trucks, and oxcarts, passing shell-shocked civilians and surly soldiers. Kennerly believed that he had survived the war by not taking unnecessary risks, and making what he called "the right choices." Speeding past columns of angry troops, who believed the United States had betrayed them, in a small Ford sedan with American flags fluttering from its front bumpers struck him as a very bad choice indeed. Martindale was afraid that the flags would attract Vietcong snipers and agreed to cover them, although, he says, "normally I wouldn't have struck the colors for anything."

Cam Ranh Bay was the best deepwater harbor in Southeast Asia, and the U.S. military had expanded its docks and built an air base and recreation center. In less than five years it had become a ruin of empty piers, weed-choked runways, and rotting barracks. Martindale and Kennerly arrived as refugees were disembarking from a U.S. Military Sealift Command freighter docked at the end of a long concrete pier. Relief workers doled out food, water, and salt tablets, military police arrested deserters, and crewmen winched passengers from the hold in cargo nets. Two barefoot girls ran down the pier screaming in agony as the asphalt scorched their feet. Their pregnant mother held a baby in one arm and the family pots and pans in the other. Martindale sprinted down the pier and scooped them up. Kennerly took a photograph of him carrying one child under each arm. A week later, the picture would hang in the White House.

Embassy officials had come from Saigon to collect American citizens and the Vietnamese employees of the Da Nang consulate. One stood on the pier, a foot propped on a rail as he coolly surveyed the scene. He told Martindale that several babies had been born aboard the U.S. freighters.

"Then you'd better get them out of here," Martindale barked. "They were born on American flag ships, so they're U.S. citizens and should be registered with the embassy."

"My God, that's *all* we need," the official said.

"They're *Americans,*" Martindale shouted. "You take care of them. It's not going to kill you to write their names down in your notebook."

Consul General Spear arrived by helicopter, and he and Kennerly flew out to inspect the refugee ships and search for Consul General Al Francis. They flew over the *Pioneer Commander*. It was carrying 140 Americans and third-country nationals, as well as 5,700 Vietnamese, soldiers and refugees. It had lacked sufficient supplies of food and water, and some refugees had died of thirst and illness, while others had been trampled to death in its dark and crowded holds. After it discharged its remaining passengers at Vung Tau, rescue workers found dozens of corpses, including several little girls still clutching their dolls. Its crew was blameless. The MSC had chartered their ship to move military supplies, not human beings. Because neither the Thieu nor the Ford administration had anticipated Da Nang falling, it had arrived off the city's shores without the food, water, sanitary facilities, and medicines necessary to carry almost 6,000 people in minimal comfort.

Kennerly asked the Air America pilot to hover above the *Pioneer Commander* so he could shoot some photographs. One of his photographs, which would also soon hang in the White House, showed refugees staring up at Kennerly. A few Vietnamese marines, furious that an American helicopter was sightseeing rather than helping them, opened fire. Kennerly heard the crack of rifles and saw muzzle flashes. The incident shook him because the men trying to kill him belonged to an elite marine division. Back in Saigon he would tell friends that the episode had given him an insight into the morale of South Vietnamese troops—namely, that there *was* none.

He agreed to take Martindale's children on his Air America plane to Saigon, where Martindale's cousin, who worked for AID, would meet them. As he and Martindale parted, he asked him what he should tell President Ford. Martindale exploded. "You tell the president to unleash the B-52s and honor our commitments to South Vietnam!

You tell him this is not the way to leave this country! That's what you tell the president. Who the hell wants to be the president of a defeated nation? Is that what he wants? Too many people have died here. Tell him to honor the peace treaty that we signed."

"Do you really think I'd tell the president *that*?" Kennerly asked.

"*I'd* tell the president that!" Martindale exclaimed.

General Weyand arrived in Nha Trang the next day, March 31, to consult with General Phu. Phu struck him as "shattered and incoherent," yet during a press conference at the Nha Trang airport after their meeting Weyand insisted that ARVN forces were "not demoralized in any sense," "performing well," "determined to slow the Communists down," and would "stand and fight." It is unlikely that he believed this, but speaking the truth would have shattered what morale remained among South Vietnam's armed forces.

Soon after Weyand left, gangs of deserters rampaged through Nha Trang. One group burst into a restaurant where Consul General Spear and his wife were dining with friends and demanded food at gunpoint. While Spear and his party were fleeing the restaurant, Nha Trang's province chief shuttered his office and discharged his staff. The next morning municipal officials fled, the police force disbanded, deserters battled air force personnel at the air base, and Vietcong operatives opened the jail, freeing prisoners who contributed to the mayhem. General Phu, who only the day before had promised Weyand that his troops would defend the city "to the last," flew to Saigon and checked himself in to a hospital, claiming "nervous exhaustion."

After hearing that Phu had fled, Spear ordered the immediate evacuation of Americans, third-country nationals, and his Vietnamese staff and their families. By now convicts and deserters controlled the streets, and military police had sealed the airfield. Despite Al Francis's warning to Spear that "the roof will fall in about twenty-four hours before you think it will," Spear had not anticipated that Nha Trang might become too dangerous for his American and Vietnamese staff to drive to the airfield. It was the first of the month, so employees had come to the consulate for their pay and retired Americans were picking up their Social Security checks. There were about 150 Vietnamese inside the compound walls, including local employees and their families and strangers who had walked in off the street because no one had locked the main gate.

Instead of leaving with his children in Kennerly's plane, Martindale had stayed to make sure that his employees from Quang Duc made it to Saigon. He was still angry at Spear for bungling the evacuation of the U.S. government's Vietnamese employees from the Central Highlands. As the evacuation from Nha Trang got under way, he turned to Spear and said, "We have a saying in the South: don't ever mistake civility for forgiveness."

Fearing that Martindale would go rogue again, Spear shouted, "I don't want you out of my sight."

"I have an obligation to the people I brought here," Martindale said evenly.

"We don't need you to be John Wayne!"

"I'm not being John Wayne. But I feel a responsibility to our allies. What if we had run out on our allies in World War II or Korea?"

"Don't give me history lessons. I'm older than you."

"Well, *somebody* here needs a history lesson," Martindale said.

Martindale helped the marine guards close the outer gate and volunteered to identify people in the crowd who had worked for the U.S. government. After making it through the gate, the French consul hugged him and said, "Cher Walter, can you believe this?"

Military intelligence agent Nelson Kieff also wanted to make sure that the Vietnamese whom he had helped evacuate from Pleiku escaped to Saigon. Unlike Martindale, he had the advantage of not being in the State Department or DAO chain of command. His boss in the Five Hundredth Military Intelligence Group was in Bangkok, and his only responsibility since arriving from Pleiku the week before had been to train Sergeant Minh, his stay-behind agent. Otherwise, Kieff was, as he said later, "free to do what I thought was right."

By mid-afternoon Air America helicopters had flown several hundred people from the consulate to the airport. Jake Jacobson, Martin's field operations officer, was monitoring the evacuation from the embassy. After receiving erroneous reports of heavy gunfire in the streets surrounding the consulate, he ordered Spear to end the helicopter airlift quickly by restricting it to Americans. The American staff rebelled, refusing to board the helicopters until the Vietnamese had departed. Spear raged against what he called their "last-man syndrome," but unless he drew the pistol he had strapped to his waist, he could not force them to leave.

Kieff and Martindale cut a hole in the back fence and roamed through Nha Trang searching for their people. Kieff came upon a group of local CIA employees standing outside the CIA billet. They complained that their American bosses had told them to gather here for evacuation but had apparently abandoned them. Kieff led them back to the consulate and slipped them through the fence.

North Vietnamese troops bypassed Nha Trang for Cam Ranh Bay and would not enter the city for several days. Nevertheless, Jacobson became convinced that they were about to assault the consulate. He called Spear and said, "Get the hell out of the city now, you and the rest of the Americans." Spear obeyed and jumped onto the next helicopter. Minutes later his deputy Phil Cook called Jacobson for instructions and was told that Spear had already left. "And you'd better get out too," Jacobson shouted. "That's an order!"

Cook summoned two helicopters. He and half the Americans climbed aboard the first as the consulate's marine guards fired warning shots over the heads of the remaining Vietnamese. Martindale and a mixed group of Americans and Vietnamese boarded the last helicopter. Among the passengers was a retired U.S. Army colonel who helped Martindale pull some of the Vietnamese evacuees into the chopper. As they were lifting off, an elderly Vietnamese man holding an infant in one arm dashed forward and grabbed the floor of the helicopter with his free hand. The colonel decided the aircraft was overloaded and stamped on his hand. Martindale would never forget the look on the man's face as he and the child tumbled onto the ground. They were among about thirty Vietnamese who were left at the consulate. Spear was also abandoning seven hundred Vietnamese who had been employed by U.S. government agencies throughout Military Region II and were being quartered in bungalows on the beach prior to a promised seaborne evacuation.

As Martindale disembarked at the airport, Spear shouted, "Get your ass over here. You're coming with me." Spear then turned to Kieff and threatened him with "a piece of my tongue" if he made any more forays into town.

Spear followed Jacobson's orders and restricted the last Air America fixed-wing evacuation flight from Nha Trang's airfield to Americans only, leaving behind the consulate's Vietnamese employees who had not yet boarded a flight for Saigon. As the Americans ran for the plane, the consulate's marine guards fired over the heads of Vietnamese. Spear would say that leaving them and their families behind had been "a bitter blow" and "very disheartening." One consulate employee told a reporter, "I'm so ashamed of the United States government that I'll never be able to work for it again."

Air America had placed pilot Marius Burke in charge of its Nha Trang evacuation. He arrived at the airport minutes after Spear had left to find himself responsible for the consulate's abandoned Vietnamese. The pilot of a Bird Air DC-8 who was flying to Saigon empty radioed Burke that he could divert to Nha Trang and take hundreds of passengers. The airport had calmed down following Spear's departure, so Burke told him to land. Spear had been silently monitoring their conversation from the radio on his plane. He broke in and ordered the DC-8 to return to Saigon empty. Burke protested, but Spear, who believed the airport was still in a state of anarchy, was adamant. "So much for quality leadership from the upper echelons," Burke thought. Before leaving Nha Trang, he and the other Air America pilots shuttled three hundred Vietnamese from the airport to a Korean LST (landing ship, tank) anchored offshore, stopping only after they ran low on fuel. The seven hundred people the consulate had abandoned on the beach hired boats to take them out to the Korean ship. Back at the airport, one of the consulate's Vietnamese employees persuaded the South Vietnamese Air Force commander to fly some of the remaining evacuees to Saigon, earning his sympathy by describing how their

American employers had betrayed them. After reaching Saigon, the employee sent Spear a note accusing him of using the consulate's Vietnamese workers "like a sponge," wringing them out and discarding them when he no longer needed them.

There were four U.S. consular districts in South Vietnam. After the fall of Nha Trang, only the consulates in Saigon and Can Tho, the largest city in the Mekong delta and its administrative capital, remained open. The U.S. consul general in Can Tho was Francis Terry McNamara, a short middle-aged man with bushy eyebrows, a fondness for Italian boots with three-inch heels, a rolling tough-guy walk, and the testy manner of Spencer Tracy in one of his ornery roles. But underneath the feisty Irish American veneer lay a kind heart and a fierce moral courage.

McNamara had been planning to send his American and Vietnamese employees and their families to Saigon so they could join the evacuation from the Tan Son Nhut airport that he assumed the embassy would be organizing. But after learning about the sudden defeat of South Vietnam's armed forces at Ban Me Thuot and the horrors of the Convoy of Tears, he told his American staff that he was thinking of loading everyone onto boats and taking them down the Bassac River to the South China Sea, where they could board U.S. Navy ships. He admitted that there were dangers. In places, Communist troops were dug in along the banks, and the river sometimes narrowed to a hundred yards or less. He would need a crew familiar with its channels, and vessels large enough to carry several hundred people each and sturdy enough to brave the open sea. Still, he argued, they would have the element of surprise because the Communists would expect them to fly. Furthermore, blockading a river was more difficult than cutting a road or bombing an airfield, and once they left Can Tho, there would be no danger of being overwhelmed by mobs of civilians and deserters. But the strongest argument for going down the Bassac, he said, was that it would enable them to evacuate more people, fulfilling their responsibility to the South Vietnamese who had been working alongside them.

His staff was an unconventional bunch. His deputy Hank Cushing was a gaunt, sharp-witted former English professor fond of quoting Dante and Shakespeare. Cary Kassebaum was a slight and thoughtful former Peace Corps volunteer with a sandy beard and Coke-bottle glasses who had come of age during the Kennedy years and still held to its ideals. Sergeant Boyette Hasty, who commanded the consulate's unit of marine guards, was a gung ho string bean who looked fifteen. David Whitten was a Vietnamese-speaking navy veteran who had spent two years in the delta advising the South Vietnamese Navy. But as unconventional as they might be, traveling for more than six hours down seventy-five miles of river through territory controlled by the Communists and doing it in open boats carrying hundreds of Vietnamese civilians struck them as harebrained, and when McNamara first proposed it, they opposed it.

They changed their minds after the botched evacuations of the Da Nang and Nha Trang consulates. On April 2, the day after Moncrieff Spear had abandoned some of his Vietnamese employees at the Nha Trang airport, McNamara told Cushing he feared that the Saigon embassy and the U.S. military would not allocate enough resources to the delta for the airborne evacuation of the hundreds of Vietnamese employed by U.S. agencies and their families. Cushing agreed that the consulate had a duty to evacuate Vietnamese tainted by their association with the United States and that going down the Bassac was the most surefire way of fulfilling it. Others on McNamara's staff also came around to supporting a riverine evacuation. They all knew that although McNamara had a reputation for being a maverick, he had proven himself to be a courageous and lucky maverick.

McNamara had grown up in blue-collar Troy, New York, as the youngest of seven children in a multigenerational household that included his immigrant grandparents and had been drawn to ships and rivers at an early age, often walking a few blocks to the Hudson River and setting out alone in a rowboat. As a teenager he had crewed on the last coal-burning tugboat on the river and on a barge plying the Erie Canal. He had left school at sixteen and lied about his age to join the navy during World War II. He entered Syracuse University after the war but after running afoul of the local sheriff transferred to Troy's Russell Sage College, a formerly all-female institution that was accepting male veterans. He rejoined the navy during the Korean War and after passing the Foreign Service examination in 1956 joined a training class of upper-middle-class Ivy Leaguers.

He began earning his maverick reputation during the early 1960s while serving at the U.S. consulate in Elizabethville in the Congo's Katanga province during a secessionist rebellion against the newly independent central government. Belgium, the former colonial power, and European mining interests supported the rebels. The United States and the United Nations backed the government. At various points during the conflict, European mercenary pilots bombed McNamara's car, and Katangan rebels mistook his jeep for a UN vehicle, opening fire on it. The colonel commanding the UN's Gurkha troops laid the blade of his curved knife against the throat of the leader of a band of squatters who were menacing McNamara's home, promising to kill him if anyone harmed the American. McNamara repaid him by standing alongside him in the middle of a road while he distributed mail to his troops as rebel mortars exploded around them. McNamara also organized the evacuation of Americans and Europeans, bringing them to the airport in armed personnel carriers manned by Swedish UN troops. As rebel bullets bounced off the sides of his armored car, the Swedes fired back, and their shell casings flipped into the back of the carrier, landing on McNamara's children.

Two senior State Department officials flew in from Washington and ordered him to encourage the locals to support the Congolese army. He told them that the Congolese army was an undisciplined armed rabble specializing in rape and pillage and that the United States should be urging the Congo's leaders to disband it. After Katanga, he refused to serve as South Africa desk officer because he could not support a U.S. policy that acquiesced in apartheid. He volunteered for South Vietnam, and in 1968 he was posted to the Mekong delta as a rural development specialist with CORDS (Civil Operations and Revolutionary Development Support) and led a team of American civilians and soldiers in Vinh Long province. The Communists had assassinated his predecessor, and the helicopter bringing in McNamara removed the man's corpse. Soon after arriving, McNamara hosted CIA official William Colby. During a boozy bull session Colby asked for his frank assessment of the war. McNamara told him that it was the height of immorality for the United States to encourage the South Vietnamese to continue resisting the Communists if it was going to abandon them. We should quit now, he said, so there would be no more unnecessary bloodshed, or plan on staying for decades, as we had in Korea.

Two weeks later, the Vietcong sprayed his compound with bullets. Six months after that, he became the first American to head a rural development team in Vinh Long to leave the province alive. He volunteered for a second tour and was appointed U.S. consul general in Da Nang. After he released a report condemning the brutality of South Korean troops fighting alongside U.S. marines, the marines' commander, General Herman Nickerson, demanded that the State Department recall him. After he had a South Vietnamese general cashiered for smuggling and pedophilia, Nickerson berated him for interfering in military affairs and said, "I bet you'd like to get rid of General Lam, too." McNamara shot back that he would, because Lam was a drug dealer who was poisoning Nickerson's marines. Nickerson leaped up from behind his desk and almost decked him.

McNamara became consul general in Can Tho in August 1974. His district encompassed the entire delta, sixteen U.S. provincial offices, and over a thousand American and South Vietnamese employees. In Can Tho he gave full rein to his eccentricities. He sheared off the tops of champagne bottles with the curved knife that Gurkha UN troops in Katanga had presented him as a tribute to his bravery and soon after arriving made a tour of the city's brothels, giving his card to the madams and urging them to contact him if their American clientele misbehaved.

After his staff agreed to support his river evacuation, he calculated that if he included all of the Vietnamese working for the U.S. government in the delta, as well as their families, it would amount to around five thousand people, an impossibly large number. He decided to put everyone into three categories. Category A would be anyone in mortal danger following a Communist victory. Category B would be those who were less threatened but whose skills, education, and facility in English would enable them to thrive in the United States. Category C would consist mostly of cleaners, guards, drivers, household staff, and manual laborers who were less likely to succeed in America and whom the Communists were less likely to punish. He asked the heads of departments at the consulate and of U.S. agencies in Can Tho to break their employees down into these categories and discreetly ask the A and B people if they wanted to leave. Once he had a master list of prospective evacuees, he planned sending some to Saigon for an early evacuation in order to reduce the number of those going down the Bassac. He recognized that there was no magic formula for determining whom the Communists might punish and who might flourish in the United States, and that he was asking Americans who had been working alongside these Vietnamese to serve as judge and jury. He faced some agonizing choices himself. He put his driver on the A list because he had served a succession of senior U.S. officials, making him a larger target than someone driving more junior Americans, but reluctantly included his maids in the C category. They were widows with children to support, but neither spoke English.

Whereas McNamara's staff saw in him courage and experience, CIA base chief Jim Delaney and his agents saw recklessness and what one termed "uncalled-for heroics." What McNamara and his staff considered a noble plan to rescue hundreds of Vietnamese, the CIA contingent considered a risky endeavor that might lead to CIA agents being shot, drowned, or left to rot in a Communist jail. They argued that the South Vietnamese Navy was certain to intercept them, that McNamara had no knowledge of the Bassac's tricky channels, and that Communists would open fire on boats filled with Americans and their Vietnamese allies, and because none of the agents had credible cover stories, they would be treated harshly if the Communists captured them.

McNamara and his staff believed that Delaney and his agents exaggerated the risk of being captured. He and Delaney were very different kinds of Irishmen. McNamara was loud and ornery; Delaney was smooth, soft-spoken, and competitive. McNamara was short and pale; Delaney was a tall and handsome redhead with chiseled features who had attended Boston College and Georgetown Law School, two of the country's most prestigious Catholic schools. Also contributing to their animosity was the fact that each relied on intelligence sources predicting different scenarios. McNamara believed Major General Nguyen Khoa Nam, a quiet and resolute officer who commanded South Vietnamese military forces in the delta and was known for his honesty and for his pledge to remain a bachelor until the war ended because he believed that the wives of highly placed officers encouraged corruption. Nam had assured McNamara that even if Saigon fell, he could hold the delta and that recent attacks on his installations had been diversionary moves. Delaney received his intelligence from a network of paid informants who had convinced him that Can Tho was in imminent danger of being overrun. Because he believed them, he understandably preferred a quick helicopter evacuation.

Their dispute escalated after the Communists shelled Can Tho on April 11. The half-hour attack killed civilians and ignited fires that raged through the city's wooden buildings. Only a change in the wind and a heavy rain saved the consulate. Delaney said it proved that a large North Vietnamese force was preparing to attack the city; McNamara's sources told him it was a diversion meant to keep ARVN forces pinned down in the delta. But, to be on the safe side, McNamara bought a flat-bottomed rice barge and began searching for other vessels. He ordered official Americans and his A-category people to withdraw from outlying provinces into Can Tho and started sending some to Saigon to join the embassy's evacuation.

Following the shelling of Can Tho, Jake Jacobson summoned McNamara to a meeting at the DAO with the service attachés and military officers from Thailand and the Seventh Fleet. During the meeting Jacobson declared his opposition to McNamara's riverine evacuation, arguing that although the Vietcong did not have a navy, they could still open fire from the shoreline. When he announced that all Americans and third-country nationals would fly out of Can Tho, McNamara shot back, "I refuse to accept that decision."

CHAPTER 6

"In the Shadow of a Corkscrew"

———┤├———

At a State Department staff meeting on April 2, one day after the Nha Trang evacuation, Kissinger argued that the United States was responsible for Thieu's mistakes because, as he put it, "we picked the little guy [Thieu]. That is what started the whole thing. After that he acted like a maniac. Unless you think he deliberately committed suicide."

Kissinger and Assistant Secretary of State Habib took turns criticizing Martin. Habib reported that after Martin had received a cable requesting his assessment of the situation, he had called the State Department asking "what this was all about."

"I know it is sort of unreasonable, when a country is collapsing, to ask the Ambassador what is going on," Kissinger remarked sarcastically, missing the point that Martin did not believe it was collapsing.

"The press is beginning to write that the Embassy is not reporting," Habib complained, "and young officers are beginning to complain that they are not permitted to send forward reports of the situation."

Lawrence Eagleburger, Kissinger's executive secretary, said that when Martin asked him, "Why do you need an assessment?" he had replied, "The Secretary [Kissinger] would like to know what the hell is going on and all we have are newspaper reports."

Several hours later, Kissinger chaired a meeting of the Washington Special Actions Group on Vietnam and Cambodia. During a discussion of whether South Vietnam would fall during the summer rainy season, Kissinger wondered if the end might come within the next three months.

"I would say we should be prepared for collapse within three weeks," Secretary of Defense Schlesinger said.

"Basically, then, nothing can be done?" Kissinger asked.

"I can't think of anything," Schlesinger replied, adding, "General Weyand, in my telephone conversations with him, is much more pessimistic than when he first got out there. He's quite grim about the situation. And he's talking mostly to those who are optimistic."

After hearing more discouraging assessments, Kissinger said, "Martin should begin preparing a plan for evacuation."

"We should push him hard on that," Schlesinger said. "We ought to clear out all non-essentials—and fast." He made it clear later that by "non-essentials" he was referring to the American employees of U.S. government agencies in South Vietnam, not the agencies' Vietnamese employees.

Kissinger raised the issue of the Vietnamese, saying, "I think we owe—it's our duty—to get the people who believed in us out," and asking if anyone had compiled a list of them.

Habib believed such a list existed but called it "limited."

"Tell Graham Martin to give us a list of those South Vietnamese we need to get out of the country," Kissinger said. "Tell Graham that we must have the list by tomorrow [April 3]."

Habib said the list had ninety-three thousand names but did not specify who had compiled it or where it was.

Kissinger asked him to get it, adding, "We'll try for as many as we can."

Ken Quinn's boss, Bill Stearman, warned that they could be talking about evacuating a million people.

Unfazed by this number, Kissinger said, "Well, this is one thing this Congress can't refuse—humanitarian aid to get people out," a remark suggesting that in addition to its humanitarian aspect an evacuation of endangered Vietnamese appealed to him as a cudgel to use against Congress. As the meeting was concluding, he said, "Let's get that list of people who have to get out and some ideas of where we should move them. We may have to ask Congress for military force to help rescue these people. I can't see how they could refuse."

According to the meeting's official Summary of Conclusions, "Embassy Saigon would prepare, by April 3, 1975, a detailed breakdown by categories and numbers of those Vietnamese the US should evacuate from South Vietnam. The breakdown is to be organized in order of priorities and should include recommendations regarding necessary arrangements with the GVN [government of South Vietnam], transport, safe havens, and staging areas." Kissinger followed up with a cable ordering Martin to make these preparations and arrange "immediately" for the departure during the next several days of "all remaining dependents of official Americans, including to the extent possible dependents of contractor personnel."

Martin did none of this. He never sent Kissinger, either on April 3 or during the following weeks, a "detailed breakdown" of endangered Vietnamese. Instead of initiating any meaningful planning for their "transport, safe havens, and staging areas," he discouraged embassy personnel from engaging in such planning. He responded to Kissinger's demands the next day with a cable titled "E and E [Emergency and Evacuation] Planning." He argued that he had to observe the "knife-edge balance" between planning for an evacuation and avoiding anything that might "set off or significantly contribute to a panic situation endangering American lives" and could have "wider repercussions on the overall political-military situation"—that is, undermine the morale of South Vietnam's government and armed forces.

Instead of the "detailed breakdown" of at-risk Vietnamese that Kissinger had demanded, he supplied estimates. He calculated that if the embassy evacuated the 17,000 Vietnamese employed by the U.S. mission in South Vietnam and permitted each employee to bring out eight family members (a number vastly underestimating what Vietnamese considered a family), it would amount to 136,000 people. Add to them an estimated 10,000 Vietnamese relatives of U.S. citizens, hundreds of high-ranking South Vietnamese government officials and their families, and you had 200,000 potential evacuees. Divide that number by half on the assumption that many would choose to remain in Vietnam, and, he wrote, "for planning purposes we should use the figure of 100,000 for [those] whose safety the USG [U.S. government] will have a definite moral responsibility." After acknowledging "major practical problems" in evacuating "such large numbers of Vietnamese nationals" and settling them in the United States, he added, "If we are to emerge with the slightest vestige of honor, given the history of American involvement in Vietnam, the only right thing to do must be to move these people to the US and resolve any legal problems by special legislation later."

Martin was offering here the same moral justifications for evacuating Vietnamese nationals as were those in Washington and Saigon who considered him their implacable foe. He was realistic about the difficulty of mounting an evacuation, recognized that America's honor was at stake, and proposed disregarding U.S. immigration regulations. Still, he refused to authorize planning and preparations for the kind of large-scale operation that could have accomplished this. The most likely explanation for his apparently contradictory behavior is either that he was determined to manage the timing and scope of any evacuation himself or that he had sent this cable so that the record would show him attempting to preside over an honorable exit. His cable was either a window on the soul of this secretive man or chaff shot up to distract his enemies and future historians.

Kissinger would later come down on the side of chaff—of Martin's cables being self-serving communications composed with an eye cocked toward future historians—later writing, "I knew very well that Martin's many hortatory messages were designed in part to create a record that might later be published—perhaps even to my disadvantage."

The same charge of composing cables and making statements at meetings with an eye toward history could also be leveled at Kissinger, whose actions, at least during the first half of April, never quite matched his own hortatory remarks about the moral urgency of evacuating America's Vietnamese allies. His comments to *Washington Post* editor Ben Bradlee during an April 9 telephone conversation also call into question his sincerity. He told Bradlee, "What worries me is, you know, there are hundreds of thousands of South Vietnamese towards whom we must *at least make a show* [italics added] of trying to save their lives."

Martin responded to the WSAG request that he evacuate U.S. dependents with a blistering April 5 cable marked "personal and absolutely eyes only for Secretary Kissinger." He reported that the CIA had recorded Major General Nguyen Ngoc Loan telling his staff that troops guarding Tan Son Nhut should be ordered to prevent any evacuation of Americans unless they were accompanied by "all the Vietnamese who wanted to go as well." Loan was the officer who had been photographed during the Tet Offensive executing a Vietcong prisoner with a bullet to the head in broad daylight on a Saigon boulevard, so Martin, Polgar, and others in Washington took his threat seriously. Referring to the Loan recording, Martin criticized the WSAG request as "the kind of action that can result in the wholly needless death of a lot of Americans, plunge this city into total chaos, and irretrievably throw away any chance we might have of salvaging anything at all of American policy interests in this area." He was also critical of the request because, he said, it had been "taken without prior consultation with me."

He blamed Habib, of course, and demanded that Kissinger "instruct my friend, Habib, to cool it a bit, to not react to panic pressures." He recommended that "some safety device be put on the 'panic button'" and threatened to resign, telling Kissinger, "You either have confidence that my judgment on the scene is quite likely to be better than that of Habib or [Deputy Secretary of State] Ingersoll in Washington or you ought to recommend to the President that he put one of them out here and relieve me." If that happened, he warned, he might go public, adding coyly, "In that case, perhaps I can make an even greater contribution by speaking out with complete candor on how we got in this current situation." He concluded, "If you and the President wish me to continue, I shall use my judgment . . . on those matters [that is, the timing of an evacuation] which can only be decided here in the light of the actual realities on the ground, and I will be grateful if you so instruct Habib."

Within hours Kissinger responded with his own blistering cable. He opened by telling Martin, "I am not at all pleased with the way we are approaching the difficult question of evacuation," saying that if they lost their "composure" over this matter, they also risked losing "lives, national dignity, and a common sense of confidence that we can manage whatever crisis the future may hold." With this in mind, he declared that he had established procedures that Martin must follow when dealing with the issue of an evacuation. He ordered, "You should comment without delay once you have received advance warning that certain measures [concerning an evacuation] may be under consideration." Once orders had been issued, he could lodge an appeal through Kissinger's deputy Brent Scowcroft. But then, Kissinger wrote, "if your appeal fails, you should execute the orders without complaint and without deviation unless extraordinary circumstances on the ground so dictate." He also reminded Martin that he had asked him to submit "urgently" a "comprehensive plan for evacuation" that would serve as the government's "basis of our overall plan . . . unless superseded in part or in whole by instructions from me."

For the next several weeks Martin continued to disregard Kissinger's requests for evacuation lists, comprehensive plans, and immediate and precipitate reductions in the numbers of Americans and their Vietnamese dependents. He knew that Kissinger would not recall him and leave the post empty at such a critical juncture. For the moment, he had beaten back Habib and the other State Department "mattress mice," but his opposition to planning an evacuation had aroused the mattress mice in his own embassy and at the DAO.

After the Communists seized Phuoc Long, the U.S. defense attaché, Major General Homer Smith, had spent sleepless nights worrying about how to evacuate the DAO's 850 American civilian employees and its 3,500 Vietnamese employees and their families. He was a logis-

tician, an expert in moving military supplies and personnel to staging areas and battlefields, and his straightforward Texan manner and
angular cowboy face reinforced his reputation for being a man who
could move anything or anyone anywhere. He had learned his trade as
a twenty-one-year-old lieutenant on a team planning the D-day invasion of France, the largest, most complicated logistical operation in
military history. During his first tour in Vietnam he had held several
demanding logistical positions, including head of mortuary affairs.
He had made himself visit the morgue every day to remind himself of
the cost of the war and because he felt duty-bound, he said, "to send
the soldiers off." He brought this same humanity and decency to his
position as U.S. defense attaché.

After reading the official evacuation plans for the embassy and the
U.S. military, he concluded that the same flaw compromised both: the
assumption that tens of thousands of evacuees could travel in convoys
of cars and buses to Tan Son Nhut and the port of Vung Tau and
that South Vietnamese police and troops would protect these facilities
and the evacuees. But if that was the case, he wondered, then why in
heaven would the United States *want* to evacuate its citizens and others in the first place? And why would anyone with a basic understanding of human nature and South Vietnam imagine that the country's
police and military would risk their lives to help the citizens of an ally
that was abandoning them to escape? His deputy, air force brigadier
general Richard Baughn, read the plans and agreed that they were
inadequate and illogical. Baughn also noticed that they made no provisions for evacuating the Vietnamese employees of U.S. agencies or
Vietnamese and Americans from the consular regions outside Saigon.

In mid-March, Smith asked three of his uniformed officers at
the DAO to produce an evacuation plan that anticipated Saigon
being in a state of near anarchy. He gave the assignment to Captain
George Petrie, Major Jaime Sabater Jr., and Marine Corps Captain
Tony Wood and told them to report to Baughn. The three soldiers
had between them about ten years of experience fighting in South
Vietnam and losing comrades and risking their lives. Sabater consid-

ered Smith's assignment a last chance to accomplish something noble before he left Vietnam forever.

Smith told them that he wanted a plan that identified the locations of Americans, third-country nationals, and Vietnamese who were most likely to suffer retribution under a Communist regime. It should provide for their transportation under hostile conditions to Tan Son Nhut and Saigon's docks, explain how these facilities would be protected, and how the DAO compound could be prepared to accommodate ten thousand evacuees for ten days. The three officers decided to call themselves the Special Planning Group (SPG) and to name their plan to fortify the DAO "Project Alamo."

Smith created a second organization, the Evacuation Control Center (ECC), and gave it the job of coordinating all seaborne and airborne evacuations mounted by U.S. government agencies and military commands, including the SPG. He also placed Brigadier General Baughn in charge of the ECC and summoned him, the three military attachés, and the ECC and SPG staff to a brainstorming session on the afternoon of April 1, just as Consul General Spear was abandoning his Vietnamese employees at the Nha Trang airport and a reliable Communist agent was telling his CIA handler that Hanoi was on a "blood scent" and would demand an unconditional surrender.

The SPG came up with the idea of turning downtown rooftops into helipads and sold the plan to Air America and the marines. It compiled a register of the addresses of Americans and third-country nationals by scrutinizing PX liquor ration cards, billeting records, and the membership rolls of the embassy's Combined Recreation Association and the Cercle Sportif. It used the U.S. mission's employment records to locate potential Vietnamese evacuees, covering a wall map of Saigon with colored pins showing where they and the Americans lived and plotting bus routes that connected the proposed collection points. Captain Wood named the routes after pioneer trails, calling them Oregon, Santa Fe, and Chisholm, and became known as the Wagon Master.

The SPG planned to collect its evacuees in forty-two DAO buses guided by an equal number of sedans. It had the sedans painted black and white and equipped with blue roof lights so that they resembled

South Vietnamese police squad cars. It designated two FM frequencies for command and control and installed an antenna on the DAO water tower to provide communication between the buses and the Evacuation Control Center. It recruited American expatriates to sit in the passenger seats of the sedans and guide the drivers down Captain Wood's trails, recruited more expats and Vietnamese DAO employees to drive the buses or ride them as armed guards, and gave them flak jackets, gas masks, and smoke grenades. The average age of the drivers and guards was forty-eight, and most had never been behind the wheel of a bus. The SPG had them move a bus back and forth in the DAO parking lot, then drive it around the compound, and finally make practice runs to familiarize themselves with the city's roadblocks and checkpoints. Major Sabater sometimes grabbed an automatic weapon and made what he called "kamikaze runs," driving over the routes after curfew to identify new roadblocks.

The SPG prepared the DAO compound at Tan Son Nhut, its "Alamo," so it could shelter ten thousand people for ten days during a protracted battle. It stockpiled chemicals to make the swimming pool water potable, pre-positioned fuel tankers, generators, and material for constructing latrines, appointed civilians to oversee billeting and sanitary and medical services, converted the DAO auditorium into an evacuation processing center, and recruited seventy American expatriates to serve in a self-defense force and trained them in the evenings. It accomplished much of this during the first two weeks of April, largely under the cover of darkness and without the knowledge of Ambassador Martin. Smith knew that Martin had no objections to revising a theoretical evacuation plan, provided it remained theoretical, but training bus drivers and putting helipads on roofs went beyond that.

Smith did not openly defy Martin, but neither did he keep him abreast of the SPG's activities. As the senior U.S. official in South Vietnam, Martin was technically his commander. But Smith also reported to Lieutenant General John Burns, who commanded the Seventh Air Force in Thailand, and to Commander in Chief Pacific Command (CINCPAC) Admiral Noel Gayler, a decorated World War II pilot who disliked Martin so intensely that he scheduled his visits to Saigon when Martin was away. (Martin, in turn, had been heard to remark that he did not want "that polo-playing admiral" in *his* country.) Brigadier General Baughn, with Smith's tacit approval, encouraged Americans working at the DAO to slip some of their Vietnamese employees and their dependents aboard the U.S. Air Force transports that would otherwise be returning empty to the Philippines. This contravened the immigration laws of South Vietnam, the Philippines, and the United States, but Smith tolerated what he termed Baughn's "covert smuggling" because, as he explained later, "my own employees had a great deal of empathy with their local national co-workers and were determined to get out as many of them as wanted to get out of the country."

Baughn believed that Americans "had an obligation to save our loyal Vietnamese" and that Martin's "head-in-the-sand policy" was putting American and Vietnamese lives at risk. When he arrived in Saigon in June 1974 to serve as deputy defense attaché, he was already disillusioned by how the architects of the Vietnam War had waged it. In his lexicon, former president Lyndon Johnson was "the Grade School Teacher," a reference to his first profession, and former secretary of defense Robert McNamara was "the Edsel Genius," a reference to the spectacular failure of that car during his leadership of the Ford Motor Company.

Baughn and Martin had been a bad fit from the start. Baughn was a decorated World War II fighter pilot, while Martin had been a U.S. Army Air Forces intelligence officer who had been, according to Baughn, "safely behind the scenes in intelligence analysis" and never facing a "do or die situation." They had served in Thailand at the same time—Martin as ambassador and Baughn as commander of a fighter squadron. Between 1965 and 1966, Baughn had flown a hundred combat missions over North Vietnam. The loss rate among his pilots matched that of some of the deadliest World War II missions, and he and his men joked that a "supreme optimist" was an F-105 pilot worrying about dying from lung cancer. He urged his airmen not to take needless risks, telling them it did not make "a damned bit of sense" to lose their lives when the Pentagon ordered them out on a mission while at the same time forbidding them to hit a nearby airfield full of parked North Vietnamese warplanes. During one four-month period he lost a third of his squadron. He blamed the empty chairs at the squadron dinner table and the agonizing letters he had to write to families on what he called his country's "asinine military policy."

As soon as Baughn arrived in Saigon in 1974, Smith's predecessor at the DAO, Major General John Murray, warned him that Martin was "a great dramatic actor," capable of being charming one moment and fixing you with his famous icy stare the next. He was a man, Murray said, who "could stand in the shadow of a corkscrew." Baughn witnessed Martin's deviousness when he substituted for Murray at a meeting of the heads of the U.S. agencies in South Vietnam. Martin opened it by saying, "I'd like to introduce you to my good friend General Richard Baughn, who I know from our days together in Thailand." Baughn had never before laid eyes on Martin, and Murray told him afterward, "You have just had some distance placed between you and the other agency heads and everyone else. They'll figure you're too close to the ambassador and will be very careful what they say to you."

General Smith hinted to Baughn that he agreed with Murray's reservations about Martin. Others were less circumspect. After Lieutenant General Louis Wilson, who headed the air force's Pacific Command, had conferred with Martin, he told Baughn, "I have now met my first egomaniac."

CHAPTER 7

Palpable Fear

Former Da Nang U.S. consul general Al Francis arrived in Saigon soon after being rescued from an MSC ship off Cam Ranh Bay. One morning, he and diplomat Ken Moorefield, who had warned the embassy of an imminent attack on Ban Me Thuot, had coffee in the embassy canteen. Moorefield had previously reported to Francis from Nha Trang and considered him a bright and decent man who was destined for a brilliant career. Francis had an unblemished record and a powerful mentor in Graham Martin, and with his rugged good looks he even looked the part of a dashing diplomat. He told Moorefield that he had just briefed Martin about his escape from Da Nang, "the chaos, the total breakdown in law and order," and how he and the other Americans "damned near didn't get out." He had urged Martin to plan for a similar catastrophe in Saigon. After Martin tried to put an optimistic spin on his account, he had raised his voice and said, "Sir, Da Nang is lost! General Truong's army is no more!" Martin smiled, shook his head, and said in a voice so faint that Francis had strained to hear him, "No. Military Region I is not lost. I have information to the contrary." He added that his sources in Thieu's palace had assured him that the government was planning to mount a counterattack to recapture Da Nang. He gave Francis a penetrating stare, inquired after his health, and suggested that he leave South Vietnam as soon as possible.

"He either will not or cannot accept the reality of what happened up there," Francis told Moorefield. "He doesn't want to hear about it. He thinks I'm sick or something. Making it up. I don't know. Jesus."

Francis had chosen to unburden himself to a man who understood Graham Martin and the Vietnam War as well as if not better than anyone serving in the embassy. Moorefield's father had been a career army officer and decorated World War II battalion commander. Moorefield had entered West Point in 1961 hoping to emulate him by commanding infantry troops in battle. At the end of his first year, President Kennedy had delivered a graduation address praising the cadets' "moral motivation" and predicting that they would experience "the greatest opportunity for the defense of freedom that this Academy's graduates have ever had." He named third world countries like Vietnam as their proving grounds and predicted that they might risk their lives, "not as combatants, but as instructors or advisors," and might "need to give orders in different tongues and read maps by different systems." He echoed the "ask not" line from his inaugural address, telling the cadets, "When you are asked by a President of the United States or by any other American what you are doing for your country, no man's answer will be clearer than your own." Years later, Moorefield could recall the timbre of Kennedy's voice, and he left the field house elated to be a member of the Kennedy generation and to be living in such "an exciting, progressive time." After Kennedy's assassination, but before President Johnson sent combat troops to Vietnam, the noted Indochina expert Bernard Fall spoke to Moorefield's political science class. He began by unveiling a wall map of South Vietnam covered with so many red pins that it reminded Moorefield of the measles. He explained that each pin represented a place where the Communists had assassinated a hamlet or village chief during the previous twelve months. Moorefield realized at that moment that Vietnam would be his war—his chance to lead men into battle.

The army sent him to South Vietnam in 1967 as an adviser to a South Vietnamese Army mobile battalion fighting in the Mekong delta. The government controlled the towns, and the Communists held the countryside. His battalion went wherever combat was heaviest. He carried a rifle and was an infantryman first and an adviser second.

For nine months he seldom saw another American. Whether or not he summoned U.S. air support or a medevac team might mean life or death for his Vietnamese soldiers; whether or not they fought bravely could mean life or death for him. He decided that to advise them, he needed to understand them, so he slept, ate, fought, celebrated, and mourned with them. They became, he said, "blood brothers in the truest sense," and he experienced an intimacy with them that he had expected to find while commanding American troops.

In the spring of 1968 the Communists attacked the provincial capital that his battalion was defending. While leading a counterattack alongside the ARVN commander, he stood up to communicate with gunships, and a bullet entered his arm and blew out his elbow. He collapsed facedown into a canal. Some of his men dashed forward under heavy fire, risking their lives to keep him from drowning. They pulled him into a paddy, stabilized him, and summoned a helicopter. He left on a helicopter with his wounded comrades. Some died during the flight, their blood mingling with his on the floor of the helicopter.

He returned a year later to command a U.S. infantry company platoon in a province northeast of Saigon. He knew the enemy, the South Vietnamese forces, and the battlefield environment. He believed himself to be superbly prepared to lead men in battle. But the war that American troops were fighting in Vietnam in 1969 bore little resemblance to his father's war. His men recognized that the goal of their political and military leaders was to avoid losing, and to hang on until a settlement could be negotiated, so not unreasonably their goal was also to hang on and not lose their lives in a war their country's leaders did not seem to care about winning. This meant that they had little tolerance for junior officers putting them in harm's way, and shortly before Moorefield arrived, a company commander had been "fragged" by a grenade—murdered by his own men.

Moorefield understood that keeping his troops at their base camp for extended periods of time gave them access to drugs and liquor but that if he ordered them to do something they viewed as unnecessarily hazardous, he might be risking his life. He steered a middle course: making decisions that demonstrated he would not needlessly endanger them while trying to convince them that remaining in a defensive posture encouraged the Vietcong to attack. His company had fewer discipline problems than others in their brigade, and his men began to resemble the band of brothers he had imagined his father leading into battle. Four months later the army transferred him to division headquarters to serve as a general's aide. He was appalled to see high-ranking officers making decisions while flying above a battlefield in helicopters and planes, zooming overhead in starched fatigues while soldiers like those in his former company fought for their lives below. He asked to be transferred back to his unit but was told he had too much experience and that there were too many newly minted captains needing command experience.

He decided that if the Vietnam War was all about career advancement, then he was finished fighting it. He left the army and back-packed through Europe before entering Georgetown University's School of Foreign Service. After completing his first year, he was tak-ing a lifesaving course at a Washington pool when he met an eccentric young man wearing black socks with his bathing suit. When they bumped into each other again a few days later, the young man invited him to meet his father, explaining that he had just been appointed ambassador to South Vietnam and might like to discuss the war with someone who had fought it.

Moorefield and Graham Martin spoke about Vietnam throughout dinner and continued their conversation while watching the Water-gate hearings on television. As Moorefield was preparing to leave, Martin asked him if finishing Georgetown was really so important and proposed that he accompany him to Saigon in ten days as his spe-cial assistant. Moorefield could think of several reasons to reject this surprising offer, not least that he had known Martin for only a couple of hours, his last tour in Vietnam remained a painful memory, and he doubted that the Paris Peace Accords would succeed. He had recently represented the voice from the battlefield on a Public Broadcasting Service program about the treaty. He had argued that allowing North Vietnamese units to remain in the South was a poison pill and had asked why, if the United States could not guarantee South Vietnam's survival with 500,000 troops, it believed it could accomplish the same thing with none?

Despite his reservations he agreed to go. It would mean entering the Foreign Service without taking the examinations, and he told himself that while serving as Martin's assistant, he might have an opportunity to influence policy. Still, he wondered why Martin had offered the position to someone with no diplomatic training, and was so determined to have him come to Saigon that after a hurried security check revealed that he had once smoked marijuana, Martin threatened not to take up the post unless Moorefield accompanied him, telling the State Department security officer investigating Moorefield, "I'd rather have an aide who told the truth than one who lied." Later, Moorefield decided that Martin might have wanted an assistant from outside the normal Foreign Service career path because such a person was more likely to be loyal, and because that was how Martin had entered the State Department, without taking the examinations and under the patronage of a powerful mentor, in his case Secretary of State George Marshall. Moorefield also wondered if Martin considered him a replacement for his two dead sons—his adopted son, Glenn Mann, who had been killed in action in 1965, and the son who had died in the car accident.

He and Martin flew to Saigon on a White House jet. After turning twenty-eight during a layover in Honolulu, Moorefield disembarked at Tan Son Nhut for the third time in five years, this time descending a metal staircase while holding the arm of the new American ambassador. Two years later, he would find himself holding Martin's arm again while walking him to a helicopter whose pilot had permission to force Martin aboard if necessary.

Moorefield spent a month living with Martin at the ambassadorial residence before Dorothy Martin arrived from the States, sharing a series of what he recalls being "pretty quiet dinners." He was a friendly and talkative extrovert; Martin was secretive and silent. If Moorefield had imagined Martin taking him into his confidence and giving him important assignments, he would be disappointed; if Martin had once imagined Moorefield replacing one of his dead sons, he had apparently changed his mind. Moorefield respected Martin for being fearless and tenacious in defending his beliefs and for being a superb writer and analyst. Most of what he learned from him he learned by reading the papers crossing his desk, particularly the cables from the State Department and his tart replies. Because Martin had once been an intelligence officer, he focused on the weekly intelligence reports from his consulates and provincial representatives, but when Moorefield compared these reports with what was happening in the field, he became skeptical of their value and suspected that much of their information came from double agents and con men.

Moorefield's two tours in Vietnam had taught him the value of going into the field, but Martin seldom left Saigon, and because he rarely traveled on official business, neither did Moorefield. It was a frustrating situation for a West Point graduate who believed that "Duty, Honor, Country" meant moving the ball toward the goalposts and that doing something and making mistakes trumped doing nothing. After a year as Martin's assistant he decided that if he wanted to prove himself as a political officer and make a career of the Foreign Service, he would need to meet the soldiers fighting the war and write his own reports. He requested reassignment and was posted to the Nha Trang consulate as a military reports officer. He evaluated and consolidated reports from U.S. provincial representatives like Walter Martindale and traveled extensively through the consular region, collecting eyewitness accounts of battles and interviewing wounded South Vietnamese soldiers and captured Communists. He returned to Saigon in December 1974 to assume the frustrating job of embassy liaison officer to the Iranian delegation to the International Commission of Control and Supervision, the organization created by the Paris Peace Accords and charged with overseeing elections that never occurred and investigating violations of a cease-fire that no one respected. A week before Da Nang fell, he had urged the Iranians to evacuate their inspectors. They resisted, saying that the U.S. embassy had assured them that ARVN had tightened its defensive perimeter around the city. He warned them Da Nang was doomed and that neither the United States nor South Vietnam was planning to rescue the Iranian inspectors. The head of the Iranian delegation withdrew his people just in time.

Moorefield's dispiriting conversation with Al Francis about Da Nang had left him concerned for the safety of the Iranian ICCS delegation in Saigon. Now that the Communists had seized half of South Vietnam and were threatening the capital, there was no longer the pretense of a peace for the Iranians to control and supervise. As their liaison officer, he felt responsible for their safety and feared that it would be on his conscience if something happened to them. He told one of the young Iranian diplomats who had become a friend, "Listen, I don't have the authority to tell you this, but you've got to get out. The South is not going to hold the line. Things are going to collapse, and when that happens, it's going to happen dramatically and it's going to be ugly. You don't have a deal with the U.S. military. They're not going to whisk you away." To his relief the Iranians left.

The embassy had a priority departure list of U.S. mission personnel who were being encouraged to leave South Vietnam and a list of "mission-essential" ones who were being asked to stay to the end. With the Iranians gone, Moorefield feared he might find himself on the departure list and began searching for a way to make himself mission essential. Al Francis meanwhile became the embassy's Cassandra, a spectral presence haunting its corridors and warning his colleagues what awaited them when the Communists attacked Saigon. His pessimism spooked Martin, who believed that the shell-shocked members of the U.S. mission from the Nha Trang and Da Nang consular districts were undermining embassy morale and should depart as soon as possible. Francis hung on until the middle of April. The day before he left, he handed Don Hays, the embassy financial officer whom Martin had ordered expelled, a check for $15,000 and asked him to spend it to help the Vietnamese employees of the Da Nang consulate escape.

Theresa Tull refused to leave Saigon until she had arranged for the departure of General Truong's children. They were staying with their mother in a house in Saigon while Truong was in a hospital recovering from nervous exhaustion, although his principal affliction was probably shame. Tull needed him to sign a letter making her the children's legal guardian and to arrange for their passports and exit visas. Martin, however, had issued a directive forbidding embassy officials to visit Vietnamese officers from their previous posts without his permission. There was talk of a coup against Thieu, and he did not want his diplomats meeting with possible conspirators. Tull explained that she was taking Truong's children to the United States and needed to see him to arrange for their departure. "Well, you know, this is a problem, Terry," Martin said. "There are rumors that people want General Truong to replace President Thieu; there are rumors of a coup that would put him in Thieu's place."

"Unfortunately, Ambassador Martin, he's not the type," she said.

Martin relented and Tull visited Truong in the hospital. After he signed a letter giving her guardianship of his children, she went to his house, where his wife introduced her to fifteen-year-old Trinh, eleven-year-old Tri, and nine-year-old Tran—the children she expected to be hers for the rest of her life. Mrs. Truong had knit a heavy sweater for each child and had packed in their bags a Vietnamese-English phrase book, some of their favorite books, recordings of Vietnamese music, several of the family's treasured Chinese-style bowls, and other mementos and keepsakes to remind them of their heritage and of the parents they might never see again.

The Truongs were willing to risk being permanently separated from their children because, like many Vietnamese tainted by their associations with the United States and the Thieu government—and like Theresa Tull, Ken Moorefield, Major General Smith, Brigadier General Baughn, Walter Martindale, Ken Quinn, David Kennerly, and other Americans who feared for their Vietnamese friends, relatives, and co-workers—they believed that the stakes were high and American "lackeys" faced execution, or at best years of imprisonment and harsh treatment in a North Vietnamese gulag.

Some Americans and Vietnamese believed that the Communists would begin seeking revenge the moment the South surrendered; others thought they would expel foreign journalists, seal the borders, and operate behind a Bamboo Curtain. Some predicted mass executions, a literal bloodbath; others forecast targeted killings. Some believed that every South Vietnamese government official, military officer, and intelligence operative would owe a "blood debt"; others thought that the Communists would punish the hundreds of thousands of "class enemies" who had worked for Americans in any capacity. Stephen Hosmer, a Rand Corporation researcher, concluded his 1970 book, *Viet Cong Repression and Its Implications for the Future,* by writing that it was "difficult to believe that the number [of executions] would be much less than 100,000."

The imagined score settling following a Communist victory in South Vietnam was sometimes called the bloodbath theory or blood-bath scenario. Some in the U.S. antiwar movement used the term derisively, insisting that only the most corrupt and wicked South Viet-namese officials would be punished and that claims to the contrary were propaganda spread by the American and South Vietnamese governments to stiffen resistance. U.S. officials supporting additional aid to the Thieu government did sometimes fall back on the bloodbath scenario. Secretary of Defense Schlesinger told a congressional committee in April that the Communists might kill as many as 200,000 people. Two days later, a Pentagon spokesman claimed that "secret reports" claimed that the Communists were carrying out "bloody reprisals" in occupied provinces. Kissinger informed the House of Representatives International Relations Committee on April 11 that he had read "plausible reports" of South Vietnamese officials being executed, adding, "We expect to see the Communists try to eliminate all possible opponents." Vietnamese newspapers reported his statements, and a headline in *Stars and Stripes,* the U.S. military newspaper that was widely read in Saigon, warned, "At Least Million Vietnamese Will Be Slaughtered."

But just because the U.S. and the Thieu governments employed the bloodbath theory did not make it entirely spurious. A January 5, 1975, memorandum from the North Vietnamese Ministry of the Interior ordered its armed forces to encourage South Vietnamese soldiers and government personnel to enter "liberated areas and join the revolution" and "punish stubborn leaders (officers from the rank of Captain up and government officials from above or on the district level up)."

The memorandum stated that South Vietnamese leaders "could be killed immediately or arrested, tried, and sentenced to death, imprisonment or reeducation camps." Ten days before Kissinger cited "plausible reports" of executions, he had read a National Security Council memorandum reporting that a double agent had provided the CIA with the "new COSVN [Central Office for South Vietnam] resolution for 1975." Under the heading "Specific missions for Party members to follow," it instructed them to "induce the masses to kill GVN [government of Vietnam] officials" and "kill some GVN officials, develop some of the progressive dignitaries and try to eliminate the reactionary ones."

Rumors circulating through Saigon in April stoked the bloodbath fears. It was said that the Communists had cut a Catholic bishop into three pieces, marched twelve naked policemen through the streets of Da Nang before beheading them, bound groups of South Vietnamese officers by their hands and feet and executed them with a single grenade, and ripped out the manicured fingernails of women suspected of prostitution, a story persuading Saigon's bar girls to cut their nails. A Buddhist monk told the embassy that Communists had executed three hundred South Vietnamese in the Ban Me Thuot market. He was not an eyewitness, but his story was included in an embassy cable cataloging Communist atrocities. Some of the atrocity stories were sketchy and unconfirmed, but the fear they inspired was real and merited. The Vietnam War was a civil war, and had neither side committed atrocities, it would have been the first atrocity-free civil war in human history.

South Vietnamese knew that the Communists had killed a quarter of a million people in North Vietnam during a 1956 land reform program that was so brutal that even General Giap, who commanded North Vietnam's army, admitted in a party newspaper that "too many honest people" had been executed, terror tactics had been "far too widespread," and torture had become "regarded as a normal practice." They knew that mass graves exhumed when Hue was recaptured from the Communists following the Tet Offensive contained the corpses of over three thousand people who had been shot or buried alive and that when Colonel Tran Van Doc defected from North Vietnam in 1969, he had estimated that if the Communists applied their own criteria for who should be included on a "blood debt" list, it would number three million people. They knew that terror was a key element of Communist strategy, that the Vietcong had executed village leaders in areas they captured during their 1972 offensive, that Communist cadres had "blood debt" lists containing the names of "reactionaries" and "class enemies," among them defectors, intelligence agents, local administrators, and teachers, and that after taking a hamlet, the Communists would execute the worst officials to make themselves more popular, and the best officials because they represented the greatest threat. They also knew that for years Communist propagandists had warned that anyone supporting the Thieu government or working with Americans would be punished, and they knew that although the spokesman for the Provisional Revolutionary Government had said during his weekly press conference at Camp Davis, "We will treat humanely, generously and honestly all those who have cooperated with the adversaries," he had added, "provided they stop sabotaging us and stop serving the interests of the Thieu administration." In other words, to escape punishment, a South Vietnamese citizen would have to become a traitor. After a defector from South Vietnam's air force bombed Independence Palace, a Liberation Radio announcer encouraged South Vietnamese Air Force pilots "to follow the example set by patriotic First Lieutenant Thanh," warning that "hesitation means committing crimes against the fatherland" and that "those who deliberately continue to oppose the people in the Liberation Armed Forces will certainly be punished."

Americans living in Saigon during the final weeks of the decent interval also knew much of this and were skeptical of Communist pledges to deal with captured South Vietnamese officials and military officers humanely. They knew that when reporters went to Hanoi to cover the release of the final sixty-seven American POWs, North Vietnamese briefers had insisted that all of the U.S. prisoners had been treated humanely, but that once the POWs had left North Vietnam, they confirmed that they had been tortured. They also knew that their nationality could make them targets. After capturing Ban Me Thuot during the 1968 Tet Offensive, the Vietcong had shot and killed three American missionaries who had surrendered with their hands raised. In Hue, they had executed three German professors who had been teaching at the university, another German national, and an American diplomat. Their killers were not rogue soldiers. An order issued to political cadres beforehand had ordered them to "annihilate all spies, reactionaries, and foreign teachers (such as Americans and Germans) in the area."

Throughout April, accounts of Khmer Rouge atrocities in neighboring Cambodia also circulated through the American and Vietnamese communities. An American tugboat captain leading convoys of barges up the Mekong to resupply the besieged Cambodian capital of Phnom Penh reported that to save ammunition, the Khmer Rouge were binding the hands and feet of their enemies together before throwing them into the river. U.S. military intelligence intercepted Khmer Rouge communications ordering its forces to execute all Cambodian army officers down to second lieutenant and their wives. A captured Khmer Rouge document said that upon entering Phnom Penh, "we will burn and destroy everything. For sure, we will burn down the markets, ration stocks etc. We will kill politicians as well as officers, ministers, and national assembly members who have no way to defend themselves."

This proved to be an accurate description of what happened after the Khmer Rouge defeated the pro-American military government in Phnom Penh on April 17. A Khmer Rouge radio station announced that members of the government had been beheaded, and *Newsweek* reported thousands of executions, adding that they might be followed by tens of thousands more. Among the rumors circulating through Saigon that later proved true was that Khmer Rouge troops had murdered the doctors, staff, and patients at the main hospital in Phnom Penh, that government officials and military officers had been forced to witness the execution of their wives and children before being killed, and that children had been forced to watch Khmer Rouge soldiers smash their parents' skulls with hammers. In a *Wall Street Journal* essay titled "Signing 100,000 Death Warrants," retired CIA analyst

Samuel Adams likened the Cambodian atrocities to what might occur in South Vietnam, writing that if you were "an enemy of the revolution" living in Phnom Penh, or Saigon, "you could face a very unpleasant fate."

Alan Carter, the director of the U.S. Information Agency in South Vietnam, received a telephone call from Washington in early April asking him to write a memorandum describing Saigon's "mood." USIA country directors routinely composed situation reports, but in this instance USIA told Carter that because State Department officials did not believe that they were receiving "accurate reports" from the embassy, he should write an unvarnished report and transmit it directly to Washington. Carter detected the hand of Martin's great bureaucratic foe, Assistant Secretary Philip Habib. When he was last in Washington, Habib had taken him aside and said, "You know, Alan, we'd like to hear from *you* once in a while." He assumed Habib meant that he wanted reports that had *not* crossed Martin's desk.

Carter had been reluctant to accept the Saigon post because of Martin's reputation for demanding absolute loyalty and for disliking reporters. Carter, on the other hand, was a well-known iconoclast who prided himself on his excellent relationships with journalists. He was sufficiently concerned about working with Martin that before agreeing to accept the post, he had lunch with him when they overlapped in Washington. He told Martin he was surprised that he had requested him for the Saigon post. "I understand you are surrounded by a bunch of people who are your acolytes," he said, "and I want to warn you that I'm unlikely to be one." Fixing him with a penetrating stare, Martin replied, "Do you think I would have accepted you if I didn't know everything about you?" When Carter repeated his warning that he was not a "yes-man," Martin said, "Exactly! I've got to have someone near me who is not an automatic yes-man."

During a staff meeting soon after his arrival, Carter made the mistake of agreeing with a young Foreign Service officer who had proposed that the embassy be more welcoming to the press. Several minutes later Martin said abruptly, "What we don't really need are newcomers telling us how to conduct our affairs." Carter cornered him afterward and accused him of undermining him. Martin insisted that he had been speaking generally. When Carter pointed out that he had been the only newcomer in the room, Martin replied, "I think your ego is large enough for you to trip over."

Carter's next mistake had been to invite a dozen members of the Saigon press corps to dinner. It was the kind of gathering that he had routinely hosted at other posts, and during it he encouraged his guests to voice any complaints, most of which concerned the ambassador. Martin heard about the party and demanded that Carter submit a memorandum describing what each journalist had said and how he had responded to their criticisms. When Carter refused, Martin accused him of being "not really interested in getting on the team" and threatened to deny him "the privilege of talking to the press."

Carter's back-channel memorandum to USIA headquarters in Washington described a mood "bordering on panic" and a city living in the lengthening shadow of a bloodbath and gripped by "a palpable fear." A March 31 *Wall Street Journal* headline, "Suppressed Hysteria Underlies Saigon Calm," coincidentally depicted the mood that Carter described in his memorandum. The undercurrent of fear running alongside Saigon's appearance of normality made Carter feel, he said later, as if he were "watching an old film roll while a new script is being written." He woke in his handsome villa and breakfasted in the patio on mango and French coffee while watching graceful Vietnamese women in their *ao dais* glide past his front gate on motor scooters. Then he walked through the gate and confronted a crowd of anxious people looking to him for reassurance or rescue.

He sensed the "suppressed hysteria" at nightclubs where young couples engaged in a parody of dancing, moving like zombies and going through the motions to reassure themselves that everything was fine. He sensed it at government offices where officials kept the bureaucratic machinery sputtering along while they planned their escapes. The "palpable fear" was evident at the Cercle Sportif, a club for expatriates and South Vietnam's elite. Waiters in white jackets still wove through the grounds with trays of gin and tonics, Frenchmen still played *boules* under the tamarind trees, and Vietnamese girls in bikinis sunned themselves by the swimming pools. But look through the bougainvillea and you saw troops digging trenches and positioning antiaircraft batteries to protect Independence Palace. Look more closely at the bulletin board and you saw a notice announcing, "Because of the current situation, the board of directors has decided to stop the admission of new members and their families for an indefinite period." Speak to the club's expatriate members and you heard that the club's Vietnamese were "scared to death."

There were suddenly more beggars in Saigon, more people selling their belongings on sidewalks, more advertisements in the English-language *Saigon Post* for foreign husbands, more Europeans flying their national flags from cars and homes so they would not be mistaken for Americans, and more Vietnamese patronizing the best French restaurants, seizing a last chance to enjoy a good meal. People hoarded rice and stood in long lines at the main post office to mail packages abroad. Women who had consorted with American men hoarded pills and spoke of suicide. Parents made their children memorize the addresses of relatives in case families became separated. Pedestrians walked faster while hurrying between markets looking for staples, illegal gambling dens operated openly, soothsayers were busier, and bar girls became more uninhibited. International flights were booked solid but left half-empty because passengers could not obtain passports and exit visas, and a Vietnam expert told *The New York Times,* "It's harder for a South Vietnamese to get out of this country, even in normal times, than for an East German to leave the Communist bloc."

While flying home with the Weyand mission, Ken Quinn composed a memorandum for Henry Kissinger, noting in a covering letter that the following were his personal judgments and had not been cleared with Weyand. After reminding Kissinger that he was the only Vietnamese speaker on the mission and had the longest consecutive service in Vietnam of any of its eight principal members, he called the situation in South Vietnam "critical" and predicted that the country "may be totally defeated in as little as three weeks." He dismissed Thieu as "discredited and almost completely ineffective." Echoing Alan Carter's report to USIA, he wrote that morale was "critically low and bordering on national despair" and that the government was "near paralysis." The only hope lay in Thieu's resigning and handing over command of the armed forces to General Truong, "the only man who has the confidence of the Army and the population." He acknowledged that Truong was currently hospitalized but argued that "a sick Truong is probably better than anyone else." Even then, he wrote, "the short term survivability" of South Vietnam in its truncated form depended on Truong being backed by U.S. airpower. Otherwise, the only way for the United States to halt the Communist offensive would be "an approach to the Soviets and Chinese emphasizing that the humiliation of the U.S. through the capture of Saigon would seriously affect our bilateral relations." The best result, he thought, would be "formation of a 'coalition government' on terms tantamount to surrender."

In a second memorandum titled "Evacuation from Saigon," he reported, "The mood among the Vietnamese is one of increasing desperation mixed with an intense and even passionate desire to avoid falling under Communist control." He listed the categories of Vietnamese who faced the greatest risk of retaliation from the Communists, calling their possible evacuation "a problem of staggering proportions," adding, "Clearly the USG [U.S. government] has some type of responsibility for the position these people now find themselves in, since most of the above people would never have become so involved with the GVN [government of Vietnam] or the USG had they known we would not continue to protect them."

Weyand's written report was less pessimistic but bore little resemblance to his parting remarks to the Saigon press corps at Tan Son Nhut, in which he had declared that South Vietnam's military forces were "still strong and have the capability to defeat the North Vietnamese." In a covering letter to Ford and Kissinger, he wrote, "The current military situation is critical, and the probability of the survivability of South Vietnam as a truncated nation in the southern provinces is marginal at best." He added that "the GVN is on the brink of a total military defeat" and proposed two measures to rescue South Vietnam: ask Congress for an emergency appropriation of $722 million "to reinforce Vietnamese capabilities," and reintroduce U.S. military airpower. He acknowledged "the significant legal and political implications" of resuming the bombing and admitted that it would take forty-five days after Congress approved any supplemental aid to deliver the equipment and supplies to South Vietnam. The principal benefits of the aid would be psychological, he said, giving a boost to South Vietnamese morale. He concluded by acknowledging that $722 million would probably not save South Vietnam, writing, "There is not and cannot be any guarantee that the actions I propose will be sufficient to prevent total North Vietnamese conquest." But the effort should be made, he said, because "what is at stake in Vietnam now is America's credibility as an ally."

The plane returning Weyand from Saigon stopped in Palm Springs on April 5 so he could brief President Ford at his vacation home. His verbal report was more pessimistic than his written one, and after he recommended renewed U.S. air strikes, Kissinger turned to Ford and said, "If you do that the American people will take to the streets again."

While driving to the press center afterward, Kissinger asked Press Secretary Ron Nessen, "Why don't these people [the South Vietnamese] die fast? The worst thing that could happen would be for them to linger on." During his press conference Kissinger urged Americans to recognize "that we are facing a great tragedy in which there is involved something of American credibility, something of American honor, something of how we are perceived by other people in the world."

David Kennerly arrived in Palm Springs in an emotional state, distressed about the fate of a country where, as he put it, "I grew up as much as I ever grew up," and of a people toward whom he felt "an almost familial attachment." He struck Betty Ford's private secretary as "pale, tired, obviously shaken." He told journalists covering Ford's Palm Springs vacation that witnessing the suffering in South Vietnam and Cambodia (which he had visited briefly on his own) had been "the worst thing that ever happened to me in my life" and described the situation as "really shitty," adding, "And you can quote me."

He knew that Weyand was recommending that Ford ask Congress to appropriate supplemental aid and that some of Ford's advisers would argue that it might save South Vietnam. When he met with Ford alone the next day, he told him the truth: the war was over and no amount of money could save South Vietnam. He showed Ford his photographs, proof of how "shitty" things were. Ford turned over one depressing image after another. He saw dead-eyed South Vietnamese soldiers fleeing the enemy, children near death in a Cambodian hospital, buses crammed with grief-stricken people escaping Nha Trang, and refugees crammed onto the decks of the *Pioneer Commander*.

"This is what's going on," Kennerly said. "Cambodia is gone [Phnom Penh would fall to the Khmer Rouge twelve days later], and I don't care what your generals are telling you, anyone who says that South Vietnam has more than three or four weeks to go is bullshitting you. The party's over." He concluded by saying, "All my friends know they're going to be killed."

It was not the plea for renewed B-52 raids that Walter Martindale had begged him to make. But telling Ford that his generals were bullshitting him was at least an antidote to Weyand's bet hedging and Martin's wishful thinking.

Ford decided to ask Congress for the supplemental aid as a matter of principle and to demonstrate to America's allies that he had tried to save South Vietnam. He was so moved by Kennerly's photographs that he ordered them hung in the corridors of the West Wing. Several days later some White House staffers complained that walking past them on their way to the White House mess was too depressing and had them removed. Ford ordered them reinstated and told Kennerly, "Everyone should know what's going on there."

While flying back to Washington from Palm Springs on Air Force One, Kennerly unburdened himself to a UPI reporter, telling him that his Vietnamese friends were "terrified" because "they know that anyone who had anything to do with the Americans has good reason to know they stand a good chance of getting greased when the Communists come." He said that many of his friends had begged him to save their children by taking them to the United States, and he asked the reporter, "How in God's name can you nicely tell a man who once saved your life while you were both covering a war with cameras that, no, you can't take his kids home to America with you?"

CHAPTER 8

Operation Babylift

The April 4 Operation Babylift flight bringing orphans to the United States would be the first U.S. government–sanctioned evacuation from South Vietnam. Major General Smith supported the Babylift flights as a way of reducing the DAO's American female dependents by sending them home as escorts for the children. Ambassador Martin called the flights "a good way to get sympathy for additional American aid to Saigon" and told a South Vietnamese official they would "help swing American public opinion to the advantage of the Republic of Vietnam." President Ford planned to meet the April 4 Babylift flight in California and carry the first orphan onto American soil. Left unaddressed was the irony of sending Vietnamese orphans to the United States on a plane that had just unloaded seventeen 105 mm howitzers, equipment likely to produce more orphans.

As more soldiers died in South Vietnam, family ties had become strained. Extended families adopted fewer children, and more ended up in orphanages. Among them were tens of thousands of the children of American servicemen and civilians, Amerasians who were outcasts in a society valuing racial purity. The six U.S. adoption agencies licensed by the government of South Vietnam had matched two thousand Amerasian orphans with parents in the United States but had been stymied by South Vietnam's insistence on exit visas and passports, documents that were difficult to obtain for orphans often lacking birth certificates. By the beginning of April, an avalanche of exit visa applications had overwhelmed clerks at the Ministry of the Interior, and the cost of bribes demanded to process them had priced out the orphanages.

Twenty-year-old Ross Meador, the co-director of overseas operations for Friends of the Children of Vietnam (FCVN), was an unlikely social worker—a lanky West Coast kid whose long blond hair, sunny disposition, and fondness for Hawaiian shirts seemed more suited to surfing than orphan management. He had postponed college to travel through Mexico and India and was searching for another adventure when a friend suggested the FCVN. He inflated his experiences as a nurse's aide in the eighth grade and persuaded the organization to give him a plane ticket to Saigon. He arrived in 1974 knowing little about Vietnam or orphans but quickly became an effective lobbyist for the FCVN at the U.S. embassy and South Vietnam's Ministry of Social Welfare. Cherie and Tom Clark, who had adopted a child through the organization, joined him in Saigon, more volunteers followed, and by 1975 the FCVN was among the most successful foreign adoption agencies. Meador divided his time between supervising the older orphans living in the organization's facility at Thu Duc on the outskirts of Saigon and badgering South Vietnamese bureaucrats and U.S. embassy officials.

In March 1975, the U.S. government waived its visa requirements for Vietnamese orphans, and Minister of Social Welfare Phan Quang Dan wrote a letter recommending that South Vietnam's government approve the departure of the two thousand orphans residing at the adoption agencies' orphanages. The embassy decided to treat Dan's letter as a laissez-passer permitting the orphans to leave for the United States, but when Meador tried to fly out his children, the commercial carriers refused to ticket them unless each had an adult escort.

On the morning of April 2, Meador heard that Ed Daly was offering to fly orphans to Oakland on a World Airways DC-8 that had just landed with humanitarian supplies. He rushed to Tan Son Nhut and found Daly holding a press conference in the DAO cafeteria. He was wearing his trademark green beret and safari suit and was already four sheets to the wind, gripping a bottle of Johnnie Walker in one hand

and a silver-plated revolver in the other that he banged on the table as he denounced Ambassador Martin for withdrawing his clearance to operate evacuation flights. He berated a nun who had been begging him to evacuate her orphans, reducing her to tears before pressing a wad of cash into her hand and bellowing, "I'm sick of these damn women. I'm not talking to any fucking women." He saw Meador and shouted, "What the hell do you want?"

"You have a plane and we have a houseful of kids."

Daly had been searching for humanitarian missions to restore his reputation after his Da Nang fiasco. He had given the wife of a physician at the Adventist Hospital a check for $10,000 to care for indigent patients and was concocting a scheme to shame U.S. corporations into donating millions to a fund for resettling South Vietnamese refugees in the United States. He pulled Meador aside and said, "I'll take care of this."

At 9:00 p.m., Tom Clark ran into the orphanage at Thu Duc shouting that the South Vietnamese government had given Daly clearance to evacuate orphans and that he planned to leave in two hours. There was no time to prepare the infants, so he and Meador decided to send out the older children. Meador dashed through their rooms yelling, "We're going to America right now!" He and Clark jammed fifty excited children into two vans. As they sped to Tan Son Nhut, Meador led them in singing "California, Here I Come," and soon a chorus of high-pitched voices was shouting, "Right back where I started from!" Among his passengers were the ten-, twelve-, and thirteen-year-old Nguyen brothers. Their father had been killed in action in 1966, and their mother had died in a car accident a year later. The oldest boy was almost fourteen, the age at which the government insisted that boys remain in South Vietnam to be available for military service.

Ed Daly stood on the running board of a jeep. He gestured for Meador and Clark to follow in their vans. Newsmen photographed him standing on the stairs of his World Airways DC-8 while welcoming the children onto a plane configured for cargo. "We don't need no stinking seats!" he shouted. "We've got blankets." As the crew was preparing to close the door, an immigration officer stormed aboard and removed the oldest Nguyen boy and his twelve-year-old brother, Than. He walked down the aisle holding each under an arm in a headlock while shouting that they were old enough to fight for their country. Daly blocked the door. As he and the officer argued, Than slipped away and raced to the back of the plane and hid. Daly took out a $100 bill. The officer slapped it away. Daly ripped the bill in two, gave one half to the oldest Nguyen boy, and told him to bring it to him when he arrived in the United States and he would help him. (The boy got aboard a later flight, had his half of the bill laminated, and brought it back to Tan Son Nhut thirty years later on a trip commemorating the Babylift flights.) South Vietnamese authorities closed the airport as Daly's plane began taxiing, citing an impending rocket attack. An air traffic controller shouted, "Do not take off, you are not cleared for take-off. Repeat. This is the tower, you are not cleared for take-off." Daly grabbed the microphone and shouted, "Oh yeah? Just watch me!"

Photographs of Daly arriving in Oakland with fifty-nine orphans appeared on front pages across the United States, diluting the impact of the Ford administration's subsequent orphan flights. Daly blasted Ambassador Martin, saying that he "should be out picking weeds somewhere." Meador thought he had demonstrated that even a drunken fool could succeed. In an opinion piece titled "The New Angels of Mercy," columnist George Will wrote, "Breathes there an American . . . who hasn't to himself said, 'Right on, Edward Daly!'"

Two days later, on April 4, the first U.S. government Operation Babylift flight left Saigon with 328 passengers on board a U.S. Air Force Lockheed C-5A Galaxy, a double-decker aircraft that was so large that jeeps could drive three abreast into its fifty-yard-long fuselage. The plane lifted off with 200 orphans and 37 official escorts. Most were American women employed by U.S. government agencies and female dependents. Among these dependents was the family of Bill Bell, the Vietnamese linguist on the Joint Military Team who had warned about an imminent Communist attack on Ban Me Thuot after the Santilli family sold its plantation. After South Vietnamese marines ran amok in Da Nang, Bell had purchased plane tickets to California for his wife, Nova, and their children, twelve-year-old Andrea and nine-year-old Michael. Several days before their departure Lieutenant Colonel Conrad Wilson, the deputy commander of the JMT delegation, informed Bell that the Thieu government had given the U.S. Air Force clearance to begin flying Vietnamese orphans to the United States. The first several hundred would be departing on April 4, and the wives of Defense Attaché Office personnel and female DAO employees would be accompanying them as escorts. Bell replied that he felt uneasy about putting his family on a plane lacking the safety features of a commercial jet. Wilson, who was under pressure from the Pentagon to reduce the number of U.S. military dependents in South Vietnam, told Bell that his family *would* be on the Babylift flight and that he should consider that an order.

Bell can remember the twenty-four hours preceding his family's departure with a clarity that escapes him when he tries to recall the hours that followed. He remembers visiting the Bachelor Officers' Quarters near Tan Son Nhut and seeing the crew of the Galaxy frolicking in the swimming pool with Vietnamese bar girls, driving his family to the DAO compound the next morning to be processed for the flight, driving past later and seeing them standing outside the base bookstore, stopping to say good-bye again, and hearing his wife say that she had bought comic books for the children, and noticing that his son was clutching a Donald Duck, his favorite.

He remembers his chauffeur Tran Van Nga driving him to Camp Davis and complaining that Americans were foolish to paint their vehicles black because it made them hotter and then wondering what his life would be like if he immigrated to the United States and expressing amazement when Bell said that because polygamy was illegal, he would have to choose between his wives. He remembers a North Vietnamese officer at Camp Davis handing him the passenger manifest for the next day's liaison flight to Hanoi, and perusing it while drinking the acidic North Vietnamese tea, and noticing that it listed a large number of senior officials from both Communist delegations flying one way. He remembers black smoke spiraling into the sky east of the runways as Nga drove him back, and his relief when Nga said that someone must be burning the pile of old tires he had seen near the runway. He remembers people rushing out of the DAO buildings and jumping into vehicles, the anguished look on the face of a friend when he asked him about the smoke, and hurrying into the JMT offices to hear air force master sergeant David Boggs say, his voice breaking, "The C-5A is down. It's bad, real bad." A voice on Boggs's radio reported that helicopters were bringing survivors to hospitals, and Bell heard himself say, "This just can't be happening. I can't lose my family like this."

While the Galaxy was climbing to cruising altitude, the locks on its rear loading ramp had failed due to negligent maintenance by U.S. Air Force mechanics. As the clamshell-shaped rear doors blew off, the decompression triggered a loud explosion that passengers mistook for a bomb. A whirlwind of debris flew through the lower cabin. Passengers not strapped down or holding on to something were sucked out; passengers unable to grab an oxygen mask passed out. Pilot Bud Traynor turned back to make an emergency landing at Tan Son Nhut, but the explosion had damaged his controls, forcing him to reduce speed and lose altitude in order to control the plane. Five miles from the runway he lost too much speed and altitude and landed in a rice paddy. The plane skidded and became airborne before crossing the Saigon River and slamming into a dike. Most of the orphans, escorts, and crew members riding in the upper level survived, most of those in the lower cargo hold perished. Nova Bell was among the forty adults who died, and Michael Bell was among the more than a hundred orphans and dependent children killed in the crash. Arriving at an accurate death toll was difficult because some children had been slipped aboard at the last minute, and no one knew how many had been sucked out after the decompression. The official death toll of 155 made it the most lethal crash in U.S. aviation history to date.

The crash site was boggy, and the nearest road was a mile away. The first medical teams and journalists arrived by helicopter. They found toys, baby bottles, luggage, and mud-covered infants. Some children screamed; others were silent and in shock. Most had only wristbands identifying the addresses of their adoptive parents. After they reached the hospital, nurses threw them in the shower and said,

"This one's alive. This one's dead." Some soldiers who had been fighting Vietcong units nearby helped evacuate the wounded; others rifled
the dead. Captain Stuart Herrington, Bill Bell's fellow interpreter on
the JMT, was among the first on the scene. He found the corpses of
two American JMT secretaries and the body of another young woman
he knew. A medic told him that rescuers had found Andrea Bell sitting
on the dike and sobbing.

Bell wandered through the DAO's labyrinthine corridors, experi-
encing what he later called "a surrealist fantasy" and a "life flashing
before your eyes" review of his life showing what had brought him
to this moment. There had been his hardscrabble childhood in rural
Texas, during which a train had hit and killed his father, an impover-
ished cotton farmer, and a neighbor had appeared at the family's back
door with a pail holding his remains.

Like many boys in the 1950s, Bell had grown up on war movies
and Westerns. His favorites starred Audie Murphy, the World War II
hero turned actor who came from his county. Bell had attempted to
join the army at fifteen, at sixteen, and finally persuaded his mother
to sign his enlistment papers on his seventeenth birthday. He soon
discovered that it was difficult to become the next Audie Murphy during the peaceful early years of the 1960s. He left the army, reenlisted
to escape a boring civilian job, and volunteered to be a helicopter door
gunner. The army sent him to Vietnamese language school instead,
and so began the rest of his life.

During his walkabout through the corridors of the DAO, he saw
himself learning Vietnamese at army language school and lying awake
in the Central Highlands and wondering how a kid from Greenwood,
Texas, had ended up speaking Vietnamese. He saw himself serving as
a plainclothes intelligence operative, studying nights and weekends to
earn a B.A. in Asian philosophy, religion, and political science from
Chaminade University in Honolulu while still on active duty, serving
as an interpreter in Hanoi during the repatriation of American POWs,
accepting the position as head interpreter for the U.S. JMT delegation, and deciding to move his family to Saigon instead of sending
them home to Tennessee. He flashed back to firefights in the Central

Highlands and saw his comrades crying over dead comrades, weeping after killing a man in hand-to-hand combat and throwing enemy corpses into pyres ignited with mosquito repellent. Because he had smelled burning flesh, seen mangled bodies, and felt the scorching heat of napalm, he could imagine Nova, Andrea, and Michael's skin blackening and curling in the postcrash fire.

He emerged to find himself outside the DAO. Rescue workers told him that the plane had crashed on its belly, where most of the wives and dependent children had been seated. A medic reported having seen Andrea at the Adventist Hospital. He found her lying on a litter outside the emergency room, fell to his knees alongside her, and wept.

The U.S. government's first official evacuation from South Vietnam had ended with American women collecting pillowcases to be used as infant body bags. What Ford, Kissinger, and Martin had imagined being a propaganda victory for the United States became one for Hanoi. North Vietnamese officials condemned the Babylift as kidnapping; South Vietnamese accused Americans of stealing their children while refusing to evacuate adults more likely to suffer reprisals. Leaders of the U.S. antiwar movement criticized the Babylift as unnecessary and culturally insensitive. Ambassador Martin accused "alarmists" of stampeding the government into a hastily organized evacuation on a military plane unsuitable for children. Some of the "orphans" disembarking from Babylift flights in the United States turned out to be the children of well-connected South Vietnamese. Like General Truong and his wife, and the parents who handed their children to O. B. Harnage on the roof of 22 Gia Long Street on April 29, their parents were prepared to risk never seeing them again so they could escape Communist indoctrination and receive a Western education.

Bell's colleague Stuart Herrington thought that the loss of so many women shattered the morale of the American community. Among eight U.S. women who had recently attended a dinner party at his house, seven had died, including the ebullient twenty-two-year-old Barbara Kavulla, a popular secretary who had stayed up late the night before while typing General Weyand's report. The disaster convinced Herrington that the American enterprise in Vietnam really *was* cursed and that evacuating his Vietnamese friends was more urgent than ever.

USIA director Alan Carter had sent his "palpable fear" memorandum to Washington on April 3, a day before the crash. Martin saw it and telephoned Carter on April 5 to complain. "You know, I never would have authorized the use of that particular plane," he said. "I've been around planes long enough [he had served in the U.S. Army Air Forces] to know that the Galaxy has problems. I never would have allowed it, but Washington didn't ask me. I'll tell you why they didn't ask me. They didn't ask me because they're getting other reports that misled them. If, for example, they hadn't felt there was 'palpable fear' here, they might have asked me."

"My God!" Carter exclaimed. "You're suggesting that I'm responsible for the crash?"

"You can read it any way you want," Martin said. "I'm telling you that if I had been consulted . . ."

Four days after the Babylift crash the morale of Vietnamese and Americans in Saigon suffered another blow. Lieutenant Nguyen Thanh Trung took off from the nearby Bien Hoa air base on the morning of April 8 with three other South Vietnamese Air Force F-5E fighter-bombers on a mission to bomb North Vietnamese positions. He turned back, claiming mechanical difficulties, and flew to downtown Saigon, where he dropped two of his four 250-pound bombs on President Thieu's Independence Palace. The first missed, exploding harmlessly on the palace grounds. The second failed to detonate. His Communist handlers had ordered him to drop his last two bombs on the American embassy. Had he succeeded, the next three weeks might have unfolded very differently. Instead, he made a second run on the palace. He had been a teenager when South Vietnamese police killed his father, a minor Communist functionary in the delta. After seeing his father's mutilated corpse, he had promised himself, he said later, "When I grow up, if I have the opportunity I will become a pilot. And I will bomb the palace of the leader of South Vietnam."

His second run on the palace was almost as ineffectual as his first.

He hit a roof, causing some minor damage. He then flew to Phuoc Long province, where he received a hero's welcome while South Vietnamese police were arresting his wife and children. His one-man raid inflicted little material damage but considerable psychological harm. Tens of thousands of people in downtown Saigon heard or witnessed the attack. The bribe price of an exit visa skyrocketed, the line of U.S. visa applicants outside the consulate grew longer, and a delegation representing the U.S. mission's Vietnamese employees met with Ambassador Martin to demand their evacuation. He promised them that *if* an evacuation became necessary, he would fly them and their families to safety, and he would not leave Saigon until they had.

On April 9, ARVN troops finally stood and fought, and fought well. The Eighteenth Division, believed to be among the army's weakest, beat back attempts by North Vietnam's troops to take Xuan Loc, a provincial capital on a strategic crossroads thirty-eight miles northeast of Saigon. During the following days Major General Le Minh Dao's outnumbered troops repulsed Communist assaults on the town, inflicting heavy casualties and boosting morale throughout the government and armed forces. The baby-faced Dao sometimes joined his men at the front, playing his guitar and serenading them. He promised a delegation of journalists that no matter how many divisions the Communists sent into the battle, he would "smash them all!"

President Thieu praised the army for recovering its "fighting ability" and announced a new "fighting administration." But because he was unable to persuade more experienced hands to move themselves up several places on the Communists' blacklist by joining the government, his new administration was a group of retreads and minor politicians. At their swearing in, he promised to never surrender and vowed to retake lost provinces. He bet everything on Xuan Loc and gave Dao the ARVN's best remaining troops. The momentum at Xuan Loc shifted after April 14, when Communist artillery blew up the main ammunition dump at the Bien Hoa air base, forcing the air force to suspend its air support of Dao's forces and reposition its planes to Tan Son Nhut and other airfields.

The Bien Hoa explosion spooked Ed Daly, who had returned to Vietnam to decide how to deploy the two World Airways planes that had been under U.S. government contract to fly into Cambodia. Moments before the blast he had received a cable from the Pentagon announcing that his Cambodia contract would end at midnight—and with it the government's insurance on his planes. He concluded that the Communists were about to take Saigon and seize his uninsured jets. After dictating an obscenity-filled telegram to President Ford, he ordered his bodyguards, two beautiful Japanese women with revolvers strapped to their waists, to rouse his air crews and tell them they were leaving. Once the crews had gathered in his suite, he shouted, "Bring out the hambones!" and one of the Japanese women opened a suitcase to reveal a dozen pistols and automatic rifles. "We may have to shoot our way out to the airport," Daly said while handing out the weapons. "I'm riding shotgun in the first jeep. Don't shoot until I do." He asked a British reporter if he would like to join them. After the reporter declined, he said, "Boy, I've got one last piece of advice for you—get the fuck out of here!"

On April 10, one day after the Eighteenth Division began its courageous stand at Xuan Loc, Brigadier General Richard Baughn, the former World War II pilot whom General Smith had placed in charge of the DAO's Special Planning Group and its Evacuation Control Center, asked representatives from the CIA, USIS, AID, the DAO, and the embassy to attend a planning meeting to discuss a U.S. mission–wide evacuation. It was the first time many had heard about the SPG and the ECC, and they struck Baughn as relieved that someone was finally taking concrete steps to plan for an evacuation. Nevertheless, the embassy's representative announced that Martin wanted any planning suspended until he had approved a written summary of their proposals. Baughn decided there was no time for such bureaucratic nonsense and continued his activities. The next day, April 11, he met with Colonel Al Gray, who commanded the marine amphibious brigade tasked with providing security for an evacuation. Like Baughn and Smith, Gray distrusted the Pentagon's official evacuation plan. This was the same document that made no provision for the evacuation of South Vietnamese, assumed that South Vietnamese troops and police would protect an evacuation of Americans, even though it did not include them, and had shocked Baughn and Smith when they first read it in January after the fall of Phuoc Long. Colonel Gray considered the plan so pointless and unwieldy that he asked one of his men to construct a wheeled cart in the ship's welding room so he could more easily throw the revised editions that arrived every evening overboard.

After visiting the evacuation sites and reviewing the SPG plan, Gray told Baughn that due to the large number of potential evacuees, and South Vietnam's precarious military situation, he wanted to fly in a marine ground security force to defend the DAO compound once the Communists attacked Saigon. He added that he agreed with a request from Air America management for a contingent of marine helicopter pilots to serve as co-pilots to the company's civilian pilots when the time came to extract people from rooftops. Baughn wrote a memorandum summarizing Gray's recommendations and sent it to the embassy's representative for approval. But instead of circulating it to Martin, as Baughn had assumed, the representative asked a lower-level official to approve it. Baughn suspected that the representative agreed with its recommendations and wanted to prevent Martin from vetoing them.

The operator at the DAO message center woke Baughn at 2:00 a.m. on April 12 to report that an urgent cable had arrived from Lieutenant General John Roberts at the Pentagon ordering him to leave South Vietnam on the next flight. After Baughn arrived in Washington, Roberts explained that while reading the outgoing cable traffic, Martin had seen his memorandum requesting the marine helicopter pilots and the security force and had telephoned Secretary of Defense Schlesinger and demanded his immediate recall. These measures were unlikely to have panicked Saigon and toppled Thieu, but Martin considered them unnecessary, and because he had not been consulted, he undoubtedly considered them a challenge to his position as the senior U.S. official in South Vietnam. The embassy claimed that Baughn had been "routinely transferred," but there was nothing routine about his hurried departure. George McArthur wrote in the *Los Angeles Times* that according to his embassy sources Martin had expelled Baughn as payback for his role in sending undocumented evacuees to the Philippines. Baughn resigned from the military soon afterward out of what he calls "complete disgust."

Instead of intimidating the Special Planning Group, Baughn's expulsion emboldened it. The Marine Corps history notes, "As a result [of Baughn's expulsion] future decisions concerning preparations of the DAO compound for evacuation and security were kept secret from everyone save General Smith and his immediate evacuation planners." Captain Jaime Sabater of the SPG told Marine Corps historians that after Baughn's expulsion the SPG did its planning at night and avoided the embassy. According to the SPG's Captain Wood, "From that moment forward everything to do with the evacuation went secret ('black') and the SPG went into deep cover."

The day after Baughn left, Martin hosted a delegation of officers from the Ninth Marine Amphibious Brigade that included Colonel Gray. The principal topic of the meeting was the advantages and disadvantages of different evacuation sites and scenarios. As the officers rolled out maps and diagrams, Martin warned them that he would not tolerate any "outward signs" that an evacuation was imminent lest they become a self-fulfilling prophecy. In his written report on the meeting, Gray criticized "a general lack of concern" on the part of "responsible officials" over the possibility of an evacuation and a "business as usual" atmosphere.

Gray was sufficiently concerned that he persuaded his commanding officer, Lieutenant General Richard Carey, to return with him to Saigon the next day and meet separately with the SPG, Major General Smith, and Martin. The SPG's preparations impressed Carey, but he noted that it had become "a kind of sneaky operation" forced into "playing a game of hide-and-seek" with Martin. He later complained that his meeting with Martin had been "cold, non-productive and . . . an irritant to the ambassador." A week later, he wrote in his log that Martin "must be convinced the time to evacuate is at hand and any further delay can only result in increased casualties," adding, "I pray for a silver tongue and the Wisdom of Solomon as he is very inflexible."

CHAPTER 9

"People Are Going to Feel Badly"

The White House announced that the purpose of President Ford's nationally televised speech to a joint session of Congress on April 11 would be to persuade lawmakers to approve the $722 million in supplemental aid to South Vietnam that General Weyand had proposed. Cynics said that Ford and Kissinger knew it was unlikely that Congress would vote for supplemental aid and that Ford wanted to pin the loss of South Vietnam on the Democratic-controlled Congress. Press Secretary Ron Nessen, who had been wounded while covering the war, privately feared that sending additional military aid to South Vietnam would only prolong the Thieu regime's "death spiral." He would later call Ford's speech "a symbolic gesture of support to prevent morale from collapsing in South Vietnam," and Deputy National Security Adviser Brent Scowcroft would admit, "Nobody thought we would get the money. It was a way to make it look as if we were serious about the whole effort," adding, "We were primarily concerned about how to get out and disengage."

With David Kennerly's photographs fresh in his mind, Ford warned Congress that "a vast human tragedy has befallen our friends in Vietnam and Cambodia." After asking for $250 million in economic and humanitarian aid and $722 million in emergency military assistance, he demanded a vote by April 19. He declared that the supplemental military aid might enable South Vietnamese forces "to stabilize the military situation" and offer a "chance of a negotiated

· 141 ·

political settlement," but if the "very worst" occurred, the aid would "at least allow the orderly evacuation of Americans and endangered South Vietnamese to places of safety." He added that the humanitarian aid was needed to fulfill America's "profound moral obligation" to South Vietnamese whose allegiance to the United States had put their lives "in very grave peril" and to guarantee "the orderly evacuation of Americans and endangered South Vietnamese." White House counselor Robert T. Hartmann would later write that the $722 million had also been a kind of "ransom," an effort by Ford to buy time to save "the remaining Americans and as many blacklisted South Vietnamese as we could get out."

Ford also asked Congress to "clarify" the law—meaning the 1973 Case-Church resolution prohibiting U.S. military activity in Laos, Cambodia, and Vietnam without congressional approval—so that U.S. troops could assist in the evacuation of Americans and endangered South Vietnamese, the implication being that Congress would be putting American lives at risk if it refused.

Washington Post Saigon bureau chief Don Oberdorfer described Ford's talk of a moral obligation as "more a statement of principle than an order for evacuation" and saw a "contradiction between what is being said and what is being done," adding that so far "hardly anything" had been done to evacuate endangered South Vietnamese. An embassy source told reporter George McArthur that although people at the embassy were compiling lists of potential Vietnamese evacuees and debating who should be included on these lists, they were doing little to figure out *how* to get them out of South Vietnam. Another source told him that some Americans were talking about evacuating thousands of Vietnamese so that after Saigon fell, they could say, "Well, we tried."

Only half of Congress attended the joint session. Some members booed and hissed. Two walked out and no one clapped. Telegrams and calls to the White House and Capitol Hill opposed sending additional aid to South Vietnam by a wide margin. Former Vietnam War hawk Senator Henry "Scoop" Jackson (D-Wash.) said of Ford's request, "It's dead. I oppose it." House majority leader Thomas "Tip" O'Neill

(D-Mass.) said it was "inconceivable" that the House would approve any supplemental military aid, and for that to happen, there would have to be "a complete turnaround" of public opinion.

On the day that Ford addressed Congress, a new Harris poll revealed that the time had passed when a U.S. president could persuade Americans to support more military assistance for South Vietnam. Seventy-five percent of respondents said that Congress had been right not to authorize the $300 million in military aid that Ford had requested in January. Since then, the hearts of a majority of Americans had become so hardened toward the South Vietnamese that when asked, "If more military aid to Vietnam and Cambodia would avoid a bloodbath for the people of those countries would you favor or oppose such military aid?" Fifty-seven percent replied that even under those circumstances they would *still* oppose any additional aid, and only 29 percent said they would support it.

There was a measure of racism behind the callousness. Unlike other Cold War refugees whom Americans had welcomed—the 40,000 Hungarians who left their country in 1956 after its failed anti-Communist uprising, and 675,000 Cubans who had fled to the United States since 1960—the South Vietnamese were Asians, and American opposition to Asian immigration had been so fierce that before passage of the 1965 immigration act immigration from Asia had been limited to 100 persons a year. War weariness was another factor. After investing so many lives and so much money in the conflict, Americans were sick of Vietnam and did not want Vietnamese refugees around to remind them of the war. By portraying the Thieu regime as corrupt, repressive, and undeserving of U.S. support, the antiwar movement and the press had also made it easier for Americans to tell themselves that South Vietnamese did not deserve U.S. citizenship. But the greatest portion of blame for this coldheartedness belonged to the U.S. political and military leaders whose bungling and lies had left Americans cynical and skeptical about anything involving South Vietnam, including its refugees.

After Ford's speech, members of Congress from both parties declared that they were primarily or exclusively interested in evacuating Americans. Senator Edmund Muskie (D-Maine) said he could "see some difficulties with respect to evacuating South Vietnamese on any massive scale." Tip O'Neill declared that "Congress will vote for the humanitarian aid but it will never vote for further military aid" and predicted that legislation would be passed to ensure the evacuation of Americans from South Vietnam, but that evacuating Vietnamese was "an imponderable issue at this time." Some questioned Ford's legal right to order troops into South Vietnam to protect an evacuation without their approval. Senator Frank Church (D-Idaho) said that Congress and the administration should act with "caution" to involve U.S. troops in an evacuation, even one restricted to Americans, because it risked "miring down U.S. troops" who might have to protect evacuation enclaves from North Vietnamese forces.

At a time when the Bien Hoa explosion was unnerving Saigon and Major General Dao's defense of Xuan Loc was faltering, the Senate Foreign Relations Committee came to the White House. The senators had requested the meeting, and it would be the first between the committee's full membership and a president in almost sixty years. Kissinger opened it by declaring that a Communist victory would put over a million of America's South Vietnamese allies in danger and that 174,000 of them would be in "overwhelming jeopardy." Senator Church protested that evacuating so many Vietnamese could reinvolve the United States "in a very long war."

Ford countered that if they tried to abandon the at-risk South Vietnamese, they might "have a hard time getting the 6,000 Americans out" and warned that if they refused his request for the $722 million in emergency aid, Thieu's government and military might take revenge against the remaining Americans. Kissinger reported that a member of Thieu's government had already warned an embassy official that "if you pull out the Americans and leave us in the lurch, you may have to fight your way out." Ford estimated that the country should be prepared to evacuate between 175,000 and 200,000 Vietnamese, adding, "We're morally responsible and we have to help the people who helped us."

Not a single senator on the committee agreed. The only excuse some could see for evacuating *any* South Vietnamese was to ensure the safe evacuation of American citizens, and the only rationale for approving $722 million in supplemental aid was if the money was essentially an unavoidable ransom.

Jacob Javits (R-N.Y.) declared that he would not vote for "one nickel for military aid for Thieu" but would approve "any ransom to get our people out." Joe Biden (D-Del.) said, "I am not sure I can vote for an amount to put American troops in for one to six months to get all the Vietnamese out," but he would "vote for any amount for getting Americans out. I don't want it mixed with getting Vietnamese out." Howard Baker (R-Tenn.) believed that evacuating Americans was "so urgent" that everything else was "secondary." Clifford Case (R-N.J.), the ranking Republican on the committee, said that the committee's members believed that the number of Americans in Saigon should be reduced to a point that the last contingent could be evacuated on a single plane. Claiborne Pell (D-R.I.) suggested that the United States should fly Vietnamese evacuees to the Indonesian island of Borneo, because it had "the same latitude [it doesn't], the same climate, and would welcome some anti-Communists."

Ford replied that the Vietnamese should not be treated any differently from Hungarians, Cubans, or Soviet Jews. "We opened our door to the Hungarians," he said. "I am not saying the situation is identical but our tradition is to welcome the oppressed."

After the meeting ended, Kissinger told White House press secretary Ron Nessen, "I personally don't believe we will get [out] anything like the 174,000." Nevertheless, he said, "we have an obligation to get out as many as we can, if we can get any out."

The Washington Post reported that at a caucus of Senate Democrats afterward, "sentiment was widespread in favor of a quick withdrawal of Americans from South Vietnam, with much opposition to any use of U.S. troops to evacuate South Vietnamese." During the meeting, James Abourezk (D-S.D.) pointed out that fifteen 747 jets could evacuate the remaining Americans. Majority Whip Robert Byrd (D-W.V.) said he was "very much opposed to the use of the armed forces to evacuate any South Vietnamese personnel" and introduced a resolution authorizing President Ford to send U.S. military forces into South Vietnam solely to rescue American citizens. Some House members went further and circulated a resolution calling for evacuating Americans "solely utilizing civilian personnel and transport."

On April 16, the House Committee on International Relations began several days of hearings to consider Ford's request for $250 million in humanitarian funds necessary for the evacuation of Americans and between 150,000 and 200,000 Vietnamese. Representative Don Riegle Jr. of Michigan, a liberal Democrat and longtime Vietnam War opponent, charged that Ford was using the Americans "as a lever to bargain out the exit of 100,000 or 200,000 Vietnamese." He called the evacuation of so many Vietnamese "a mistake" and suggested that the administration "scale down" its list of endangered Vietnamese to between 1,000 and 2,000. He predicted that trying to rescue hundreds of thousands of Vietnamese could result in the deaths of five thousand American soldiers.

Congress failed to authorize Ford's request for $722 million in supplemental aid but endorsed $200 million for humanitarian assistance on the understanding that the administration would accelerate the departure of U.S. citizens. The Senate and House bills prohibited Ford from increasing the number of U.S. military personnel involved in the evacuation beyond those needed to evacuate Americans. The Senate bill required that U.S. troops leave South Vietnam once Americans had been evacuated.

It was too late for Nixon's letters to Thieu promising swift retaliation if North Vietnam violated the cease-fire to influence Congress. Erich von Marbod told his friend Nguyen Hung that Weyand had handed copies to President Ford and that Ford had seemed "moved" by them. But after Secretary of Defense Schlesinger briefed Senator Henry "Scoop" Jackson on their contents, Jackson said that they simply demonstrated that Nixon had made secret commitments to Thieu without consulting Congress, and therefore Congress was under no obligation to honor them.

Schlesinger and Chairman of the Joint Chiefs of Staff General George Brown agreed with the politicians urging a rapid evacuation of

Americans. At a meeting of the National Security Council on April 9, Schlesinger had said the administration should recognize that South Vietnam was "gone" and that more aid was justified only as a way of "buying time, partly to get out the Americans." At a meeting of the Washington Special Actions Group on Vietnam and Cambodia on April 17, he said, "I think we ought to get out what Americans we can, and soon," adding, "I don't think we can get many Vietnamese out, even under the best of circumstances." In fact, he argued, the administration did not have the authority under U.S. law to evacuate anyone *but* Americans.

Kissinger believed that Schlesinger had less than honorable reasons for insisting on the rapid evacuation of Americans, writing later, "The careful record established by the Pentagon of its repeated requests for a speedy evacuation guaranteed that Ford and I would be held accountable should anything go wrong at the last minute."

After the dispiriting April 17 WSAG meeting, Kissinger cabled Martin, "You should know that at the WSAG today there was almost no support for the evacuation of Vietnamese and for the use of American force to protect any evacuation. The sentiment of our military, DOD [Department of Defense] and CIA colleagues was to get out fast and now." He said that in light of this he was ordering Martin to accelerate the evacuation so that only two thousand official and private U.S. citizens remained in South Vietnam by April 22. Minutes later he sent Martin a second back-channel cable warning that "interagency pressure for immediate evacuation of US personnel has now become irresistible" and that "drastic action will be required if we are to have any chance of providing for those Vietnamese who have relied on us." He added that the "drastic actions" he was contemplating included "initiating discussions with the Soviet Union and the PRC [People's Republic of China] in order to work out some arrangement which would permit the departure of substantial numbers of Vietnamese who would be endangered and to whom we are most deeply obligated."

At a WSAG meeting four days later, on April 21, General Brown reported that according to General Vien, South Vietnam's chief of staff, a mob at the Nha Trang airport had shot three of his generals as they were boarding helicopters and that Vien had warned that Americans attempting to leave from Tan Son Nhut might suffer a similar fate. In light of this, Brown said that it was "ridiculous" to imagine that the U.S. military could execute an all-day evacuation from Tan Son Nhut. Instead, it would be lucky to manage two waves of helicopters, enough to collect the last remaining Americans. Schlesinger recommended evacuating the remaining Americans on a few C-130s, even if that meant abandoning the Vietnamese. NSC staffer William Smyser reminded Schlesinger that Ambassador Martin had promised to evacuate the U.S. mission's Vietnamese employees and their families and that if most accepted his offer, America would have to evacuate upwards of 100,000 people.

The next day, April 22, NSC staffer William Stearman sent Kissinger a memorandum titled "Evacuation or Rescue of Vietnamese." He predicted, "We will be able selectively to evacuate only relatively small numbers of endangered Vietnamese (e.g. employees of the U.S.)." If the administration wanted to save substantially more, he believed that it should be willing to accept "the random evacuation or rescue of large numbers of Vietnamese." He also predicted that "most Vietnamese who want to escape will have to do so by water," estimated that the tens of thousands of Vietnamese refugees who put out to sea could pose "operational problems" for the U.S. Navy, and asked, "Do we pick them [the refugees] up or not?" And if we decided to pick them up, should the navy move close enough to the shoreline to pick up people whose vessels might sink if they braved the open sea? And then what should they do with these evacuees, people for whom, Stearman wrote, "we would assume a certain responsibility" by having rescued them. One solution, he said, might be "to take as many as possible to Guam or other non-Vietnamese islands to await resettlement in the U.S. or other countries." He closed by suggesting that at the next WSAG meeting Kissinger should ask its members, "Do we want to make every effort to rescue Vietnamese escaping by water?" And if so, how close ashore could navy vessels go, and where should they take the people they rescued?

At a WSAG meeting on April 23, Schlesinger again opposed any large-scale evacuation of Vietnamese nationals, saying, "But the U.S. is going to be accountable for all these Vietnamese. Don't forget that." Kissinger replied darkly, "It's *me* who's going to be held accountable."

Members of the Ford and earlier administrations had cited the bloodbath scenario as a reason for supporting the Thieu government, but now that a genuine bloodbath was under way in Cambodia, it was seldom mentioned at these meetings as a rationale for rescuing large numbers of South Vietnamese. Instead, discussions of their fate in Washington were largely dispassionate and bloodless. Representative Don Riegle spoke of evacuating 2,000 South Vietnamese instead of 200,000 as if the difference scarcely mattered. Stearman's NSC memorandum mentioned the "operational problems" the U.S. Navy might face when thousands of South Vietnamese attempted to escape by water, and presented Kissinger with a choice between ordering the navy to steam closer to shore and rescue them and allowing their vessels to flounder in the open sea—a choice between saving them and letting them die of thirst or drown.

As the end neared, Kissinger became more insistent that the United States had an obligation to evacuate its South Vietnamese allies. On April 19, he told the WSAG that he hoped for "a collapse under controlled conditions" because it promised "the greatest chance of getting the most people out." He asked Senator Ted Kennedy (D-Mass.) to assist in persuading Congress to support an immigration parole for endangered Vietnamese, telling him during a telephone call, "We really owe it to the fifteen years of effort to get some of the key people out." During an April 22 meeting with Republican congressional leaders, he said, "We want to take out the people most likely to suffer," and at a WSAG meeting that same day he asked General Brown, "How many Vietnamese have we gotten out so far?" When Brown admitted that they did not have any "reliable figures," he asked plaintively, "Anybody have any ideas on how we could get more Vietnamese out?"

As John Gunther Dean, the U.S. ambassador to Cambodia, was preparing to leave Phnom Penh on April 12, five days before it fell to the Khmer Rouge, he received a letter from Deputy Prime Minister

Sirik Matak, replying to his offer to evacuate him and other senior members of the pro-Western government. After thanking Dean for his "offer to transport me towards freedom," Matak wrote, "I cannot, alas, leave in such a cowardly fashion." He continued, "As for you, and your great country, I never believed for a moment that you would have this sentiment of abandoning a people which has chosen liberty. . . . You leave, and my wish is that you and your country will find happiness under the sky. But, mark it well, that if I shall die here on the spot and in my country that I love it is too bad, because we are all born and must die one day. I have committed this mistake of believing in you, the Americans. Please accept, Excellency, my dear friend, my faithful and friendly sentiments."

Kissinger was so moved by Matak's letter that he included it at the conclusion of his April 15 statement to the Senate Appropriations Committee. On April 21 the Khmer Rouge shot or beheaded Matak, and four days later CIA director William Colby told the WSAG that the CIA had "good evidence that the [Cambodian] Communists" had ordered their cadres "to 'secretly eliminate all senior enemy commanders and those who owe us a blood debt.'" Kissinger was probably thinking of Matak, and of himself, when he told his staff, "I think people are going to feel badly when it's over. I don't think there would be many heroes left in this."

By the third week of April, Kissinger was beginning to recognize that it was not enough to "make a show" of trying to save at-risk Vietnamese, as he had told Ben Bradlee on April 9, and that his peace of mind and place in history might depend on whether he avoided a bloodbath in South Vietnam, and if not, how many Vietnamese he saved from it. His ability to accomplish that might rest on how adeptly he handled the prickly Graham Martin and how successfully he resisted pressure from Capitol Hill and the Pentagon to evacuate only Americans. And so throughout the second half of April he pushed Martin to comply with the Pentagon's evacuation targets for Americans, but did not push him too hard. He pushed back against General Brown and Schlesinger, who were demanding an immediate evacuation of the remaining Americans, but not too much. He sent tough-sounding cables to Martin demanding that he meet various evacuation targets for American evacuees, but then accepted Martin's repeated failure to meet these targets with a surprising degree of tolerance and equanimity. Several times during these final weeks he said or wrote that he hoped for what he called a "controlled situation" in South Vietnam. By this he meant a slow-motion negotiated surrender by South Vietnam that would avoid an American humiliation, provide time to evacuate South Vietnamese allies wishing to leave, and avoid the kind of bloodbath that had claimed the lives of Matak and other Cambodian political and military leaders. If Kissinger's "controlled situation" occurred, it would be his second decent interval and would require a skeleton staff of Americans at the embassy and other U.S. agencies who could participate in negotiations and facilitate a final and orderly evacuation.

Schlesinger pushed back against Kissinger's endgame strategy by planting an article in *The New York Times* designed to increase the pressure on him for an immediate and total evacuation of Americans. It began, "Defense Department officials concluded today that the situation in South Vietnam was deteriorating so rapidly that the United States must plan on the immediate evacuation of all Americans and their dependents," and reported that in "urgent" White House discussions Secretary of State Kissinger was "opposing proposals for complete evacuation of the 2800 Americans and 1200 Vietnamese dependents [of Americans] still in Saigon." It added that President Ford had said that no plans had been developed for the large-scale evacuation of Vietnamese.

Kissinger complained about the article to Deputy Secretary of Defense William Clements, remarking sarcastically that the gist of it had been that "Defense wishes total evacuation, but that son of a bitch Kissinger, who is thinking of national honor and dignity of the United States, won't permit it." He added, "You guys over there really ought to be ashamed of yourselves. I'm trying to leave [us] a little self-respect." He asked Clements if he did not think they all had a duty to "honor the sacrifice" of Americans killed in the war and avoid "the disgrace of the United States of packing up and leaving everybody." Clements said that *he* agreed with him, and Kissinger conceded that his anger was really directed at Schlesinger.

As the April 14 meeting between the president and the Senate Foreign Relations Committee was ending, Senator Javits had voiced a suspicion shared by other senators that Ambassador Martin had become a loose cannon, telling Kissinger, "We think you should be sure through someone other than Martin that your orders are being carried out."

Kissinger cabled Martin afterward, "It was apparent from that meeting that their full concern is with the evacuation of Americans. . . . In light of the situation we are facing here, I simply must have by the close of business Washington time on Tuesday [April 15], a detailed plan for reduction [of the Americans] in as expeditious manner as possible." Martin failed to execute this order, as he would future ones from Kissinger and Scowcroft directing him to reduce the number of Americans.

The timing and urgency of evacuating Americans dominated many of the communications between Martin and Kissinger. On April 10, Kissinger had ordered him to reduce the number of Americans to those who could be evacuated in a single lift. After acknowledging Martin's "strong views" against reducing U.S. personnel, he said, "But I want you to know that the order for the immediate reduction comes personally from the President." He added, "He [Ford] feels very strongly about this" and "on this one there is now no more flexibility."

Martin replied the next day that he had "strong views" that a rapid drawdown of Americans would be "detrimental to U.S. policy" and would guarantee "that some of our Americans were killed in the wholly unnecessary panic which would have ensued." A day after that, he cabled Scowcroft that because he was confident that he could "anticipate events with sufficient precision to at least stay ahead of the point where there would be serious danger to American lives . . . in order to keep the Mission going, I will not reduce to exactly 1250. . . . I shall not rpt [repeat] not so inform [State] in order to keep pressure on to get some decisions out of Potomac Debating Society Department [that is, the State Department]."

Following the meeting with the Senate Foreign Relations Committee on April 14, Kissinger informed Martin that "the U.S. political situation will not permit withdrawals at the rates you propose" and that because the issue of the number of U.S. citizens and dependents in South Vietnam was "rapidly becoming the focal point of congressional debate on the President's request for military and economic assistance to Viet-Nam," he must accelerate his schedule for the evacuation of American citizens and submit a proposal to reduce their number to two thousand by close of business (COB) on April 18, Washington, D.C., time.

Martin ignored Kissinger's request. The next day Kissinger pushed back the deadline, demanding that he reduce the Americans to eleven hundred by COB on Tuesday, April 22. Martin ignored him again, leading Ford to complain about Martin's practice of constantly increasing the number of Americans remaining in South Vietnam and to tell Kissinger, "He always ends up higher. I don't like that."

Kissinger replied, "I agree. He has not carried out orders." Even so, Kissinger did not push him very hard to obey those orders.

In a back-channel cable to Kissinger, Martin complained about being "hounded" to reduce the number of U.S. citizens, writing, "My situation reminds me of the chap who has his staff progressively removed, yet his national HQ supervisor demanded more and more. Then he got a cable saying his supervisor had been informed the office was dirty. The local man called back, and asked how the hell he could do all that and keep his office clean too. Back came a cable suggesting that he stick a broom up his ass so he could sweep up the office as he went about the rest of his duties."

After recounting this fable, he asked permission to ignore Kissinger's cables concerning the number of remaining Americans so he could "work on reporting the substantive issues which are of vastly more importance." He concluded by criticizing Kissinger for failing to make preparations to receive the increasingly large numbers of Vietnamese refugees who were reaching the Philippines, Guam, and Wake Island, suggesting that "it would be helpful if a bit more of your attention was focused on that end." Several hours later he cabled, "I have an exhausted staff and I am not repeat not going to reduce the U.S.

government side, either direct hire or contractors, any more as long as you want us to continue the airlift." He ended, "I think we have really come to the end of the road on any further pressure on us here about the American community."

To read Martin's insubordinate cables to Kissinger is to understand why Secretary of State Dean Rusk recalled him from Bangkok in 1967. He had defied Rusk then for some of the same reasons that he was defying Kissinger and Schlesinger now: because he believed that his experience as an intelligence officer gave him a superior understanding of military affairs and that he had a duty to resist orders that he considered inimical to U.S. interests and the safety of his staff. He expressed this in an April 15 cable to Kissinger, telling him, "There are only two important considerations I keep in mind, the safety of the people under my charge and the integrity of U.S. policy." He added, "The relatively few people about whose opinions I really care will not change their opinions of me. Even the sly, anonymous insertion of the perfumed icepick into the kidneys in the form of quotes from my colleagues in the [State] Department are only a peculiar form of acupuncture indigenous to Foggy Bottom [the State Department] against which I was immunized long ago."

He reassured Kissinger that he was "leaning over backward" to be "a dispassionate observer viewing Vietnam as from a seat on the moon." He reminded him that while some in the U.S. mission were sending out their dependents and shipping their possessions home, he was not, adding that "the most calming influence in Saigon is my wife who goes about her regular way, making appointments for weeks in advance, and who has refused to pack anything at all although we would hate like hell to lose our most valued possessions."

His defiance of Kissinger's orders complicated their already tricky relationship. Martin was a decade older and considered himself more knowledgeable and experienced in military and diplomatic affairs. Kissinger claimed to admire Martin's intellect and toughness but told Ford and Scowcroft that he worried he was becoming unhinged and sometimes referred to him as "the Madman," saying, for example, "I talked to the Madman."

Kissinger pursued a strategy of flattering Martin in cables and meetings while in private questioning his stability. During a conversation with Scowcroft and Ford on April 8, he said, "We have two nutty ambassadors. Dean [John Gunther Dean, U.S. ambassador to Cambodia] wants to bug out. Martin wants a new version of the Easter Rebellion [the Irish Republicans' revolt against British rule]. He is supporting Thieu too strongly." He praised Martin as "a gutsy guy" but said he was "heading for a debacle" and criticized him for failing to plan for an evacuation. As the end neared, he feared that Martin might emulate "Chinese Gordon," the British military officer and adventurer whose courageous but foolhardy defiance of orders to evacuate the last group of British officers and civilians from Khartoum during the Mahdist revolt in 1885 had led to a yearlong siege culminating in their massacre and his heroic death. Kissinger compared Martin to Gordon several times in April, telling Senator Ted Kennedy, "Our problem is to prevent panic at the other end [South Vietnam] and we have an Ambassador there who might like to go out like Chinese Gordon but I cannot say that publicly."

Among Martin's contributions to the impression that he was becoming "nutty" was his April 9 cable proposing a campaign to persuade American businessmen to invest in South Vietnam. It was said to "jar" Ford, according to an article in *The New Republic,* and prompt others in his administration "to wonder if Martin was in possession of his faculties." Also contributing to the impression that Martin had lost touch with reality was the cable he sent to James Akins, the U.S. ambassador to Saudi Arabia, asking him to use his "finesse" to persuade the Saudi government to extend a billion-dollar loan to South Vietnam. He called the loan "a good bet" for the Saudis and argued that the lost provinces in the North had been "an economic drain" on South Vietnam and that what remained was "the economic heartland," a region that could be "economically viable in a very short time."

It was too late to recall Martin, so Kissinger defended him, particularly when Schlesinger was on the attack. During a conversation with Ford on April 18, Kissinger praised him as "a noble American" for "trying to hold things together and get people out." He came to his defense again at a meeting the next day, telling Schlesinger, General Brown, and others that Martin was getting as much flack in Washington as he was, adding, "I told him that the only difference between us is that they will hang him a little lower than they hang me." When Schlesinger criticized one of Martin's insubordinate cables as "a rather obnoxious, flamboyant telegram" and asked Kissinger to respond with "a stern cable," Kissinger shot back, "Look, Graham gets lots of abuse. He doesn't need any more from here. . . . I think he's doing a good job under the circumstances."

He reported this exchange back to Martin, telling him, "You may think I am perpetually harassing you. However, when you get back here you will find that the record shows that I defended you and your approach without exception. I continue to believe you are playing a heroic and patriotic role."

Martin responded, "I don't think you are perpetually harassing me," adding, "I think we can keep under control both the Washington mattress mice and the situation here. Sometimes, it is a bit like an Algerian egg dance, but so far I haven't broken any yet."

During Kissinger's congressional testimony on April 18, Representative Don Fraser (D-Minn.) told him that many on Capitol Hill lacked confidence in Martin "based on our experiences with him." Although Martin had spent the previous week refusing Kissinger's orders to reduce the American community in South Vietnam, Kissinger loyally praised him as "a disciplined Foreign Service officer who will carry out his instructions with great competence." He also argued, more truthfully, that for the United States to recall its ambassador at the same time that President Thieu was replaced, as many people were recommending, "is not the best way to maintain a controlled situation."

Instead of threatening Martin, Kissinger suggested to him they were allies, both battling the State Department mattress mice while trying to honor America's responsibility to the South Vietnamese. He praised Martin for handling the tumult in Saigon as admirably as a "field commander" and "playing a heroic and patriotic role."

Meanwhile, Martin was bombarding Kissinger, Scowcroft, and

the State Department with a stream of assessments and predictions that would prove to be spectacularly wrong.

He reminded Kissinger's deputy Brent Scowcroft that he had been "watching our friends in Hanoi with a certain intensity since 1936" and argued that because "for three decades they have tried to avoid the image of naked military power," it was "not in their character to make an immediate smash at Saigon."

He insisted that the South Vietnamese Army was "eager for revenge" and could "surprise the hell" out of the pessimists in Congress who had voted against additional military aid.

He told Kissinger in mid-April that "panic in Saigon arising from our actions in Washington . . . is a far greater worry to me than North Vietnamese capabilities." And on April 25, five days before South Vietnam's unconditional surrender, he cabled Kissinger, "We will have the appearance of a legal transfer [of power]" resulting in "the preservation of stability in Saigon," and boasted that "events have validated what I have felt all along—that . . . we could really count on the DRV [Democratic Republic of Vietnam—that is, the North] desire for a peaceful evolution . . . to avoid [a] massive attack on Saigon."

CHAPTER 10

"No Guarantees!"

—| |—

The circuitous journey bringing CBS Saigon bureau chief Brian Ellis from England to Saigon was not that unusual for a restless young man during the 1960s. After serving in the Royal Air Force he had roamed through Africa, the Middle East, and North and South America before following his English girlfriend to Florida and marrying her. He began as a cub reporter in West Palm Beach, started a newspaper in the Bahamas, joined the staff of the CBS Miami affiliate, and was promoted to the network's Atlanta bureau chief before being transferred to Saigon as bureau chief in 1972.

He was the kind of matey and gregarious Englishman who makes friends easily, and he quickly became devoted to his twenty Vietnamese translators, cameramen, reporters, and fixers, and they to him. They invited him to their homes, fussed over him, and risked their lives for him. When he was racked with pain from a kidney stone after spending weeks behind Vietcong lines, soundman Mai Van Duc tracked him down to a remote coastal town and chartered a plane to evacuate him to Saigon. Soundman Doan Van Hai mothered him, insisting that he fortify himself with a large bowl of *pho,* the popular Vietnamese noodle soup, before heading to a battlefield. His secretary, Miss Pham Thi Yen, was so intelligent and hardworking that he trusted her to speak for him and make decisions in his absence. The softhearted Nguyen T. Nguyen persuaded him to film stories in Saigon's orphanages, leading him and his wife to adopt a malnourished girl.

He woke in his room at the Hotel Continental on March 31 to hear an account on the radio of Da Nang's horrific last hours. He promised himself that he would evacuate Duc, Hai, Yen, Nguyen, and the others before a similar anarchy gripped Saigon, sparing them whatever punishment the Communists were planning for class enemies who had worked for an American news agency and from what he had experienced during the Blitz. His father had been overseas with the British army, and his mother had raised him and his brother while serving as an air raid warden in Canterbury, England. When the sirens wailed, she dashed to work, and Ellis and his brother ran to a bomb shelter.

He asked his contacts at the embassy if they could include his employees and their families in the official U.S. evacuation; they replied that Ambassador Martin was discouraging evacuation planning. He asked if his American personnel should consider leaving; they said, "That's something you yourself need to decide." He asked how he should evacuate his high-risk Vietnamese; they said, "Legally."

He and AP bureau chief George Esper calculated that if they evacuated the Vietnamese employees of every U.S. television, radio, and print news agency in Saigon, including their families, and were generous in their definition of "family," it would mean taking out about two thousand people. Because such an evacuation would violate U.S. and South Vietnamese immigration laws, they would also have to do it clandestinely. After President Ford asked Congress for $722 million in supplemental aid to South Vietnam and demanded a vote by April 19, Ellis telexed CBS News Division president Richard Salant a warning that once the South Vietnamese learned there would be no additional aid, the situation in Saigon could turn ugly. He reported that he and the other bureau chiefs had concluded that chartering planes to evacuate their employees would work only "if the embassy says it will help us, and it says it won't." Instead, he hoped to launch a seaborne evacuation before Congress rejected Ford's request.

He drove to Vung Tau, the port on the South China Sea fifty miles south of Saigon and found that anyone with a boat was demanding large down payments to buy black-market fuel, life vests, medical supplies, food, and portable toilets and provide reimbursement in case the authorities seized their vessels. While he was searching for a ship, he was also organizing an emergency airlift of 150 U.S. news agency employees from Phnom Penh. The reports of Khmer Rouge atrocities there spooked his Vietnamese employees, and they started asking him if CBS planned to evacuate them from Saigon.

The reports also unsettled the network and print executives in New York. The networks contacted White House press secretary Ron Nessen, a former NBC correspondent in Vietnam, and asked him what the government's reaction would be if they evacuated their Vietnamese employees. Nessen sent a memorandum to Deputy National Security Adviser Brent Scowcroft inquiring what would happen "if a planeload of Vietnamese employees of the networks showed up by charter plane at Clark Air Force Base in the Philippines without proper visas or passports." Nessen added that the networks wanted reassurance that the U.S. government would not penalize a charter airline for flying them to the Philippines. Two days later, a member of Scowcroft's staff told Nessen that giving the news agencies a green light would be "highly improper" and that the Philippine government had already complained about undocumented Vietnamese arriving at Clark. Scowcroft followed up in person, telling Nessen that the administration could not "make exceptions to U.S. laws and regulations for the employees of the U.S. networks" nor encourage them to violate Vietnamese regulations.

The media executives decided to defy the government and organize their own evacuation. CBS executive Sid Feders called Ellis on April 14, and using an informal code to confuse the South Vietnamese security services that CBS assumed were tapping its Saigon bureau's phones and reading its telexes, he reported that the executives wanted Ellis to head a committee in Saigon to coordinate "all future shipping needs" (that is, the evacuation of Vietnamese employees). Ellis suspected that NBC and ABC had voted for him so that their bureau chiefs would be free to cover the news.

Martin heard about the committee and instructed his press secretary, John Hogan, to invite Ellis to meet with Deputy Chief of Mission Wolfgang Lehmann at the embassy. Lehmann spoke to Ellis of "contingency plans" and an evacuation being "a work in progress." He said that an early draft of who *might* be on evacuation lists included some news agency people and suggested that the agencies send him a list of their employees. Ellis was even more encouraged after receiving a telex from Feders saying, "Tell your daughter the next time you see her that the man was going to help all her friends." He interpreted it as meaning that the White House had promised to evacuate the CBS employees. But less than an hour later Feders telephoned to report that Assistant Secretary of State Philip Habib had informed the CBS Washington bureau that the embassy's evacuation list would not include the agencies' Vietnamese. Feders added that the executives in New York had voted 8–1 against mounting an independent evacuation, but because CBS had cast the dissenting vote, the network wanted Ellis to continue searching for a way to evacuate his own employees.

On April 16, Ellis telexed an anguished letter to Senate majority leader Mike Mansfield and House Speaker Carl Albert imploring them to persuade the administration to include the Vietnamese employees of the American news agencies in any evacuation. He reminded them of the risks these Vietnamese had taken and the "invaluable contribution" they had made to U.S. reporting. Several hours later, he received a call from Martin's secretary, Eva Kim, inviting him to meet with the ambassador. He had seen Martin at official functions and had been impressed by his silver hair, elegant suits, courtly manners, and how closely he matched the classic image of a crusty old-school ambassador. He arrived to find Martin sitting at his desk in shirtsleeves and reading a document. Without looking up, Martin nodded his head toward a chair, indicating where Ellis should sit. His face was ashen, and the room reeked of cigarette smoke. An autographed photograph of Richard Nixon shared space on his desk with one of his late adopted son, Glenn Mann. After several minutes of awkward silence, he fixed Ellis with a penetrating stare and waited for him to speak.

Ellis explained that he had come as chairman of the press evacuation committee, not as a journalist. To emphasize this point, he placed his reporter's notebook on his desk so Martin could see that he would pick it up only to make a note when they were discussing an evacuation. He began by asking Martin to clarify the contradiction between Habib's statement to the news agency executives that the embassy would not evacuate their Vietnamese and Lehmann's statement to him that their inclusion was "likely."

"Don't you mean *if* there's an evacuation," Martin said. "But if you have people who want to leave, they should leave now."

"But what about the Vietnamese? They can't leave now."

"That's not the embassy's problem."

Martin locked eyes with Ellis and warned him against organizing his own evacuation. "Such efforts are bound to fail," he said, a statement showing that he was either ignorant of the underground railroads or chose to ignore them. He condemned freelance evacuations for "sending a bad message, a defeatist message to the South Vietnamese."

Holding his stare, Ellis replied that he could appreciate his concerns but could not rule out that he and the other bureau chiefs might organize their own evacuation if the embassy refused to assist them.

Martin surprised him by summoning him back the next day. He was standing by the window holding a clunky radiophone. He waved the phone at Ellis and said, "You'll be getting one of these." He remarked casually that Kissinger had given him the green light to evacuate American journalists. Ellis assumed that the news executives in the United States had pressured the White House.

"Will there be any seats for our Vietnamese employees?" he asked.

"No. No seats for the Vietnamese," Martin said.

Ellis asked if that was likely to change. Martin said it would not and announced that he was putting Ellis in charge of implementing the evacuation of American journalists, *if* such an evacuation proved necessary. He handed him a 1973 pamphlet titled "Standard Instructions and Advice to Citizens for Normal and Emergency Situations." A map identified "civilian assembly points," and a recently prepared insert explained that when Americans believed an evacuation was imminent, they should tune in to Armed Forces Radio. When the announcer said, "The Temperature in Saigon is 112 degrees and rising" followed by Bing Crosby's "White Christmas," everyone should report to their assembly points. The amateurish nature of the scheme shocked Ellis, but he agreed to organize the American newsmen, hoping to find a way to include his Vietnamese. He telexed a summary of the meeting to Feders, who replied that network executives had lobbied Kissinger, only to be told, "No Vietnamese."

The next morning Eva Kim summoned Ellis back for the third straight day. As he walked in, Martin was talking with his press attaché, John Hogan. After Hogan left, Martin said, "I'll strike a deal with you. I'll help you get your Vietnamese out." Part of the deal was that Ellis had to manage their evacuation. "You're the man that the news agencies have already put in charge," he said, "and besides, I don't want to be getting phone calls at all hours from a dozen or so bureau chiefs wanting to know when they can get their seats and how many." He explained that he had "found some seats" for the news agency Vietnamese on the U.S. Air Force transports flying back to Clark Air Base and asked how many Ellis needed. Ellis said that if all the agencies participated, there would be between eight hundred and twelve hundred evacuees, a number including spouses and children, as well as parents, grandparents, brothers and sisters, aunts and uncles, and so on.

Martin shook his head. "No. You'll have to be much tougher than that. I can't get you so many seats." He could promise only around twenty a day, he said, explaining that Hogan would call Ellis every morning with a specific number, but first Ellis would have to submit a list of his evacuees to the embassy. "I want to know who you're taking," he said. "I don't want to see any maids or girlfriends. And don't take anyone who's in the military."

Ellis knew that the number of seats he could wring out of Martin could determine whether or not he had to split up families. They dickered over seat numbers and luggage, agreeing on one small carry-on bag per person and that Ellis would be responsible for deciding the order in which the news agency employees departed.

As Ellis reached across the desk to shake hands, Martin said, "Now you understand, of course, that you are not going to be able to tell anyone, and I mean anyone, about how you are getting these people out, or who is helping you." He had to insist on this, he explained, because by helping Ellis evacuate his people, he would be violating South Vietnamese immigration law and the U.S. War Powers Act, which prohibited U.S. officials from using the military to exfiltrate foreign nationals from a war zone.

Ellis thought, "Oh no, this isn't good," and said that the other bureau chiefs and U.S. executives would want to know the details before entrusting him with their people.

Martin took a long drag on his cigarette and blew a cloud of smoke upward. After a long pause he said, "Okay, that I can understand. But can you guarantee, can you promise me that none of them will ever let the cat out of the bag?" He had to know that Ellis could not promise this and that once he told the other bureau chiefs and they informed their bosses in the States, keeping the evacuation secret would be difficult.

Ellis protested that he did not think the ABC and NBC bureau chiefs would be pleased that he was in charge of the evacuation.

"If they balk at your offer or talk openly about it, tell them they won't be getting any seats from you," Martin said. "Remind them that you're the one with the seats, and if they don't like it, threaten to give them to other deserving Vietnamese." Here was the hard-nosed Graham Martin that Ellis had expected.

As Martin shuffled papers and puffed on his cigarette, Ellis struggled with his conscience. He finally shrugged and said, "Okay." Martin looked up and they exchanged a firm, lingering handshake. Martin warned Ellis that he was on his own and that if the South Vietnamese authorities caught him, he would not be able to help him. For the first time, Ellis detected a faint smile.

Ellis wondered why Martin had changed his mind. Had Kissinger or Ford buckled to pressure from the network executives? (This might explain why Martin had rebuffed NBC's bureau chief Art Lord in the beginning of April but was now cooperating with Ellis.) Or was Martin doing it on his own? And why was he willing to break the law to evacuate South Vietnamese citizens working for a press corps

he detested when there were thousands of Vietnamese whose current
and former employment with the U.S. mission placed them at equal
or greater risk?

The next year, Martin would tell Congress that Kissinger "had
requested that we do what we could to facilitate the escape of Vietnamese nationals of the American press and TV offices in Saigon."
Still, he could have stalled Kissinger, as he did throughout April when
Kissinger was badgering him to reduce the number of Americans in
South Vietnam. Ellis later wondered if Martin had decided to help
him because his evacuation was small and more easily concealed, and
would not hamper the smooth running of his embassy, and because
evacuating these particular Vietnamese might inhibit the Saigon press
corps from criticizing him.

Ellis told Sid Feders that he had a plan that might work but did
not disclose that it involved Martin. After being briefed about the
evacuation, one reporter assumed that Ellis had bribed Thieu, another
speculated that he had leased a submarine, another wondered if he had
persuaded a platoon of Vietnamese rangers to overpower the perimeter
guards at Tan Son Nhut by bribing them with seats on a DC-6 chartered by the CIA. When Ellis made a test run to Tan Son Nhut, two
reporters tailed him, and he noticed them inspecting the registration
decal on his van, hoping to identify its owner.

His agreement with Martin seemed straightforward. Martin would
provide seats on the planes, and Ellis and Press Secretary Hogan would
drive the evacuees to the airport. But the more Ellis imagined what
might go wrong, the more worried he became. He wondered what he
should say if the MPs detained him at the Tan Son Nhut gate, or do if
the embassy bus had departed and the plane failed to arrive, or if there
were not enough seats on the plane, or if some people changed their
minds at the last minute and decided not to leave. His employees were
not strangers. They were people he cared about deeply—people who
had entrusted him with their lives.

He called Martin and asked him to promise that the first group
would get through.

"No guarantees!" Martin snapped.

At midday on April 19, Ellis summoned his employees to the CBS office on the second floor of the Caravelle Hotel. An editor took the phones off the hook and watched the Teletype for urgent messages. The Vietnamese were silent and stood. Ellis was nervous and his mouth was dry. He spoke slowly, pausing to sip from a coffee mug. He announced that he had arranged to evacuate them and their families during the next twenty-four hours. They could each take a small bag and should pack their passports, birth certificates, and marriage licenses. There was a long silence as they realized they would have to decide whether to leave their country forever.

Senior reporter Nguyen Khiem Cat asked if they were going to America. Ellis said it was their final destination, but there might be intermediate stops. Cameraman Pham Boi Hoan asked what they would do in America. Ellis said they would remain on the CBS payroll, and the network would offer most of them jobs. Hoan smiled and said, "That's good, that's good." Reporter Nguyen T. Nguyen kept saying, "Thank you, boss . . . Thank you, boss." Soundman Mai Van Duc wiped away tears. Secretary and office manager Pham Thi Yen threw her arms around him. He sensed that she was as frightened by the future as she was relieved to be going.

Hogan called that evening to offer him fifty seats on two planes leaving the next day. Hogan also promised to accompany him on the first run. Ellis decided to make his employees the guinea pigs and evacuate them first. If anyone was arrested, he wanted them to be his people rather than those from another network. He told his first fifty to gather at a corner in the Cholon Market at noon. The neighborhood was busy with buses and minibuses, and he reckoned that the DAO's gray school bus would attract less attention there.

The next day he stood outside the bus, counting off his employees as they boarded. Khiem Cat wept in relief as he climbed the steps. He had many high-ranking government officials among his confidants and believed that the Communists would find his name on Rolodexes throughout Saigon. He told Ellis, "You're saving my life."

Ellis worried that the MPs at the gate would storm the bus and arrest everyone. None of his people had exit visas, and some were of military age. Hogan was so calm and practiced that Ellis assumed him to be a veteran of similar missions. As they approached the gate, Hogan ordered the driver to pull into the middle of the road. That way, he explained, the bus would block both lanes, creating an instant traffic jam and making the MPs eager to wave them through. As they rolled to a stop, Hogan jumped out and thrust a wad of papers with U.S. embassy letterheads and official-looking stamps at a startled MP. As the soldier leafed through them, Hogan told Ellis, "Most of these guys can't read English, but they'll be impressed by these documents." He pretended to be impatient, checking his watch and pacing back and forth while announcing that his passengers were embassy employees going to the Defense Attaché Office for reassignment. Another policeman boarded the bus and walked slowly down the aisle, staring at the silent passengers but not demanding visas or identification.

The MPs let them pass, and they drove to the Air America terminal. The air force loadmaster was Major Robert Delligatti, a stocky joker who had escaped the West Virginia coalfields to play on an undefeated U.S. Air Force Academy football team. He had covered the name tag on his overalls with a piece of gray tape that he termed a "security measure." He explained that his superiors knew that he was engaged in unauthorized evacuations and wanted to prevent him from being traced back to his unit. He boarded the bus and delivered a tongue-in-cheek safety briefing that he concluded by saying, "Be sure to have your tickets and boarding passes ready and have a nice flight."

He pointed to two C-130 transports sitting on the tarmac with their engines running and shouted, "Thirty people in that one; twenty in the other." Ellis noticed another bus pull up near one of the planes and disgorge dozens of Vietnamese, each clutching a single bag. An air force officer identified them as DAO employees, and during the next several days Ellis noticed buses, troop carriers, and trucks bringing evacuees to the flight line. His friend Jim Eckes, who managed a charter airline, said that some U.S. agencies had been evacuating their Vietnamese employees since early April and that neither Martin nor the Thieu government had known about it.

As the CBS employees boarded the plane, Ms. Yen gave Ellis a doleful look, as if to say, "Why don't you come with us?" Khiem Cat shook his hand and said gravely, "My family thanks you." Reporter Nguyen waved and shouted, "See you in America, boss!"

But would he? Ellis knew only that his employees would land at Clark Air Base, but then what? When he asked a crew member about their destination, the man smiled and said, "Disneyland!"

He was relieved they were escaping but sad that his friendships with them were ending. He returned to an empty office and telexed CBS executive Feders, "Fifty Birds have flown and now working on second crop." After Hogan confirmed that the plane had landed, he telexed, "All our children made it across the highway safely. . . . They [are] all your wards but they may not surface for a couple of days. Please please we must maintain closed mouth policy that they do not exist . . . keep the lid on til my pipeline runs dry."

He began making runs to Tan Son Nhut with the employees of other news agencies. He persuaded a travel agent to print up phony tickets for domestic flights that he flashed at the MPs. He filled a bus with cameramen and their families, pointed to the cameras dangling around their necks, and said they were flying to the delta to cover a story. The other news agencies padded their lists with household servants, cousins, and grandparents-in-law. He brought them to Tan Son Nhut anyway. If he came with extra people, Delligatti found room for them, sometimes boarding them two to a seat.

As the North Vietnamese Army neared Saigon, the air force pilots kept their engines running and turned around quickly, and the checkpoint police became more tense and unpredictable. The DAO had bribed their commanders with money and promises of evacuation, but once these officers departed, a more volatile contingent of unbribed junior officers took over. They questioned the manifests and boarded the buses to search for military-aged men, sometimes ordering everyone to disembark for questioning and arbitrarily arresting "deserters." The harassment was blackmail, a message that they also wanted to escape. Ellis handed out "facilitating fees" in soon-to-be-worthless piastres. During one standoff an MP pointed a revolver at the head of

CBS cameraman Mike Marriott and pulled the trigger. There was a click and the gun failed to fire.

Ellis found himself in what he termed "a dreadful and conscience wrenching position," forced to make life-and-death decisions because of the promises, encouragement, and inducements that the U.S. government had offered to the South Vietnamese over the years. Casual friends, relatives of relatives of the news agency evacuees, and strangers accosted him in the street and at his hotel. The doormen and bellhops at the Caravelle sold his room number. He took a room at the Majestic and moved between it and another room at the Continental, but businessmen and bureaucrats who had heard his name whispered by friends tracked him down, telephoning at night or banging on his door. They offered him gold, cars, and antiques. An acquaintance mentioned an ivory chess set. The owner of a restaurant he frequented handed him a list of ten people and a large check written on a Paris bank. He took their names but refused the check. Bar girls held out photographs of themselves with the U.S. servicemen who had promised to marry them. Americans begged him to evacuate girlfriends and mistresses. One Vietnamese man burst into his office and demanded nine seats. Leaning across his desk so their noses almost touched, he said, "I no get seats your family will be sad because I come back and shoot you." He pointed his index finger, cocked his thumb, and said, "Bang!" Another man solemnly handed him a letter promising that if he evacuated him and his twenty-six family members, they would "love you and call our future babies after you name." Otherwise, he warned, "Viet Cong cut off all my heads."

Ellis recognized a man who barged into his room at the Hotel Continental as the officer who provided an English translation of Lieutenant Colonel Hien's daily ARVN press briefings. The officer demanded seats for himself and Hien. Ellis refused, saying that he could be arrested for assisting in the desertion of a South Vietnamese officer. The officer became agitated and Ellis stalled, promising to check on his seat numbers and suggesting that he return in several days. The officer returned the following evening wearing military fatigues and carrying a sidearm. He demanded eleven seats and threatened "big trouble" if Ellis did not produce them. He sat on the corner of the bed, tapping his foot and unbuckling his belt so that his revolver rested on one knee. The phone rang, breaking the tension. It was the CBS night editor calling with messages from New York. Ellis pretended it was his contact at the embassy promising extra seats and asked the officer to return later. As soon as he left, Ellis alerted Martin, who promised to handle the situation. Hien continued delivering his briefings until the end, spinning fantasies about Communist reversals and ARVN triumphs. A CBS reporter saw him at the embassy on April 29 boarding a helicopter.

Ellis hated to refuse anyone, and he could not risk someone becoming angry and alerting the police. He equivocated, saying that finding seats was difficult but promising to try, and sometimes Hogan did produce more seats. The extra seats forced Ellis to choose. He filled some with his own special cases and the relatives of the first batch of CBS evacuees whom he had left behind because he had been adhering to Martin's rule of immediate family only. Before allocating the others, he paced his room at night, struggling with decisions he likened to the thumbs-up or thumbs-down determining the fate of a Roman gladiator. At first, he denied seats to unaccompanied children on the grounds that they would be better off with their parents. But after comparing their parents' situation to that of adults on a sinking ship desperate to put their children into a scarce lifeboat, he decided that he would do the same for his children and sent them out unaccompanied.

Martin would later credit him with evacuating 595 people. But because he had padded his lists and crammed extra people onto the buses, Ellis thought that the actual number was closer to 700. After Martin retired to North Carolina, Ellis called to thank him and to admit having padded his lists.

"Oh, I knew that all along," Martin said breezily.

"But if you knew, why on earth didn't you stop me?"

"If you were finding room for all those people on those planes, why on earth would I?"

In Martin's 1976 congressional testimony he called Ellis one of his "Scarlet Pimpernels." He recited a couplet from the book—"Is he in heaven?—Is he in hell? / That damned, elusive Pimpernel"— and boasted, "My Young Pimpernels did a magnificent job." He also claimed that he had turned a blind eye to some underground railroads and in some instances had supported and assisted them.

Martin's first "Scarlet Pimpernel" operation had involved a Pentagon decision to remove the fuel rods from the nuclear reactor at Dalat University in the Central Highlands. The United States had provided the university with a small reactor to support its medical and agricultural research but not with the expertise to remove its rods from their lead-lined barrels. On March 31, two U.S. Air Force C-130 transports flew to Dalat from a base at Johnston Island in the Pacific. The DAO had devised a fail-safe plan that called for the first plane to land with a contingent of U.S. Navy SEALS and technicians from the Atomic Energy Commission. The second plane was to circle overhead while the SEALS loaded the nuclear rods onto the first one. If the first plane suffered a mechanical failure or was hit by North Vietnamese ordnance, the second would land, collect the rods, and fly them back to Johnston Island. If the first plane accomplished its mission, the second would remain airborne and return without stopping in Saigon. Foreign Service officer Lamar Prosser, the senior U.S. government official in Dalat, protested this arrangement to Martin, saying that if the operation went smoothly, he wanted the second plane to land and evacuate his Vietnamese employees, the director of the institute, its faculty members and their families, and a group of French nuns, flying them all to Saigon.

Martin took Prosser's side, but the DAO refused to budge. The quarrel went to the Pentagon, where Secretary of Defense Schlesinger supported the DAO. Martin cabled Kissinger that he would deny the first plane clearance to leave Dalat until the second one had landed, collected Prosser's evacuees, and was airborne. The Pentagon capitulated, and the second plane flew the Vietnamese and the French nuns to Saigon. Martin was so secretive and opaque that his motivations in this and other instances can be hard to discern. The same humane impulses that might explain his willingness to allow Ellis to inflate his numbers may also explain the Prosser incident, or perhaps he was more willing to support an evacuation within South Vietnam's borders. And he undoubtedly considered the Pentagon's refusal to fly out Prosser's people a challenge to his position as the senior U.S. official in South Vietnam.

By evacuating South Vietnamese civilians employed by the U.S. news agencies, Martin had broken American and South Vietnamese laws. In order to fly Prosser's people to Saigon, he had defied the Pentagon. He had repeatedly said in cables and at weekly staff meetings that the United States had a moral duty to evacuate endangered South Vietnamese. When someone mentioned evacuating a thousand Vietnamese at a meeting in late March, he had jumped in and said, "Oh, no, we have to have a plan in place to evacuate everyone. Their lives will be in danger in the unlikely event that the country falls. So I want you guys to draw up a plan to evacuate 250,000 people." Naval attaché Cornelius Carmody thought that taking out 250,000 people was madness and wondered if Martin had "lost it."

Martin also broached the subject of an evacuation with Kissinger's assistant Brent Scowcroft, telling him in an April 7 cable that America "clearly owes protection in case of danger" to about 175,000 Vietnamese, calling the obligation "clear and immediate," and saying that only a sealift or a "jumbo airlift" could fulfill it. Four days later, on April 11, he promised a delegation representing the U.S. mission's Vietnamese employees that he would evacuate them and their families and would be the last man out. One day after that, he asked Rear Admiral Hugh Benton, the CINCPAC liaison officer for evacuation matters, to develop a plan to send a million Vietnamese to the United States.

There were two ways to evacuate large numbers of Vietnamese. The first required a large-scale military intervention during which U.S. troops occupied Tan Son Nhut airport and the port of Vung Tau and loaded evacuees onto American planes and ships. This would risk the lives of American troops and anger Congress. The second possibility, which Martin considered more promising, was that North Vietnam would choose negotiations over a direct assault on the city, leading to weeks or months of talks that would allow ample time to evacuate hundreds of thousands of South Vietnamese. But leaving nothing to chance, Martin began casting around for ways to accomplish a large-scale evacuation in the absence of any negotiations. In mid-April he summoned Carmody and asked what he knew about amphibious operations. Carmody replied that he knew a lot because he had previously captained an LST, a vessel designed to land cargo directly onto a beach.

Martin was ecstatic. "That's perfect!" he exclaimed. "You know about beaching these ships and stuff?" Carmody replied that he had beached many of them. "Absolutely wonderful! Call a helicopter to come get you and fly you down to Vung Tau and let me know if you think that the beaches down there would be suitable for an amphibious landing. We could get thousands of people off on just one LST."

South Vietnamese forces held the port of Vung Tau and the highway connecting it to Saigon, but the Communists controlled much of the surrounding countryside. The Air America operations officer warned Carmody that he would be risking his life by flying low over the beaches. Carmody's pilot made several low passes anyway, and Carmody saw uniformed North Vietnamese soldiers looking up while shielding their eyes from the sun. When he returned to the embassy an hour later, Eva Kim said, "Oh, the ambassador is just pacing back and forth waiting for you." Carmody reported that the slope of Vung Tau's beaches was too gentle for amphibious landings. Martin questioned him closely but finally accepted the bad news.

Martin had sent Carmody to Vung Tau on April 14, two days after he had ordered General Baughn expelled for making evacuation preparations. The contradiction between these moves indicates the distinction that Martin drew between planning for a theoretical evacuation and making concrete preparations to execute these plans—preparations such as those being made by the DAO's Special Planning Group. He was therefore willing to send Carmody to Vung Tau to evaluate the possibility of a large-scale sealift of South Vietnamese and willing to send an embassy representative to a meeting to discuss evacuation planning with Brigadier General Baughn and others. But once Baughn appeared to go behind his back and propose measures such as bringing in marine helicopter pilots and a ground security force—measures that Martin believed risked alarming the South Vietnamese, much like painting an *H* on rooftops—he had expelled him.

On April 13, *The Washington Post* ran a front-page profile of Martin highlighting his elusiveness and the contradictions in his nature and policies that baffled some observers. The profile spoke of his "leathery face and unsettling eye" but also described his "bland expression." It called him a "highly controversial figure" but acknowledged that he had "an almost impossible job." It mentioned his surprising strategy of pressing businessmen to make long-term investments in South Vietnam, implying that this might explain why some observers, including members of his staff, believed that his "reasoned judgment" had been "impaired" and that he was "as mad as a March hare and just about as elusive." But it added that others praised him for being "determined and wily."

Two days before the *Washington Post* profile appeared, Martin gave a rare on-camera interview to Garrick Utley of NBC News. Utley had jump-started his career while covering the Vietnam War in the mid-1960s and had returned to witness its death throes. According to his diary, Martin faced the camera with "a riveting stare that defies contradiction." After Martin said, "I have always believed in the importance of telling the American people the full truth," Utley wrote that Martin spoke "passionately about the importance of not abandoning South Vietnam." He compared the mood in the United States to the America First isolationism of the 1930s and offered, Utley said, "the now worn argument that with just a little more perseverance we will one day be able to leave the South Vietnamese on their own, etc., etc." Martin agreed to speak on background off camera, and Utley noted "a distinct change" in his tone. He was more pessimistic and said he feared that someone in Washington would "push the panic button," starting a precipitous evacuation of Americans and setting off "a violent reaction." Utley believed that had Martin been truthful, he would have said something like "I don't believe this [the perseverance argument] at all. But I say it because I still hope. I do not want to be remembered for going out like this, ending my career as the ambassador who pulled down the American flag over Saigon."

Few of Martin's detractors have painted him as callous or wicked. The evidence that he believed that the United States had a moral responsibility to evacuate endangered Vietnamese is extensive, and unlike some in Washington and Saigon voicing this sentiment, he had proven himself willing to violate American and South Vietnamese immigration regulations to achieve it. On April 19 he responded to a query from Kissinger about evacuating the news agency Vietnamese by cabling, "We are already in business with Brian Ellis and I think the relationships will be wholly satisfactory." He brushed off Kissinger's request for more details, saying, "It would be just as well if you didn't know. I think if you leave it to me we can have all these employees out." He cautioned that the operation required the deepest secrecy and that if anyone in the media revealed what was happening, "that will have put an automatic block on our ability to remove the rest of them."

The day before, he had cabled Kissinger, "It is also beginning increasingly likely to appear that drastic action will be required if we are to have any chance of providing for those Vietnamese who have relied on us," and had urged Kissinger to initiate "discussions with the Soviet Union and the PRC" to facilitate "the departure of substantial numbers of Vietnamese who would be endangered and to whom we are most deeply obliged."

But although Martin believed that an evacuation was a moral imperative and was willing to assist in the evacuation of certain classes of people, such as the Vietnamese working for the U.S. news agencies and the relatives of U.S. Foreign Service officers, he did not believe that the situation was sufficiently urgent to begin taking concrete steps to prepare for a large-scale evacuation. In early April, he had insisted that the South Vietnamese military could fight the Communists to a standoff and hold Saigon and the delta. Later in the month, when this seemed unlikely, he embraced the notion that the Communists preferred negotiations to a frontal assault on Saigon and that this would lead to a coalition government or, at worst, a slow-motion surrender, providing ample time for evacuating large numbers of South Vietnamese.

CHAPTER 11

Playing God

As Saigon's mood oscillated between denial, despair, and "palpable fear," and while Kissinger, Schlesinger, and Martin were debating how many Americans and South Vietnamese to evacuate, the humanitarian mutiny of the "American Schindlers" was proving to be largely immune to interference from the White House or the embassy. There may have been no one more determined to evacuate Vietnamese than Walter Martindale. After Consul General Spear ordered the last Air America flight from Nha Trang restricted to Americans only, Martindale had promised himself not to leave South Vietnam until he had evacuated the rest of his Quang Duc evacuees to Saigon and then to the United States if they so desired. Some were among the 250 evacuees whom Spear had abandoned in Nha Trang airport. They had traveled from there to Cam Ranh Bay, where they joined 40,000 other refugees who were boarding four U.S. freighters chartered by the Military Sealift Command. They were told that their destination was Vung Tau, Saigon's nearest port, but while they were at sea, the Thieu government ordered them taken to Phu Quoc, a remote teardrop-shaped island off South Vietnam's west coast known for its peppercorns, pungent fish sauce, and fearsome prisons where France and South Vietnam had incarcerated their most incorrigible Communists. The prisons had closed following the Paris Peace Accords, but the government had decided to reopen them as refugee camps.

Martindale persuaded Jake Jacobson, Martin's special assistant for field operations, to make him a special field operations officer, a vague title allowing him to do more or less as he pleased. After learning that the government had interned some of his people on Phu Quoc, he marched into Jacobson's office and announced that he was going there "even if I have to go in a rowboat." Jacobson knew him well enough to know that he was not joking. He put him in charge of a hastily manufactured mission to study the feasibility of identifying former U.S. government employees interned on Phu Quoc and relocating them to Saigon. On April 13, Martindale flew to the island on a commercial flight along with what he called his "identification team," a contingent of Montagnard bodyguards, friends from the national police, and Vietnamese from Quang Duc and other captured provinces who could identify their comrades and co-workers.

After arriving, he performed a delicate dance with the island's senior military official, South Vietnamese Navy captain Nguyen Van Thien. Thien said that while "in principle" Martindale could remove his people, he was afraid that doing so might incite the other refugees to riot. To prevent that from happening, Martindale proposed moving them gradually and in small groups from the larger camps to a staging area near the airport. Thien agreed, and Martindale visited six of the fourteen camps and located 52 U.S. government employees and 235 of their dependents. Consul General Moncrieff Spear's former assistant was still so furious over his treatment that he refused to speak with Martindale. Others described a hellish journey from Cam Ranh Bay. They had spent two days at sea with little food or water before anchoring off Phu Quoc and then waiting days to disembark while the sun scorched them and renegade soldiers robbed them.

Martindale gave them cash from the embassy's emergency fund and promised to fly them to Saigon. He asked four members of his identification team to remain, visit the other camps, compile a list of U.S. government employees and their dependents, and begin transferring them to a holding camp he had set up near the airport. He wrote in a report to Jacobson that most of the employees he had met were "sick, emotional, and scared." Some had wept with relief upon seeing him. Others had cried "bitter tears" and "expressed disbelief that we, the Americans, had abandoned them."

He persuaded a pilot with the charter company Bird Air to fly him back to Phu Quoc on a rattletrap World War II–vintage DC-4. He jammed so many people onto his first evacuation flight that the pilot taxied back and off-loaded some. He returned three more times on successive days, stopping only after Bird Air ordered its planes out of Vietnamese airspace. He pulled strings at the DAO so he could transfer the evacuees with intact families directly onto U.S. Air Force transports leaving Tan Son Nhut for the Philippines. The other evacuees fanned out across Saigon to search for their relatives. When they were ready to depart, he manufactured bogus visas and passes to get them back into Tan Son Nhut. He purloined Ambassador Martin's personal stamp and another belonging to a high-ranking Vietnamese police official under what he admits being "questionable circumstances" and used them to emboss his fake visas and passes. He provided similar documents to friends in Saigon, friends of friends, and anyone he thought might face retaliation from the Communists. He turned his apartment building into a safe house, filling its empty apartments with evacuees and throwing down mattresses in its hallways and on the roof. He slipped some of his people onto the embassy buses that were shuttling Ambassador Martin's "special cases" to Tan Son Nhut. Others he smuggled into the airport himself, stuffing them into the trunk of the new Peugeot he had bought as a wedding present for his Franco-Vietnamese fiancée, who had decided to remain on her family's coffee plantation.

He made mistakes. He refused to evacuate the eighteen-year-old brother of a friend because the boy was old enough to fight for his country. He soon regretted his decision and tried to compensate for it when two Vietnamese MPs boarded an embassy bus to search for draft-age males. After an American diplomat fingered one of Martindale's evacuees, a fourteen-year-old boy traveling with his mother, Martindale lost his Irish Cherokee temper. "You're *not* letting them take that kid!" he shouted. "Do you want to die in Vietnam? Well, you're not getting off this bus alive if they take that kid." The boy remained on the bus.

He accelerated the pace of his evacuations after noticing that the Israeli and West German ambassadors had left their Mercedes limousines in front of the American embassy, keys in their ignitions and flags on their bumpers, and after hearing that the French ambassador had evacuated his mistress but not his wife. He became even more concerned when his friend Nay Luette, a Montagnard who had formerly served as minister of tribal affairs, gripped his hand and begged him to evacuate a hundred Montagnard boys and girls, saying that he expected a bloodbath and wanted to save "the seed" of his people. Martindale reported his request to Jacobson, who like many former U.S. military officers was devoted to the Montagnards. Jacobson shook his head and said, "Walt, I'm afraid that we're the only people in this embassy who give a damn for the Montagnards." He urged Martindale not to lose hope and claimed to have "inside information" that a negotiated settlement was imminent.

Between April 6 and April 18, the U.S. Air Force evacuated 2,776 South Vietnamese and third-country nationals from Tan Son Nhut on transport planes that had arrived from the Philippines with supplies and would have otherwise returned empty. Hundreds more Vietnamese left during this period on "black flights" involving U.S. planes that had flown into Tan Son Nhut empty for the specific purpose of evacuating Vietnamese employed by the CIA, the DAO, and other U.S. agencies.

The DAO's underground railroad smuggled many of these evacuees into Tan Son Nhut. It owed some of its success to Andy Gembara, the burly Ukrainian American army intelligence agent who had become so alarmed by the embassy's slipshod evacuation planning in March that he and Colonel Bill LeGro had started evacuating Vietnamese employed at the DAO. After serving two earlier tours as an airborne infantry officer, being wounded, learning Vietnamese, marrying a Vietnamese woman, and coming to admire her people for "their toughness, love of family, and stoicism," Gembara was determined to rescue deserving South Vietnamese. He hired a Vietnamese forger to make a copy of the U.S. consular stamp that he believed "looked even better than the real thing." He scrounged up a refrigerator truck and drilled airholes in its floor, transformed a van into an ambulance, painting red crosses on its sides and putting a flashing blue light onto its roof, and modified a pair of jeeps to resemble those used by the ICCS delegations, painting them gray and adding the ICCS logo to their doors. He gave priority to his former comrades in the Military Security Service (MSS). Some were so high on blacklists that the Communists had infiltrated hit squads into Saigon to kidnap or execute them. One squad had grabbed General Le Van Hoc, a former head of the MSS counterintelligence unit, snatching him off a downtown street and spiriting him to Hanoi, where he died under torture. Military intelligence operative Mike Gill's driver also disappeared. His body surfaced several days later, and Gill and Gembara suspected the Communists or a band of ARVN deserters had killed him. His death and Hoc's disappearance convinced Gembara that evacuating his people before Saigon fell was not enough; he had to do it before the Communists got them first.

He lent his refrigerator truck to other underground railroads and struck a deal with CIA agent John Limbeck, a fellow Ukrainian who worked in the agency's logistical department. Limbeck feared that CIA chief of station Polgar would rescue his friends and high-ranking government officials while abandoning many of the agency's Vietnamese, including the men working in his warehouse. He offered Gembara supplies from the warehouse in exchange for evacuating his workers. Gembara told him that he and the others running the DAO's evacuation were taking amphetamines to stay awake and were perpetually thirsty. What they needed was water and more pills. Limbeck gave him the only liquids left—bottles of whiskey and cognac and crates of San Miguel beer—and threw in several boxes of opera glasses. Gembara could not imagine how the CIA had planned to use them, perhaps explaining why so many remained. He handed them out as bribes to bemused roadblock MPs.

Gembara became an accomplished briber. He bribed the colonel commanding the military police detachment at Tan Son Nhut by evacuating the man's family and then bribed him again by evacuating his second family. He bribed down the chain of command because there was no guarantee that a senior officer would be on duty when he needed him. By the third week in April, several back-to-back twenty-four-hour days and a sudden proliferation of roadblocks manned by unbribed officers had left Gembara stressed and emotional. He drove sixty evacuees to a C-130 transport, only to find a CIA agent was loading it with President Thieu's furniture. The plane's ramp was down and its engines were running. The CIA truck was on one side; Gembara's bus was on the other. He and the CIA agent were armed, exhausted, and angry. Had they been adversaries in a Western, they would have been reaching for their six-shooters. The air force loadmaster said that the embassy had ordered Thieu's furniture evacuated. Gembara complained to LeGro, who checked with the embassy and radioed back to say that Thieu's furniture had priority. Gembara stood down but was furious that the CIA, which was moving slowly to evacuate its Vietnamese agents and members of South Vietnam's Central Intelligence Organization, was saving Thieu's furniture.

Like Walter Martindale, Bill Bell was determined to see the war through to the end. Several days after the Babylift crash that had killed his wife and son, he had flown his daughter, Andrea, to a hospital in California for treatment. His superiors on the Joint Military Team urged him to stay with her. Instead, he left her in the care of her maternal grandparents and returned to Saigon. He wanted to help the forensic experts at Tan Son Nhut identify Nova and Michael and wanted "to save as many people as possible to justify my being over there and getting my family killed." He believed that his fluency in Vietnamese and contacts with the military on both sides of the conflict obligated him to help Americans and South Vietnamese survive "the fire that was coming." After the forensic experts identified his family's remains, the Communist delegations at Camp Davis invited him to a traditional *chia buon,* a sharing of the grief ceremony. Their sympathy and humility struck him as sincere, reminding him of their shared humanity and "the futility of war."

While he had been in California, his colleague Captain Stuart Herrington had represented the U.S. JMT delegation on the April 11 liaison flight to Hanoi. The opportunity to visit Hanoi on these flights had been one of the things attracting Herrington to the JMT. Despite spending several years immersing himself in Vietnam's language and culture, he felt that he knew only half the country, and the liaison flights promised a window on the rest. He had joined the army in 1967 as an intelligence officer, serving in Berlin and then transferring to the reserves to escape Vietnam. Procter & Gamble hired him, but he soon regretted becoming a soap salesman and returned to active duty. After months of intensive language training, he went to South Vietnam as a district intelligence officer, advising South Vietnamese militia forces, immersing himself in village life, and fighting with South Vietnamese troops. He wanted the South to win but respected the enemy for its "tenacity, aggressiveness, and bravery." On the way home from his first tour in 1970, he had landed at Travis Air Force Base in California and entered a restroom crowded with soldiers exchanging their uniforms for civvies. He overheard one soldier say, " 'Nam was a bummer, a bad trip"; another said he would tell people that he had served in Korea. None of them expressed pride in having fought in Vietnam. He left Travis scared for his Vietnamese friends and wondering how much longer Congress would underwrite this unpopular war.

When he had landed in Hanoi in 1974 on his first liaison flight, Gia Lam airport had been deserted except for a few Soviet helicopters and colorless except for red flags fluttering over its faded stucco terminal. The city had struck him as dingy and cheerless, and the contrast with Saigon reminded him of that between East and West Berlin. Major Huyen, his escort on this and later visits, led him through an art museum filled with exhibitions extolling Ho Chi Minh before treating him to lunch at the drab Hoa Binh Hotel.

He arrived in Hanoi on the April 11 liaison flight expecting the usual sightseeing and knickknack purchasing followed by lunch at the Hoa Binh, a routine rendered still more surrealistic by the fact that North Vietnamese troops were flagrantly violating the very treaty responsible for these flights. He found Hanoi transformed, with smiling soldiers and civilians strolling under streets hung with red-and-gold banners proclaiming, "Giant Victories." He and Major Huyen had developed a cordial relationship based on an unspoken mutual respect, but as they drove from the airport, Huyen suddenly said, "Our Foreign Ministry has denounced the American scheme of a refugee-orphan airlift as a crime similar to those committed during the Hitler era." Herrington shot back that he had always considered Huyen "an educated and intelligent person" and did not think he believed such nonsense. Huyen glared at him and fell silent.

Lunch was acrimonious. The North Vietnamese gloated, telling the South Vietnamese delegation, "We scared the hell out of your soldiers so that all they did was run, run, and run." As Herrington parted from Huyen at the airport, he suggested that instead of vilifying Americans for evacuating anti-Communist South Vietnamese, North Vietnam should be thanking them for removing so many potential opponents, and said, "You should let us take out our Vietnamese friends and depart in peace." Huyen flashed a thin smile and said, "We have been trying to get you to leave our country for twenty years. You may therefore rest assured that when you are finally ready to go, we will not stand in your way."

A week later, on April 18, it was Bill Bell's turn to travel to Hanoi on the liaison flight. While perusing the manifest, he noticed that three senior Communist officials, including the influential Colonel Tu, were flying one way. He alerted Colonel Jack Madison, who commanded the U.S. JMT delegation, that the Communists were using the flights to evacuate their senior cadre and that Tu's inclusion indicated an imminent attack on Saigon. It had been his experience, he said, that North Vietnam's leaders were willing to suffer huge battlefield losses when the dead were poor rural teenagers but would be reluctant to risk the lives of senior cadre. He suggested keeping the senior Communist officials at Camp Davis as human shields, arguing that the longer they delayed their departure, the more time they would have to evacuate the U.S. delegation's South Vietnamese personnel.

Madison passed Bell's recommendation up the chain of command and received approval for the plane to develop mechanical difficulties. After circling Saigon, it returned to Tan Son Nhut, where mechanics made a show of examining it. When Madison declared the flight canceled the Communists stood on the runway fuming and accusing him of bad faith and deception.

Since returning from California, Bell had assisted Herrington in evacuating the Vietnamese wives of former or current U.S. servicemen. Some of the women had been living temporarily with their parents until their husbands completed an overseas posting; others had been visiting relatives and were unable to get exit visas. Herrington and Bell dressed the wife of an air force sergeant in a nun's habit and slipped her onto a bus that was bringing nuns and orphans to a Babylift flight. As the nuns carried the orphans aboard in cardboard boxes, Herrington distracted the police while the sergeant's wife climbed a metal stairway to the flight deck and hid until takeoff. Sometimes Herrington and Bell rode the buses bringing orphans to the flight line and persuaded their drivers to make a short detour to collect the wives of U.S. servicemen whom they had hidden behind the terminal. If an immigration official boarded a bus to make a head count, the wives hid under the skirts of the American women who were escorting the orphans.

Colonel Madison asked Herrington and Bell to expand their operation and evacuate the U.S. JMT delegation's Vietnamese employees and their families. Madison was a tall, gangly West Point graduate with a sweet smile and a kind heart who had advised South Vietnamese troops in 1963, returning four years later to command a battalion in the Central Highlands. Behind the "Duty, Honor, Country" motto of West Point is an assumption that the three are a harmonious triad, but sometimes its graduates must choose. This had happened to Madison during his second tour in Vietnam when he concluded that instead of trying to win the war, the Johnson administration simply wanted to avoid losing it until negotiations ended it. Because his battalion's area of operations included a major infiltration zone, his men had the dangerous assignment of engaging enemy soldiers and pushing them back across the border. Instead of sacrificing his teenage draftees in a war their leaders had no strategy for winning, Madison placed his personal honor and his duty to his men first. He discouraged what he called "bayonet stuff," and targeted infiltrators with artillery and air strikes, "anything to avoid casualties among my guys."

Several years later, Madison had been on track to make general when an assignment officer at the Pentagon offered him command of the U.S. JMT delegation. He protested that he had been to Vietnam twice while some at his level had yet to go. After the officer promised him a pick of assignments when he returned, he reluctantly accepted the assignment. He reported to Dr. Roger Shields, the deputy secretary of defense for POW and MIA affairs, but was also under the command of Ambassador Martin and Major General Smith, a situation enabling him to play them off against each other. His previous two tours in the country had left him with what he called "a deep emotional connection" with the South Vietnamese, and he was upset when Martin refused to evacuate the U.S. delegation's Vietnamese interpreters, drivers, secretaries, and MIA experts. He considered Martin's excuse that their departure could lead to the collapse of the Thieu government ridiculous because, he thought, "everything was collapsing anyway!" In 1967 he had engaged in some low-level shenanigans to keep his teenage draftees out of harm's way; eight years later he was ready to do it again to evacuate his Vietnamese employees. He called Deputy Secretary of Defense Shields, explained the situation, and proposed evacuating his people aboard the transports returning to the Philippines. If anyone questioned the operation, he would point out that if the Communists won, the United States would need their expertise to continue negotiating on MIA issues.

Shields said, "Do it!" and promised him a chartered plane to fly the JMT delegation's Vietnamese to Guam.

Madison gathered his Vietnamese employees and said, "You should consider this top secret, but I want to know which of you wants to leave because the Communists are going to come waltzing in here any day now." Most asked to leave. They would be easy to evacuate because they had passes permitting them to enter Tan Son Nhut, but their families would have to be smuggled onto the base. Madison gave this job to Herrington and Sergeant Bill Herron. Herrington asked Andy Gembara if he could borrow his notorious freezer truck. Gembara said he could have it, but only for a few hours because it was in demand from competing underground railroads.

Although Gembara had drilled airholes in its floor, Herrington was so nervous about suffocating his evacuees that he assembled them at a safe house three minutes from the airport. On his first run he packed everyone in so tightly that they had to stand. Before closing the door, he said that as he neared the gate, he would lean back from the cab and hit the side of the truck three times, "Bang! Bang! Bang!" After that, there could be no noise, and mothers must clap their hands over the mouths of their infants and children. His first two runs went smoothly. He banged on the truck and everyone quieted. The MPs saw a uniformed U.S. Army officer and waved him through. Because the JMT had its own dedicated plane, he drove straight to the flight line and delivered everyone to Madison and Colonel Harry Summers, the second-in-command of the U.S. delegation. But when he returned to the safe house for the third time, the evacuees warned him that neighbors had reported suspicious activities to the police, and they had summoned the owner of the house to the local station. Faced with imprisonment for assisting an illegal operation, the man jumped into the back of the truck and arrived in Guam with the clothes on his back.

Herrington had some special cases that he was determined to evacuate regardless of the dangers or laws that he might be breaking. Major General Smith had forbidden anyone in his command to evacuate members of the South Vietnamese military, but Herrington was torn. Although assisting desertion in wartime was a serious offense, he also believed that the Communists were certain to execute or imprison South Vietnamese intelligence officers, and knew that not evacuating military personnel with their families meant depriving their wives and children of their sole wage earner, perhaps splitting up families for years if not forever. During his earlier tour he had become friends with

Lieutenant Tuan, who had led an intelligence platoon. Tuan had written to him, saying, "Dear Captain, If you are able to help my family and me please come to Bien Hoa. You know the house. If you can't help us, we are dead for certain." Tuan was a Catholic who had fled the North, a marked man for sure. After considerable soul-searching, Herrington decided to evacuate him and other military friends. He assumed that the government had tapped the U.S. delegation's phones, so he met his prospective evacuees in person to agree on a code. He told them that if he called to invite them to a party at his quarters, the time and date of the event would indicate when they should arrive at a prearranged safe house.

Bill Bell also faced some agonizing decisions. He glanced out his office window one morning to see a Vietnamese lieutenant colonel standing outside the door, as if debating whether to come inside. Bell recalled seeing him at the DAO accompanied by a plainclothes U.S. intelligence operative who had identified him as Lieutenant Colonel Pham Xuan Huy, a legendary intelligence officer who had erected a memorial to a heroic American pilot. Bell thought that Huy was a candidate for a Communist death list and assumed he was too proud to ask someone at the JMT to help him but was hanging around hoping that someone might volunteer. Bell told himself that one of the Americans who knew and admired him would surely rescue him. Instead, everyone abandoned the man who would become Bell's father-in-law.

Madison recruited Bell and marine gunnery sergeant Ernest Pace to operate the JMT's second underground railroad. Pace was also a Vietnamese linguist and, according to Bell, "a hard-drinking and fun-loving Marine." They drove day and night, losing sleep and missing meals while collecting the relatives of JMT employees who had missed the first evacuation flights. Bell also evacuated his landlady and her neighbors, Special Branch policemen whom he knew from his earlier tour, and a friend's daughter who worked for *Stars and Stripes*—an obvious "class enemy." As Bell loaded her into the trunk of his car, he realized while closing it that his friend might be seeing his daughter for the last time.

He and Pace also evacuated CIA sources who feared the agency would abandon them, anyone carrying a GE Slimline radio, because they knew that the CIA issued them to its Vietnamese agents, and the Vietnamese wives of American officers who had kept their marriages secret because they feared they would lose their security clearances for cohabiting with a woman who had not been vetted. They began by evacuating people they deemed to be endangered but were soon helping anyone who wanted to leave. If they could fit six people into whatever vehicle they were using and only four showed up, they offered places to anyone standing around. "It was fill it up, get in, who wants to go to the United States," Bell recalled. "Bam! Bam! They'd jump in and we'd take off." The more people he evacuated, the better he felt about leaving Andrea in California.

As he and Pace drove farther into Saigon's sketchier and more distant neighborhoods, they shifted from trucks to cars to navigate the narrow streets. Their favorite vehicle was a black Ford LTD with a large trunk that an American had abandoned in the DAO parking lot. Pace played the chauffeur, while Bell sat ramrod straight in the backseat, wearing his parachute wings and decorations and staring straight ahead. The MPs saw a bigwig and waved them through, and they drove their people to a hangar where they handed them over to a little African American air force enlisted man wearing a bandanna around his head. Every time Bell watched his evacuees following the airman to the plane, like baby ducks behind their mother, he felt a surge of pride.

He tried to keep his operation on the down low, but the word spread. One man offered him diamonds; another promised to sell him a Ming dynasty vase for $20. Phones at the JMT rang with calls from Americans in Bangkok begging him to track down a girlfriend, wife, in-law, or ARVN comrade. He went to houses where several generations waited in a single room, sitting on their suitcases, scared to go but terrified to remain. He drove into dodgy neighborhoods filled with ARVN deserters to collect bar girls described as "close female friends." During his last runs North Vietnamese rockets whistled overhead and exploded nearby, showering the streets he had just left with metal shards.

After Madison had flown the U.S. JMT delegation's Vietnamese and their families to Guam, Major General Smith asked him to help evacuate the families of South Vietnam's 150-man JMT delegation. Madison informed Colonel Nghia, their commanding officer, that although for the moment his men could not accompany their families, he would try to evacuate them later. During the next four days Nghia arranged to have his men's families brought to the Tan Son Nhut soccer stadium. Herrington scrounged up a bus with embassy license plates and drove them from the stadium to the flight line, where they boarded the planes that Madison and Summers had wrung out of the air force.

Herrington had the painful job of standing by the door of the bus, counting people off, and enforcing Smith's prohibition on evacuating military personnel, watching as Colonel Nghia's men embraced their wives and children for what might be the last time. One parting between a colonel and his family was particularly excruciating. The wife was pregnant and one of the children seriously ill. The colonel and his wife hugged, wept, and hugged again. Unable to watch any longer, Herrington told him in Vietnamese, "Go, Colonel. Get on the bus with your family."

"My duty requires that I stay and fight," he said. "I can't desert my country at this desperate moment."

"That's very noble of you, but President Thieu has left, and some generals left this morning. [In fact, Thieu would not leave until the next day.] Your family needs you more than your country right now. I'm not going to say it again . . . but get on the bus. Get on the bus!"

The colonel burst into tears and boarded with his family.

Colonel Summers had been standing nearby and asked what had happened. When Herrington explained, he became furious and said, "You encouraged the desertion of an officer. You know what the rules are. Shame on you!"

The incident haunted both men for years. Two decades later, Summers recounted it in a magazine article. He admitted that "nothing that officer [the Vietnamese colonel] could have done would have changed anything," and concluded, "In hindsight, Captain Herrington did the right thing." He also admitted that he had himself violated the prohibition against evacuating the military. One case involved a pregnant waitress at the DAO mess who was days from delivering her child. She refused to leave without her husband, a marine sergeant who had just turned up after being reported missing. "So we just bundled her husband up and put him on an airplane and shipped him out of [the] country," Summers wrote. "We figured they could lose a Marine sergeant and it wouldn't hurt too bad."

As Herrington was escorting some evacuees to the flight line, he discovered that a wealthy Saigon surgeon had bribed an officer in the Vietnamese JMT delegation to put him and his family on the manifest. Herrington considered it the kind of corruption that had ruined South Vietnam. He was so angry that he flagged down a pickup truck and ordered the surgeon and his family dumped outside the gate. Minutes later he felt awful. To ease his conscience, he approached a forlorn-looking young couple who were sitting alone under a tree. She said that her boyfriend was a law student and they saw no future for themselves in a Communist country. Some friends who had promised to get them on a plane had failed to appear. Herrington handed them the flight manifest and told them to add their names to it. Pointing to a staging area where families of the Vietnamese JMT delegation were boarding a bus, he said, "Just get over there and join that line." She blinked back tears and said in perfect English, "We will always think of you as our guardian angel and remember you in our prayers."

Herrington realized that he was playing God. He might have condemned the surgeon and his family to years of privation and imprisonment while giving the young couple the chance at a new life in the United States. He never forgot any of them. Twenty years later he received a phone call from a woman asking if he was the American captain who spoke Vietnamese. After he replied in Vietnamese that he was, she asked, "Do you remember that law student and his girlfriend? Well, I was that girl." She reported that she and her boyfriend had married, had children, and now lived in Seattle, where he practiced law. "I just wanted to tell you that we took advantage of that opportunity you gave us," she said.

Although Martin had fired Don Hays for participating in an unauthorized evacuation, Hays soon became involved in schemes that could have led Martin to expel him again. While having lunch with an American secretary in the recreation center restaurant, he overheard Wolfgang Lehmann saying, "Goddamn it! I'd like to find the defeatist who's telling all these secretaries to leave," and realized that Lehmann was talking about him. One of the embassy communication officers had recently handed him a cable from the State Department authorizing the immediate departure of the dependent families of U.S. government employees in South Vietnam. The officer told him that Martin had ordered him not to distribute it and to destroy the original. Hays ran off copies and put one in every in-box during the lunch break. Some secretaries showed the cable to their bosses and received permission to depart.

Hays's wife was security officer Marvin Garrett's secretary. Garrett struck Hays as loud and brash, "the kind of guy who might get you in trouble if you went barhopping with him," but he also admired him for being decisive and candid. Because Garrett's last evacuation scheme had led to Hays's expulsion, he was wary when Garrett summoned him to another late-night meeting in his office. Garrett had gathered an eclectic group from across the mission that included Ken Moorefield, two Seabees, a marine guard, and someone from Alan Carter's USIA office. Garrett declared, "Since the ambassador has frozen me out of his thinking on any evacuation, refusing to even discuss it with me, we're going to have to plan it ourselves."

He said he was not asking them to launch an evacuation without Martin's approval, at least not yet, but to prepare for it discreetly. He gave Hays the assignment of transforming the embassy compound into a helicopter evacuation site in case the land route to Tan Son Nhut became impassable. Hays asked a contact at AID to send over a work crew of Seabees. They modified the embassy gates, reinforced the roof, moved utility poles farther from the walls to prevent them from being climbed, and strung concertina wire across the wall. While Hays was on the wall supervising the work, his boss Hank Boudreau saw him and shouted, "What the hell are you doing?" Boudreau was close to Martin, so Hays told him he was carrying out a work order. Who had signed it? Boudreau asked. "You did!" Hays shouted. "Or at least it looks like your handwriting." Boudreau harrumphed and walked on.

Hays's wife was eight months pregnant. The embassy doctor had told her, "I don't want to end up delivering a baby on a helicopter," so Hays bought tickets out on Pan Am for her and their daughter. The airport was chaotic. Vietnamese shouldered their way into the check-in line and threw bribes at ticket agents. Police and immigration officers were so distracted that Hays boarded the plane with his wife and daughter. He considered leaving with them, but had he done so, several hundred more Vietnamese might have ended up in Communist reeducation camps, including the husband of his daughter's kindergarten teacher.

The teacher was a New Zealander, like Hays's wife. She had finagled visas and passports for herself and their two children and had flown with them to New Zealand on the assumption that her Vietnamese husband, who worked for Esso as an engineer, would soon follow. But Esso refused to help him, and the New Zealand embassy would not issue him a passport or visa. He appealed to Hays because their wives were friends. Hays told him that the Royal Australian Air Force was operating daily flights to Bangkok. Their plane was parked on the far edge of Tan Son Nhut, and they were boarding anyone who showed up. To get past the MPs, a South Vietnamese citizen needed a ticket, passport, and exit visa, but Hays had noticed the MPs waving through the Japanese ambassador and suggested that the engineer borrow a black Mercedes, affix a Japanese flag to its bumper, hire a driver, and wear a dark suit and a homburg. "Go racing through the checkpoint," he said. "Have the driver wave but don't stop until you reach the Australian plane." After Hays joined his wife in New Zealand a month later, she told him that the teacher and her husband had invited them to dinner. As soon as they arrived, the engineer handed Hays the homburg and said, "You saved my life."

CHAPTER 12

"Godspeed"

———⊣⊢———

As General Dao's troops retreated from Xuan Loc, the price of a seaworthy boat rose. CIA station chief Polgar strapped on a revolver and shipped his household goods home, and a police major suffered a breakdown in front of the American consulate, yanking people out of the visa line and shouting, "You can't leave this country! I'll arrest you all!"

The Washington Post described Martin as "dazed and confused" and in "deep personal anguish" over the fate of the U.S. mission's Vietnamese. Still, he insisted that work continue on a new bathhouse for the recreation center pool and that the embassy keep normal hours and close on weekends. He strong-armed USIA head Alan Carter into appearing on South Vietnamese television on April 19—the same day that embassy buses began taking Brian Ellis's evacuees to Tan Son Nhut—to declare that rumors the embassy was organizing an evacuation were false. Carter insisted that there was "absolutely and equivocally no truth" to the claim that Americans would leave if Congress failed to appropriate additional military aid for South Vietnam and that the departure of U.S. citizens was "routine," adding, "If you were to visit Ambassador and Mrs. Martin's house you would see that nothing has been packed," and that "the same is true of my house."

The relationship between Martin and the commander in chief of U.S. military forces in the Pacific, Admiral Noel Gayler, had been strained ever since Gayler kept Martin waiting before their initial meeting in Honolulu. Gayler was a decorated naval fighter pilot who had shot down five Japanese Zeros, winning the Navy Cross. His contemporaries considered him a maverick, and he has described himself as "a loose cannon." Like Martin, Madison, and Baughn, he blamed President Johnson and Secretary of Defense McNamara for their "disastrously bad strategy" in Vietnam. He found Martin "not an easy man to communicate with," and during their telephone conversations in early April he was unable to shake Martin from what he called his "curious idea that somehow or other there was a political fix coming, and [that] an armistice had been arranged." Because Gayler commanded all the military forces from the West Coast of North and South America to the Indian Ocean, including those assigned to the Defense Attaché Office in Saigon, he considered himself the final authority on any evacuation from South Vietnam involving the U.S. military. Martin, however, insisted that as senior U.S. official in South Vietnam *he* should have the last word on anything involving U.S. civilian and military personnel there, including an evacuation. When Gayler pressed him to estimate how many people the military might have to evacuate from South Vietnam, Martin's answers were so vague and evasive that Gayler finally flew to Saigon to resolve what he called "a very considerable conflict between the ambassador and me on making preparations [for an evacuation]."

He met with Martin in the embassy on April 19 along with Major General Smith and air force lieutenant general John Burns, who commanded the Seventh Air Force from Thailand. The White House, Congress, and the Pentagon had been exerting pressure on all three officers to evacuate U.S. citizens from South Vietnam. One obstacle to accomplishing this had been Martin's insistence that a large-scale evacuation of Americans would destroy morale and lead to revenge attacks against those who remained. Another had been the reluctance of American civilian contractors and government employees to leave South Vietnam. Many of them had invested years in the war, and like Bill Bell they wanted to see it through to the end. Those working for the U.S. government also feared that being designated "non-essential" would damage their careers. At a gathering of CIA agents at the Duc

Hotel, the agency's Saigon hostel, Polgar had stoked these fears by urging the agents to leave, followed by an admission that he could not guarantee that doing so would not become a black mark in their files.

A third of the approximately seven thousand Americans residing in South Vietnam at the beginning of April were civilian contractors who were filling jobs previously performed by the U.S. military. Martin dismissed them as "lotus eaters," and Stuart Herrington thought they represented "the largest group of undisciplined and overindulgent foreigners to hit a foreign capital since the Red Army descended on Berlin in 1945." Hanoi accused them of being America's "secret army." If so, they were a spectacularly unfit one, a hodgepodge of retired military men, long-term expatriates, and adventurers attracted by generous pay, the whiff of danger, and a chance to live a comfortable life on the cheap. Many had married Vietnamese women, fathered children, and become devoted to their Vietnamese families. They resisted going "home" because for many of them South Vietnam *was* home. In mid-April the U.S. Immigration and Naturalization Service (INS) agreed that the embassy could "parole" certain categories of South Vietnamese, giving them U.S. entry visas, and that any American citizen in South Vietnam legally married to a Vietnamese woman could bring out his wife and her immediate family. But because the INS parole did not include common-law wives, grandparents, siblings, or draft-age brothers, few Americans accepted it, and even if they did, their families still needed South Vietnamese passports and exit visas.

On April 14, Smith had called together the heads of the DAO's contracting firms and urged them to persuade their employees to leave. They complained that their people had been unable to get passports and exit visas for their Vietnamese families. Smith next summoned retired U.S. military personnel to the DAO auditorium. He had already suspended their PX and commissary privileges, but to no avail. They insisted that they would not leave without their wives' and girlfriends' families, and one man shouted, "What is it you don't understand about loyalty to one's family?"

Just before Gayler, Smith, Burns, and Martin met at the embassy on the morning of April 19 to decide how to persuade the contractors and other American civilians to leave South Vietnam, a cable arrived from the Justice Department's Immigration and Naturalization Service offering a possible solution. The INS had previously insisted that an American relative seeking to sponsor a South Vietnamese citizen had to be physically present in South Vietnam. Its April 19 cable said that it would now permit an American living anywhere in the world to sponsor visas for their Vietnamese in-laws and relatives. Candidates for this immigration parole would have to appear at the embassy to be screened, and their American sponsors would have to agree, the cable said, to be "responsible for the cost of transportation, care, maintenance and resettlement."

During the April 19 meeting at the embassy, Smith said that the INS cable meant "we can start to move people out of here in large numbers" and that "anyone in the States—any American anywhere, or his Vietnamese wife—can vouch for people here and the INS will let them in." It also meant, he said, that an American citizen could evacuate his wife's grandparents and second cousins, or anyone else he wanted, as long as he signed an affidavit promising to support them in the United States. Turning to Martin, he added, "I really think this might solve the problem with the contractors, Mr. Ambassador."

Martin wanted to get Washington off his back and reluctantly agreed. Before the meeting ended, Gayler suggested that they compose an affidavit of support saying that the signatory promised to support the family members listed below after they arrived in the United States. Eva Kim typed it onto a stencil and mimeographed a sheaf of copies. She handed a stack to Smith. Each had the potential to change dozens of lives. Smith returned to the DAO and told his staff to sign them for whomever they wanted to evacuate, relatives or not, as long as none were military personnel.

The affidavits quickly circulated through the DAO and other U.S. mission agencies. Suddenly, any Vietnamese who could persuade an American to sign a legally unenforceable affidavit stating that they were family members—genuine or "adopted"—and promising to support them could leave on a U.S. Air Force plane. Within hours Americans began bringing Vietnamese whom they claimed to be their relatives or adopted children to the Evacuation Processing Center that the DAO had set up in its auditorium. Some Americans agreed to support dozens of bogus "adopted" children—adopting lovers, bar girls, maids, and friends. A few adopted anyone willing to pay for their signature. The evacuation became larger but no less capricious, favoring Vietnamese who could find an American to adopt them and sign their affidavit. Because any American could sign one, every American could play God, and because Vietnamese evacuees still needed to get past the MPs and into Tan Son Nhut, the number of South Vietnamese riding into Tan Son Nhut on the underground railroads doubled, tripled, and more each day, and the number of evacuees boarding U.S. military planes for the Philippines and Guam jumped from several hundred a day to several thousand.

Later on April 19, Martin received two cables from Deputy National Security Adviser Brent Scowcroft that further expanded the evacuation. On April 16, Ken Quinn had concluded that Saigon might fall before his relatives and friends, and those of other Foreign Service officers, could escape. He waited until late that evening, when he knew Scowcroft would be alone, before going upstairs to his office to make his pitch. He told him that Martin was resisting a large-scale evacuation and informed him of the State Department cafeteria group and the similar one in Saigon involving Lacy Wright that was ready to facilitate the departure of the relatives of U.S. government personnel. Scowcroft presented Quinn's case to Ford that same evening. Ford approved the evacuation of the relatives and decided to expand it to include high-risk Vietnamese who were not related to U.S. government employees. David Kennerly also played a role in Ford's decision. After hearing that the Pentagon was urging Ford to evacuate Americans as quickly as possible, he had what he calls "a real heart-to-heart" with Ford during which he warned that the Communists might execute some of their South Vietnamese friends. Ford replied, "Goddamn it, we're going to get as many Vietnamese nationals as we can out."

Scowcroft's first cable to Martin on April 19 had instructed him to evacuate the Vietnamese relatives of State Department employees and had included a preliminary list of their names and addresses. His second cable expanded the evacuation and said, "One thing left out of last cable we sent you was that Henry [Kissinger] said you can, at your own judgment, begin to move out Vietnamese in the high-risk category. He does not want to second guess you in this area. You must be the judge on when and how fast to move such high-risk elements and CIA assets."

Until April 19, Lacy Wright, Shep Lowman, and the others who had met with Ken Quinn at a deserted office in the embassy in early April had been puttering along in first gear: identifying safe houses, collecting lists containing the names of endangered Vietnamese employed by the U.S. mission and politicians and intellectuals believed to be Communist targets, receiving the names of Vietnamese related to State Department personnel supplied by Quinn, and coordinating their activities with the embassy's fourth-floor Evacuation Control Center manned by Mel Chatman and Russell Mott. They and Chatman and Mott had arranged for the DAO buses to transport the embassy's "special cases" to Tan Son Nhut; these included Brian Ellis's U.S. news agency personnel. Scowcroft's two April 19 cables expanded the scope of what Wright and Lowman could do. They now had permission to begin moving more of the Vietnamese on their lists to Tan Son Nhut for evacuation, using whatever buses Chatman and Mott could commandeer from the DAO.

Martin immediately complied with Scowcroft's first cable, and Wright, Lowman, Don Hays, and others in the U.S. mission began collecting the State Department and other U.S. government relatives and bringing them to Tan Son Nhut. But Scowcroft's second April 19 cable had given Martin the job of determining which Vietnamese qualified as "high-risk" and when they should be evacuated. Martin was slower and more cautious about moving out people in this category because he continued to believe that a large-scale evacuation would ignite panic, leading to the collapse of civil authority and the army, and that it was unnecessary because the Communists favored negotiations over a direct assault on Saigon.

As Ken Moorefield was casting around for a way to include himself on the embassy's list of "mission-essential" personnel who would
be permitted to stay until the end, he had noticed that every day the
line of Americans and Vietnamese outside the consulate stretched farther down the street. He approached his friend Consul General Walter
Burke and proposed opening a branch of the consulate at Tan Son
Nhut so that evacuees could be processed there before going directly
to the flight line. Burke agreed and gave him an emergency consular
commission and seal. On Friday, April 18, Moorefield opened his
consular office at the Evacuation Processing Center inside the DAO
auditorium.

The DAO already had a team there processing its American and
Vietnamese evacuees. There was also a contingent of agents from South
Vietnam's Ministry of the Interior who were under orders to prevent
the departure of military personnel, draft-age males, and security risks.
During Moorefield's first morning in the auditorium, he tried to follow the State Department's guidelines, clearing only Vietnamese with
papers showing them to be the dependents of an American citizen
through marriage, birth, or adoption. He sent the others back downtown to obtain these documents from government ministries. They
returned empty-handed and complaining of astronomical bribes. By
afternoon he had decided to ignore the State Department guidelines.
He told the secretaries he had brought from the embassy to type up
forms saying, "I've lost my paperwork but I'm an American dependent," "This is my legally adopted child," "We are legally married but
have lost our paperwork," and "Those listed below are the family members of the following American citizen." After an evacuee signed the
appropriate form, Moorefield fixed his consular seal on it, making its
holder and those named on it eligible for places on an evacuation flight.

The Ministry of the Interior agents questioned some of his evacuees, slowing the processing and sometimes refusing to issue laissez-
passers. He counterattacked by setting up a maze of lines that wound
back and forth inside the auditorium, making it difficult for the agents
to know who had been processed. He channeled the easiest cases into a
line that dead-ended at their desks, keeping them busy and distracted

while he approved the more questionable individuals. By the end of his first day he had processed three hundred people.

News of his generosity spread, and Vietnamese began stopping Americans in the street and asking them to sign an affidavit of support. His adoption and marriage forms had anticipated Gayler and Smith's affidavit by a day. After the crowds in the auditorium grew larger and more unruly, Smith moved the processing center to the gymnasium in the DAO annex, a nearby complex of recreation facilities known as Dodge City.

The air force began landing two transport planes an hour to accommodate the increased numbers of evacuees, and Moorefield began operating on a twenty-four-hour basis, keeping his evacuees overnight to avoid having any plane leave with empty seats. On April 21, the air force evacuated 249 Americans and 334 "others," mostly Vietnamese. The next day it flew out 550 Americans and 2,781 others; the day after that, 190 Americans and 5,574 others; and on April 27, 219 Americans and 7,359 others. Moorefield, Martin, Ellis, and others spoke of "seats," but the air force relaxed its post-Babylift crash insistence on physical seats and loaded evacuees on the planes' steel floors, throwing cargo nets over everyone to prevent them from being hurled into the cockpit if a pilot slammed on the brakes.

The embassy believed it had sent Moorefield to Tan Son Nhut to expedite the evacuation of the Vietnamese family members of American citizens. He was soon processing Vietnamese who worked for private American companies and charities, or who had close American friends or any connection with the United States that might put them at risk. He called the embassy and asked for guidance. When none was forthcoming, he applied what he calls his own "remedies."

The Saigon press corps was oblivious to Moorefield's operation. A front-page article in *The Washington Post* on April 19 reported that "the most sober view is that if there is an emergency in Saigon, the United States will get out its own citizens and leave behind the Vietnamese," and that "the specter is raised by well-placed observers of Americans climbing aboard helicopters and flying away while U.S. Marines push away and possibly gun down their frantic and enraged former allies." Citing "many informed observers," the article predicted that "as things stand now, a few thousand Vietnamese at most might be evacuated, and even that seems improbable." Two days later, almost three thousand Vietnamese flew out of Tan Son Nhut, yet George McArthur, who had excellent sources at the embassy, reported, "It is hardly likely that more than a few thousand [Vietnamese] will be successfully evacuated." Apparently, the underground railroads running to Tan Son Nhut really *were* underground, as was the scope of Moorefield's operation.

On April 22 the U.S. Justice Department put a legal face on what Moorefield and others had been doing by announcing that with the approval of the Senate Judiciary Committee it was waiving immigration restrictions for 130,000 refugees from Indochina. It amounted to the largest exception to American immigration regulations since the Cuban exodus of the early 1960s. The Justice Department was responding to pressure from Ford and Kissinger and playing catch-up by giving ex post facto legal status to the thousands of evacuees and "adoptees" who were arriving at transit camps in the Philippines and Guam. Included in the 130,000 emergency immigration paroles were 50,000 for people in a so-called high-risk category. On April 26, former ambassador Dean Brown, whom Kissinger had had brought out of retirement and placed in charge of the evacuation and humanitarian assistance to South Vietnam, sent Martin a plaintive cable saying, "It is essential that we get a better grasp on how you are handling the high risk category." Brown asked what Martin's "ground rules" were for granting an immigration parole and requested that he estimate what percentages were "embassy and other USG [U.S. government] employees, political/intellectual, and the other categories of high risk under which you operate." He asked for "a better understanding as to how you reach decisions," adding, "I assume someone gives a parole document to the parolee and that there is a numerical count maintained." He also requested that Martin "send me soonest cumulative total and a daily report."

Martin ignored him. There was no breakdown of how many current or former U.S. government employees versus intellectuals were

being evacuated, nor any "ground rules" for choosing high-risk people, largely because Martin had discouraged the kind of planning that
would have required such rules. The U.S. Air Force was doing the
evacuee count, and Moorefield and his team of young diplomats at
Dodge City, as well as Americans in the Defense Attaché Office and
on the Joint Military Team, were deciding on the spot who was "high
risk." At first, the DAO and the JMT had filled a disproportionately
large number of seats because they were based at Tan Son Nhut and
could easily put their people onto planes. After other agencies in the
U.S. mission complained, the embassy initiated a quota system that
imposed some sporadic fairness.

Moorefield feared that if he flooded the system with too many
people, it would collapse, and if he processed any South Vietnamese
military personnel, the government would shut him down. Undercover government intelligence agents mingled with the evacuees and
had already arrested a government minister. Immigration officials also
boarded planes, questioned passengers, and had to be bribed with
promises of evacuation for their families. Moorefield installed himself
in an office adjacent to the gymnasium so he could interview the more
problematic evacuees in private. He told an ARVN colonel who had
commanded a unit that he had once advised, "I can't send you out,
because if I do, the police may shut us down and no one will get out."
(Moorefield returned to Vietnam in 1995 and learned that the colonel
had died in a concentration camp.) The deputy commander of Military Region II appeared wearing civilian clothes and burst into tears
and shouted, "They'll kill me!" when Moorefield said it would be too
risky to evacuate him.

Moorefield and the young Foreign Service officers who had volunteered to assist him had minutes to break up families and decide who
should go to America. He begged family heads to make these decisions, telling a man who had brought seventy family members, "Look,
you may be qualified to leave, but I can't send out seventy people from
your family. . . . You'll have to decide; you'll have to tell me how this
is going to work." If a family asked his advice, he suggested leaving a
healthy wage earner behind to provide for the young and elderly. As a

last resort he made the decisions himself. He tried to create two economic units: a group of elderly family members who remained with
one or two young men, and a second group that went to America and
included young people with marketable skills and a good command
of English. He had minutes to decide who would start a new life in
the United States or live in a Communist Vietnam; which members
of a family would stay together or might never see one another again.
He had a soft spot for young women who brought letters from their
American "husbands" professing their love but saying they had to support their families in the United States. There were thousands more
like them in Saigon, and he wished he could send them all to America.

He looked up from his desk one morning to face a tall, imposing
Irish nun in her mid-forties wearing full habit. "You *must* help me,"
she said. "I've got a whole orphanage of Amerasian kids and staff who
are going to be at great risk." She wanted seats for eighty orphans. The
Babylift crash had led to accusations that Americans were "stealing"
Vietnamese children, and Moorefield knew that the government was
touchy about the evacuation of undocumented children. Sending out
eighty Amerasian children at once would ring alarm bells. He told her
he could not process so many unaccompanied children.

She returned the next day, planted herself in front of his desk,
fixed him with a penetrating stare, and said, "You *are* going to help
us." After she returned again, he realized that he was facing an implacable force of nature. "Look, I need you to create small families with
a man and woman dressed in civilian attire," he said. "They can each
claim four or five orphans as family members. I'll approve these 'families' one by one and put them on flight manifests fast, before anyone
begins asking, 'What the hell are all these Amerasian kids doing with
these couples?'" She recruited other nuns, members of her staff, and
American friends to pose as parents. They staggered their arrival at the
gymnasium, and during the next two days Moorefield flew out eighty
Amerasian orphans.

The air force loadmasters were also generous in defining "family."
After perusing the thirty-two adoption affidavits signed by a single
American, one of the airmen said, "Do you know you are only allowed

to take immediate family members of American citizens out? Are all these people related to you?" The American said they were, directly or by adoption. He had listed the ages of his thirty-two adoptees. One was an elderly Catholic priest.

"What in the hell is this?" the airman asked. "Here's this eighty-year-old priest."

"Well, that's my adopted son."

The airman burst out laughing and said, "You guys got in here; we'll do our best to get you out."

Whenever he could escape from Dodge City, Moorefield evacuated his own special cases. An embassy friend who had left earlier with his Vietnamese wife had asked him to rescue her parents and relatives. Her father was a senior bank official, a guaranteed class enemy. Moorefield arrived at their house to find that the family had packed its suitcases and lined them up in the foyer. As he walked in, the father said, "Ah, Mr. Moorefield, we knew you would eventually come for us." He was moved to tears by their trust and relieved not to have betrayed it.

The gymnasium became noisier, hotter, and more crowded by the day. Women wailed, babies cried, toilets overflowed, people tripped over discarded luggage, and loudspeakers blared an announcement on a perpetual loop asking everyone to limit themselves to a single Sprite or Coke. When the Ministry of the Interior agents who had manned desks in the auditorium appeared with their families, Moorefield stamped their papers. Gaggles of bar girls moved through the lines, waving affidavits of support signed by their American lovers and clients. He stamped their papers, too. He turned away the policemen and military officers who offered him bribes and a Chinese businessman who promised to make him a wealthy man. He believed that making these life-and-death decisions was easier for him because he had made similar ones while leading troops in battle. But the stress of deciding the fate of so many people, and of witnessing so much anger and love, sacrifice and treachery, corruption and decency, sometimes overwhelmed members of his team. One junior diplomat jumped up and shouted, "I can't take it anymore! I quit!" Another hurled a Coke bottle against the wall and began screaming insults at the Vietnamese crowding around his desk.

Joe McBride, the Foreign Service officer who had been shocked by the embassy's luau party after Phuoc Long, joined Moorefield's operation. He saw the Dodge City processing center as an opportunity to rescue thousands of deserving Vietnamese and was disgusted by the American drug dealers, deserters, and black marketers who had come out of the woodwork and appeared at his desk demanding evacuation. He had orders to send out every American, so he processed them, but reluctantly. One man came through his line several times with different "families" who had obviously bribed him to sign their affidavits. The third time he appeared, McBride grabbed his shirt and said, "Listen, you fucker, if I see you here again, I'm going to make sure personally that you never get out of this country, even if I have to tie you to a fucking tent post."

It was the kind of behavior one might expect from a self-proclaimed "contrarian." McBride was the product of an Irish Catholic father and a blue-blooded Yankee mother. He had chafed against both backgrounds and had attended Brandeis, a Jewish institution as far as he could get from his Catholic prep school. The Foreign Service had been a childhood dream nurtured by his maternal grandfather, who had been a "Thomasite," one of the idealistic young Americans who had gone to the Philippines after the Spanish-American War to launch an English-language public school system, or as McBride put it, "teach our little brown brothers how to be good white men." AID had hired him out of graduate school and sent him to the Mekong delta in 1969 to serve on a joint military and civilian program charged with pacifying the countryside. He called it "the place I wanted to be, the job I wanted to be doing, the adventure I'd been seeking, and the country where I felt I could make a difference." He joined militiamen on night ambushes, made Vietnamese friends, and had an official cashiered for corruption. He turned down a promotion to district officer because he thought he was becoming too emotionally invested in South Vietnam, "too upset by all the lying, cheating, and stealing on the American side—the way people told their bosses, 'Okay, we're winning, now give me my next promotion.'"

A senior AID official who had brought his pregnant Vietnamese girlfriend and her mother to the Dodge City processing center rubbed McBride the wrong way. Exhausted by the stress of making these decisions, and upset that he was not rescuing more deserving Vietnamese, he shouted, "What the fuck, we'll send out you and your girlfriend but not her mother. Tough luck. Good-bye." Next in line was a Vietnamese man who said, "Sir, I know you won't consider my humble case." He handed McBride a sheaf of documents indicating that he had risked his life while working for several U.S. agencies. McBride evacuated his entire family. (They kept in touch afterward, and one of his sons became a managing partner at the consulting firm McKinsey.) After processing one of his former interpreters who had risked his life while working in a dangerous province, McBride accompanied him to a plane and saw a group of the DAO's cleaning women climbing aboard. He exploded at their American sponsor and called the embassy to complain. One of Martin's acolytes said, "Don't worry, Joe, we know what's going on."

One night McBride woke in the villa where he was sleeping to hear a commotion in the street. He went downstairs and saw, illuminated by the moon, a column of ARVN troops staggering down the boulevard. They wore blood-soaked bandages and were carrying their wounded. They struck him as used up and badly used, and he was irate that brave men like these were being abandoned while their commanding officers found seats on evacuation planes. But when Wolfgang Lehmann asked him if he was ready to leave, he said, "Nah, send someone else. I want to see this through to the end."

Martin had supported President Thieu longer than events warranted. He had even intervened to persuade General Nguyen Cao Ky to postpone a possible coup against Thieu. In mid-April he had driven to Ky's villa in a dented Volkswagen with Charles Timmes, a retired

U.S. general who had trained many of South Vietnam's military leaders and now served as a liaison between them and the CIA. Martin had disguised himself in a sports jacket and had pulled a cap down over his forehead. He greeted South Vietnam's former prime minister by saying, "You must be surprised to see a man like me at your house."

Ky considered the remark condescending but let it pass, partly because Martin's appearance was so shocking. His eyes were sunken and red-rimmed, and he appeared to have shriveled since Ky last saw him. Without promising to support Ky's rumored coup, he gave him the impression that the Ford administration wanted Thieu to resign. Timmes spread a map out on the floor, and for several hours he, Martin, and Ky discussed how Ky would stop the North's advance so that South Vietnam would have a strong hand in any negotiations. As Martin was leaving, he said, "It's not easy, you know. Give me a few days—then we'll see what we can arrange." He was just vague and encouraging enough to persuade Ky to delay his coup.

By the third week in April, Kissinger and Ford had soured on Thieu, and on April 20 Martin went to the palace and encouraged him to resign, warning that if he did not, his generals would push him out. Thieu replied that he would do what was best for his country. Martin cabled Kissinger, "I went home, read the daily news digest from Washington, took a shower, scrubbed very hard with the strongest soap I could find. It didn't help very much."

Thieu announced his resignation during an emotional ninety-minute speech on April 21. He blamed the United States, and speaking as if addressing the U.S. Congress and the American people, he said, "You have let our combatants die under a hail of shells. This is an inhumane act by an inhumane ally." He read aloud from the letter that von Marbod had given Weyand in which Nixon had promised "severe retaliatory action" if North Vietnam attempted to occupy the South. The letter had not swayed Ford or Congress earlier that month, and was unlikely to do so now. Thieu also blamed his generals, charging some with being "cowardly." He demanded his people's pity, telling them, "Over the last ten years, all years, months, days, and hours in my life have been bad, as my horoscope forecast." After promising to "stay close to you in the coming task of national defense," he declared, "I am resigning but not deserting." The next morning the South Vietnamese Communists' Provisional Revolutionary Government issued a statement calling his resignation "a ridiculous puppet dance" and "a clumsy trick manipulated by the United States to keep the Thieu clique without Thieu."

Xuan Loc fell the same day that Thieu resigned. South Vietnam had committed the last of its reserves to the battle, and Major General Dao had lost a third of them. He fought to the end and spent seventeen years in a concentration camp. But instead of immediately attacking Saigon, the NVA paused for five days. Optimists in Saigon and Washington concluded that the Communists were waiting to negotiate with Thieu's successor, and the BBC raised hopes by calling the lull in the fighting "a de facto ceasefire." In truth, the NVA had advanced so quickly that it had outrun its supply lines.

Vice President Tran Van Huong succeeded Thieu. He was reputedly honest and capable but almost blind, afflicted by high blood pressure and diabetes, and appeared a decade older than his seventy-one years. Hanoi had claimed to be ready to negotiate with a "peace cabinet" but dismissed Huong as another American puppet. He had done little to further the chance of negotiations by declaring in his inaugural address on April 22, "Saigon will become a mountain of our bones and a river of our blood. And we will stand and fight together to the last drop of blood."

The next day, April 23, President Ford addressed a student audience at the Tulane University field house. He had complained beforehand to aide Robert Hartmann about spending "so much time worrying about a war that's over as far as we're concerned."

"Well, why don't you just say that?" Hartmann asked.

Ford said it might upset Kissinger.

"What do you care whether Henry likes it or not?" Hartmann asked. "You're the President, and if that's the way you feel, say it."

While flying to New Orleans, Ford added a statement to his speech saying that the Vietnam War was "finished." Press Secretary Ron Nessen knew it would electrify the crowd, writing later in his memoirs,

"From my first day in the White House I had a fantasy that at some point I would stand up in front of a news conference and announce the end of the Vietnam War."

Ford told the students, "America can regain the sense of pride that existed before Vietnam, but it cannot be achieved by re-fighting a war that is finished as far as America is concerned." When he uttered the word "finished," they jumped to their feet and cheered. Ford called it "probably the best reception" he had received from an audience since becoming president.

During the flight back to Washington, a reporter asked if Kissinger had approved the speech. "No! Absolutely not!" Ford exclaimed.

He was right about the line upsetting Kissinger. According to Hartmann, Kissinger "ranted and raved" at a meeting the next day, telling Ford, "This has got to stop. I can't hold my head up in front of all these ambassadors with a major statement like this and I don't know about it. I've just lost face."

Ford's speech devastated morale in Saigon, dashing whatever hopes Thieu's resignation had raised. Three U.S. allies who had contributed troops to the war—Australia, New Zealand, and the Philippines—evacuated their citizens, closed their embassies, and abandoned their Vietnamese employees. Canada, Britain, and other European democracies followed suit. The Vietnamese working for the Canadian embassy returned in the morning to find the building locked and deserted. The British left behind Indians and Hong Kong Chinese holding British citizenship. They stood outside the embassy waving their passports as the ambassador climbed into the limousine taking him to the airport.

Two days after Ford's Tulane speech, Thieu flew into exile in Taiwan on a plane provided by the embassy. He arrived at Tan Son Nhut inebriated and with so many relatives and bags heavy with so much gold (they clinked as his bodyguards carried them to the plane) that the pilot needed the entire runway to lift off. Thieu's bodyguards Hieu and Nguyen had been at his side for ten years. The Communists were certain to punish them for protecting his life, but after they had carried his booty onto the plane, he gave each man 5,000 piastres, a pitifully small sum, and left them standing on the tarmac.

Martin saw Thieu off. He said "Godspeed" and jerked away the metal staircase with a surprising burst of energy for someone who looked so sick and frail. CIA agent Frank Snepp, who witnessed the scene, wrote that Martin had pulled away the stairs "as if he was severing the umbilical that had kept us attached to South Vietnam." Thieu was not the only one making a well-timed exit. Soon after his departure so many senior officers had deserted their posts that an American reporter walking down the corridors of the Ministry of Defense heard a cacophony of telephones ringing on empty desks.

CHAPTER 13

"Make It Happen!"

——| |——

Pan Am flight 841 from San Francisco landed at Tan Son Nhut on April 22 after stops in Honolulu, Guam, and Manila. Most of the twenty passengers scattered across the 747's 375 seats were hoping to evacuate friends and family members from South Vietnam and then depart two days later on Pan Am flight 842. During the two-and-a-half-hour flight from Manila, they discussed their strategies for accomplishing this. Tra Dong, a young Vietnamese flight attendant, said she was planning to slip her three sisters aboard and hide them in the lavatories while immigration officers walked down the aisle making their final inspection. A South Vietnamese colonel who had been posted to the United States for training said that although he had decided to return to Saigon and remain there with his family, he wanted to evacuate his five-year-old son. He and Tra Dong made a deal: he would smuggle her sisters into Tan Son Nhut and hide them in the Pan Am cargo hangar, and she would smuggle his son onto the plane. Because the jumbo jet would be on the ground for only two hours before returning to Manila that day, they agreed to honor their bargain on flight 842 on April 24.

The other passengers included four Vietnamese women who held U.S. citizenship and were coming to rescue their families, and six American diplomats who had left posts around the world so they could evacuate their Vietnamese friends. All were violating a State Department order forbidding personnel to travel to South Vietnam except on official business. Two of the diplomats, Lionel Rosenblatt and Craig Johnstone, had gone AWOL from their State Department desk jobs and were traveling on their personal rather than their diplomatic passports, hoping that might mitigate the damage they were inflicting on their careers. Both were Foreign Service highfliers in their early thirties. Johnstone was on the staff of Kissinger's National Security Council, and Rosenblatt was an assistant to Deputy Secretary of State Robert Ingersoll. They gave themselves a fifty-fifty chance of being expelled from the Foreign Service and similar odds that the Communists would take Saigon and imprison them before they could leave. Johnstone believed that because of his experience in Vietnam, facility in Vietnamese, and familiarity with Saigon, failing to rescue his friends would be "repugnant." Rosenblatt wanted to evacuate his former comrades to settle a debt of honor he had incurred when his Montagnard guards saved his life during a Vietcong assault on his villa. When he told Johnstone that he was flying to Saigon to rescue his people, Johnstone replied, "Yes. That sounds like the right thing to do," and agreed to join him.

During the flight he and Johnstone drew up lists of their prospective evacuees. Each contributed ten names. If everyone on them wanted to leave and bring out ten family members, it would mean spiriting two hundred people out of South Vietnam. While they were in the air, the State Department cabled Martin requesting that he order embassy security officers to find and expel them. After reading the cable, Martin asked Lehmann, "Who do these guys think they are? They're not welcome here." Lehmann barged into a meeting of the political section and asked Joe McBride and the others if they knew Rosenblatt and Johnstone, demanding that they report any sightings. Martin asked the South Vietnamese police and security agencies to join the hunt. Rosenblatt thought it was not "a friendly thing" to do, because if the South Vietnamese arrested them, they could have been sitting in a South Vietnamese jail when the Communists marched into Saigon.

Rosenblatt was a founding member of the State Department cafeteria cabal. He had become less sanguine about what the group could accomplish after Ken Quinn delivered his gloomy report on the state of the embassy's evacuation planning. The final straw had come on April 18, when he read a cable from Kissinger to Martin saying, "There is strong domestic and congressional concern that we must put a higher priority on ensuring the safety of Americans in Vietnam." This meant an "accelerated departure," Kissinger said, so that no more than 2,000 Americans remained by April 22. In the same cable Kissinger asked Martin for "more details of what you have in mind for evacuation of Vietnamese," adding, "We are particularly concerned about the safety of Vietnamese associated closely with us, including our employees, and relatives of American citizens and resident aliens." In his response, Martin cited Ford's pledge to protect Vietnamese who have been associated with the United States—a number that he estimated could involve as many as 200,000 people. In light of this large number, Martin said, "We do not believe it feasible to try to assume responsibility to lift all the Vietnamese to whom the President refers directly from Saigon," adding, "We will instruct our own local employees to make their way to designated spots on the coast where they may be evacuated. Many may not make it, but we do owe those who do the chance to escape."

But what Martin considered a realistic way to satisfy his and Ford's humanitarian instincts, Rosenblatt viewed as a callous strategy promising to leave tens of thousands of Vietnamese stranded. Furthermore, if Martin was prepared to tell the embassy's Vietnamese employees to make their way fifty miles to the coast through Communist-controlled territory, then the people whom he and Johnstone wanted to evacuate would likely receive even less consideration.

After Pan Am flight 841 landed at Tan Son Nhut on April 22, immigration officers ordered its pilot to park half a mile from the terminal to prevent unticketed passengers from sneaking aboard. Thousands of Vietnamese stood on the other side of the airport security fence, guarded by soldiers with submachine guns as they watched passengers disembark. One American remembered them being extraordinarily quiet, standing "like ghosts." Sometimes one cried out, "Can you help me?"

Vietnamese who had talked or bribed their way into the terminal mingled with the flight crew and departing passengers. A woman cornered flight attendant Valerie Chalk, tugging at her sleeve and begging her to put her four-year-old daughter on board. Chalk asked flight attendants Gudren Meisner and Pam Taylor to help. The mother bent over and kissed her daughter before gently shoving her toward Chalk and Meisner. Each grabbed a hand and knifed through the crowd and past immigration officers. If challenged, they planned to say that she was an unescorted minor whose ticket was on the plane.

A middle-aged American and his Vietnamese wife asked Taylor for a similar favor. The woman pointed to a skinny boy standing next to their luggage and explained that he was their fourteen-year-old son and that she and her husband had been able to afford only exit visa bribes for two of their three children. They had brought him hoping to get him on the plane. Meisner and Taylor tried to walk him past the immigration desk, but he was too big to hide behind their skirts and a policeman turned him back, dismissing Taylor's claim that his parents were on the plane. The flight attendants persuaded the Pan Am baggage handlers to drive them to the cargo hangar. From there they made a dash for the plane. Some troops in a jeep intercepted them and ordered them back to the terminal. Taylor took the boy inside and said, "Thursday. Day after tomorrow, we come back. You be here?" He nodded and she promised to evacuate him then.

The ground hostess who had accompanied passengers from the terminal whispered to Taylor and Meisner that she would stay on the plane. The infant she was carrying in her arms and the toddler hidden behind her skirt were her own, and she had pretended to be bringing them aboard for a passenger. Her husband was fighting with the army, she said, and she had not had time to explain to him or her parents that she had decided to put her children's future ahead of her marriage, ahead of everything. The flight attendants seated her children with other Vietnamese passengers, and she hid in a toilet while immigration officers made a final check. The flight attendants alerted the pilot, and he ordered the door closed and started the engines.

Rosenblatt and Johnstone were unsure how to evacuate their two hundred Vietnamese. Before leaving Washington, they had collected dozens of expired U.S. passports from friends with an idea of turning them into documents convincing enough to get their people out. Not knowing that Martin had ordered them detained and expelled, they went straight from the airport to the embassy to confer with Lacy Wright and others. As they were climbing a back staircase, they ran into Joe McBride. "You'd better get the hell out of here," he said, explaining that their arrest and deportation had been discussed at that day's staff meeting. He suggested that they funnel their people through the Dodge City gymnasium, bringing them to him or Ken Moorefield.

They went underground. Rosenblatt shaved off his bushy mustache, and Johnstone began wearing a heavy French overcoat, an absurd garment given Saigon's steamy April weather. They carried two clunky French-style briefcases and borrowed a friend's 1940 Citroën. Another friend at AID gave them access to an apartment building whose American residents had left. Jim Eckes of Continental Air Services, who was playing a role in several underground railroads, lent them a white van with his company's logo and Huu, a fearless young Vietnamese driver who asked only to be evacuated with her family in exchange for her services.

They met some of their friends at the cathedral. It was dark and empty, but they still whispered. They did not pressure anyone to go but pressed them to make a quick decision. They told those who wanted to leave to return the next day with their families and a single suitcase. The disguises and clandestine meetings were melodramatic, but the stakes were too high to leave anything to chance. Some friends asked for a few weeks to put their affairs in order. "No, no, no, we're not here for long," they said, "and we don't think the situation is that stable."

They picked up their people from the cathedral or main post office and drove them to the apartment building. Once they had collected enough for an airport run, they led them out the back entrance and piled them into Huu's van. Upon reaching the gate, she grabbed a fistful of piastres from a shoe box and thrust them at the MPs. Sometimes she waved a sheaf of Air Vietnam tickets for Can Tho that Johnstone had bought with his American Express card.

At first, Rosenblatt manufactured counterfeit exit visas and laissez-passers on an ancient typewriter at the safe house, embossing them with a stamp purloined from the consulate. But after escorting his first group into the processing center, he realized that he needed only to hand Moorefield or McBride affidavits of support. One evacuee changed his mind after noticing that many of the others were wealthier and spoke better English. "I don't qualify," he told Rosenblatt, "and I'm worried I'll starve to death." Rosenblatt handed him a $20 bill and told him to accept it as a symbol that he would stand behind him after he arrived in America. The man took it, boarded the bus, and became a machinist in Minnesota.

Rosenblatt and Johnstone took catnaps and ate nothing in two days except a bowl of soup. They decided that the cloak-and-dagger meetings at the cathedral were too cumbersome and drove directly to their evacuees' homes and gave them five minutes to decide whether or not to go. By April 24, they were returning to collect the grandparents, siblings, and aunts and uncles whom they had left behind. They also evacuated strangers, among them a group of American-educated pharmacists and some pedestrians who had seen the Continental Air Services logo on their van, assumed they were going to the airport, flagged them down, and left with the clothes on their backs. By the time they departed on April 25, they had evacuated more than their planned two hundred people. They feared that if they stayed longer, they might end up occupying seats on an evacuation helicopter that could have gone to two Vietnamese. They finagled places on a chartered plane flying Air

America executives to Singapore. It lacked authorization to land, so they were met by policemen pointing submachine guns.

Kissinger summoned them to his office after they returned to Washington. Before they went in, his assistant Lawrence Eagleburger warned them that Kissinger was unpredictable and the meeting could turn nasty. He advised them to accept their dressing-down and say as little as possible.

An article about their mission had appeared in *The Washington Post,* and Kissinger asked if it was true. When they admitted it was, he said, "You realize that you were disobeying a direct order from the United States government, *my* order. I'm trying to create a disciplined foreign service and you guys just picked up and did what you wanted."

They followed Eagleburger's advice and said nothing.

Kissinger continued, "You did a very admirable thing. I'm very proud of you. If more people had done what you had done we would have had a better evacuation." Turning to Eagleburger, he said, "If I get another memorandum like this one from the personnel people, chastising the only people who have done the honorable thing, it'll be *you* who'd [be] dismissed."

He turned to them and asked what they would like to do next.

Johnstone said he wanted to return to being a political officer in Central America. Kissinger nodded at Eagleburger and said, "Make it happen," and it did.

Rosenblatt said, "We've got around 125,000 Vietnamese on our hands and I'd like to work on the refugee task force until every last woman and child evacuee is out of the camps. And I'd like a staff of twenty to help me."

"A staff of twenty!" Kissinger exclaimed.

Rosenblatt explained that he did not want Americans on his staff, only Vietnamese, Cambodians, and Lao.

Kissinger turned to Eagleburger and said, "Make it happen!"

Eagleburger protested that it was going to be difficult. Rosenblatt replied that the people he wanted to hire had all been employed by the U.S. government in their native countries, so why couldn't they be government employees here?

"Make it happen!" Kissinger said, and it did.

Like Rosenblatt and Johnstone, Don Hays had been too busy to eat or sleep much during this final week, and he was concerned that time spent eating and sleeping might mean leaving hundreds of South Vietnamese behind. In addition to his embassy day job, he helped friends at AID evacuate the families of their Vietnamese staff, collecting them in buses, maneuvering them through checkpoints, and delivering them to Dodge City. Because AID had made its own arrangements with the U.S. Air Force, Hays did not send his people through Moorefield's processing center. In fact, although Hays had been living in Moorefield's building since his wife left for New Zealand, the two men had been so busy with the evacuation that they seldom met.

On April 22 embassy security officer Marvin Garrett summoned Hays and some Seabees and mission wardens to a secretive 1:00 a.m. meeting at the recreation center restaurant. Garrett poured Hays a triple scotch and handed him a T-bone steak off the fire. It was the first real food he had eaten in days. Garrett said that Thieu's resignation and loss of Xuan Loc meant that the end was near. He had found a way to evacuate some of his most endangered employees on a special black flight and wanted Hays to give them their severance pay so they could use it to launch their new lives in the United States. Hays said, "I'll give it a try," and slipped the rest of the T-bone into his jacket pocket.

After the Justice Department authorized an immigration parole, Martin started fulfilling his pledge to evacuate some of the embassy's Vietnamese staff and their families. Hays sometimes rode on the buses to Tan Son Nhut with Martin's evacuees. He was as generous as Moorefield, turning a blind eye to men of military age and not questioning his passengers about their relationships to embassy employees. He resented Martin's prohibition against evacuating the military because it could mean splitting up families, perhaps forever. He became so distressed by this that he sometimes lost his temper. As he was picking up evacuees in front of a hotel, an Agence France-Presse photographer began taking pictures. Knowing that Martin would continue his selective evacuation only if it remained secret, Hays ordered the photographer to leave. The man protested and said, "I'm only interested in the news." Hays shouted, "I'm only interested in your blood," and picked up a two-by-four and chased him down the street.

On April 24, one day before Rosenblatt and Johnstone escaped to Singapore, the last Pan Am flight landed at Tan Son Nhut. Among its passengers was Richard Armitage, a former U.S. Naval Academy linebacker, fluent Vietnamese speaker, and multi-tour veteran of South Vietnam's riverine wars. He was coming on a secret mission to save South Vietnam's navy authorized by Secretary of Defense Schlesinger. After graduating from Annapolis in 1967, Armitage spent five of his next seven years in South Vietnam, repeatedly choosing combat and danger over safety and career. In 1968, he had requested transfer from a U.S. destroyer patrolling off the coast of Vietnam to one of the South Vietnamese Navy's river patrol boats. He advised an ambush team, slept on the dirt floors of village huts, wore black pajamas, and learned to speak flawless Vietnamese. He avoided using the term "adviser" because it connoted superiority and instead introduced himself to Vietnamese naval officers as their "comrade in arms." They called him "Tran Van Phu," an honorific name evoking a famed seventeenth-century Vietnamese naval hero.

There was a Lawrence of Arabia flavor to the way Armitage submerged himself in an alien culture, acquiring an honorific title and earning the respect of the men he was advising. But whereas Lawrence had been short and slender with a long thin face, Armitage had a broad face, bull neck, and the brick-wall build of a linebacker. His bull-in-a-china-shop look was deceiving. It suggested a man relying on muscle and physical supremacy, not someone possessing a keen intellect and cultural sensitivity similar to T. E. Lawrence's.

He had resigned from the navy after the Paris Peace Accords, a treaty he compared to "getting a lady pregnant and leaving town." He also resigned because while he was attending an anti-insurgency course in the States, his superior officer had pressed him not to volunteer to return to South Vietnam as one of the fifty uniformed American military personnel permitted by the Paris Peace Accords, arguing that a posting in Vietnam would hurt his career because he needed experience on warships. Armitage shot back, "Well, what other war are you fighting?"

He returned to Vietnam as a DAO civilian adviser to South Vietnam's navy, visiting navy bases, collecting and analyzing intelligence, briefing Ambassador Martin, and suffering wounds while traveling on ammunition barges to Cambodia. In the summer of 1974, as the fighting intensified, he visited the front lines with Erich von Marbod, who had been sent by Secretary of Defense Schlesinger to determine how much aid South Vietnam needed. By December 1974, Armitage had concluded that South Vietnam's military was losing its will to fight. The Pentagon brushed off his warnings, and he resigned, returned home to California, and spent the next several months worrying about his Vietnamese friends. After the defense of Xuan Loc collapsed, he called von Marbod and said, "Erich, I hope people are listening. It's over."

"Ricky, we've been looking for you," von Marbod said. "Get your ass to Washington."

When Armitage arrived, von Marbod explained that Schlesinger wanted them to go to South Vietnam, destroy high-tech U.S. military equipment, and encourage South Vietnamese air and naval units to escape with their planes and ships before the Communists seized them. He would save the air force; Armitage would use his contacts at naval headquarters to save the fleet. Von Marbod stopped in Thailand on his way to Saigon, while Armitage flew directly to Saigon on the last Pan Am flight.

Pan Am station manager Al Topping was planning to fill most of the seats on the plane that had brought Armitage to Saigon with his Vietnamese employees and their dependents. Topping was a tall and distinguished-looking African American in his mid-thirties, younger than most managers of busy Pan Am stations. He had been working as a ticket agent for United Airlines at Kennedy Airport when his life changed because his dry cleaner failed to finish his uniform on time. After he wore a business suit to work, his supervisor said he preferred him in it and promoted him to customer service. He met VIPs flying through Kennedy and impressed a Pan Am executive who offered him a job as a sales representative in San Francisco. He took it, moved into management, became director of operations for South Vietnam and Cambodia, and arrived in Saigon in 1972, when it was busy with cargo and civilian flights. The Pan Am station manager was a big deal, an ambassador from one of America's most iconic and prestigious companies. Topping attended diplomatic events, joined the Cercle Sportif, lived in a spacious villa across from the American embassy with his wife and children, and achieved his dream of becoming a disc jockey by hosting a Saturday evening program on the U.S. Armed Forces station that he called *Al Topping with Good Vibrations*.

By 1975 he and his maintenance manager were the only Pan Am Americans left in Saigon. He was younger than most of his Vietnamese mechanics, ticket clerks, and office and sales managers, but they called him "Uncle Al," as if he were a beloved family member. He was smitten by what he called "these very special people" and found it painful to ask them to sell tickets on Pan Am planes and service them but not escape on them. He knew that the Communists would view them as traitorous as Vietnamese working at the embassy, and raised the subject of an evacuation with executives at the New York headquarters. They asked how many he wanted to evacuate. All sixty-two of them, he said, and their families. They replied, "Yes. Let's get them all out," and said they would trust him to figure out how to do it and when—trusting him with the lives of sixty-two people about whom he cared deeply.

He gathered them at Pan Am's downtown office at the end of March and said that the company had decided to evacuate them and their families. "I can't tell you when it's going to happen or how," he said, "but believe me it's going to happen."

New York promised him a dedicated plane if he could not fit everyone on a scheduled flight, but he still needed to get his people into Tan Son Nhut. He hit upon the idea of "adopting" them before General Smith and Admiral Gayler proposed it to Martin. Pan Am had flown two chartered 747s with more than six hundred orphans and escorts to the United States during the Babylift, and he reasoned that if adopted orphans, some long out of diapers, could leave without exit visas, then why not his employees and their families? It was the kind of harebrained scheme you might expect from a corporate manager who doubled as a disc jockey. He sent his human resources manager, Xuan Nguyen, to the Ministry of the Interior to ask his contacts there how Topping could adopt his employees. Nguyen returned with a stack of adoption forms and told Topping to sign one for each employee and their dependents. Topping gave Nguyen the job of compiling a roster of the employees' family members. After he came up with 700 names, Topping insisted that he cut it in half. Pan Am in New York had said immediate family members only, and he needed to fit everyone onto a single 747. The next day Nguyen handed him a list of 360 names. Topping tried not to imagine the painful negotiations that had produced it.

Topping signed the forms and Nguyen brought them to the ministry with cash for the fees and bribes. After the forms came back signed and stamped, Topping sent his family home to the States and moved into a trailer at the airport. He spent restless nights sleeping in a flak jacket and listening to distant explosions. He assumed Hanoi would want to take Saigon before the Communists' May Day celebration and scheduled his evacuation for the April 24 flight. The day before, the Federal Aviation Administration prohibited U.S. commercial flights from landing in Saigon. Pan Am executives persuaded the State Department to designate flight 842 a government charter on the pretext that some embassy employees had purchased tickets. Topping had accepted a thousand reservations for the flight but assumed that few Vietnamese would get exit visas and arrive to claim them. The April 22 flight had left largely empty despite being overbooked, and he assumed the same thing would happen again. To be safe, he asked Pan Am to put a second 747 on standby in Bangkok.

He alerted his employees on April 23 and suggested they sleep at the downtown office or the airport. He decided not to notify Ambassador Martin, even though the flight was technically a State Department charter. Instead, he called a friend at the embassy who agreed to provide four buses to carry his people to Tan Son Nhut. News of the evacuation spread through the Pan Am grapevine, and he received calls all night from former employees begging to be included. He had to say no. He had already promised to evacuate 360 of his employees and dependents on a plane seating 375 people, and he might have to accommodate hundreds more depending on how many people claimed their reservations.

The next morning an envious crowd watched as the Pan Am employees boarded the buses. Telex machines chattered away on empty desks, and a sign on the front door said, "Temporarily Closed." Topping met the buses at the airport gate. He handed an MP a stack of forms showing that he had adopted all the passengers. Soldiers boarded the first bus and walked slowly along the aisle, glancing down at the adoption papers and up at the passengers. The bus was stifling, over a hundred degrees. Everyone stared straight ahead. No one said a word. They were the most terrifying minutes of Topping's life. He had "adopted" several military-aged men, and the MPs would have been justified in arresting them, and him. Instead, they disembarked and waved them through.

The buses drove straight to the plane. The landscape was flat, and the four-story-high 747, painted in Pan Am's blue-and-white livery with an American flag on its tail, was visible for miles. It was such an inviting target that during the Babylift flights Topping had ordered that only one 747 could be on the ground at once.

The flight attendants from the April 22 flight, including Pam Taylor, Gudren Meisner, and Tra Dong, had returned from Manila. Taylor searched the terminal in vain for the teenage boy she had promised to evacuate. The security was tighter, and the crowds outside the fence were larger and more menacing. Meisner replaced the Vietnamese ticket agents at the counter so they could slip aboard the plane and hide. Topping did a masterful job of choreographing the departure. Pan Am employees working as liaison officers in the control tower left at the last minute to board one of the buses heading to the plane. Vans raced across the tarmac, bringing Pan Am mechanics, baggage handlers, ticket agents, and caterers from the cargo hangar. Tra Dong's sisters arrived in one. The colonel whom Dong had met on the previous flight had kept his word and smuggled her sisters into the airport. She had borrowed flight attendant uniforms from Pan Am crews who were on layover in Manila. Her sisters threw them on and made a show of helping passengers up the stairs. The skirts were too long for them, and they stumbled in the oversized high heels. When no one was looking, they pulled them off and bounded up the stairs two at a time.

Topping had also agreed to evacuate some of the Adventist Hospital's Vietnamese staff. They pretended to be patients and arrived in ambulances, lights flashing and sirens wailing. Some limped up the stairs; others came aboard on stretchers. About 50 passengers walked from the terminal holding boarding passes. The other 950 people with reservations had not appeared. Because the flight was a charter, commercial rules were suspended, and Topping loaded some passengers two to a seat and put others in the aisles and galleys. He noticed that several of his employees had brought extra family members and that two soldiers from the airport detachment had changed into civvies and boarded. He let everyone stay.

An immigration officer walked down the aisle and announced that anyone without an exit visa would have to disembark. Passengers threw their remaining piastres into a pillowcase and bought him off. A soldier stationed at the foot of the stairs began checking papers, and the crew placed a garbage can at his feet so evacuees could fill it with their soon-to-be-worthless currency. After removing the wheel blocks, three maintenance workers crawled into the plane through its electrical box. The ground traffic controller jumped onto the landing gear after using his wands to direct pilot Bob Berg toward the runway. Berg came to a full stop so the controller could climb into the wheel well. From there the man pushed aside a panel and slithered into the cabin. After Berg had reached the runway, the air traffic controllers claimed that there was enemy activity nearby and put him on a ground hold. They were furious that the same Pan Am employees who had been sitting next to them in the tower minutes before were escaping.

After the plane had been on the runway for forty-five minutes, Jim Eckes, the Continental Air Services manager, handed an ARVN officer holding a walkie-talkie $200 and said, "Ask the tower to let that plane take off. Offer them this money. Let 'em drink to our health. Let 'em do what they want with it." The officer spoke to the controllers, and Pan Am's last flight from Saigon finally took off. Eckes had been close to Topping and the Pan Am employees. He thought, "Now all my pals are gone, all my friends," and began crying.

Ross Meador, the long-haired West Coast youth who had become a co-director of the Friends of the Children of Vietnam, evacuated his Vietnamese employees. He had accompanied a group of FCVN orphans to California on the April 5 Babylift flight. His parents had urged him to stay, but like Bill Bell he insisted on returning and moved into the FCVN orphanage at Truong Minh Ky Street, the last one remaining open following the departure of many of the organization's orphans and staff on the Babylift flights.

He discovered that because of the backlash against the orphan flights, formerly sympathetic government officials were refusing to provide adoption certificates and exit visas for the FCVN's remaining orphans. As the military situation deteriorated and reports of Khmer Rouge atrocities spread, he began caring for more and more children. Women arrived at the FCVN compound in the final hours of their pregnancies and left their babies. Physicians at the city's hospitals implored him to collect babies being left in their maternity wards. Nuns from rural orphanages arrived penniless and abandoned their malnourished charges. Packs of homeless children camped in the lane outside the FCVN villa. Mothers held their babies up against the windows of Meador's van whenever he left the compound, screaming and begging him to take them. Some hurled their infants over the compound's wall at night. The next morning the staff found them lying in the courtyard and wailing, or dead if they had hit a patch of concrete.

By April 21, Meador and his staff were caring for 180 orphans. The Ministry of the Interior was refusing to approve their adoption, and the crowd outside the compound had become so menacing that the DAO offered him a handgun. Vietnamese staff members reported that their relatives were begging them to stay home, complaining that they were putting themselves and their families at risk by continuing to associate with Americans. Meador promised to evacuate them and stopped at the AID office daily to ask when they would begin evacuating non-governmental organization (NGO) staff. He was always told not yet. He concluded that the NGO Vietnamese would always be at the bottom of any AID or embassy list and decided to evacuate them himself. He put five staff members on the floor of his van, threw blankets and suitcases over them, and headed for the airport. When they were several hundred yards from the barrier, he heard gunfire and a bullet whizzed through the car, missing him by inches. A middle-aged man on a motorcycle in army fatigues pulled alongside, pointed a revolver at him, and shouted, "Pull over, I go too!" Meador swerved, hitting the motorbike and sending it careening off the road. He was so unnerved that when he saw soldiers manning a machine gun nest near the Tan Son Nhut gate, he slammed on the brakes and reversed back onto the highway.

The next day he hid his staff members underneath a group of orphans whom he encouraged to be noisy and unruly. The soldiers let them pass, and he used the same ruse several times, sometimes bringing along Americans who had volunteered to "marry" or "adopt" his Vietnamese employees and sign their affidavits. He married some staff members and adopted others. Sister Therese, a nun in her forties, married a nervous Vietnamese man in his early twenties. Moorefield, McBride, or whoever signed their papers gently suggested that perhaps she should make him her adopted son.

An American physician at the Adventist Hospital contacted Meador on April 22 and proposed a collaboration. The hospital had requested a U.S. Air Force medical-evacuation plane from the Philippines and planned to put some of its Vietnamese staff aboard. The physician offered to include Meador's sickest children. Meador arrived at the hospital with his children to see members of its medical staff wrapping bloodstained bandages around each other, setting splints, and attaching IVs to arms. They rode to Tan Son Nhut in ambulances with Meador's orphans, sirens wailing and bringing traffic to a halt. Meador followed in his van, laughing and cheering. The MPs saluted as they sped through the gate.

Meador still had 184 orphans. Mr. Thanh, an FCVN guard and translator, came to his rescue. After Thieu resigned and Huong assumed the presidency, Thanh found that he had friends among the new ministers. He persuaded one to write a letter on official stationery stating that the new government would not interfere with the evacuation of the FCVN orphans. AID agreed to provide seats on a plane, supply four buses for an airport run on April 26, and permit them and their seventeen American and Vietnamese escorts to land in Guam without documentation.

Meador stayed up all night, making up names for the children that he put on armbands and writing notes on their medical conditions. The AID buses had sealed windows to prevent mothers from slipping their infants inside and armed guards to prevent anyone from forcing their way aboard. Meador followed in a van filled with food and medical supplies for the flight. The MPs expected the convoy and raised the barrier as it approached the gate. When Vietnamese attempted to run into the airport after the buses, the police turned fire hoses on them.

The airport had become grimmer and the crowds more unruly. Soldiers had shot several people attempting to scale the perimeter fence, and their bodies lay draped across the barbed wire. Meador and the orphans waited hours for a plane, long enough for a baby girl with an IV in her arm to die in Cherie Clark's arms. She and the other American staff flew out with the orphans. Meador wrestled with his conscience. He was a military-age American male, and there was a risk that the Communists would identify him as a CIA agent and execute him. On the other hand, the FCVN villa was filled with equipment and supplies that should be distributed to the other orphanages and hospitals before looters got them. He decided to stay.

There were dozens of other American civilians who, like Meador and Al Topping, operated freelance underground railroads. Some had the support of their bosses; others, like Rosenblatt and Johnstone, and the five Americans working for Alaska Barge & Transport (ABT), defied their superiors.

The ABT Americans operated the barges that had been chartered by the U.S. Military Sealift Command to transport ammunition and supplies up the Mekong River to Cambodia. They met for lunch on April 24 at the United Seamen's Service Club in Newport with Bill Ryder, the MSC's South Vietnam operations officer. Before leaving the club, which would close for good that afternoon, they would cast a vote that would determine the future of more than twenty-five thousand South Vietnamese. When asked later to reflect on the role that Bill Ryder played in rescuing these people, U.S. Navy attaché Carmody said that had Ryder been in the military, he would have recommended him for the Congressional Medal of Honor.

Ryder was an unlikely-looking hero: a slight, wiry man in his late forties with a receding hairline and a deceptively mild disposition who had spent a quarter century at sea on U.S. merchantmen or at MSC headquarters in Washington. He had volunteered to serve in South Vietnam because the pay was good and he was sick of his desk job, not because he supported a war that he thought every American president since Kennedy had lied about to the American people. The MSC was a civilian branch of the U.S. Navy responsible for chartering merchant ships from American maritime companies to transport cargo and military supplies for the U.S. military and government agencies. Most of its vessels in South Vietnam operated from the port of Vung Tau or from Newport, a large military terminal of piers and warehouses north of downtown on the Saigon River that was also headquarters for South Vietnam's navy.

By March, Ryder and Dan Berney, who headed the MSC in South Vietnam, had concluded that the most pressing question for them was not when Saigon would fall but how they could evacuate their Vietnamese employees before it did. In early April they moved their offices from the downtown riverfront to Newport to put them closer to their ships and make it easier to cultivate Vietnamese naval officers and the commander of the terminal. Several days before the April 24 Seamen's Club luncheon, ABT had canceled the contracts of its American and expatriate employees, stopped their pay, given them airline tickets, and ordered them to leave South Vietnam. By April 24, the Americans and expatriates operating the tugboats and barges had already evacuated most of their Vietnamese friends and family members. Now they were deciding whether to remain and risk their lives to evacuate Vietnamese strangers.

Five of the expatriates who captained the tugs that pulled the ABT barges had already chosen to remain and continue working without pay so they could evacuate South Vietnamese. During their April 24 lunch Ryder told the American barge workers that although the MSC had ordered him to leave, Rear Admiral Hugh Benton, whom the navy had sent to the embassy to coordinate an evacuation with the Seventh Fleet, had asked him to remain so that the MSC's freighters, tugs, and barges could participate in an evacuation. Ryder promised them that if they voted to stay, he would too, but they should realize that attempting to escape down the Saigon River on tugs and barges filled with thousands of anti-Communist refugees could be a dangerous enterprise. Their safest choice would be to obey the company and leave. All five voted to stay if he did. They said they needed him to coordinate with Admiral Benton and trusted him to tell the embassy to go to hell. He needed them because he had been in South Vietnam less than two years while they had years in the country and had good relations with the port commander and his staff.

Three of the MSC freighters that had evacuated refugees from Da

Nang and Cam Ranh Bay had been resupplied, repaired, undergone extensive cleaning, and were docked at Newport. Each could carry ten thousand evacuees. The U.S. Joint Chiefs of Staff feared that if they remained at Newport, they might be shelled and captured, and if they waited too long before putting to sea, the Communists might board them as they steamed down the Saigon River. On April 23, the Joint Chiefs ordered Ryder and Dan Berney to send all three freighters out to join the U.S. naval task force in the South China Sea.

Berney, Ryder, and navy attaché Carmody had been planning to load them with thousands of evacuees, including the families of the river pilots, the Newport post commander, and others with a connection to the MSC. Carmody believed that Martin would approve the operation because earlier that month he had told his military attachés, "I want you guys to draw up a plan to evacuate 250,000 people." Carmody went to Martin and proposed using the three MSC freighters at Newport to evacuate 30,000 people. He told Martin that he had calculated the risk of coming under enemy fire from the riverbanks, and of triggering a panic by boarding so many people at once, and believed it was worth the gamble. He pointed out that U.S. Air Force transports had been flying Vietnamese out of Tan Son Nhut without inciting riots, that Newport was a closed military facility farther removed from the city than the airport, and that the freighters could be loaded and depart under cover of darkness.

Martin dismissed his arguments and ordered the MSC freighters to leave empty. In a caustic cable to the State Department defending his decision, he said, "I will once again take time I could better use in other ways to explain why we are not using the MSC lift here." He argued that the embassy could evacuate everyone through Tan Son Nhut if that proved necessary, and that although South Vietnam's government had so far overlooked the violation of its immigration laws by Americans who were evacuating their Vietnamese dependents, sending out so many of its citizens at once on the MSC ships could provoke the government into cracking down. He added that everyone on his staff was in agreement that loading evacuees at Newport "would trigger the kind of panic we saw at Da Nang." He closed, "We have had the quietest night anyone can remember as far as military actions are concerned—almost an undisclosed ceasefire—which I had been counting on."

He sent a second cable to Washington reporting that he had ordered one of the MSC freighters to transport seven thousand Nung (ethnic Chinese the United States employed as guards in South Vietnam) to Phu Quoc and that if this intra-Vietnam transfer proved successful, he might resort to a "dodge," and fill up the ship with endangered Vietnamese when it returned, "and instead of going to Phu Quoc, transfer [them] to other ships outside Vietnamese waters." He did not tell Ryder and Berney about his "dodge." Instead, they saw him ordering two empty freighters to sea that could have carried thousands of evacuees to safety. Berney lodged a protest with Admiral Benton, and Benton persuaded the Joint Chiefs to modify Martin's order to permit two of the three ships to remain at Newport for at least another day in the hope that Martin might change his mind. Martin did not, and ordered the two ships to leave Saigon empty and reach international waters by 11:00 a.m. on April 25.

Berney and Ryder encouraged the master of one of these freighters, the *Green Wave,* to board some seven hundred Vietnamese passengers before leaving Newport on April 25. They suggested that once he had cleared South Vietnam's territorial waters, he should inform the embassy that he had conducted a "stowaway search" and had discovered seven hundred stowaways. It was a completely illegal scheme. They were violating South Vietnamese law by encouraging the evacuation of citizens lacking exit visas and passports, and because some of the evacuees were in the armed forces, they were also guilty of encouraging desertion in wartime. They would be sending the refugees to the Philippines, where they would be illegal immigrants upon their arrival. From there the refugees would continue on to the United States without visas or sponsors. To accomplish this, they were using a ship that the U.S. Navy had chartered at a per diem cost of $12,000 and sticking American taxpayers with the bill. Ryder expected the U.S. Navy to bring them up on charges unless South Vietnamese authorities jailed them first. Berney alerted Rear Admiral Benton to their scheme the night before the *Green Wave* departed so he could tell the Seventh Fleet's task force to be prepared to receive the ship after it reached international waters.

On the evening of April 24, Berney and Ryder gathered hundreds of the *Green Wave*'s prospective stowaways in the MSC offices to conceal them from the South Vietnamese Army stevedores who might attempt to block the ship's departure unless their families were included in the evacuation. After the evacuees boarded in the middle of the night, the ship started down the Saigon River at 5:30 a.m., passing downtown while it was still dark. Half an hour later, the second ship departed empty. Upon reaching the three-mile limit, the master of the *Green Wave* notified the embassy that he was carrying seven hundred stowaways. With their evacuation a fait accompli Benton persuaded Martin to claim that he had approved it. It was either that or admit that Berney and Ryder had outfoxed him. Still, there was grumbling at the embassy and Pentagon and talk of bringing Berney and Ryder up on charges.

Benton followed up with a message to CINCPAC warning that the task force should prepare to receive tens of thousands of refugees who were likely to travel down rivers and put out to sea in anything that floated. He cabled, "Possibility substantial outflow of South Vietnamese refugees via water craft to offshore U.S. ships in near future," adding that a dozen MSC merchantmen were in the vicinity and could accommodate 58,000 people and that "approximately 1000 refugees aboard MSC ship SS *Green Wave* on route Subic [the U.S. Navy base in the Philippines] with Ambassador Martin's approval."

CINCPAC replied that Berney or Ryder should join the Seventh Fleet's command ship, USS *Blue Ridge,* and set up a command post to coordinate the activities of the MSC ships. Berney went because he was ill, leaving Ryder in Newport to manage the evacuation on the barges. Berney was relieved to be leaving because, he admitted later, "I was scared silly."

CHAPTER 14

"I Won't Go for That"

——— ┤├ ———

After Phnom Penh fell to the Khmer Rouge on April 17, rumors of widespread executions swept through Can Tho, terrifying the Vietnamese working at Terry McNamara's consulate and other U.S. agencies. During a staff meeting earlier that month, McNamara had suggested that if the Communists seized the Mekong delta, some of his American consulate employees should stay behind to act as witnesses to any atrocities. He argued that their presence might inhibit the Communists, and if not, they could testify at war crimes trials. Although the Communists might imprison them, he doubted they would "kill them out of hand." Afterward, his deputy Hank Cushing, the former English professor, was grinning when he told McNamara, "You scared the shit out of them." McNamara's suggestion reinforced his staff's preference for an evacuation down the Bassac River, which was undoubtedly his goal.

The Khmer Rouge victory gave McNamara his vessels. A friend in AID who had been sending supplies up the Mekong to Phnom Penh offered him two LCMs (landing craft, mechanized), the World War II workhorses that had landed troops and tanks on invasion beaches. Both were sitting idle in Saigon and were perfect for McNamara's scheme. They were eighty feet long, could carry several hundred people, and had a shallow draft, two strong diesel engines, and armor plating and high walls filled with sandbags that would protect the crews and passengers against small-arms fire. McNamara agreed to take them, and their crews drove them down to Can Tho.

On April 22, McNamara sent Averill Christian and David Sciacchitano from his staff to Saigon to check that the embassy was evacuating the Vietnamese whom he had already sent there. They found that instead of the well-planned and comprehensive embassy evacuation operation they had anticipated, the U.S. mission's agencies and individual Americans were competing for seats on the U.S. Air Force transport planes. Meanwhile, the Can Tho Vietnamese were stuck in hotels, at the bottom of the evacuation totem pole. They complained about the situation to Jacobson, who struck Sciacchitano as glassy-eyed and detached from reality. He told them, "Everything will be all right, there's no problem . . . nothing's going to happen. . . . Your people aren't in trouble. Why bother getting them out? There won't be a bloodbath. . . . It's all a bunch of nonsense. Go back to the Delta. The big transport planes and helicopters will get you out."

McNamara found their report so alarming that he helicoptered to the embassy the next day to inform Jacobson that he had his ships.

"Terry, you're not going out by boat. It's too risky," Jacobson said. "You've got to go out by air, and you'll only be able to take Americans because you won't have enough helicopters."

"No. I won't go for that," McNamara said, adding that he would disobey any order to that effect and that given what was happening in Phnom Penh, leaving any of his people behind amounted to signing their death warrants.

Jacobson suggested that he plead his case to Martin. During McNamara's eight months in Can Tho, Martin had always been away or too busy to see him, so he was surprised when Eva Kim immediately ushered him into his office. He told Martin that obeying Jacobson meant abandoning his employees. "I'm not going to do it, Mr. Ambassador," he said. "I've got about five hundred locals who deserve to get out, and I'm getting them out."

Martin jumped up from behind his desk and said, "Let's go and see Lehmann." With McNamara in tow he stormed into Lehmann's office. "What's this about Terry being told he can't get his Vietnamese out of the Delta?" he demanded.

"Oh, no, that isn't right," Lehmann stammered.

"Tell Jacobson it's OK," he said before abruptly marching out.

Lehmann knew Commodore Thang, who commanded the naval detachment at Can Tho. He suggested that McNamara cultivate him, because his friendship might prove invaluable during a river evacuation.

McNamara returned to Jacobson's office to report that he had secured Martin's support.

"That's all very well," Jacobson said. "But when the time comes and you have to get out of there, and the pressure is on and the time is short, don't be surprised if you get an order saying that you have to go by helicopter, and you won't be able to take any Vietnamese."

It seems odd that Martin would order Ryder and Berney's MSC freighters to travel down the Saigon River empty yet would support McNamara's evacuation down the Bassac. But there were differences between these schemes. McNamara's operation did not threaten to spread panic in Saigon, and it involved evacuating Vietnamese working for the U.S. government, instead of private American contractors. It is also possible that there really *was* no rational explanation for why Martin treated these two requests so differently. Both were judgment calls involving the increasingly erratic judgment of a prickly, sickly, stubborn, chain-smoking insomniac whose pride and temperament made it hard for him to second-guess himself.

After returning to Can Tho, McNamara accelerated his preparations. He persuaded the manager of the Shell Oil dock to fill the LCMs' fuel tanks and docked one LCM and his rice barge, the *Delta Queen,* near the consulate at the Delta Compound dock. He parked the other at the Shell Oil dock near Coconut Palms, the CIA living quarters and club that were serving as temporary housing for Vietnamese evacuated from outlying provinces. He took command of the Delta Compound's LCM and rice barge and put a former South Vietnamese Navy lieutenant commander in charge of the other LCM. He summoned Sergeant Hasty, the youthful string bean who commanded the consulate's marine guards, and announced that his men would be protecting an evacuation down the Bassac River. "It sounds dangerous, sir," Hasty said, "but no guts, no glory!" He turned smartly on his heel and marched out of McNamara's office. He had just married his Vietnamese girlfriend and was planning to put her mother and siblings aboard one of the LCMs.

CIA base chief Jim Delaney and his agents were less enthusiastic. They continued to believe that McNamara's scheme was needlessly risky and placed them in additional peril because of their profession. In mid-April, Delaney had asked his deputy to compile a list of the base's key indigenous personnel (KIP)—Vietnamese who had served in sensitive positions—and bring them into Can Tho from the provinces. Delaney's KIP were similar to McNamara's A- and B-list evacuees, and like McNamara with his C-list he had excluded from his KIP category cooks, drivers, and guards. His list was shorter than McNamara's A- and B-lists because he had already sent many of his KIP to Saigon and because McNamara's priority evacuees included third-country nationals, U.S. citizens, and the Vietnamese relatives of U.S. citizens.

Delaney and McNamara continued arguing about the evacuation. The consulate's walls were thin, and CIA agent Jim Parker overheard one of their exchanges. After Delaney insisted that helicopters were "the safest, surest means of evacuation," McNamara shouted, "There are not enough helicopters to go around; there are too many Vietnamese that we must get out." When Delaney asked which Vietnamese McNamara was planning to evacuate, McNamara shouted, "I do not answer to YOU. . . . If we have to evacuate, this consulate goes out by boat down the Bassac River. Period. End of discussion."

Delaney lowered his voice and said, "That is ridiculous. We might have to fight our way out and we are not combatants. . . . We go out by helicopters."

McNamara shouted that the Air America helicopter pilots were "wild, uncontrollable animals," and he did not want them deciding who went and when. "We control our own destiny if we go out by boat," he said. "I have many, many Vietnamese—and Cambodians—I am obligated to get out, and going by boat is the only way we're going to do it."

McNamara reminded Delaney that he was "the senior man on the scene here." Delaney replied in an even voice, "I have *my* people to protect, and I have helicopters. My people go out by helicopter."

McNamara screamed, "You will do what I say." There was a loud crash that sounded like McNamara's large glass ashtray hitting the floor, followed by McNamara screaming, "Get out of my office!"

Delaney continued to prepare for a helicopter evacuation. He told his agents to carry their passports so they could be ready to leave at a moment's notice and ordered the trees surrounding the Coconut Palms tennis court felled so helicopters could land on it. He asked agent Jim Parker to contact CIA deputy air operations officer O. B. Harnage and request that he base three Air America helicopters in the delta on a twenty-four-hour basis.

None of the CIA agents in Can Tho had more at stake in the evacuation than Parker, who was planning to bring out the two Amerasian children that he and his wife had agreed to adopt. Until recently Parker had been based in Vi Thanh, a remote provincial capital encircled by Communist forces. After Phuoc Long fell, the embassy had withdrawn the other official Americans from the province, leaving him on his own, a situation that suited a man who had spent his life seeking adventure and courting danger. He had grown up in North Carolina near Fort Bragg, watching military planes taking off and wishing he was aboard them or jumping from them and seeing trains and Greyhound buses speeding away and wanting to be on them. When he was fifteen, he and a friend had hitchhiked to Florida, caught a boat to Havana, and stayed in a waterfront neighborhood of flickering neon, cigar smoke, and prostitutes. After he returned home, his parents packed him off to a military academy. During his sophomore year at the University of North Carolina, he and some friends left to drive a beat-up jeep through Central America. They ran afoul of pre-Sandinista rebels, escaped to Miami, and returned to Chapel Hill in time for the next semester. Midway through his final exams he enlisted in the army, and by the fall of 1965 he was a lieutenant leading an infantry platoon in Vietnam.

His troops saw a tall, outgoing man with an easy smile, "a man's man." But his laid-back cool concealed a sensitivity at odds with the Vietnam War. The moral dilemma of fighting an enemy that was indistinguishable from the civilian population made him uneasy, and orders one night to shoot anyone violating a 9:00 curfew in a peaceful-looking village set him worrying that his men would kill a schoolboy running an errand for his mother, or a woman returning late from work, and he prayed, "Please, Lord, don't test us tonight." Around midnight a man appeared on a trail they were watching but vanished before Parker's men could open fire. They grumbled about it the next morning, but he was relieved. Another evening his men wounded a suspected Vietcong sniper. The man groaned in agony and cried for help all night, but Parker and his men remained in their positions, fearing a trap. The next morning they found the corpse of an unarmed young man next to a bag of rice. Parker saw him and thought, "I've come halfway around the world to kill a laborer."

He was wounded, crawled through Vietcong tunnels, and lost his best friends, Harold Ayers and Miguel Castro-Carrosquillo. He placed them in what he calls "a closed and locked compartment in the back of my mind." But sometimes they escaped. Two days after their deaths his superior officer announced that the commander of U.S. forces in Vietnam, General William Westmoreland, was coming to award medals to his unit. There were none pending, so Parker had to choose the men least likely to protest participating in a charade. Westmoreland arrived by helicopter with an entourage of reporters and photographers. His uniform was crisp, his jaw prominent. One of his arms was cradled in a sling, an injury suffered on a Saigon tennis court. As flashbulbs popped, he walked down a line of soldiers, pinning Silver Stars on their shirts. As soon as his helicopter lifted off, a major retrieved the medals. Parker told a friend that he had become "a little sick of this war" and could not find much in it to make him proud. In fact, he said, it was "one big fucking waste."

He returned to the States, served a stint as a drill instructor, and left the army rather than return to Vietnam as a replacement. He worked in his father's lumber mill, finished college, married, joined the CIA, and served as a case officer in Laos while his wife lived in Thailand. He asked to be reassigned to Vietnam because "naive as it might sound," he said, he felt he could make a difference. He also had "a lot invested" in the country, including Ayers and Castro-Carrosquillo. The CIA posted him to Chau Doc, a remote provincial capital on the Cambodian border. Saigon Station ("an insulated, bureaucratic institution") ignored his reports and in 1974 transferred him to beleaguered Vi Thanh. The agent he was replacing warned him that it was the most dangerous provincial capital in the country. The Vietcong controlled the countryside, and venturing out was evidence of a death wish. He recommended that Parker double the size of his night guard and keep a loaded revolver handy. "It's all over," he said in parting. "The country's lost."

Despite months of combat and losing Ayers and Castro-Carrosquillo, Parker felt comfortable among Asians. He and his wife, Brenda, had adopted two Thai orphans, and his favorite place in Vi Thanh became a shady orphanage run by Filipino nuns that sat across the river from the town. He spent hours there playing with the orphans, giving them piggyback rides, and throwing them parties with gifts and ice cream. He also spent his days playing chess, Ping-Pong, and tennis with Loi, who commanded his detachment of Nung guards. Their friendship was one of equals, although the tall and rangy Loi usually beat him at tennis. Loi slept outside his bedroom window, and when the Vietcong fired rockets into Vi Thanh and Parker failed to wake up because he had his windows closed and air conditioner on, Loi broke down his door and threw his body across him.

Parker believed that Asians like Loi could sense that he liked them and in turn felt comfortable around him. This probably explains his friendship with Brigadier General Le Van Hung, who commanded the Vi Thanh–based ARVN Twenty-First Division. During lengthy dinners at Hung's quarters they discussed their families, Vietnamese history, and American literature. Hung spoke softly, flashing a pained smile while agonizing over his casualties and complaining about his limited resources. He knew that Parker would report his observations back to the CIA and hoped they might lead to more American military assistance. He was candid, and his predictions were accurate. By the winter of 1975 he had become the CIA's best source of intelligence in the delta.

After Ban Me Thuot fell, the high command put Hung in charge of defending Can Tho and transferred him there. He was courteous and correct with Delaney but clearly preferred dealing with Parker. Delaney ordered Parker to close down Vi Thanh and move to Can Tho so that Hung could brief him. Soon after leaving Vi Thanh, Parker returned to distribute severance pay to his employees and to ask his KIP to move to Can Tho for possible evacuation. Loi gave him a meaningful stare, waiting to be included in the invitation. When Parker called him into his office to receive his money, he refused to take it, burst into tears, and said he wanted to continue working for Parker. Parker's eyes watered and his voice broke. He increased Loi's severance pay, but not enough to ease his conscience. Like many of the guards working for Americans, Loi was a Nung, an ethnic Chinese minority known to be fierce fighters and fiercely loyal. The Communists despised them, and a Nung working for the CIA was doubly damned. Parker capitulated and told Loi to drive the two KIP interpreters to Can Tho. After he arrived, Parker nourished his hopes, telling him to return to Vi Thanh, collect his family, and come back to Can Tho.

By mid-April, Vietnamese officials in Can Tho were abandoning their offices, the line of visa applicants at the consulate was lengthening, and the pile of car and apartment keys that departing CIA agents had left on Jim Delaney's secretary's desk was growing higher. CIA station chief Tom Polgar chose this moment for what he imagined being a morale-boosting visit. Instead, his briefing confirmed the agents' suspicions that Saigon Station was either dangerously out of touch or deluded about conditions in the delta. Polgar assured them that there was "nothing to worry about" and promised that there would be work in the delta "for generations of CIA case officers." The agents recalled Terry Balls making a similar boast when he delivered his optimistic briefing in February. They had considered it nonsense then, and it seemed even more absurd now.

When Polgar said "South Vietnam will survive," agent Tom Fosmire interrupted to say that he doubted that South Vietnam's military had sufficient morale to survive.

Parker told Polgar that after fighting for decades to unify the country, he doubted that the Communists would halt outside Saigon and "sue for peace."

Polgar brushed off their objections and said that South Vietnam had "a bright future."

Parker and Fosmire met at the CIA club afterward. They agreed that either Polgar was crazy or they were. "But crazy or not," Fosmire said, "the North Vietnamese are going to win this war, flat out, whether that desk warrior likes it or not."

In mid-April, Jim Parker received his first angry and expletive-filled briefing from Brigadier General Tran Van Hai, who commanded the Seventh ARVN Division, the unit responsible for protecting the northern approaches to Can Tho. Hung had given Parker an introduction to Hai. The two generals could not have been more different. Hung was sensitive, reticent, and soft-spoken; Hai was a pudgy-faced, hard-eyed man who had acquired an impressive lexicon of battlefield obscenities from his American advisers. He greeted Parker by condemning the United States for "abandoning us on the fucking battlefield, in our darkest hour . . . just political shit on top of political shit, so that it all stinks," adding that there was "not a breath of honesty or honor among you guys. And that includes you, you turdy American piece of shit."

When Parker attempted to steer the conversation to the military situation, Hai said, "You want information, U.S. government man. I want helicopter parts. I want ammunition." He was a chain-smoker, never without a cigarette. He stared at Parker and said through a cloud of smoke, "You Americans don't always keep your word to us Vietnamese 'slope heads.'"

O. B. Harnage was the man in the white shirt leaning down to pull a passenger aboard a helicopter perched on a Saigon roof in Hugh Van Es's iconic photograph. Here he is standing in front of the U.S. embassy Air Operations headquarters at Tan Son Nhut.

President Gerald R. Ford meets with (from left to right) Graham Martin, ambassador to Vietnam, army chief of staff General Frederick Weyand, and Secretary of State Henry Kissinger in the Oval Office on March 25, 1975. During this meeting Martin predicted that South Vietnam's armed forces would give the Communists "a helluva scrap."

U.S. POWs held in Hanoi by the Provisional Revolutionary Government of South Vietnam (Vietcong) being released during the implementation of the 1973 Paris Peace Accords. Bill Bell (far right) acted as a translator at the release ceremony.

(ABOVE) Walter Martindale on board the USS *Blue Ridge* on May 1, 1975. Martindale led his Vietnamese friends and staff to safety in a hastily assembled convoy after the Communists overran Quang Duc province.

(RIGHT) Tom Glenn in Saigon in 1974. Glenn headed the National Security Agency detachment in South Vietnam. The U.S. embassy in Saigon discounted and dismissed his warnings that the Communists would attack Saigon in April 1975.

(BELOW) James Parker in Vi Thanh. When he arrived in the besieged provincial capital in 1974, the CIA agent he was replacing told him, "It's all over. The country's lost."

Da Nang deputy consul general Theresa Tull with Lieutenant General Ngo Quang Truong, Military Region I corps commander, at the U.S. Consulate General's July 4, 1974, reception in Da Nang. Before leaving Da Nang for good in late March 1975, Tull agreed to evacuate three of Truong's children and raise them as her own in the United States.

(ABOVE, LEFT) Air America pilot Marius Burke several days before the fall of Da Nang. On April 30, he spent fourteen hours in the air and was the last Air America pilot to stop flying.

(ABOVE, RIGHT) Ken Moorefield (in sunglasses) leading a patrol in South Vietnam during the war. After leaving the U.S. Army, Moorefield ran into Graham Martin's son in Washington, leading to a dinner with Martin and his surprising offer to Moorefield that he accompany him to Saigon as his special assistant.

Vietnamese fleeing Da Nang crowded onto a ship preparing to dock at Cam Ranh Bay on March 30, 1975. Soon after David Kennerly took this photograph, renegade South Vietnamese marines opened fire on his helicopter.

U.S. consul general Al Francis waves from a tugboat in Cam Ranh Bay shortly after escaping from Communist forces in Da Nang. Francis would later complain to Ken Moorefield that Martin was dismissing his warning that the collapse of South Vietnamese forces that had occurred in Da Nang could be replicated in Saigon.

Refugees riding on the back of a truck between Cam Ranh Bay and Nha Trang on March 30, 1975. David Kennerly took this photograph while driving to Cam Ranh Bay with Walter Martindale. The scenes along the highway reminded them of World War II newsreels of refugees fleeing the Nazis.

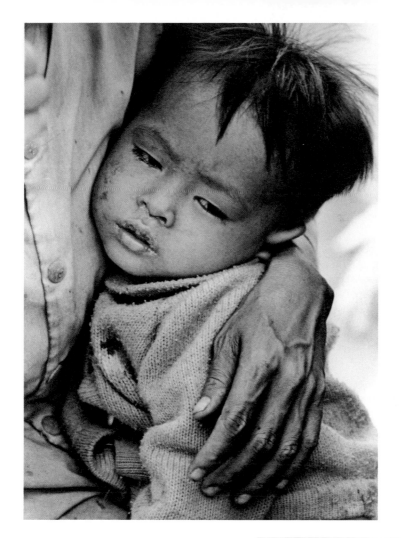

(ABOVE) A sick Vietnamese child in his mother's arms at Cam Ranh Bay on March 30, 1975. A week later this photograph and others taken by David Kennerly would be hanging in the White House on orders from President Ford.

(RIGHT) David Hume Kennerly aboard a U.S. Army helicopter in the Central Highlands of South Vietnam, 1971. Kennerly was White House photographer under Gerald Ford and a member of the last presidential fact-finding mission of the war.

President Gerald R. Ford carries a Vietnamese orphan from the Pan Am jet that brought approximately 325 South Vietnamese orphans to San Francisco International Airport. The flight landed one day after the catastrophic crash of the Babylift flight that killed Bill Bell's wife and son.

South Vietnamese babies on a chartered Pan Am 747 flying from Saigon to the United States during Operation Babylift.

Bill Bell's wife, Nova, and his children, Michael and Andrea, in Saigon during March 1975. Nova and Michael died in the April 4, 1975, Babylift crash. Bell accompanied Andrea back to California for medical treatment but then returned to Saigon so he could help evacuate his Vietnamese friends.

(RIGHT) Ross Meador with three of the orphans he supervised at the Friends of the Children of Vietnam orphanage.

Al Topping was the Pan Am station manager during Operation Babylift and also evacuated over 300 of his Vietnamese employees by "adopting" them. He is standing in front of the former Pan Am office during a visit to Saigon (now Ho Chi Minh City) in 1990. Note that fifteen years later the Pan Am logo is still above the front door.

Erich von Marbod (in beret) inspecting a South Vietnamese Army forward position. South Vietnamese troops had presented him with a paratrooper uniform and urged him to wear it because men dressed in civilian clothes attracted the attention of Communist snipers. This position was overrun by North Vietnamese forces on April 28, 1975.

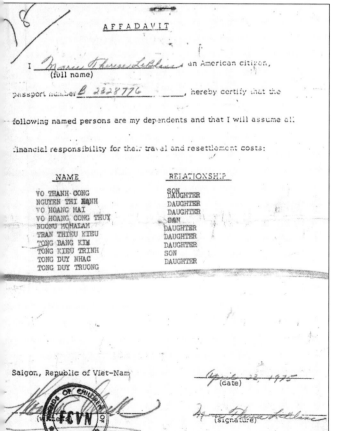

An affidavit of support signed by Sister Marie Therese LeBlanc, who worked at the Friends of the Children of Vietnam. Notice that she has named ten children as her sons and daughters and has agreed to assume financial responsibility for them. This was the affidavit of support that Major General Homer Smith proposed at a meeting with Graham Martin and others at the U.S. embassy on April 19, 1975.

The staff of the CBS Saigon bureau. Brian Ellis is standing at the far right, next to the wall. His employees were people he cared deeply about. In April 1975 they entrusted him with their lives.

(RIGHT) CBS Saigon bureau chief Brian Ellis and CBS news correspondent Ed Bradley on assignment in Vietcong territory in 1973. Their Vietcong translator is sitting between them.

(BELOW) Some of the U.S. news agencies' Vietnamese employees on a bus taking them to Tan Son Nhut for evacuation.

Colonel John Madison, the chief of the U.S. delegation to the Four-Party Joint Military Team, standing next to North and South Vietnamese representatives to the JMT during a meeting in Hanoi in late 1974.

The Vietnamese employees of the U.S. delegation to the JMT and their families at Tan Son Nhut in late April 1975. Colonel Madison had arranged to have them secretly assembled there and evacuated on U.S. Air Force transports that were otherwise returning largely empty to the Philippines.

Remains of the rocket that killed marine guards Charles McMahon and Darwin Judge during a surprise Communist rocket attack on Tan Son Nhut early on the morning of April 29, 1975. McMahon and Judge were the last U.S. service members killed in action in South Vietnam.

(RIGHT) Colonel John Madison (right) and Captain Stuart Herrington of the U.S. delegation to the JMT upon arriving at the U.S. embassy on the morning of April 29, 1975. They had been told that they would remain at the embassy to negotiate with the Communists after other American personnel had been evacuated.

John Madison speaking with marine corporal Kevin Maloney on the USS *Okinawa* on April 30, 1975. Maloney was in command of a marine detachment guarding the U.S. compound at Tan Son Nhut and later helped Ken Moorefield lead a convoy of buses through Saigon on April 29, 1975.

Can Tho consul-general Terry McNamara at helm of an LST during the evacuation that he led down the Bassac River on April 29, 1975. Several armed members of his consulate staff are standing in front of him.

South Vietnamese clamber aboard one of Bill Ryder's barges at a wharf in downtown Saigon. The high sandbag walls had been added to protect the ordnance that the barges had formerly carried up the river to Cambodia.

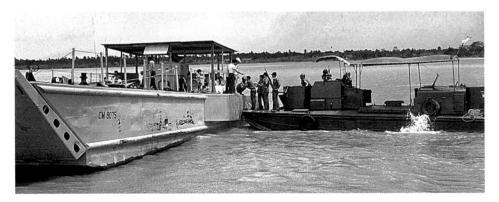

A South Vietnamese Navy gunboat intercepting Terry McNamara's LST on April 29, 1975. An hour later, Commodore Thang arrived on the scene and ordered the gunboat to permit McNamara to proceed down the river. A week earlier McNamara had evacuated Thang's family, telling him, "If we do have to evacuate I'm intending to go down the river and we may need your help."

The MSC freighter *Pioneer Contender* loaded with refugees off the port of Vung Tau on the morning of April 30, 1975. On the top deck is the bridge where CIA agent James Parker stood while seeing Vietnam for the last time.

South Vietnamese attempting to scale the walls of the U.S. embassy on April 29, 1975. The two Americans looking over the top of the gate are attempting to pick out any of their employees from the crowd and help them into the embassy compound.

The U.S. embassy in downtown Saigon. The helipad can be seen on top. The building was sometimes likened to a giant toaster or air conditioner.

Evacuees crowded into the U.S. embassy's recreation area while awaiting transportation to the U.S. fleet.

Evacuees boarding a U.S. Marine helicopter in the embassy parking lot on April 29, 1975.

Evacuees who had been helicoptered from the embassy assembled on the deck of the USS *Okinawa* on the morning of April 30, 1975.

Graham Martin being interviewed by journalists on the USS *Blue Ridge* on the morning of April 30, 1975. A reporter described his eyes as "flat" and his skin as "chalky." He mumbled the answers to a few questions before bumming a cigarette from a journalist.

Lt. General Ngo Quang Truong's children outside Theresa Tull's home in Washington, D.C., on July 4, 1976. General Truong and his wife managed to escape South Vietnam, and Tull remained close to the family.

His division faced General Tich, the best field general in the North Vietnamese Army. "You know what the slogan of his division is?" Hai asked. "'Obliterate the enemy.' That's me. You know what the slogan of the army helping us is? 'Fuck your friends.'"

Parker helicoptered to Hai's headquarters several times a week to listen to his arias of insults. Hai criticized the United States for not sending troops into Cambodia to destroy North Vietnamese sanctuaries, calling it a "simple military situation" and asking, "What do you think of that, CIA man?" Parker thought about the tens of thousands of U.S. troops who had died trying to keep South Vietnam's corrupt government afloat, but held his tongue. Like other Americans serving out the final days of Kissinger's decent interval, his job was to accept the blame and do penance for the mistakes and broken promises of Americans who had long since left or had made a mess of the war without leaving Washington.

During one briefing Hai shouted at Parker that the American government "stinks like leper shit" and that Americans had violated a soldier's code of honor by abandoning their comrades in arms on the battlefield. Hai would have preferred to tell Kissinger or Martin that they stank of leper shit, but had to settle for Parker. Another time he stood up, and putting a hand on the butt of his revolver, he said, "I should kill you in the name of all the good men who died in this war."

After Congress rejected Ford's request for $722 million in additional aid, Parker wondered if Hai really might shoot him. The Air America pilots flying him to Hai's headquarters preferred not to remain on the ground because it put their helicopters within range of North Vietnamese artillery. This time Parker told pilot Cliff Hendryx that he was afraid Hai might become violent and persuaded him to stick around. Hendryx set down near Hai's tent so Parker could make a quick escape, and he and his co-pilot held automatic rifles at the ready. Hai glared at Parker before standing up and approaching him. His right hand was inches from his sidearm, but instead of shooting him, he delivered a tirade that concluded with his calling Senator Frank Church, who had loudly opposed Ford's request for $722 million in emergency assistance, "worse than Hitler."

On April 17, Hai told Parker that the North had massed fresh units and additional armor, artillery, and portable bridges across the border in Cambodia. It was a larger force than necessary to defeat Hai's division, so he assumed Saigon was the target. Two days later, he told Parker that once the North had placed heavy attack tanks and bridging units in front of these fresh troops, an attack on Saigon was imminent. On April 22 he reported that this repositioning had just occurred and fresh troops had fallen in behind the tanks. He predicted that Saigon would fall in seven days. Raising a cup of lukewarm coffee, he proposed that he and Parker toast all the soldiers who had died in the war. Nine days later he committed suicide by drinking a shot of whiskey laced with poison.

Delaney believed Hai's forecasts but was in a bind because Saigon Station was discouraging reporting that contradicted Martin and Polgar's line that the Communists intended to capture Saigon through negotiations. When Parker reported Hai's predictions, Delaney sometimes made a show of putting his hands over his ears, signaling that he did not want to hear anything contradicting the "party line"—a gesture perfectly symbolizing the reaction of earlier American military and political leaders to bad news from Vietnam. Delaney's and Parker's earlier cables had tempered Hai's brutal message, but they relayed his warning that the Communists would take Saigon on April 29 in unvarnished terms. To Parker's surprise, neither Saigon nor Langley pushed back. The CIA graded intelligence reports on a scale from one to twenty with twenty being the highest score possible. After Saigon fell, Parker's report received a twenty.

After weathering Hai's verbal abuse, Parker often stopped on his way into Can Tho from the airport at a small wooden bungalow where he received another lecture about American treachery from "Chau," the mother of two Amerasian children whom he and his wife, Brenda, had agreed to adopt. "Is this the American way to be a friend?" she demanded. "You don't care about us. You used us. Yes, you and your countrymen. I cry inside all the time. I will die soon because of you. You destroyed my life. My country. We trusted you. You used us and now you leave. Good-bye, Vietnam. Sorry."

He listened without complaint because she was right. Two Americans had impregnated her and broken their promises to marry her and bring her to the United States, leaving her alone to raise her two outcast Amerasian children.

For weeks Parker had been trying to avoid meeting someone like Chau. Every morning he walked into the consulate past a gauntlet of young women waving the tattered letters from former American lovers that they hoped to transform into visas and plane tickets. He knew that he was susceptible to their entreaties and avoided reading their letters or meeting their eyes. On April 14, his friend Glenn Rounsevell asked him if he would consider adopting the two Amerasian children of a female acquaintance. Rounsevell, who knew Parker was partial to orphans, said that the woman was already in the consulate and waiting to meet him. Parker found a beautiful woman in her early thirties sitting in an interview room off the lobby. She said that she adored her children, was afraid that the Communists would harm them, and had heard that after taking over the North in 1954, the Communists had murdered some Franco-Vietnamese children. After crying, "I don't want my children to die!," she burst into tears.

Parker suggested that the Communists might not take the delta.

She predicted that soon a North Vietnamese official would be sitting in this same room, interviewing her and weighing the fate of her children. "Let them live!" she begged. "Send them to your wife!"

Parker visited her home and found "grand-looking, healthy, everyday children." The house was bright and neat. Toys and stuffed animals filled her children's rooms—proof of how much she loved them. The four-year-old girl had penetrating, intelligent eyes that reminded him of his daughter. The two-year-old boy was rambunctious and beguiling. Parker was smitten. He called Brenda and she agreed to take them. Her only concern was that Chau might reach the United States and try to reclaim them. She said that Chau must agree that the adoption would be final, adding, "I will not be used."

Parker stopped at Chau's house to become acquainted with his future son and daughter. The girl gripped his hand, examining his fingers and watching his lips as he spoke. Her brother tried on Parker's glasses and rummaged through his pockets. With each visit Chau became angrier and more emotional. He sensed her beginning to hate him.

He asked her to take the children out of school so they could be ready to leave at a moment's notice. She packed their clothes and birth certificates into two small plastic suitcases plastered with Disney cartoon characters and lined them up by the door so they could grab them and run. When he left her house for the last time, he looked back to see his future daughter standing in the doorway next to her Disney suitcase, ready for America.

CHAPTER 15

Kissinger's Cable

NBC Vietnam War correspondent David Butler has written that if Ambassador Martin's critics among the "aggressive young activists" in the U.S. mission could have read the "eyes only" cable that Martin received from Henry Kissinger on the morning of April 25, they might have been "more forgiving of the ambassador's calm, his seeming inaction."

More than any single cable, this one would determine how many Vietnamese would escape during the next five days, and when. It began, "We have just received a reply to our initiative to the Soviets which is quoted below." The "initiative" was an oral note—a written but unsigned document that has the diplomatic status of a conversation. President Ford had addressed the oral note to Soviet leader Leonid Brezhnev, and Kissinger had delivered it to Soviet ambassador Anatoly Dobrynin on Friday, April 18. It asked that the U.S.S.R. "use its good offices to achieve a temporary halt to the fighting" and said that a "temporary cease fire" would "save lives and permit the continued evacuation of American citizens and the South Vietnamese to whom we have a direct and special obligation." In exchange, Ford said, the United States was "prepared to discuss the special political circumstances that could make this possible," an artfully couched promise to seek Thieu's resignation and his replacement by a leader prepared to negotiate with Hanoi.

The note cautioned that "the situation in Vietnam has now

reached a point, that the United States and the USSR must consider the long term consequences of further developments there for Soviet-American relations," a veiled threat that the current détente between Washington and Moscow could be imperiled unless the U.S.S.R. used "its good offices to achieve a temporary halt to the fighting." Kissinger had helped engineer the détente, and it had culminated in President Nixon and Soviet premier Brezhnev signing the 1972 Strategic Arms Limitation Talks Treaty. The two nations had also signed agreements on East-West trade, human rights, and other areas of dispute, ushering in a hoped-for era of peaceful coexistence. The détente had become frayed since then, but encouraging the Soviet Union to exert pressure on Hanoi remained Kissinger's last best hope for a cease-fire.

After delivering Ford's oral note to Dobrynin, Kissinger expanded on the arguments for a temporary cease-fire in Vietnam, telling Dobrynin that the United States was not going to the Chinese but directing its appeal solely to Moscow "because it is in our long term mutual interest that the situation be brought to its conclusion in a manner that does not jeopardize Soviet-American relations."

He did not cable the text of the oral note to Martin until Wednesday, April 23. At that time he informed Martin that Dobrynin had reported that the note was receiving "urgent study" in Moscow and had been passed to Hanoi.

The Soviets answered on April 24, telling Kissinger that "the position of the Vietnamese side on the question of evacuation of American citizens is definitely favorable" and that Hanoi would not "put any obstacles" in their way. In what Kissinger considered the most significant sentence in their response, the Soviets stated, "It was emphasized [by Hanoi] that in the struggle for achieving a political settlement, the [North] Vietnamese side will proceed from the Paris Agreement, we are also told that the [North] Vietnamese do not intend to damage the reputation of the United States."

Kissinger read the Soviet reply to an April 24 afternoon meeting of the National Security Council. He said that he interpreted it as meaning that "as long as we keep the dialogue going we have an assurance against military action as we pull our people out." He added that the possibility of tripartite negotiations between North and South Vietnam and the PRG "gives us the hope of a coalition solution which can be better than surrender."

President Ford suggested that the Communists' willingness to negotiate might explain the lull in the fighting following Thieu's resignation and said, "This looks like they are willing for an agreement within the framework of the Paris Accords and that we can keep our people there, and reduce them until such time as we decide to remove them." Although the Soviet note had mentioned only the evacuation of American citizens and not Vietnamese, Kissinger told the NSC that he interpreted it as saying, "Get them [all] out."

After the meeting Kissinger drafted a cable to Martin that due to the twelve-hour time difference arrived in Saigon on the morning of April 25. Kissinger opened by stroking Martin's ego, telling him, "I want you to know that in sending you the details of my negotiations, I am doing something I have never done before." He then offered an interpretation of the Soviet reply that vindicated Martin, saying that it indicated that "we will be permitted to continue our evacuation, including the evacuation of Vietnamese, unimpeded," and that the PRG was prepared "to undertake negotiations in the tripartite formulation." He gave Martin's ego a final stroke by adding, "The Soviet reply indicates to me that your judgment about the time we have left is correct."

Although Kissinger embraced the Soviet reply to the oral note as an encouraging development, one that might facilitate the evacuation of endangered South Vietnamese, he still feared that once most of Saigon's American residents had been evacuated, Secretary of Defense Schlesinger and Chairman of the Joint Chiefs Brown, with the support of Congress, would end the airlift, abandoning thousands of Vietnamese. With this in mind, he told Martin that reducing the nongovernmental and nonessential Americans to around eight hundred by Sunday, April 27, would be "satisfactory." He followed this with a revealing sentence, saying, "There is a great deal to be said for trickling Americans out slowly after Sunday to keep the airlift going and thus stay within the literal terms of the Soviet note." He was referring here to the Soviet statement that Hanoi's position was that "the question of evacuation of American citizens . . . is definitely favorable."

Kissinger knew that Ford was insisting on evacuating the remaining Americans and that Schlesinger and Brown wanted to accomplish this as quickly as possible. Still, he was encouraging Martin to "trickle" out the remaining Americans slowly so that the airlift of endangered South Vietnamese could continue. Kissinger had spoken of America's "moral responsibility" to rescue its Vietnamese allies in press conferences, at meetings, and in cables that he knew would be part of the official record. But giving Martin a green light to slow the evacuation of Americans to a trickle, an order that he knew Martin would embrace, demonstrates that not only did he believe the United States had a responsibility to evacuate endangered Vietnamese but was prepared to encourage Martin to discharge it. He explained himself a decade later, writing, "We would not be able to evacuate any South Vietnamese friends unless we prolonged the withdrawal of Americans, for Congress would surely cut off all funds with the departure of the last American."

In his reply to Kissinger's cable, Martin urged him to keep the ambassador's role in the evacuation secret. He reported that to date (April 25) twenty-one thousand Vietnamese had departed on U.S. military planes and that "99% of this movement was illegal in accordance with Vietnamese law." He closed by saying, "You are quite right that I feel as you do, a very heavy moral obligation to evacuate as many deserving Vietnamese as possible. I feel it so deeply that I refrain from commenting about it or putting it in the official reports to the Department which some damn fool leaks to the press and endangers cutting off our ability to continue as we are."

More evidence that Kissinger viewed the airlift of Americans as a cover for rescuing South Vietnamese can be found in his April 23 telephone conversation with Senator Strom Thurmond of South Carolina—a conversation also showing that not every U.S. senator was as opposed to evacuating Vietnamese as members of the Foreign Relations Committee. After telling Thurmond that the administration was "continuing to reduce" the American population, Kissinger said,

"Between you and me, we're taking out many Vietnamese." Thurmond replied, "I'm glad. They stood by us and we should stand by them." Kissinger responded, "Not everybody in Washington feels that way."

Another senator who *did* feel that way was Edward Kennedy. Kissinger called him on April 21 to ask that he lobby his fellow senators to support giving the administration parole authority to admit Vietnamese refugees. Kennedy said that he was interested in "initiatives" that could provide "protection of the population there." Kissinger replied, "We really owe it to the fifteen years of effort to get some of the key people out." Kennedy agreed, saying, "I think that is right."

The Soviet response to Ford's oral note convinced Kissinger and Martin that an emergency evacuation of the remaining Americans was less urgent. By holding out the promise of a lengthy period of negotiations, it made expending the time and effort needed to plan an emergency evacuation seem unnecessary. Martin spelled this out in a cable to Kissinger, writing that "the need for [an] emergency evacuation appears more and more remote."

On April 26, a day after suggesting that Martin trickle out Americans, Kissinger cabled, "Do not worry about arrangements for the onward movement of evacuees. That is our problem and we will take care of it. Just keep the evacuees coming and do not slow down." He closed, "I may have an odd way of showing it, but you have my full support."

Kissinger's April 25 cable had been "eyes only" for Martin, but he showed it to Polgar, at the same time threatening to "cut off your balls and stuff them in your ears" if he shared it with anyone. Polgar shared the gist of it with others anyway. Those who were privy to it displayed a confidence and preternatural calm that puzzled, distressed, and angered their subordinates and others. When a foreign diplomat informed Wolfgang Lehmann that he and his staff were departing the next day, Lehmann, who knew about the cable, said, "No, you don't really have to go. We're staying. The North Vietnamese aren't going to take Saigon. There'll be an arrangement."

Several hours after receiving Kissinger's cable, Martin had lunch in the embassy canteen. He shared a table with a CIA agent who said that he was setting up a network of stay-behind agents. Martin smiled and said that he doubted that would be necessary, adding, "I hope we'll all be staying on." Later that afternoon he told Marius Burke, the Air America pilot whom he had forbidden to paint an *H* on rooftop helipads, that he had "good information" that Saigon was "off-limits" to the North Vietnamese. He cabled Admiral Gayler on April 27, "Through other channels we have increasing evidence that Hanoi has given tacit acquiescence to permitting evacuation operations to continue uninterrupted while the political solution in Saigon continues in a way they deem favorable." On April 28, with South Vietnam's surrender two days away, he cabled Kissinger that he believed there would be an official American presence in Saigon for "a year or more."

After reading Kissinger's April 25 cable, Polgar told his two American secretaries that he thought they would all be in Saigon for at least another six months and suggested they cancel their plane reservations. He also modified his plan to evacuate the CIA's U.S. and Vietnamese employees from Bien Hoa, telling his agents there that because he foresaw the formation of a coalition government, they should stash their Vietnamese in safe houses instead of moving them to Saigon.

CIA agent Don Kanes arrived in Saigon from Can Tho on April 25. He told Polgar that Jim Delaney had sent him to facilitate the departure of the Can Tho KIP. "Well, I guess you might as well," Polgar replied, "but it looks like the deal is being set." He told Kanes that as soon as retired general Duong Van "Big" Minh became president, there would be negotiations and a coalition government, adding, "The North Vietnamese don't want the world to see them marching into Saigon."

"I don't think they're worried about their image," Kanes said.

The next day Kanes heard the same line from Charles Timmes, the retired general who advised Martin on military affairs. "The fix is in," Timmes told him. "Big Minh will become president, and there'll be some adjustments."

Polgar had cultivated a professional friendship with Colonel Janos Toth, the Hungarian military attaché. When they met at Polgar's villa on the afternoon of April 25, Toth reinforced the Soviet reply, saying that according to his "friends in the North" Hanoi preferred negotiations to an assault on Saigon. The Communists had three preconditions: Thieu's departure; a new government in which the North had "confidence"; and a declaration from the United States that it would stay out of Vietnamese affairs, recall its military advisers, and reduce its embassy to a conventional size. Toth said that the PRG delegation at Camp Davis wanted Polgar to serve as an intermediary in talks between them and the Saigon government. Polgar trusted Toth because they were fellow Hungarians. He returned to the embassy in an ebullient mood, telling CIA agent Frank Snepp, "You see, I was right. There's a chance for some kind of deal. They want me as an intermediary."

Polgar had been optimistic about negotiations even before reading Kissinger's cable. For several weeks *New York Times* correspondent Malcolm Browne had been serving as his secret intermediary with Phuong Nam, who handled the PRG's press relations at Camp Davis. Browne told Nam that according to Polgar the United States wanted a peaceful end to the war, the safe evacuation of Americans, and negotiations leading to a coalition government. Browne reported to Polgar that Nam had hinted that all this was possible but remained vague about how to accomplish it. After reading the Soviet note, Polgar infected Browne with his optimism, leading Browne to tell UPI reporter Peter Arnett, "Peter, there will be no final battle, believe me. I am plugged in better now with all sides than I have ever been in my life."

Martin could not resist gloating. Hours after receiving Kissinger's cable, he told Scowcroft, "Events have validated what I felt all along— that as long as progress could be made we really could count on the DRV [Democratic Republic of Vietnam] desire for a peaceful evolution insofar as the transfer of power . . . to avoid massive attack on Saigon."

He dispatched a self-congratulatory cable to Kissinger the next day, writing that the Soviet note "clearly indicates that there will be no interference with the evacuation of Americans" and reminding him, "I have always believed this." He predicted that the Communists would show "considerable patience" as they followed a strategy of using "the threat of their military dominance in the environs of Saigon to force the pace of political evolution in Saigon to the formation of a Big Minh government to be followed by negotiations." During that evolution he "saw no reason why the United States would not keep an embassy here." He called Kissinger's earlier question of how he and his staff planned to leave "a bit premature" and predicted that after General Minh's inauguration the embassy would remain "for a considerable period." He closed by reminding Kissinger, "You once paid me a very great compliment—that I was one of the very few people you knew capable of totally dispassionate and objective analysis." He said that in recent weeks he had recalled that praise and had "tried to keep even more aloof from emotion than usual," adding, "It turns out I have been right so far, which is unforgivably infuriating to the bureaucracy."

Kissinger shared his optimism. He alluded to Ford's oral note to Brezhnev and Brezhnev's reply during his conversation with Ted Kennedy. When Kennedy asked if declaring Saigon an open city was under consideration, he replied that they were "waiting some possible moves and are in touch." When Kennedy asked if the negotiations would be just "window dressing," he said, "I don't think so," adding, "Incidentally, this is a strictly private conversation."

One day after receiving the Soviet reply, Kissinger briefed Ford and Scowcroft on its implications, on France's attempts to broker a cease-fire, and an encouraging approach from the PRG representative in Paris. Ford said it all sounded "encouraging and interesting" and asked, "If it developed would we keep an embassy there?"

Kissinger encouraged Martin's optimism. In a "Sensitive via Martin Channels" cable of April 26 he said, "My thinking regarding the political evolution in Saigon is that following the formation of a Minh government, there will be negotiations which will result more or less rapidly in an agreement on a tripartite government [North, South, and PRG]." After pointing out that this new government would be "two-thirds 'Communist' and one third controlled by them," Kissinger said that they would then have to decide about the future of the embassy. He believed that at some juncture "the North will decide to prevent the future evacuation of Vietnamese" and that the United States would then have to decide "whether to close the embassy or maintain a token presence." He asked Martin to give him his "considered judgment" on what might happen and do it by "the opening of business here on Monday." This meant Monday evening Saigon time, several hours after General Minh would be inaugurated and North Vietnam would attack Tan Son Nhut.

During a White House meeting on April 29, and at a later press conference, Kissinger would say that throughout the morning of April 28 in Saigon he had believed it was "highly probable" that the war would end in a cease-fire and negotiated settlement. Years later, however, he claimed that despite the Soviet note he had been skeptical that Hanoi would negotiate, calling it a "slim hope." He had been "certain," he wrote, that Le Duc Tho, with whom he had negotiated the Paris Peace Accords, "would never acquiesce in a gradual transfer of authority or any autonomous political structure in Saigon, however temporary—not even an autonomous Communist one," and that "Hanoi would take no chances on the emergence of Titoism in South Vietnam." But these ex post facto assertions are unconvincing when measured against his cables to Martin, his conversations with Ford and Ted Kennedy, and his actions following the Soviet response of April 24. These all suggest that Moscow and Hanoi had bamboozled him, as well as Martin, Ford, Polgar, and others, into believing that a cease-fire and negotiations conducted within the structure of the Paris Peace Accords would be the Vietnam War's most likely outcome.

For Kissinger, a cease-fire followed by negotiations and a slow-motion surrender was an appealing scenario. It would affirm the value of his détente with the Soviet Union, spare the United States the humiliation of a panicky evacuation, allow it to rescue its South Vietnamese, preserve the fiction that the Paris Peace Accords remained in effect, and reassure its Cold War allies. For Martin, it would prove that he had been right about Hanoi's reluctance to capture Saigon by force of arms and correct to have resisted a precipitous drawdown of the mission's U.S. employees. And it would save him from becoming the man who had concluded a glittering diplomatic career by losing South Vietnam.

Because Martin, Kissinger, and Polgar wanted to believe that Hanoi preferred negotiations, they inflated the importance of anything appearing to confirm it. They were encouraged by a *New York Times* story from its Moscow correspondent reporting that "well-placed sources" in the Kremlin had said that based on recent cables from Soviet diplomats in Hanoi, North Vietnam had decided not to attack Saigon during "the current campaign." Martin cabled Kissinger that France's ambassador to South Vietnam, Jean-Marie Mérillon, had told him that the French had advised Hanoi "not to press an immediate military attack at the moment" and to follow "a negotiating track" that promised "results much more favorable to Hanoi in terms of world public opinion." The current lull in the fighting, Martin said, appeared to confirm that Hanoi was listening to the French. Mérillon was so confident that negotiations would occur that on April 24 he recommended that the ten thousand French citizens in Saigon remain because a cease-fire appeared "imminent."

But on April 25, the same day that Martin received Kissinger's cable, the Communist delegations at Camp Davis began digging bunkers, and U.S. intelligence intercepted a message to Hanoi from a member of North Vietnam's delegation saying that if Communist forces had to shell Tan Son Nhut, they would consider it an "honor" to lose their lives "for the total victory of the campaign." It would later be revealed that on April 25 the commander of the North Vietnamese armed forces, General Van Tien Dung, had ordered his army to attack Saigon on April 29. His 1977 memoirs confirmed that the talk of negotiations, a tripartite government, and a cease-fire had been part of a disinformation campaign orchestrated by Hanoi, abetted by Moscow, and aimed at persuading South Vietnam to relax its defensive planning. France would later acknowledge that it had been "outrageously deceived."

Martin had canceled the Joint Military Team's April 18 liaison flight to prevent the Communist delegations from evacuating their senior cadre. But after receiving Kissinger's encouraging cable, he decided that the Friday, April 25, flight should proceed as planned. Bill Bell and Colonel Harry Summers, the second-in-command of the U.S. JMT delegation, flew to Hanoi to represent the United States at the weekly JMT meeting. Summers headed the Negotiations Division for the U.S. delegation, a job that entailed persuading the Communist delegations to reveal the location of American MIAs. He anticipated that while he was in Hanoi, the Communists might attempt to negotiate a cease-fire and political settlement with him. Before leaving, he asked Jim Devine, the embassy's chief political-military officer, "What are my negotiating instructions?"

"Damned if I know," Devine said.

But what was he supposed to do? Summers asked.

"Do the best you can," Devine suggested.

After boarding the plane, Bell noticed that the Communists were sending their senior cadre to Hanoi. He assumed that they would be briefing the Politburo on conditions in Saigon and the preparations being made to defend it. The passengers sat facing each other on benches along the side of the C-130. The members of South Vietnam's delegation were subdued and expressionless, already resigned to defeat. (Bell had recently evacuated their families.) The PRG and North Vietnamese delegations were usually somber and poker-faced. On this day they were ebullient and chatty. They pretended to be concerned about the American delegation losing face, a bogus solicitousness that Bell found harder to swallow than their customary lectures about the glories of socialism. Colonel Nguyen Tu, who headed the DRV North Vietnamese delegation, told him and Summers, "You Americans should not feel so badly, you did everything you could." Summers pointed out that the U.S. military had never lost a major battle. "Yes, that is correct," Tu replied, "but it is also irrelevant." This succinct exchange would become a frequently quoted epitaph for the Vietnam War, following Summers through his distinguished career as an author, academic, columnist, and television commentator on international affairs.

Bell and Summers noticed that the Communists had augmented their customary program of humiliations. Instead of eating lunch at the usual hotel, they were told that they would be eating at the Thong Nhat Hotel, a term meaning "reunification" in Vietnamese. Bell noticed that sacks of rice had been placed throughout the lobby where the delegations could see them. Their labels said "donated by the people of China," a reminder to the South Vietnamese of who had the more generous ally.

The rumors that Thieu's resignation had paved the way for a coalition government had led Bell and Summers to anticipate important deliberations with North Vietnamese officials. But after an uneventful lunch their hosts announced that the liaison meeting had been canceled and drove Bell and Summers to the airport through streets filled with celebrating crowds. Bell noticed that Colonel Tu and other senior cadre were not returning to Saigon.

After the plane reached cruising altitude, Major Huyen, now the highest-ranking member of the North Vietnamese delegation, approached Summers and Bell. After some small talk about the weather, his demeanor abruptly changed. He raised his voice, snapped to attention, and emphasized every word. Summers recognized a Communist "teaching point," the moment when a junior official communicated a series of prepared remarks.

Huyen asked Summers and Bell to relay three points to the White House: the United States had three days to "dismantle and remove" the Defense Attaché Office; the U.S. delegation to the JMT should remain in Saigon and continue working on POW/MIA issues; and, he said, "the American Embassy shall be allowed to work out its future with the new government in Saigon."

Bell and Summers agreed that although Huyen had been vague about the composition of this "new government," he had been specific about the fact that the DAO had to leave and that the U.S. JMT delegation should stay. To pass the time during the remainder of the flight, Bell borrowed a copy of *Stars and Stripes* from a crewman. The front page carried a photograph of the pilot of the Babylift plane that had crashed, killing Bell's wife and son. An accompanying article contained an eyewitness description of the crash site. It mentioned that the pages of a Donald Duck comic book had "flipped in the breeze." Bell spent the rest of the flight staring into space.

Bell and Summers believed that the Communists had presented them with the terms for the withdrawal of U.S. personnel from South Vietnam, but Martin saw Huyen's conditions differently. He seemed unconcerned that the Communists had given the United States three days to dismantle the DAO, seizing instead on the fact that they had asked the American JMT delegation to remain and had invited the embassy to "work out its future" with the new government. He took Huyen's statement as proof that Kissinger's approach to the Soviet Union was working and that Brezhnev had persuaded Hanoi not to attack Saigon. He apparently did not wonder why, if the Communists were serious about a cease-fire and political solution, they had used the liaison flight to evacuate the senior cadre who would be the obvious people to engage in these negotiations.

Bell recognized Huyen's terms for what they were: an ultimatum laying out what the United States must do prior to a Communist victory. He resumed spiriting Vietnamese into Tan Son Nhut and onto planes, work that now seemed even more urgent and timely. Back at the DAO, Summers ran into Erich von Marbod, who had just arrived on his mission to prevent the Communists from capturing the South Vietnamese Air Force. He told von Marbod that the Hanoi trip had been such a "screwed up situation" that he could have given the Communists a nuclear ultimatum and they would have believed him.

"Then why didn't you?" von Marbod asked, a question Summers took as being "only half in jest."

Summers called Colonel Clint Granger, an army buddy serving on the National Security Council, and said that he was appalled at having been sent to Hanoi without any negotiating instructions. He told Granger that he would be returning to Hanoi on the Friday, May 2, liaison flight, adding, "For God's sake, give me some guidance on what to talk about."

CHAPTER 16

Richard Armitage's
Courageous Silence

—||—

After Thieu's resignation North Vietnam's army slowed its advance, encouraging Washington and the embassy to anticipate a slow-motion surrender at the bargaining table. Government troops still held the road to Vung Tau, the post office delivered mail, newspapers published, and bureaucrats showed up for work. Residents of Saigon saw artillery flashes on the horizon and heard distant shell fire, but that was all. It was believed that because ICCS inspectors from Poland and Hungary lived in Saigon, and because North Vietnamese and PRG officials were based at Tan Son Nhut, the Communists would not shell the city. This notion vanished in the early morning hours of Sunday, April 27, when North Vietnamese gunners fired Soviet-built 122 mm rockets into densely populated neighborhoods, killing ten civilians and igniting a firestorm that destroyed five hundred homes in the Chinese neighborhood of Cholon. One rocket hit the top floor of the Hotel Majestic, a grand old colonial building on the riverfront, killing an employee and destroying the penthouse suite that the government had been remodeling to serve as a venue for the anticipated negotiations. The suspicion that Hanoi might have been signaling a lack of interest in such negotiations by hitting the suite was countered by the fact that rockets are imprecise weapons and that one had almost killed the Polish ambassador who lived one floor below the penthouse. His spokesman condemned the rocket as "the work of a misguided person" and exclaimed, "Why, our ambassador was asleep on the fourth floor!"

Communist artillery spotters meanwhile were infiltrating the refugee columns entering the city. Some ARVN soldiers became suspicious when an officer wearing an unfamiliar insignia was confused by the price of coffee in a café near Tan Son Nhut. Under questioning by MPs, he admitted being sent to target South Vietnam's Joint General Staff. JMT linguist Stuart Herrington lived nearby, and the incident convinced him that an all-out attack was imminent. He was the evacuation captain for a building with sixty apartments that had been occupied by Americans but were now home to their guards and servants. He had a master key and walked through the building after the rocket attack, making a head count and reassuring everyone. A maid and her three sons had installed themselves in the home of her former employer, a man she called "my fiancé." Herrington had seen him in a line of evacuees at Tan Son Nhut and winced when she said that he was flying her to the United States and marrying her. The next day Herrington threw a blanket over her and her sons and smuggled them into Tan Son Nhut. One of her fiancé's American co-workers was on her flight and was so disgusted that he gave her the man's address and telephone number in the States, despite knowing that he was married.

North Vietnamese troops resumed their advance on Saigon after the rocket attack. Some tied down South Vietnamese forces on the perimeter; others headed for the center down Route 1, the divided highway connecting Bien Hoa to Saigon. ARVN ranger and airborne units mounted a defense that was all the more courageous and inexplicable given that many of their senior officers had fled. One junior officer told a reporter, "We, the young ones, are expected to keep fighting. But how can we fight when there are no generals to lead us anymore?" An enlisted man said, "If our officers stay with us next time we will fight the Communists. Otherwise, we will surrender."

North Vietnamese troops made repeated attempts to take the Newport Bridge, only to have South Vietnamese soldiers, sailors, and combat police push them back. As they were mounting their heroic defense, deserters were looting the Seamen's Club. Communist commandos attacked an ARVN communications center on the southern outskirts of Saigon, and several Americans at the DAO had breakdowns and were medically evacuated. A U.S. Army engineer drank himself into oblivion and was locked up. Embassies burned files, ashes fell on downtown streets, a man stabbed himself to death on the steps of the National Assembly, and Ambassador Martin appeared on South Vietnamese television on April 27 to deny that he was evacuating American personnel. His skin was gray, the texture of parchment. Speaking in a ponderous voice, he said, "I, the American ambassador, am not going to run away in the middle of the night. Any of you can come to my home and see that I have not packed my bags. I give you my word." He called Major General Smith afterward and said, "We'll be here until July or August," adding, "I'm not at liberty to tell you how I know that." He was so convincing that Smith flew his wife back from Thailand.

Martin cabled Kissinger on April 27, "It may also be possible a few more rockets will be launched this evening. It is [however] the unanimous opinion of senior personnel here that there will be no direct or serious attack on Saigon." George McArthur echoed Martin's assessment in a *Los Angeles Times* article datelined the same day, writing, "It appears evident—since almost all analysts concede that Hanoi probably has the strength to take Saigon within 48 hours—that the North Vietnamese are willing to negotiate their way into the city. Therefore, the analysts see the fresh ground attacks as merely a tactic to tighten the Communist ring around the capital and not the start of a major offensive."

Tom Glenn, the young cryptologist who headed the National Security Agency station in South Vietnam, had predicted the North's attack on Ban Me Thuot and the current offensive against Saigon. He certainly belonged to the U.S. government's "senior personnel." Yet contrary to what Martin had told Kissinger, Glenn had warned him on April 27 that his signals intelligence showed Hanoi preparing to attack Saigon.

Two days before delivering his warning to Martin, Glenn had heard a knock on his office door at the DAO and had looked through the peephole to see Colonel Al Gray, who commanded the U.S.

Marines ground security force that would protect Tan Son Nhut during an evacuation. Glenn had met Gray in the late 1960s, when they were both running around South Vietnam with radios and antennas while intercepting Communist communications. He almost had not recognized Gray because he was wearing an aloha shirt, shorts, and flip-flops to comply with Martin's insistence that he and his men wear civilian clothes while in Saigon. During the next several days Glenn had watched as Gray and his men prepared the DAO for a siege and evacuation. They filled drums with gasoline, wired them together, and stationed them along the perimeter fence. They transformed the parking lot into a helicopter landing zone by driving the remaining cars, including Glenn's Japanese compact, into the side of a building, and then smashing them together so that they occupied as little space as possible. They drove the larger cars, including Glenn's Ford, onto the tennis courts, using them as battering rams to demolish the nets, fences, and poles. The urgency and single-mindedness of their preparations reflected a pessimism that equaled Glenn's.

By the time Glenn met Martin on April 27, he was desperate to persuade him to launch an evacuation. He and his two communicators had been living in their offices at the DAO, sleeping fitfully, and surviving on cigarettes, black coffee, and a diet of mustard, relish, and canned Vienna sausages scrounged from a hotel bar. He was feverish, suffering from a chronic cough, finding it hard to focus his eyes, and beginning to hallucinate. Martin, too, was on the verge of a collapse and plagued by a severe case of bronchitis that had turned into pneumonia.

Glenn told Martin that intercepts of North Vietnamese communications showed that the Communists had surrounded Saigon with sixteen to eighteen divisions and that some enemy units were two kilometers from Tan Son Nhut. Their assault would start within several days, he said, commencing with a rocket and artillery bombardment of Tan Son Nhut.

Martin dismissed Glenn's signals intercepts as part of a Communist deception campaign orchestrated to intimidate South Vietnam's government into accepting a disadvantageous political solution. Throwing an arm around his shoulder, he said, "Young man, when you're older you'll understand these things better."

Glenn hurried to Tom Polgar's office and delivered the same briefing. Polgar showed him a cable that Martin had just sent to Washington reporting that the Communists' skillful use of "communications deception" had duped some in Saigon into believing an attack was imminent.

"What evidence does Martin have to support this?" Glenn asked.

Polgar ignored the question and said, "I'll bet you a bottle of champagne—vintage your choice—that we'll both be here at our desks this time next year."

"I finally understood what was going on," Glenn wrote later. "The embassy was a victim of what sociologists now call *groupthink syndrome*—firm ideology, immune to fact, shared by all members of a coterie. The ambassador, and therefore his subordinates, could not countenance the prospect of a communist South Vietnam and therefore dismissed evidence of the coming disaster."

A day after wagering Glenn a bottle of champagne (a wager he would never settle), Polgar became less confident that the next year would find him in Saigon. French ambassador Jean-Marie Mérillon reported that the Communist JMT delegations had refused to commit to negotiating with General Minh if he assumed the presidency, and a member of Poland's ICCS delegation warned him that the time for negotiations had passed and withdrew his offer to serve as an intermediary.

Polgar began hedging his bets. During a meeting in Martin's office on the morning of April 28, he supported embassy security officer Marvin Garrett's request to cut down the giant tamarind tree in the embassy parking lot so that helicopters could land there.

"There is no way, Tom, that I'm going to have that tree brought down until it's apparent that we've lost every one of our options," Martin said. "If we've got to leave, we're going to do it with dignity." He walked over to his window and exclaimed while staring down at the visa seekers and supplicants gathered outside the gate, "For God's sake, look at that crowd below! Don't you see that once that tree falls, so does America's prestige? I have given these people my word that we will not run away in the middle of the night. I have told them to come to my home and see that I am not packed and ready to leave. Don't you understand that once that tree falls the word will go out that the Americans have cut down their biggest tree so that helicopters can land and take away the ambassador?"

"Listen to reason, Graham," Polgar implored. "If we have to pull the plug those big choppers are going to have no place to land if that tree is still there. Simple as that. If that tree doesn't go a lot of our people are going to get trapped and maybe some of them are going to get killed."

Polgar ordered his agents to trim the tree's rear branches so it would be easier to fell when the time came but would appear unchanged when Martin looked out his window the following morning.

The CIA's Can Tho base chief, Jim Delaney, had sent agent Glenn Rounsevell to Saigon on April 27 to check on the fifty key indigenous personnel whom he had had sent there expecting that the embassy would evacuate them. After serving in the delta for three years, Rounsevell knew most of the KIP and wanted to make sure they escaped. He had spent two Cold War decades with the agency while becoming increasingly cynical about the Vietnam War—a cynicism that President Ford had reinforced with his remark at Tulane that the war was "finished as far as America is concerned." Upon hearing this, Rounsevell had thought, "Wait a minute, if the war is finished, then what am I doing here working with a South Vietnamese colonel to erect a high-security fence to discourage infiltrators?" The next day, a Vietnamese Air Force major had asked him, "So why did we fight this war, then? Why all the bloodshed?" Rounsevell had no answer.

Rounsevell checked in to the CIA's Saigon hostel, the Duc Hotel. Vietnamese wandered through the lobby at all hours, clutching one of Major General Smith's affidavits and searching for an American to sign it. Rounsevell put his name to dozens. A pretty teenager said, "I'll do anything, *anything,* if you'll help get me and my family out." He scrawled his signature on her affidavit and asked for nothing.

He discovered that few of his Can Tho people had made it onto the embassy evacuation lists and that those who had were moving further down them as cooks, barbers, and girlfriends sponsored by Americans living in Saigon advanced. His friends in the embassy reported that Polgar and Martin were insisting that an evacuation would be unnecessary because North Vietnam preferred negotiations and that Martin was walking around in a daze, high on the amphetamines he was taking for his illnesses.

Rounsevell delivered a dispiriting report to CIA base chief Delaney that reinforced Delaney's determination to evacuate his American agents and Vietnamese KIP by helicopter. He asked Rounsevell to arrange for a U.S. Navy ship with a helipad to be stationed offshore so it could receive the Can Tho KIP. Rounsevell raised the subject with Rear Admiral Benton, who said, "You're the first guy who's given me a straight request. Where do you want it?"

Jacobson heard about Rounsevell's request and alerted McNamara, who immediately grounded every Air America helicopter in the delta. Jacobson summoned Rounsevell to his office and accused him of going behind McNamara's back.

"Saigon's going to fall in two days," Rounsevell said. "Poof. Gone. It's now or never. We're just trying to do in the delta what you're doing here—getting people out while we can."

Back in Can Tho, McNamara and Delaney traded accusations of bad faith that ended with McNamara shouting that Delaney was fired. Lehmann and Jacobson brokered a truce. McNamara agreed to permit a helicopter evacuation of the CIA's KIP provided that Air America scattered its landing zones across the surrounding countryside and that helicopters flew directly out to sea and low enough to avoid South Vietnamese radar. In exchange, Delaney agreed to send his American agents out on McNamara's LCMs. The fact that their greatest source of friction involved the best way to evacuate their American and Vietnamese employees reflects well on both men.

Air America pilot Marius Burke flew to Vung Tau on April 26 to oversee the evacuation of the Vietnamese families of the company's Filipino mechanics. Most of the mechanics had lived in Vietnam for years, married local women, and were threatening to strike unless Air America evacuated their families. Even though the company would be crippled without them, the embassy and the DAO had not included their dependents on any evacuation lists. The Philippine government was more sympathetic and sent an LST and a senior Foreign Ministry official, a Mr. Sabalones, to Vung Tau. About a thousand of the mechanics' relatives had arrived on April 25 expecting to board the workboats that Burke had hired to take them to the LST. Vietnamese officials stopped them from leaving because they lacked passports and exit visas, and they spent the night sleeping on the beach. The next morning, the Filipino mechanics began refusing to service Air America aircraft.

Had Burke failed to get their families aboard the LST before it weighed anchor, the Saigon evacuation might have unfolded differently. With fewer Air America helicopters available to extract people from rooftops, Hubert Van Es might not have taken his iconic photograph, Dr. Huyhn might never have treated patients in Atlanta, and Janet Bui might not have become a biotech researcher in Southern California.

Burke took Sabalones aside and said, "Hell, let's just load them up in helicopters and fly them directly out to the ship." The young diplomats on Sabalones's staff were appalled at the prospect of flouting South Vietnamese law, but he asked Burke, "You could do that?"

Burke said, "Sure!" and summoned three Air America helicopters to Vung Tau. They shuttled six hundred relatives to the LST before nightfall. Burke loaded the remaining four hundred onto a barge and motored them out to the LST after dark. The next morning Sabalones asked Burke if there was anything he could do for him in return.

"As a matter of fact, there is," he said. He proposed that Sabalones evacuate the families of Air America's Vietnamese personnel and some of the company's nonessential employees.

Sabalones said his LST had room for an additional four hundred people, but before boarding them, he would need a letter from the U.S. embassy promising to accept responsibility for them after they arrived in the Philippines.

Burke called Jacobson and explained the situation. So far, Jacobson's approach to the evacuation had been erratic. He had permitted Martindale to fly to Phu Quoc and collect his former employees, but that had involved moving evacuees around within South Vietnam. On April 1, he had panicked and ordered an Americans-only evacuation from Nha Trang. He had vetoed McNamara's plan for a riverine evacuation, only to have Martin overrule him. Because he owed his current position to Martin, he tried to act as he imagined Martin would have wanted, and so he told Burke, "Not only no, but HELL NO! For all I know you could be putting ARVN soldiers on board. I wouldn't touch that with a ten-foot pole!"

Like many Air America pilots, Burke had a chip on his shoulder when it came to State Department personnel like Jacobson. Some of the resentment stemmed from the fact that although the pilots were not handsomely paid, they considered themselves more dedicated and committed to the Vietnamese than U.S. military or government personnel, not least because they were volunteers. Burke claimed to fly "for the love of the people" and for the camaraderie and danger rather than the money. After Jacobson refused his request that the embassy assume responsibility for the Air America dependents, he said, "If you won't send me a letter so our Vietnamese families can leave on the LST, would you at least send me a photograph of yourself?"

"Why do you want it?" Jacobson asked.

"So I can make copies and distribute them to our flight crews. That way, when the evacuation begins, they'll know who *not* to pick up."

As Dan Berney and Bill Ryder's *Green Wave* "stowaways" were reaching international waters on April 25, Richard Armitage, who had arrived on the last Pan Am flight the day before, was meeting at South Vietnamese naval headquarters in Newport with his friend Captain Do Kiem, the deputy chief of naval operations, and with Commander Chung Tan Cang, who headed South Vietnam's navy. Armitage told them that the Pentagon wanted them to order their ships to sea if the Communists attacked Saigon, and proposed that their vessels proceed to Con Son Island and rendezvous there with a U.S. warship that would escort them to the Philippines. He was in effect asking them to commit an act of treason by removing an entire branch of South Vietnam's armed forces before an official surrender. Their decision would determine whether thousands of Vietnamese sailors and civilians became American citizens and whether Kiem would spend years in a concentration camp, like other military officers of his rank, or teach mathematics and science at a New Orleans high school and become the grandfather to six American-born children.

Cang and Kiem agreed to evacuate South Vietnam's fleet. Two days later, on April 27, Armitage returned to Newport to hash out the details. He suggested that Kiem tell the crews of the smaller patrol boats to report to their bases for "reasons of security" so they could travel together in convoys and meet the larger vessels off the coast. Kiem proposed canceling long-term repairs, concentrating on fixing his most seaworthy vessels, and shortening the length of offshore patrols so his warships could quickly return to their ports.

They danced around the issue of the sailors' families. Armitage had suggested that the crews in the delta return to their bases with their families but had not said what would happen to those families once Kiem ordered the fleet to sea. The Pentagon had given him the authority to evacuate South Vietnam's navy—not as many family members, friends, and other civilians as Kiem's officers and men could cram aboard each vessel.

Armitage knew that the sailors would not abandon their families, and Kiem knew that Armitage knew this. But each was reluctant to say it. Kiem also knew from articles in U.S. newsmagazines that a majority of Americans opposed admitting large numbers of Vietnamese refugees to their country. Gathering his courage, he said, "You know of course that they'll come. The sailors won't leave without their families."

Armitage thought, "Of course I know that. I've lived with these fellows long enough to know that." But by admitting that he knew it, he could be responsible for sending tens of thousands of unauthorized refugees to the United States. Forbidding Kiem to include the families was also not an option. The sailors would defy him or attempt to escape with their families on small vessels or through the airport, leaving their ships behind.

He stared at Kiem and remained silent. As he had intended, Kiem interpreted his silence as approval. "He didn't say yes, and he didn't say no," Kiem remarked later while recalling Armitage's courageous silence.

By saying nothing, Armitage had opened the door to thirty thousand new American citizens, although at the time he was not sure how many ships would escape and with how many passengers. Later during their conversation Kiem said, "Of course we have room for more than just the crews and their families," adding that although the families would have priority, he also intended to evacuate "friendly non-naval personnel."

Again, Armitage remained silent.

Erich von Marbod had stopped in Thailand to persuade his friend General Kriangsak Chomanan to permit South Vietnamese Air Force planes to land at Thai bases. The next day he was in Saigon, explaining his mission to Graham Martin. He had seen Martin three weeks earlier when staying at his residence while serving on the Weyand mission. He was shocked by how much Martin had deteriorated. His skin was even grayer, and he looked more sick and exhausted.

Martin warned him that by emasculating South Vietnam's armed forces, he might be sabotaging the chance for a negotiated peace. He expected a cease-fire within three days, he said, followed by a coalition government, and after that, he told von Marbod, "you will have all the time in the world to salvage American matériel."

Von Marbod persuaded a Vietnamese Air Force pilot to helicopter him to the front lines. A young airborne lieutenant agreed to accompany him as a guide. After arriving at the battlefront, von Marbod interviewed a senior officer who told him that he had sent a battalion of teenagers to help the Eighteenth Division hold Xuan Loc and that only a third had survived. Another officer reported that although President Ford had declared the war "finished," he and his men would fight to the death. Von Marbod met a soldier who had lost a leg but had insisted on remaining and was firing on enemy positions. His bravery left von Marbod "overwhelmed and ashamed." The helicopter that had brought him to the front failed to return. He assumed it had been diverted or shot down. The airborne lieutenant who had guided von Marbod to the front found a soldier who was willing to brave enemy fire and drive him back to Saigon on the back of a motorcycle. North Vietnamese troops were certain to overwhelm this position soon, and von Marbod urged the lieutenant to return with him. "I can't go," he said. "I can't leave my country." He handed von Marbod a letter to his wife in Paris on a folded piece of paper and asked him to mail it. He explained that they had been living there before he volunteered to return and fight for his country. It was a farewell note from a man expecting to die.

During the next several days von Marbod met with Nguyen Cao Ky, who had formerly served as South Vietnam's prime minister and air marshal. Although Ky was not on active duty, he maintained considerable control over the VNAF. Von Marbod also met with the current commander of the VNAF and his staff at his headquarters at Tan Son Nhut. He convinced Ky and the VNAF commander that while U.S. aircraft belonging to the VNAF should be used to fight the Communists, they should never be surrendered to enemy forces. He then provided them with the map coordinates and landing strip information for three Thai air bases where VNAF pilots could land their aircraft. He promised that the air defense weapons at these bases would be "cold," that U.S. Air Force personnel would sign for the U.S. aircraft, and that the planes would be returned to the VNAF if the military situation at Tan Son Nhut "stabilized."

Von Marbod saw Martin again at the embassy three days later on April 28. Since their previous meeting Martin had read Colonel Summers's report of his April 25 liaison flight to Hanoi during which the North Vietnamese had requested that the U.S. JMT delegation remain in Saigon and that the embassy stay and negotiate a "new role" for itself—developments that had confirmed Martin's belief that a cease-fire and negotiations were imminent. He told von Marbod, "We have a deal," and showed him Kissinger's April 25 cable. He repeated his earlier admonition that von Marbod not do anything to degrade South Vietnam's armed forces, because their aircraft and ships were certain to be valuable bargaining chips. He predicted a cease-fire within three days, followed by thirty days to form a coalition government.

Von Marbod accepted Martin's invitation to have lunch at the residence and was shocked to see that his wife was still there. "For Christ's sake, Graham," he said, "put Dottie on a plane now!" Martin shook his head. She was staying because her presence reassured the Vietnamese.

After lunch von Marbod returned to the front lines to search for evidence of Martin's imminent cease-fire. He flew over North Vietnamese armored columns traveling bumper to bumper toward Saigon and landed at a medical aid station where he reported seeing "the dead and the wounded, the dying and the insane," but no indication of any cease-fire. He landed at the Bien Hoa air base, heard sporadic gunfire, and saw crates of helicopter parts, electronic equipment, and U.S. high-tech gear. The officers had fled, leaving a few enlisted men to wander across the runway. Upon returning to Saigon, he asked Armitage to assemble a team and fly to Bien Hoa and remove or destroy the equipment.

Armitage persuaded four U.S. servicemen to accompany him. They found the hangars and warehouses deserted except for a few ARVN stragglers. Armitage promised to fly them back to Saigon if they protected his team and helped pack up or destroy the equipment.

Back at Tan Son Nhut a DAO intelligence officer showed von Marbod intercepts of North Vietnamese radio communications ordering its troops to take the Bien Hoa air base and kill everyone inside.

Von Marbod radioed Armitage and said, "Ricky, I can't tell you why, but I'm sending a helicopter to pick up you and the guys." He did not mention the radio intercepts on an open line because it would tell the Communists that their communications had been compromised.

"I've got a problem with that plan," Armitage said. "If we try to jump on a chopper we'll be shot by the thirty Vietnamese soldiers who are here protecting us from the bad guys. I gave them my word, Erich, and we're too many to fit into a helicopter."

Von Marbod called Seventh Air Force headquarters in Thailand and arranged for a transport that had been heading for Saigon to divert to Bien Hoa. It landed just as North Vietnamese troops appeared on the far side of the runway. The pilot lowered his ramp and slowed without coming to a full stop. Armitage and his team sprinted across the tarmac and clambered aboard as the Communists opened fire. An ARVN soldier on a motorcycle gunned his engine and sped up the ramp. As the pilot corkscrewed into the air, North Vietnamese troops swarmed across the runway.

When CIA agent Jim Parker returned to General Hai's headquarters outside Can Tho on April 26, he found a wasteland of dismantled tents and empty bunkers. A North Vietnamese armored column was kicking up clouds of dust on the horizon while heading for Saigon. The following evening Parker told his bodyguard Loi, who had arrived from Vi Thanh with his family, that he should bring them to his apartment in the CIA's Coconut Palms compound the next evening. By then, he said, he would have finished flying the KIP to the fleet and could put Loi's family onto one of McNamara's LSTs. Chau's house was dark when he drove past, so he decided to return the next day to visit his children. He telephoned his wife in Thailand and said that he would be home soon, bringing the two newest members of their family.

Before boarding an Air America helicopter the next morning, he experienced a sense of dread that he remembered feeling before setting off on hazardous missions in Laos. He had been planning to deliver his first group of KIP to the ship that Admiral Benton had promised Glenn Rounsevell, but the navy air controllers knew nothing about his mission. The USS *Vancouver* finally agreed to let him land. Armed marines surrounded his helicopter and escorted him to the captain. Parker explained that the embassy had approved his flight, the Vietnamese were U.S. government employees, and he had to return to Can Tho to coordinate the rest of the evacuation. The captain was suspicious but grudgingly agreed to accept his Vietnamese.

Parker spent the remainder of the day in Can Tho, coordinating the other flights. The Air America pilot assigned to fly the last group of KIP to the *Vancouver* was supposed to land on the roof of the American club when he returned. He told Parker that he was unfamiliar with Can Tho and might have difficulty locating the club after dark. Parker agreed to go along and guide him back. As soon as they landed on the *Vancouver,* marines escorted Parker to the bridge. The captain told him that no one on the fleet knew anything about his "ratty-looking people" and that he was going to transfer them and Parker to an MSC freighter, the *Pioneer Contender.* "Now, go say good-bye to your helicopter," he said. "You belong to me. And to those people of yours down there."

Parker imagined Loi and his family waiting for him in his apartment, and Chau and her children standing next to their plastic suitcases by their front door. He protested that he had important business at the consulate.

The captain promised to send a workboat to collect him from the merchant ship the next morning. Parker could then summon a helicopter to collect him from the *Vancouver.* "It is the best deal I'm offering," he said, "and I have been very good to you. Plus, you don't have any choice."

Parker joined the Vietnamese in the loading area where they were waiting for the workboats. The marines were guarding them with drawn weapons. "Hey!" Parker said. "These are not VC. They are pretty good people."

The crew of the *Pioneer Contender* were haunted by the rapes, executions, and suffering they had witnessed on their ship during the evacuation from Da Nang. Despite multiple cleanings their ship still smelled faintly of feces and death. After arriving on the ship, Parker told Captain Ed Flink that his refugees were U.S. government employees whom the Communists might execute. Flink said that he had heard *that* story before. He grumbled about accepting Parker's people but provided them with food and medical care, treating them more humanely than the *Vancouver* had.

While helicopters were collecting the CIA's KIP on April 28, Terry McNamara had been attending Major General Nguyen Khoa Nam's weekly briefing. When he and Nam had coffee alone afterward, he was torn over how much to tell him about the consulate's evacuation. Nam had forbidden the departure of military-aged men, and McNamara knew that some of the men on his A- and B-lists were military aged, including his translator. He decided to inform Nam that he was reducing the consulate's American personnel, but not reveal that he had already sent some of his Vietnamese employees to Saigon or that he was preparing to take more down the Bassac. They had become good friends, and as they parted, Nam said in a pleasant but firm voice, "If you have to go suddenly, please do not attempt to evacuate any military—particularly officers." As they shook hands, Nam held McNamara's hand for several extra beats.

McNamara felt guilty about deceiving Nam and considered returning and telling him the truth. He asked his driver Phuoc to stop and spent several minutes by the side of the road wrestling with his conscience. He rolled down his window and felt a gathering wind and watched it rustle the palm fronds as thunderheads rose in the sky. At that moment, he wrote later, he had "realized how much I had grown to love Vietnam." Although he had found Africa fascinating, he thought that there was "something special about Vietnam," something that had enabled it and its people to suck him "further into its spell." He decided to place his evacuation ahead of his friendship with Nam and told Phuoc to drive on. Three days later Nam shot himself.

CHAPTER 17

Eighteen Optimistic Minutes

——┤├——

At 10:00 p.m. on April 27, members of the National Assembly who had not yet fled South Vietnam (about two-thirds of them) ignored their constitution's succession procedures and voted unanimously for a resolution stating that "the President of the Republic of Vietnam transfer all the powers of the president to General Duong Van Minh in order to carry out the task of seeking ways and means to restore peace in South Vietnam." Minh had told an American television newsman earlier that day that he preferred to assume the presidency the following day because the stars were out of alignment for an April 27 inauguration. President Huong, the antique politician who had succeeded Thieu, postponed Minh's inauguration until late on the morning of April 28 because more time was required to arrange a respectful ceremony and, he argued, "we cannot hand over the responsibilities of power like a handkerchief." The inauguration was postponed until late afternoon because Minh was having difficulty assembling a government. Many experienced politicians had already departed, and the others were reluctant to accept a post promising to lengthen their incarceration in a Communist prison.

Minh had maintained a back-channel dialogue with Hanoi, his younger brother was a senior officer in the NVA, and he was the acknowledged head of a neutralist "Third Force" supposedly capable of uniting Communists and anti-Communists in a government of national healing and reconciliation. Because of these factors he believed, as did Graham Martin and other optimists, that once he assumed the presidency, the Communists would agree to a cease-fire and negotiations. His supporters praised him for accepting the presidency at such a perilous moment; his detractors thought his Third Force was nonsense and that he was politically inept and quite stupid.

His most distinguishing features were his purported honesty and his size. He was large for a Vietnamese man, six feet tall and two hundred pounds, leading to his nickname, Big Minh. He had served as president for several months after participating in the 1963 coup against President Diem, but his current power base consisted of a dwindling number of Vietnamese and Americans who believed he could pull a coalition government out of his hat. His supporters touted him as a serene Buddhist who would have preferred to raise orchids and play tennis at the Cercle Sportif, an image somewhat at odds with the fact that he had strangled a guard while escaping from a Communist prison and had been one of the principal plotters in the 1963 coup toppling President Ngo Dinh Diem, reputedly giving the signal (two raised fingers) that resulted in Diem and his brother-in-law being murdered while in army custody.

At 5:00 p.m. on April 28 two hundred members of South Vietnam's remaining political and military elite arrived at Independence Palace wearing uniforms and tailored dark suits covered with medals and ribbons. Liveried footmen opened limousine doors, and members of Minh's cabinet lingered outside, whispering and intriguing as if preparing to launch a long and prosperous chapter in their nation's history. After they took their seats under the Great Hall's chandeliers, Minh addressed them in a heavy, halting voice—"as if delivering a hopeless prayer," one observer said.

He said, "The order to our soldiers is to stay where they are, to defend their positions, to defend with all their strength the territory remaining to us." He declared, "Our soldiers fight hard," although discarded boots and uniforms already littered streets near the palace.

They did not sound like the words of a leader seeking negotiations, but then he added, almost as an afterthought, "I accept the responsibility for seeking to arrive at a cease-fire, at negotiations, at peace on the basis of the Paris Accords. I am ready to accept any proposals in that direction." Claps of thunder and a howling wind from the first storm of the monsoon season almost drowned him out as he proclaimed, "Citizens, brothers, patriots! In this difficult hour I can only beg of you one thing: Be courageous, do not abandon the country, do not run away."

Headlines in *The Saigon Post* the next morning (its last day of publication) proclaimed, "Ceasefire Likely" and "Saigon Residents Feel Sense of Relief, Hope." But Radio Liberation called his inauguration a trap "set up by the lackeys of the United States" and "a scheme of the Americans" and attacked Minh for being "no longer a member of the Third Force but an American lackey." *New York Times* reporter Malcolm Browne telephoned Polgar to report that a Communist spokesman had told him that Minh was an unacceptable negotiating partner. Polgar's other intermediary, his fellow Hungarian Colonel Toth, stopped taking his calls.

At 6:08 p.m., eighteen minutes after Minh had finished speaking, five captured American A-37 fighter-bombers attacked Tan Son Nhut. Lieutenant Trung, the turncoat who had bombed Thieu's palace on April 8, had trained a group of VNAF defectors and North Vietnamese pilots and flew the lead warplane. His squadron attacked the South Vietnamese Air Force flight line, dropping 250-pound bombs, firing cannons, and narrowly missing Major General Smith's office. The attack commenced minutes after Richard Armitage had landed at Tan Son Nhut following his narrow escape from the airfield at Bien Hoa. As Trung's squadron approached at five hundred feet, von Marbod turned to Armitage and said, "I thought South Vietnamese pilots knocked off at 6:00 p.m." When the raid ended, von Marbod said, "It's over. We're getting out tomorrow."

Tom Glenn had been walking to the men's room down a corridor in the sprawling DAO headquarters. He passed some workmen on stepladders who were threading wires through the ceiling. One said they were connected to explosive charges and joked, "Last man out lights the fuse and runs like hell." As a bomb exploded nearby, the urinal lurched from the wall toward Glenn. He staggered outside as Lieutenant Trung's planes were diving for a second attack.

Twenty-eight hundred people were inside the DAO awaiting evacuation. A bomb fell on open ground near the Evacuation Processing Center, rattling the gymnasium and sending overhead fluorescent lights crashing to the floor. One slammed into Joe McBride's shoulder. He wrapped the consular stamp around his wrist with duct tape and jumped up from his desk. Holding the stamp high in the air, he shouted, "I'm still working! Look, the stamp's still here!"

Ken Moorefield grabbed his revolver and dashed from his side office into the gym. Another explosion shook the room and McBride shouted, "Let's get out of here." They hustled everyone into a sturdier building across the street and told them to lie down in the hallways. Moorefield doubled back to the processing center for his consular stamp. While he was outside, two planes dove toward him. He remembered calling in air strikes on Communist positions and thought, "Well, now I know how scared and utterly defenseless the Vietcong must have felt."

Bill Bell had been erecting a sign over the entrance to the combined mess identifying it as the new headquarters for the U.S. delegation to the Joint Military Team. The delegation's commander, Colonel Jack Madison, assumed they would be staying after a Communist victory and wanted to consolidate their offices and living quarters in the mess hall. Bell watched as the A-37s attacked the VNAF flight line, releasing their bombs and circling for a second attack. One peeled off and seemed to be tracking him. He moved right and it did the same; he moved left and it did too. It finally released a bomb that fell into a patch of open ground, throwing up a shower of rocks and dirt. He had witnessed numerous sorties against Communist positions, but this was his first time as a target. Nothing had prepared him for the terror of having a plane dive at him, guns blazing, and he wondered, "How in the world did they put up with this during all the years when we had air superiority?"

When Ross Meador left the Friends of the Children of Vietnam orphanage that morning, babies in cardboard boxes had been wailing and toddlers stumbling down hallways. After helping to put them on an evacuation flight, he returned to a building that was suddenly so empty and quiet it gave him the willies. As the A-37s hit Tan Son Nhut, a group of Vietnamese nuns had been loading the villa's incubators and refrigerators into their truck. They sped away, leaving Meador alone with the FCVN's senior Vietnamese nurse. The power failed after sunset. Fearing that the Communists were about to seize the airport, he and the nurse spent the night huddled together and made love.

Earlier that day, Jim Devine, the embassy's political-military officer, had called Walter Martindale to join the embassy's "skeleton team" after Saigon fell. "You have to tell us now if you're willing to stay," Devine said. "Yes or no." Martindale said yes. He had already evacuated his children and most of his friends and believed he could help others escape. He was at Tan Son Nhut when the A-37s attacked. He hurried back to his apartment building and strode through the hallways, shouting to the Vietnamese whom he had encouraged to move into the empty apartments, "Don't worry! Don't worry! I'll get you out. . . . I'll get you out!"

After Jacobson refused to give Marius Burke a letter guaranteeing visas for Air America's Vietnamese employees and their families, Burke continued searching for ways to evacuate them. He saw a solution when retired Foreign Service officer Jim Collins returned to Saigon on a mission to rescue orphans being housed at the military academy in Vung Tau. Rear Admiral Benton had promised Collins a barge so he could transfer the children to an MSC freighter. Burke agreed to fly Collins to Vung Tau on condition that he evacuate some of the Air America Vietnamese personnel and their families on his barge. When the A-37s hit Tan Son Nhut, Burke had just dropped Collins at Vung Tau and was heading back to Saigon. He landed on one of the U.S. Navy ships and decided to return to Vung Tau in the morning.

The ARVN troops guarding Independence Palace fired off rounds at the departing A-37s. Some hit the U.S. embassy. Diplomats and CIA agents grabbed weapons and dove to the floor. Someone screamed,

"They're in the halls! They're in the halls!" and marines in flak jackets dashed up stairways.

Don Hays was in the embassy recreation center, surrounded by anxious Vietnamese. The evacuees he had been managing at the DAO evacuation center had become so dehydrated and famished while waiting to board planes that he had driven to the embassy and persuaded the manager of the recreation center's restaurant to have the cooks make five hundred sandwiches. When the attack commenced, he led the Vietnamese in the recreation center into the restaurant. He put the children in a windowless bathroom and told the adults to turn over the tables and take cover. After the raid ended, two of his supervisors, Hank Boudreau and Al Jazynka, happened to be walking past as he was loading his sandwiches and jugs of juice and water into a station wagon. Jazynka asked, "Why the hell do you have to bring them all that?"

"Because they're dehydrated and I'm afraid they're going to become sick and we don't have any doctors or running water there," Hays replied.

"Stop being so serious, Don," he said. "Come with us, we're going to a cocktail party."

Hays slugged him. After Jazynka struggled to his feet, Hays turned to Boudreau and asked, "Why didn't you stop me from doing that?"

"Because I thought you wouldn't do it."

Hays assumed it was the end of his career, but neither man reported him.

Dr. Lem Hoang Truong's position as acting head of the Ministry of Administrative Reform and Civil Service made her the government's highest-ranking female member. Like many Vietnamese her age, she was acquainted with political violence and realized what might happen to her following a Communist victory. During World War II she had seen Japanese soldiers cut off the hands of militants; after the war French police had shot and killed her father. Yet unlike other civil servants of her rank, she had not hired a boat or bought plane tickets. Because she was South Vietnam's top civil service reformer, she believed she had to lead by example.

Like many families, hers was split over whether to become exiles. Her mother was desperate to leave, but her husband leaned toward staying. Like her, he was a devout Catholic, and because the church hierarchy had decided to remain after a Communist victory, he believed that he should stay. The couple had been living in different homes because her government job provided her with a house near Independence Palace where she lived with her mother, two young daughters, and a four-month-old baby girl. Her thirteen- and fifteen-year-old boys lived with her husband in the family home.

One of her American friends, Dr. John Evans, had formerly served as a technical adviser to her ministry. He had returned to assist in the evacuation and had come to her office several hours before the raid on Tan Son Nhut to inform her that Ambassador Martin had just received an urgent telex from Secretary of State Henry Kissinger directing the embassy to evacuate her and her family and tell her that a position awaited her on the faculty of the Federal Executive Institute in Virginia, where she had previously studied. Evans was emaciated, fidgety, and under great stress. She asked him to inquire if the embassy would also evacuate her senior staff. Many were former military officers whom the Communists were certain to treat harshly. He promised to speak with Jacobson and call her the next morning. Moments after she returned home from her office, Tan Son Nhut came under attack. She and her daughters and mother spent a sleepless night in their shelter.

All across Saigon families like hers huddled behind shuttered doors and windows, debating whether to leave or stay, trying to calculate how tainted they might be in the Communists' eyes, how far down the purges might reach, and who among their American friends and contacts might help them. They wondered if everyone in the family should leave, if some should stay, if some of the elderly should be left on their own, and if they should evacuate their younger children with friends or relatives or entrust them to strangers. Which was worse, they wondered, never to see your children again or to have them indoctrinated and raised by the Communists?

An hour after the attack ended, Martin convened a meeting of his senior staff in the sixth-floor communications room. He spoke by radio to Major General Smith at Tan Son Nhut, using a microphone and loudspeaker so that Polgar, Lehmann, and the others could listen. Smith reported light damage to the runways and said the transports could resume landing.

Polgar, who believed that the attack had been Hanoi's response to Minh's inauguration, said, "You can bet that some cadre in the palace got a copy of his speech in advance." (In fact, Hanoi had started planning the attack on April 19, and its timing, coming just minutes after Minh's inauguration, had been coincidental.) Martin disagreed. The Communists claimed to favor a political solution, he said, and were "not the kind of people to change their minds." He telephoned Kissinger and predicted that despite the bombing he expected the Communists to answer Minh's speech with a "political initiative."

Minutes later he cabled Kissinger and complained that the DAO was jumping to the conclusion that the A-37s were captured VNAF planes. Instead, he said that "when all the evidence is in," he believed it would be revealed that they were piloted by disaffected South Vietnamese pilots showing "bitter resentment" at the way the war had been conducted. He told Kissinger that "we do not expect any interference" with the C-130s that were scheduled to commence their evening runs to the Philippines and that during the next twenty-four hours he hoped to evacuate "at least 10,000 or more of our Vietnamese employees and high risk Vietnamese."

He went on to describe what he thought would happen in the days and weeks ahead. He forecast that Minh would recognize the PRG as a legitimate government leading to three Vietnams—North Vietnam, South Vietnam, and areas in the South controlled by the PRG—and that a negotiated cease-fire and the formation of a national council of reconciliation would follow. He predicted that the new coalition government would have a "60-40 lineup," with the 40 percent or less being Communist because, he insisted, the Communists "are simply not in that much of a hurry." After "a year or more" they might "begin to tighten the screws on the administration of Saigon." Nevertheless, he thought that "they will wish to show a gentle face for a while." He argued that the new 60-40 administration would be counting on the United States "to help them buy a little more time" and that closing the embassy and making "an immediate or precipitate" departure would "pull out the rug" from under this coalition government. He declared that given that "we still have a functioning Republic of Vietnam, and will for quite a while," there was no U.S. policy interest "in either leaving in pique or trying to create conditions that would force our departure." Instead, the embassy should remain open, and the United States should provide "a modicum of relief and rehabilitation" to the people of South Vietnam. He reported that 825 Americans assigned to the U.S. mission remained in Saigon, adding, "We cannot do with any less." He concluded by telling Kissinger that he could take either his advice or that of those on the Washington Special Actions Group, "who have not, it seems to me, crystal balls of the first quality." As an exercise in wishful thinking, Martin's April 28 cable may be unequaled in State Department history. Not only would nothing that he predicted happen, but during the next forty-eight hours the exact opposite would occur.

Kissinger cabled back that in the judgment of officials attending the Washington Special Actions Group meeting that morning, "we could have as little as one to three days before a military collapse and Tan Son Nhut become unusable." He added diplomatically that this was "at some variance" with Martin's cable. In response to Martin's arguments for maintaining a large diplomatic presence in Saigon, he said, "It is my feeling that Minh will be pushed fairly rapidly into giving in to a pro-Communist or Communist dominated government and our people would end up as hostages."

Martin would be spectacularly wrong about how the war would end, but he was right to be concerned about the Pentagon's reaction to the attack. Two C-130s had been minutes from landing at Tan Son Nhut when it began. Smith asked them to remain in a holding pattern while his people assessed the damage. In the meantime, the Pentagon decided to suspend the flights indefinitely, leaving over three thousand evacuees stranded at the airport.

Washington was twelve hours behind Saigon, so it was early on the morning of April 28 when Ken Quinn heard that the Pentagon had stopped the flights and was recommending that Ford halt the evacuation of Vietnamese by fixed-wing planes and concentrate on rescuing Americans. He called Lacy Wright, who confirmed that thousands of Vietnamese were stuck at Tan Son Nhut. Quinn ran into David Kennerly's office and explained the situation. Kennerly hurried into the Oval Office and told Ford that a reliable source had informed him that thousands of refugees were stranded at Tan Son Nhut.

Ford ordered the flights resumed. The two C-130s that had been in a holding pattern landed and collected 360 evacuees, leaving 2,800 at Tan Son Nhut. Admiral Gayler informed Smith that beginning the next morning and continuing for twenty-four hours, there would be an around-the-clock airlift of sixty C-130 sorties. Ten thousand people would be evacuated, including the remaining DAO staff, at-risk Vietnamese, and all U.S. civilians and government personnel except those needed to staff a bare-bones embassy.

Before returning to his residence for the night, Martin told his staff to prepare to move American citizens, third-country nationals, and the U.S. mission's Vietnamese employees and their families to Tan Son Nhut the next morning. Jim Devine, the embassy's political-military counselor, passed the word down the chain of command, telling everyone to contact the people on their evacuation lists and begin assembling them in the embassy and agency compounds so that buses could take them to Tan Son Nhut. The embassy's plan depended on fixed-wing planes continuing to land at Tan Son Nhut, the roads between downtown and the airport remaining open and safe, and South Vietnam's police and military remaining a cohesive and dis-ciplined force prepared to protect an evacuation that did not include them—precisely the scenario that Generals Smith and Baughn had considered so unrealistic when they read a version of this plan following the fall of Phuoc Long.

At 11:25 a.m. Washington time on April 28, five hours after the raid, Ford asked Kissinger if the A-37s had inflicted enough "major damage" to impede the next day's ambitious airlift.

"No. They hit the Vietnamese Air Force side," Kissinger said.

"How many are out now?" Ford asked, referring to the evacuees.

"Thirty-five to forty thousand," Kissinger said. "It's remarkable."

Ford agreed, saying, "It really has been magnificently done."

The evacuation would have been far less "magnificent" had Bill Ryder, Walter Martindale, Al Topping, Richard Baughn, Homer Smith, Ken Moorefield, Andy Gembara, Bill LeGro, Lionel Rosenblatt, Craig Johnstone, and others followed State Department guidelines and obeyed Ambassador Martin and the immigration laws of the United States and South Vietnam. By April 28, according to U.S. Air Force records, 43,439 evacuees had left Tan Son Nhut on chartered aircraft or U.S. Air Force planes. About 5,000 had been Americans. Most of the rest were South Vietnamese. If you also counted those who had escaped on the CIA's and the DAO's black flights, or had hidden behind the skirts of Pan Am flight attendants, or left on Ed Daly's flights, and all the others not making it onto the official list, the actual number of evacuees leaving in the thirty days prior to April 29 probably approached 50,000.

Ken Moorefield felt responsible for the Vietnamese and Americans who were marooned in the Dodge City processing center. He recruited a consular officer to help him break into the commissary. They carried sacks of rice and beans to the mess hall and persuaded some former army cooks among the evacuees to make dinner for several thousand people. After everyone had eaten, Moorefield walked around the DAO's perimeter fence, checking for incursions. As he approached the main gate, a man shouted that he and forty people were trapped outside. Moorefield could see them lying flat on the ground. He realized that if there was another air strike, they would be exposed; if North Vietnamese troops attacked or South Vietnamese troops mutinied, they would be caught in cross fire, but if they stayed in place, North Vietnamese sappers might infiltrate them.

Major James Kean, the commander of the embassy's marine guards, had sent sixteen of his men to the DAO to help manage and protect the Dodge City processing center, direct traffic, and erect a barbed-wire defensive perimeter around the compound. Two of these marines, Lance Corporal Darwin Judge and Corporal Charles McMahon, manned a forward position just inside the perimeter fence and adjacent to the road leading to the main gate. Moorefield walked back down this road to warn them that he was about to escort forty Vietnamese civilians into the DAO. He noticed that their skin was pale, marking them as recent arrivals. They struck him as very young (Judge was nineteen, and McMahon was twenty-one), very nervous, very green, and lacking the experience to distinguish friendly Vietnamese from the enemy. As he spoke, they flicked their eyes back and forth between him and the buildings they were guarding.

"Guys, look, I'm going to go out there and collect these Vietnamese families so they can be processed," he said. "Things are tense and we don't know what's going to happen tonight. You don't want them in front of you if something happens, and if there's any combat, you could have sappers coming with them, so stand fast because I'm bringing them in."

They stood fast. They were good boys, both of them. Judge was an evangelical Christian and a former Eagle Scout, newspaper boy, grocery bagger, and snow shoveler for the elderly of Marshalltown, Iowa. McMahon was a local football hero whom the Boys' Club of Woburn, Massachusetts, had named "Boy of the Year." They had fired their weapons in anger for the first time that evening, pumping off some shots at the A-37s. After the attack ended, Judge had persuaded Sergeant Kevin Maloney, who commanded the marine guard unit at the DAO, to accept Christ as his savior. Until the previous day, Maloney had been Ambassador Martin's personal bodyguard. That morning Major Kean had exiled him to the DAO because of some shenanigans that could have led to his court-martial. Kean had promised to "lose" his paperwork if he behaved. Maloney admitted being a "hard-drinking, hard-living type of Marine." But thanks to Judge, he says, "I became a believer that day."

Moorefield rounded up the Vietnamese and walked them through the gate and past Judge and McMahon. He added them to the others without checking their papers and left the DAO at midnight, driving through the curfew-emptied streets and scattering packs of cigarettes at roadblocks. Before falling asleep, he packed a getaway bag with a pistol, ammunition, currency, passport, and his West Point class ring.

Jake Jacobson convened an evacuation planning meeting at the embassy that commenced around midnight. He presided because Martin had returned to his residence. Lacy Wright, Shep Lowman, USIA head Alan Carter, and a dozen other senior officials attended. Jacobson reported that the White House had approved an evacuation of ten thousand people the next day on U.S. Air Force transports and said that Martin believed that the Communists would hold off for another forty-eight hours before deciding whether to attack Saigon. In the meantime, Martin wanted these ten thousand to be genuine high-risk people, no household staff and personal friends. Jacobson turned to Lowman, who had been compiling and collecting the embassy's lists, and said, "See if you can dredge up the names of 2,000 Vietnamese who *really* deserve help."

As the meeting was ending, Lowman asked Alan Carter to give him a list of his "priority" evacuees. Carter, who had already gathered over a hundred of his most endangered employees at the USIA office, exclaimed, "For God's sakes, Shep! I turned a list in days ago!"

So many Americans had wanted to save as many Vietnamese as possible that they had flooded Lowman and his team with lists. "Our tabulations have broken down," Lowman admitted. "We'll have to start again."

CHAPTER 18

Frequent Wind

———┤├——

At 1:00 a.m., Stuart Herrington, Jack Madison, and Harry Summers of the JMT began busing evacuees from the Dodge City processing center to the Tan Son Nhut flight line. Smith had told them to expect sixty sorties of C-130s during the next twenty-four hours, with the first transport arriving at 1:30 a.m., and they wanted to marshal the evacuees near the runway so the planes could make a quick turnaround. Before returning to Dodge City, Herrington stopped at Judge and McMahon's post and asked, "How are things going, guys?" They answered, "Fine, sir, no sweat."

At 3:58 a.m., North Vietnamese gunners fired a barrage of rockets into Tan Son Nhut. One landed on Judge and McMahon. Sergeant Maloney found them first. The blast had scattered pieces of McMahon across the ground. Judge lay next to a pile of burning motorcycles. His ammunition belt was so hot from the explosion that it burned Maloney's hand as he dragged him away from the fire. Before the day ended, Senator Richard Schweiker (R-Penn.) would accuse the Ford administration of having sacrificed Judge's and McMahon's lives, and risked those of other Americans, "as a subterfuge to evacuate South Vietnamese," and charge that it had been "madness" to have "stalled" the evacuation of Americans to rescue Vietnamese.

Another rocket exploded near Smith's quarters, pitching him and his wife out of bed. More rockets hit the control tower, a fuel truck, and the Evacuation Processing Center. Erich von Marbod's toilet shot into the air, gushing water across the floor. He jumped into a flight suit, threw a submachine gun over his shoulder, and staggered outside, his ears still ringing. Colonel Madison grabbed his helmet and sidearm, ran to the chapel where the mess hall's waitresses and cooks had been sleeping, and led them into a bunker. His sardonic sense of humor had survived, and he turned to Sergeant Ernest Pace, the JMT linguist who had helped Bell on his evacuation runs, and said, "Call up the Communist delegations and tell them they're violating our 'privileges and immunities.'"

Stuart Herrington ran to Judge and McMahon's post, arriving as an ambulance was removing their remains. A marine standing by a smoking crater said, "I'm Sergeant Maloney, squad leader, manning my post. My two men are dead." The ambulance delivered their bodies to the morgue at the Adventist Hospital. They would be left there, and instead of the negotiations with the Communists that Martin, Polgar, and Kissinger had imagined dragging on for months, the only talks between the United States and Hanoi would concern the repatriation of their remains.

Herrington and Maloney jumped into a ditch as 120 mm artillery shells slammed into the South Vietnamese Air Force flight line. One shell exploded so close that Herrington heard shrapnel pinging against the chain-link fence. He grabbed a helmet that was lying on the ground and shoved it on. When he returned to the DAO, Smith's wife screamed. It had belonged to Judge and had a hole in one side and was smeared with his blood.

The VNAF unraveled. As the shelling continued, many of its aircraft headed for Thailand. Some pilots were acting on their own; others were obeying commanders who had promised von Marbod that they would not allow the Communists to capture their most sophisticated warplanes. Soldiers and airmen fought to get aboard transport planes. The crew of one overloaded C-130 pushed soldiers off its loading ramp as another plane spun off the runway and burned. Some pilots jettisoned their ordnance and external fuel tanks onto Tan Son Nhut's runways and taxiways. By 7:00 a.m., a disabled F-5 fighter and hundreds of mutinous soldiers and airmen blocked the last active runway. Their actions were not hard to parse. After capturing ten VNAF intelligence personnel at the Da Nang air base in March, the Communists had executed them on the flight line. This may also explain why VNAF commander Lieutenant General Tran Van Minh and thirty armed members of his staff burst into the DAO at 8:00 a.m. and demanded evacuation to the American fleet. Smith ordered his assistant air attaché, Lieutenant Colonel Richard Mitchell, to disarm them. "If they refuse, tell them I'll have them shot," Smith said. General Minh and his staff surrendered their weapons, and Mitchell locked them in an office.

Former VNAF air marshal Ky arrived at the headquarters of South Vietnam's Joint General Staff to find it virtually deserted. The former chief of staff, General Cao Van Vien, had resigned the day before and flown to the American fleet. His successor, General Vinh Loc, had told his troops not to "run away like rats" and had then joined Vien on the fleet. As Ky was leaving, he met General Truong, the former commander of Military Region I who had entrusted his children to Theresa Tull. Truong had been released from the hospital and given an empty office in the building. He told Ky, "I don't know what to do anymore." Ky said, "Come along with me then," and they flew to the fleet in Ky's helicopter.

Ross Meador and the Vietnamese nurse woke in the FCVN orphanage to the explosions at Tan Son Nhut. He walked onto a balcony at daybreak and saw two men breaking into the compound. They wore black pajamas and could be looters or Communist soldiers. He fired off a shot with his revolver and they fled. He was so unnerved that he drove downtown to have breakfast at the Duc Hotel and ask the CIA agents there what was happening. He was eating alone in the restaurant when an agent ran in yelling, "Let's go! Let's go!" Meador protested that he had not finished breakfast. "I don't know what you think is going on here," the agent shouted, "but if you don't leave now, you're never leaving. This is it, the final evacuation!"

Jim Parker woke with the sun. The sea was empty to the horizon. The *Vancouver* had weighed anchor during the night, stranding him on the *Pioneer Contender*. The communications room was the size of a closet and had a single portable radio. The seaman on duty could not communicate with the navy, only with the Military Sealift Command. Parker listened to the chatter on the MSC frequency and realized that an evacuation was under way and that MSC tugs would be bringing refugees out on barges. He slept a few more hours and returned to the bridge. There were still no ships in sight. He assumed that by now McNamara and Delaney would be heading down the Bassac and that Loi would be waiting for him in his Coconut Palms apartment, telling his anxious family that his friend Jim Parker would not desert them. Chau's children would be sitting by their plastic suit-cases in their immaculate little house while she wept and cursed him, another American who had betrayed her.

Air America pilot Marius Burke helicoptered from the fleet to Vung Tau. The docks were deserted, and there was no sign of Jim Collins and his Vietnamese orphans. Burke continued to Tan Son Nhut. By the time he landed, VNAF pilots had stolen four Air America helicopters. One had crashed and lay on its side, its rotors spinning while it exhausted its fuel. The Air America fuel truck was locked. No one could find the keys or hot-wire it because its battery was dead. This would mean that throughout the day Burke and the other Air America pilots would have to fly to the fleet to refuel. Because no one had alerted the U.S. Navy that civilian Air America pilots were an integral part of the evacuation, some were harassed and detained when they first landed on the ships.

Don Hays, the young diplomat whom Martin had ordered out of the country a month earlier, was at Tan Son Nhut supervising the embarkation of people on the embassy lists. He lined up his evacuees in the DAO corridors according to the numbers on baggage tags attached to their shirts. When the first rockets hit Tan Son Nhut, they screamed and ran in every direction, reminding him of "a jarful of lightning bugs." By daybreak he had resigned himself to becoming a POW. He called the embassy and told Wolfgang Lehmann that rockets and artillery shells were still hitting the air base. Lehmann said that

Ambassador Martin planned to inspect the damage personally and that the rocket attack was not happening anymore. Hays thrust the phone out the window and bellowed, "Listen to the 'non-happening' rocket fire!" Lehmann accused him of panicking and hung up.

NSA head of station Tom Glenn signed off for the last time at 6:10 a.m. "Have just received word to evacuate," he told NSA headquarters. "Am now destroying remaining classified material. Will cease transmission immediately after this message. We're tired but otherwise all right. Looks like the battle for Saigon is on for real." Glenn telephoned the general commanding South Vietnam's twenty-seven hundred cryptologists, only to learn that he had fled to the American embassy. A squad of U.S. marines burst into Glenn's office shouting that armed South Vietnamese Air Force pilots had forced their way into the building. They hustled him into another office and locked him inside. There was no telephone, and now he had no way to help evacuate the Vietnamese cryptologists.

Tom Polgar, who had bet Glenn a bottle of champagne that they both would be in Saigon the following year, woke to the explosions and stuffed his camera, passport, and checkbook into an airline shoulder bag. Despite Martin's insistence that an assault on Saigon was unlikely, his secretary, Eva Kim, had already packed a similar escape bag. Polgar arrived at the embassy at 5:00 a.m. Martin appeared soon afterward. His bronchitis and pneumonia had left him speaking in such a faint whisper that when he telephoned Major General Smith, Polgar had to listen on an extension and repeat his words.

At 7:30 a.m., Martin received a note from President Minh requesting that all DAO personnel leave South Vietnam within the next twenty-four hours "in order that the question of peace for Viet Nam can be settled early." Martin promised to comply and cabled Kissinger, "In view of the above, I repeat my request to permit me and about 20 of my staff to remain behind, at least for a day or two, to at least give some dignity to our departure."

The National Security Council convened in the White House Situation Room at 7:32 a.m. Saigon time. Ford decided that this would be the last day for evacuating Vietnamese and that all the remaining Americans should depart except for a small group at the embassy. Kissinger recommended leaving a skeleton staff of 150, saying it would signal that the United States had not abandoned Minh and might lessen the chances of his turning on the United States. He continued pushing for the evacuation of Vietnamese and suggested filtering Americans out with them because, he said, "if the Americans get out on the first aircraft the situation will be out of control. We have to space them out. The people who should stay to the end are the team to handle the evacuation of Vietnamese. The others should go."

Kissinger cabled Martin that Ford had decided that if Tan Son Nhut remained open for fixed-wing planes, he should evacuate high-risk Vietnamese, all the DAO Americans, and all but the "bare minimum" from the embassy. He continued, "While you should not say so, this will be the last repeat last day of fixed-wing evacuation from Tan Son Nhut." He added that should Tan Son Nhut become too hazardous for fixed-wing planes, "You are immediately to resort to helicopter evacuation of all repeat all Americans, both from the DAO compound and from the embassy. . . . Suppressive fire will be used as necessary in the event of helicopter evacuation."

Kissinger's cable reinforced Martin's determination to continue the fixed-wing evacuation. He met in his office at 8:00 a.m. with Polgar, Jacobson, Alan Carter, Joe Bennett, and his military attachés. Smith called Jacobson to report that ordnance, vehicles, wing tanks, and armed soldiers were blocking the runways and that he had ordered the Special Planning Group buses and Air America helicopters to begin collecting Americans, third-country nationals, and Vietnamese and bring them to the DAO for a helicopter evacuation.

After Jacobson repeated Smith's report to the room, Polgar interjected that a CIA agent at Tan Son Nhut had just notified him that the runways were a mess.

"How do you know for sure?" Martin demanded. After all, this was only one man's opinion.

Polgar replied that if Martin would not believe an eyewitness report, perhaps he should see for himself.

"I can tell you this," Martin said, "before I make any decision I'm going out to Tan Son Nhut to have a look. I refuse to run away from this thing."

Before leaving, Martin received another call from Kissinger. After hanging up, he announced to the room that Ford wanted to continue the fixed-wing evacuation and reduce the embassy to 150 people—"a small hard core."

To comply with Ford's directive, many of the Americans who had already reported for duty would spend the next several hours inside the embassy, poring over staff rosters and debating who among the U.S. mission's remaining 750 Americans should be included in this "hard core."

Alan Carter had told a hundred of his employees and their families to assemble for evacuation at the USIA office. A hundred and fifty Vietnamese with CIA connections had gathered at the Duc Hotel. Similar groups awaited evacuation in other U.S.-owned or U.S.-leased buildings across Saigon. Their American friends and bosses had steered them to these staging areas in the belief that buses would take them to Tan Son Nhut or the docks. But because of the attack on Tan Son Nhut and the increasingly chaotic streets, and because fewer trained escorts and drivers than anticipated had reported to the embassy and the DAO to drive the Special Planning Group's buses—because they either could not reach the DAO, were obeying the government's sudden twenty-four-hour curfew, or had already been evacuated—there were fewer buses than anticipated. Six never left the embassy motor pool, and the SPG's bus routes had to be reduced from twenty-eight to fourteen. Meanwhile, some of the people who should have been directing buses to the embassy safe houses, finding drivers for the idle buses, or themselves driving evacuees to the docks or walking them to the embassy were themselves inside the embassy. By the time Ford ordered a total evacuation of Americans, the crowd surrounding the embassy wall had become much larger and more unruly, and Saigon's streets more dangerous, making it more difficult for Americans to leave the embassy and assist their Vietnamese evacuees, although some did. Meanwhile, the Vietnamese gathered in the safe houses and staging areas continued to believe that the promised buses would arrive, and were reluctant to venture into the streets and get themselves to Tan Son Nhut or the river docks without an American escort. It was a textbook demonstration of the truth of Prussian field marshal von Moltke's maxim that "No battle plan survives contact with the enemy."

Jacobson wanted Martin to helicopter to Tan Son Nhut, but the Air America controller did not have a spare aircraft. Two helicopters were in Can Tho, VNAF pilots had hijacked four more, and many pilots had not yet arrived on base.

When Martin heard this, he said, "Goddamnit, I'll drive. That way I can get the feel of the atmosphere in town."

Jacobson warned him that Vietcong units had been sighted near the airport and urged him to wait for a helicopter.

"Well, we all make mistakes, don't we, Jake?" he said. "Someone call my car. I'm going."

He drove to Tan Son Nhut in his armor-plated Chevrolet sedan. His marine escorts retracted its fender flag stanchions to avoid announcing his presence. An advance jeep of two marines probed the streets and roadblocks, radioing back instructions in code. More sedans filled with marines, fingers on triggers, preceded and followed him.

The South Vietnamese police and MPs manning the Tan Son Nhut gate refused to admit Martin. He sat alone in the backseat for twenty minutes while authorities were contacted and pressure applied. As columns of black smoke spiraled into the air from damaged VNAF planes, he told himself that no matter what happened, he was sure to receive "sledgehammer blows from the idiot leftist press" and "the perfumed ice pick to the kidneys from State Department enemies."

Promises were made and threats delivered, and he was finally admitted to Tan Son Nhut. Major General Smith had assembled a group of American and Vietnamese officers in his operations bunker. They told Martin that a fixed-wing evacuation would be madness under present conditions. Martin turned to Colonel Le Van Long, the head of intelligence for the ARVN Joint General Staff, and told him to call his office and *demand* that his troops restore order. Long said that no one was answering the phones and that even his switchboard operators had fled.

Smith broke in and said, "Either we go with Option Four [the helicopter evacuation] or we're going to look pretty stupid, or pretty dead."

Martin asked to confer with him privately. Once alone in Smith's office, he said that he was determined to evacuate ten thousand Vietnamese that day and that only the C-130s could accomplish this. He called the White House on Smith's scrambler phone and asked Scowcroft to confirm to Smith that President Ford had agreed that the fixed-wing airlift should continue. Scowcroft replied that Ford wanted the planes to continue flying "as long as feasible."

As he and Smith were walking back to the operations room, he repeated his conversation with Scowcroft. When Smith protested that the runways were blocked, he said, "If we can't, okay, but let's try." Then, speaking with more passion and force than Smith had ever witnessed from him, and even though he was speaking in a whisper, he said, "Everybody—the Pentagon, Schlesinger, the Joint Chiefs, and CINCPAC—is going to ask us to get the Americans out fast and leave the Vietnamese. We have thousands of high-risk Vietnamese here; we have to pull out as many as possible." He repeated himself several times, warning that Schlesinger, CINCPAC, and the Joint Chiefs were going to exert enormous pressure on them all day—pressure they must resist. Leaving the high-risk Vietnamese behind would be "unconscionable," he said, one more ghastly mistake capping the thousands of others that the United States had made in Vietnam.

Erich von Marbod had been sitting at a desk in the corner of the operations room. After walking past without acknowledging him, Martin suddenly turned, smiled, and putting an arm around his shoulder asked if they might have a word outside. They stood talking next to Smith's bunker for several minutes. As a shell slammed into the Air America hangar, sending fireballs shooting into the sky, Martin said, "You have friends at Seventh Air Force headquarters. Can you ask them to send for a plane to pick up Dottie?"

"Goddamn it, Graham! Don't you realize what's happening?" von Marbod asked. "Look at the runway. We're catching a ration of shit." The time when a plane could land and pick up Martin's wife had obviously passed.

"I've just told the president we'll go fixed wing," Martin replied coldly. As he spoke, more shells hit the VNAF flight line.

Smith, Martin, and the White House had agreed that even if Martin and his "hard core" of diplomats departed, the U.S. delegation to the Joint Military Team should move to the embassy and continue to pursue MIA issues and mediate negotiations between General Minh and the Communists. Colonel Madison thought that staying in Saigon under the auspices of a peace agreement that the Communists had blatantly violated was lunacy. When Smith asked him to move his men to the embassy, he imagined himself standing alone at the gate when the Communist tanks arrived, holding up his Paris Peace Accords documents and demanding that they honor his "privileges and immunities."

The American JMT delegation had shrunk to Madison, Colonel Summers, Captain Herrington, Bill Bell, and two enlisted men, Ernest Pace and Bill Herron. After a breakfast of bacon and eggs and champagne liberated from the DAO snack bar, they loaded a Land Rover, sedan, and jeep with typewriters, medical supplies, and rations, put on helmets and slipped on their Four-Part Joint Military Team armbands—bright orange with a "4" in the middle—and attached flags carrying that same symbol to their vehicles. Herrington doubted that the flags and armbands would protect them. He feared disgruntled ARVN troops more than Hanoi's soldiers and was secretly rooting for the Communists to take Saigon quickly and impose some order.

Sporadic Communist artillery shells and rockets continued hitting the VNAF flight line as the JMT's three-vehicle convoy drove through the main gate and past the sign proclaiming, "The noble sacrifices of allied soldiers will never be forgotten." The day was overcast and windless, with a low, leaden sky that trapped the heat and humidity. Herrington swerved into a ditch to avoid some looters who were dismembering a stalled car. Past the airport, the traffic thinned and police remained on duty at some intersections. Uniforms, helmets, and boots abandoned by deserters littered sidewalks. Loudspeakers broadcast Minh's acceptance speech and the national anthem on a continuous loop.

Martin returned to the embassy around 10:00 a.m. He called Smith to report having just received a cable from Scowcroft confirming that the C-130s should resume landing, then called Smith back minutes later to remind him that he wanted large numbers of Vietnamese included in the evacuation.

Smith called Admiral Gayler in Honolulu and described the conditions at Tan Son Nhut. "The helicopters should begin now," he said. "Period. Or I don't know what, exclamation point!"

Gayler said that he would recommend that the Joint Chiefs activate Option IV, or "Frequent Wind," the helicopter evacuation from Saigon. Smith reported this to Martin, giving him a chance to save face by making the same recommendation to Kissinger.

"It's not their decision," Martin snapped, meaning that it was his.

Smith replied that landing planes at Tan Son Nhut had become impossible.

"Well, you're probably right—for the wrong reasons," Martin said, wanting to have the last word. "We could get them in but we couldn't control the boarding."

Martin called Kissinger at 10:48 a.m. and requested Option IV, making the decision his own.

Kissinger asked that he complete the evacuation within daylight hours.

When Martin said this might not be possible, Kissinger resorted to flattery, saying, "Graham, you did your best and it was excellent."

Martin shot back, "I don't like much A for effort." He followed up with a cable saying, "I repeat my request to permit me and about twenty of my staff to remain behind, at least for a day or two to at least give some dignity to our departure and to facilitate an orderly disposition of our extensive properties here."

Ford had become increasingly concerned about the safety of U.S. citizens. He vetoed the idea, and Kissinger called Martin back and said, "The President insists on total evacuation."

Martin argued that he should remain in Saigon with a small team to help Minh and keep the evacuation going.

"Now, Graham," Kissinger said, "we want all our heroes at home."

During the National Security Council meeting that morning, Ford had asked Joint Chiefs chairman Brown, "Are you ready to go to a helicopter lift?" Brown had said, "Yes, if you or Ambassador Martin say so, we can have them there within the hour." Instead, more than three hours would elapse between when Martin agreed to go to Option IV and when two helicopters landed at Tan Son Nhut bringing Lieutenant General Richard Carey, commander of the Ninth Marine Amphibious Brigade (MAB), and Colonel Al Gray, who was commanding the MAB's five-hundred-man ground security force. And it would not be until an hour later, at 3:12 p.m., that Gray's troops began arriving in the larger CH-53 Sea Stallion helicopters and the first groups of seventy evacuees began boarding these helicopters. After learning about the delay, Kissinger said, "We've screwed up everything else in this war—why not that?" An investigation revealed that the delay had occurred because the marines and their helicopters were positioned on different vessels and had to be "cross-decked"— brought together on the same ship—and because of a misunderstanding between the navy and the air force over whether the L in "L-Hour" meant when the helicopters were launched or landed in Saigon.

The JMT was unpacking its equipment in the embassy's fifth-floor military affairs office when Wolfgang Lehmann burst in and said, "New orders from Washington. We're all leaving." He suggested that because they were already at the embassy and many of them spoke Vietnamese, they could help manage the evacuation.

Herrington looked out a window to see streamers of shredded documents falling like ticker tape and black smoke spiraling into the air as diplomats destroyed their files. In the recreation area over a thousand evacuees sat on suitcases and cardboard boxes filled with photographs, memorabilia, diplomas, jewelry, and cash—the kinds of valuables people grab when homes burst into flames. A gate connected the recreation area, with its pool and restaurant, to the parking lot and chancery. Herrington could see that the larger helicopters would have to land in the parking lot and that the JMT would need to control the people in the recreation center, breaking them into helicopter loads and feeding them into the parking lot through the gate or over the low roof of the embassy fire station. He turned to Lehmann and said, "The only way we're going to get control of the crowd is to promise that everyone inside the compound will be evacuated."

Lehmann checked with Martin and reported back that he had promised that everyone inside the embassy compound would be flown to the fleet.

Herrington, Bell, Madison, and Summers went downstairs and circulated through the crowd in the recreation center. The evacuees were nervous and fearful. Herrington thought it would not take much to start a riot. He and the others confiscated weapons and large suitcases and threw them into the swimming pool. They removed a large antenna that risked snagging one of the helicopters. They promised the twenty embassy firemen that they would put their families on the first helicopters if the firemen agreed to leave on the last ones so they could extinguish any fires if one of them crashed. They barged in on a group of American contractors who had pulled meat from the lockers in the recreation area restaurant and were grilling it over burners while swilling liquor stolen from the bar. They locked up the liquor and shooed the contractors outside. They walked through the crowd repeating the same message: hand over your weapons, calm down so we can organize you into helicopter loads, everyone will get out.

Summers climbed onto the roof of the soft drink stall and shouted through a bullhorn, "Every one of you folks is going to get out of here. Let me repeat that: all you people here with us today are going to be flown to safety and freedom. Not one of you will be left behind. I will only go after the last of you has left. And the United States ambassador has assured me he will leave right at the end, after you and me. On that we give you our solemn word." He climbed down and walked through the crowd saying, "Don't you worry," and "Sure, you'll get a job in the States."

Herrington had written to his parents in April that he was "doubtful about my ability to walk out with my personal honor" and was "extremely worried" that he was "going to be made to abandon our people, our employees, their families, my friends," and be told, "Save the Americans and the hell with everyone else." Now, relying on Martin's promise, he shouted through a megaphone in Vietnamese that within twenty-four hours everyone who could hear him would be safely aboard U.S. Navy ships. "There is plenty of time! Don't worry about it! No one will be left behind!" he yelled. "We will remain with you! We will be the last to leave!"

He and Summers were promising to evacuate everyone inside the compound, villains and saints alike. They were promising evacuation to third-country nationals: to Korean diplomats and intelligence agents, a German priest, the young Filipino rock musicians who had arrived lugging their instruments and speakers, the Japanese ambassador who was wearing a white helmet and a bulletproof vest, and the ICCS Hungarians who were terrified that Communist soldiers would mistake them for Americans. They were promising to evacuate everyone who had gotten into the embassy compound because of what Vietnamese called "Big Nose Syndrome," that is, their Caucasian features. They were promising to evacuate Ross Meador, Brian Ellis, the American women who had arrived in high heels and long dresses, as if flying out first class on a commercial airliner, the American contractors who sat by the pool drinking and spraying around champagne stolen from the Combined Recreation Area restaurant while singing, "We're going home in freedom birds / Doo dah, doo dah," to the tune of "Camptown Races," and the young Vietnamese women who, upon hearing that everyone was going to the United States, had ditched their paunchy middle-aged American husbands and lovers because they no longer needed them.

They were promising to evacuate Thu Minh Nguyen and her six children. Her husband was still fighting with the army and had ordered his family to escape without him. She had driven her children to the Khanh Hoi wharf, but they had been terrified by the sight of people falling into the water and drowning while trying to board barges. After that, she had used the family's gold to buy forged documents stating that her husband worked for the embassy.

They were promising to evacuate Y. I. Ching, an American merchant seaman of Chinese descent who had returned from his native Hawaii to rescue his Vietnamese wife and their five children. He had collected them in Bien Hoa two days before and taken sanctuary in the embassy.

They were promising to evacuate Binh Pho, a young architecture student who had slipped into the compound with his girlfriend thanks to the help of a friend who had a relative working at the embassy. After making it inside, Pho's friend said, "Let's have a party, we're in America now." They sat around the swimming pool drinking, and Pho and his girlfriend made paper airplanes out of their soon-to-be-worthless piastres, sending them soaring into the muggy midday air.

They were promising to evacuate the upper-class Vietnamese women who had come wearing their fur coats and had jammed multiple rings on their fingers and slipped dozens of bracelets on their wrists to prevent them from being stolen from their luggage. They were promising to evacuate the former mayor of Saigon, General Minh's relatives, President Thieu's cousin, a millionaire who had played tennis with General Westmoreland, Bui Diem, the former ambassador to Washington, portly General Quang, Thieu's former national security adviser, who had arrived in a civilian suit with a wad of cash peeking out from his breast pocket, and others whose presence here appeared to confirm the truth of the Vietnamese saying that only when the house burns do you see the faces of the rats.

The biggest rats stood out because the American newsmen and diplomats knew them. But most of the Vietnamese in the recreation area were embassy employees and their families, friends of Americans, friends of those friends, and anyone lucky enough to have arrived early. Some had been on evacuation buses that had dropped them outside the embassy after the Vietnamese MPs had prevented their buses from entering Tan Son Nhut; others were people whom Air America pilots had collected from rooftops and brought here instead of Tan Son Nhut; others had persuaded the marine guards that they worked for a U.S. agency or were related to someone who did.

Many feared that the small Air America Hueys that were landing on the embassy roof to discharge evacuees from nearby helipads were also shuttling people out to the fleet. They began pushing and shoving to get closer to the gate separating the recreation area from the rest of the compound. Herrington waded into the crowd with a bullhorn. Speaking Vietnamese with a fluency that amazed architecture student Binh Pho, he said, "Hey everybody, stay in line. You don't have to elbow each other to try to get in. What we have here is about 3000 people and we have 24 hours to evacuate." He promised that helicopters would soon begin landing again on the roof and at ground level, adding, "My calculation is that the helicopters will come and go in fifteen-minute intervals, and right now it's three in the afternoon and we'll be out of here easily within twenty-four hours. There's plenty of time, don't worry about it." The crowd calmed down, and although Pho and his girlfriend were near the gate, they hung back to help manage their friends' children.

While the JMT was promising to evacuate everyone, a work party of marines and Seabees began cutting down the huge tamarind tree in the parking lot. Weeks before, contractors from Pacific Architects and Engineers had surveyed the compound as a possible evacuation site and had recommended that the embassy keep several chain saws at hand. Instead, there was only one and it immediately broke. It took this impromptu work party more than an hour to fell the tree with fire axes and sweep up the chips and branches so that the helicopters' rotor wash would not blow them into the faces of the evacuees.

Martin had ordered that the evacuation be first-come first-served and that no preference be given to Americans. Some in the U.S. mission were ignoring him and putting their Vietnamese friends and co-workers at the head of the lines leading to the parking lot and the roof. Nevertheless, during a meeting in his office Martin said, "I'm not aware that anyone is being given priority in terms of seat space. Everybody is supposed to be equal here." One of Marvin Garrett's mission wardens shot back, "Obviously you don't know what's happening out there."

CHAPTER 19

Ken Moorefield's Odyssey

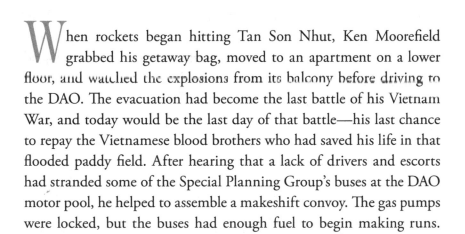

When rockets began hitting Tan Son Nhut, Ken Moorefield grabbed his getaway bag, moved to an apartment on a lower floor, and watched the explosions from its balcony before driving to the DAO. The evacuation had become the last battle of his Vietnam War, and today would be the last day of that battle—his last chance to repay the Vietnamese blood brothers who had saved his life in that flooded paddy field. After hearing that a lack of drivers and escorts had stranded some of the Special Planning Group's buses at the DAO motor pool, he helped to assemble a makeshift convoy. The gas pumps were locked, but the buses had enough fuel to begin making runs. He persuaded a middle-aged Vietnamese man whom he had met in a ditch where they had both taken shelter from the bombardment to drive a bus. By mid-morning he and the SPG's captain Tony Wood had left Tan Son Nhut in charge of a three-bus convoy. Wood had recruited Sergeant Maloney, the now born-again Christian who commanded the DAO's marine guards, to lead the buses with him in one jeep while Moorefield brought up the rear in another jeep.

The streets were already busy with people who were ignoring the curfew to search for food, relatives, and escape. At some roadblocks security forces waved the buses through; at others they stopped them and hassled the drivers. Some soldiers robbed pedestrians, looted stores, and stole civilian clothes from washing lines and tailors' shops; others fought on, mounting a brave rear-guard defense. Moorefield and Wood collected evacuees from the SPG's downtown pickup locations and brought them to the DAO, where they came under sporadic artillery fire. Moorefield believed that a North Vietnamese forward observer was targeting the buses.

Wood and Maloney exchanged their jeep for a Chevrolet with flashing police lights and led the empty buses and Moorefield back into town. Just beyond the gate they stopped for a roadblock. As traffic backed up, a sniper opened fire. Maloney grabbed his rifle, and he and Wood ran toward the gunfire, hoping to hunt down the sniper. Moorefield intercepted Maloney and persuaded him to return to his jeep and keep the convoy moving. In the meantime Moorefield's driver had vanished with his jeep, taking his getaway bag with his West Point class ring. He jumped into the passenger seat of Maloney's jeep, and they continued into Saigon, stopping at the SPG collection points and filling up the three buses.

They returned to find a new and un-bribed MP detachment manning the gate. A nervous young lieutenant stood in the road with his arm extended, his palm facing outward. After Moorefield stopped, he shouted, "You turn around!" Moorefield said he was an American official and wanted to drive a short distance to a U.S. military facility. The lieutenant drew his .45, pointed it at Moorefield's head, and ordered his men to lock and load. One of the American bus drivers got out and began to argue. The MPs shouted, "We're not letting you in," and fired at his feet.

Fearing a massacre, Moorefield led his convoy back into the city. Pedestrians pounded their fists on the sides of his buses. An ARVN officer waved a revolver and threatened to shoot him unless he evacuated his family. The buses were low on gas and Moorefield overheard a dispatcher at the Evacuation Control Center warning drivers to avoid the embassy because a mob had surrounded its walls. The dispatcher radioed Moorefield and said that the ambassador wanted him to collect his household staff from his residence. Moorefield remembered that a fuel truck was usually stationed there and agreed to go. He collected some of Martin's staff, gassed up the buses, and called the embassy to ask what he should do with his three busloads of evacuees.

Jim Devine answered and suggested putting them on one of the MSC barges that should have arrived by now at the Khanh Hoi wharf in downtown Saigon. This was the first that Moorefield had heard about Bill Ryder's barges, and he was upset that the embassy had kept him in the dark.

At Newport earlier that morning Bill Ryder had destroyed his files and asked his tugboat and barge captains to board evacuees onto the barges and the Korean LST *Boo Heung Pioneer.* Most of his Vietnamese employees had already left as stowaways on the *Green Wave,* so many of the barges and the LST would be evacuating port officials and members of the military and their families. The LST's Korean officers had already left, so Ryder persuaded Nguyen Bao Truc, a former navy commander and future Lodi, California, school janitor, to pilot the ship down the Saigon River.

The LST cast off at noon. The tugboats and barges followed within the hour. Each of the five tugs towed a two-thousand-ton barge capable of carrying six thousand people. The barges had transported munitions to Cambodia, and to protect their crews and cargo, the Military Sealift Command had surrounded them with ten-foot steel walls filled with sandbags. Ryder had promised Lacy Wright and AID officials Mel Chatman and Russell Mott, who were operating the embassy's Evacuation Control Center, that he would evacuate any U.S. mission Vietnamese personnel unable to reach Tan Son Nhut. The battle for the Newport Bridge had made it too dangerous to bus evacuees to Newport, so Ryder agreed to collect the embassy's people at the Khanh Hoi wharf. As he was preparing to leave Newport, two CIA officers radioed to report that they had collected five hundred of the agency's up-country employees and their families in a fleet of yellow school buses and wanted to put them aboard the barges. Ryder told them to meet him at Khanh Hoi.

Martin and Jacobson feared that Ryder's barges would ignite riots and had kept them a closely guarded secret, alerting Lacy Wright and a select group of embassy officials but not Alan Carter, Ken Moorefield, and others. As a result, many of the people boarding them at Khanh Hoi would be passersby, deserters, those hearing rumors about them, and embassy employees whom Lacy Wright and Joe McBride would drive there. Because no one knew how many barges would arrive, they fought to get aboard the first ones, and because there were no stairs or gangplanks, evacuees had to climb over the barge's ten-foot-high sandbag walls. Ryder saw a grandmother holding an infant fall between the pier and the barge. They never resurfaced, and he realized at that moment that he would never forget them. Nor would he forget that once his barge became overloaded, he and his crew had threatened to shoot anyone attempting to board it, nor that they had fired into the water to discourage people from swimming after them, nor that he had asked himself, "Who the hell am I to play God?" But at least he had been an egalitarian God who had dispensed with VIP lists, visas, and bribes.

His tug pulled its barge into the middle of the river and waited as the others docked their barges. By the time the last tug arrived around 5:00 p.m., the crowds had thinned, and its captain was shouting through a bullhorn that anyone wanting to go to the United States should jump aboard. AID officer Mel Chatman, who had driven to Khanh Hoi, called the embassy evacuation center and said, "We've got two huge barges here. Call everyone and tell 'em that if they got any people who are still looking for a ride, we've got the space. All they gotta do is get down here to Khanh Hoi."

Some Vietnamese at the Khanh Hoi wharf hesitated, immobilized by the irrevocability of their decision. Like many on April 29, they had to choose between living in a Communist Vietnam or as exiles in the United States. Those boarding a bus for Tan Son Nhut could change their minds during the drive or after arriving at the airport, and some did. But anyone boarding one of Ryder's barges could not. Climb aboard, and you faced a perilous journey down the Saigon River; stay on the dock, and you might face years in a concentration camp, or worse. Climb aboard, and you could become an American citizen and never see your country again; stay on the dock, and you might become a second-class citizen in a Communist Vietnam, an exile in your own land. Some people stepped back from the edge of the dock and returned home, telling themselves they could leave later, as many would try to do in the coming months and years. And so the last barge departed from Khanh Hoi with room to spare, while a mile away several thousands were besieging the embassy.

Soon after Moorefield left Ambassador Martin's residence, Martin arrived to collect his poodle Nit Noy ("little thing" in Thai) and destroy classified documents. He had asked his marine bodyguards to drive him, but the moment they opened the embassy's rear gate, the crowd surged forward and Major Kean ran over and said, "Sir, with all due respect, there is no way in hell that you are going to drive that car out of here. I recommend that you move back upstairs."

"I am going to walk once more to my residence," Martin said. "I shall walk freely in this city. I shall leave Vietnam when the President tells me to leave."

He and his bodyguards slipped through the door connecting the embassy's recreation area to the French embassy. After paying his respects to Ambassador Mérillon, he walked four blocks to his residence, collected Nit Noy, and supervised the marines as they destroyed classified documents. After returning to the French embassy, he considered asking Mérillon to allow him to move into his wife's bedroom. That way, he reasoned, he could force Washington to keep the helicopters flying until they had evacuated the Vietnamese inside the embassy, leaving him the honor of being the last man out. But even for a man who had defied McNamara and Rusk, disobeying Kissinger and Ford at this crucial moment was too much, so he returned to the embassy with Mérillon's parting gift, a large head of the Buddha.

After leaving Martin's residence, Moorefield had led his buses toward the embassy, only to find that the crowd surrounding its walls made driving inside impossible. He led his convoy to political officer Shep Lowman's villa to see what Lowman suggested. Lowman begged him to evacuate the fifty embassy employees, intellectuals, and politicians whom he had told to gather at his villa. "Shep, I don't have room," he said, "and if I try to squeeze them on, we'll have a riot on our hands."

He continued to the Brink Hotel, now a bachelor officers' quarters. A hundred and fifty Vietnamese sat in the courtyard, lobby, and ground-floor public rooms. Some were hotel employees; others said that their American friends had told them to come with their families and await buses for Tan Son Nhut. Moorefield thought they were doomed. He picked his way around them to the reception desk, avoiding their eyes. He called Martin's office and told Eva Kim that he had several hundred people in his buses and had just encountered 150 more at the Brink Hotel. "What am I going to *do* with these people?" he asked. After putting him on hold, she returned a minute later and reported that no one could help him. He walked back through the courtyard murmuring, "Stand fast. Stand fast. Stand fast," and thinking, "There's no plan, or if there was, it's been overtaken by events. And now I've got three buses filled with people."

He returned to find a mob besieging the buses. The metal grilles covering their windows could be lowered six inches for ventilation, and a mother had slipped her infant into one bus through this opening and was screaming, "My baby's on the bus!" Instead of driving to the wharf through Saigon's chaotic streets, Moorefield decided to park near the embassy and walk everyone to the main gate. He assumed that the bus drivers would follow his jeep. Instead, they lost him in the traffic.

One of these buses had collected a contingent of journalists from the Caravelle Hotel that included Ed Bradley of CBS, Hilary Brown and Ken Kashiwahara of ABC, and Keyes Beech, a veteran *Chicago Daily News* war correspondent. They had ridden in Moorefield's haphazard convoy for several hours, witnessing his standoff with the MPs and becoming increasingly impatient as they waited outside the Brink Hotel, Lowman's villa, and the ambassador's residence. Their American expat driver had careened through Saigon's narrow streets, sideswiping cars and knocking over the carts of sidewalk vendors. He had no ignition key and had to hot-wire the bus whenever they stopped. Several times he turned around to shout, "If there's a bus driver aboard I'd be glad to let him take the wheel."

After becoming separated from Moorefield, he and the other drivers headed to Khanh Hoi, believing that Moorefield had gone there. They had the misfortune to arrive as a large crowd was battling to get aboard an overloaded barge. The driver of the journalists' bus suggested that they either try to board it or wait for a helicopter. Ed Bradley thought that no helicopter pilot in his right mind would land in the middle of this mob, and he and the other Americans stayed on the bus. Some Vietnamese passengers disembarked, quickly realized their mistake, and ran back. Ken Kashiwahara noticed a helicopter flying toward the embassy and persuaded their driver to head there. As they were leaving, Bradley saw one of the Vietnamese passengers attempting to rejoin them. The man carried a suitcase in one hand and was holding on to his wife with the other. She was dragging along their two children so that the family resembled a string of paper dolls. Decades later, Bradley could still see the terrified expression on the man's face as the bus pulled away.

Other Americans who drove, guarded, or rode in the evacuation buses witnessed similar heartbreaking scenes. DAO intelligence operative Frank Aurelio had persuaded Nelson Kieff, the plainclothes military intelligence agent who had rescued people from Pleiku and had teamed up with Martindale during the Nha Trang evacuation, to serve as an armed guard on an SPG bus. Aurelio told Kieff that the Vietnamese driver had been trained and given a predetermined route and list of evacuees. Kieff's job would be to prevent unauthorized passengers from boarding his bus. Crowds besieged his bus the moment it stopped, crying and begging to be allowed inside. It was half-full when Kieff picked up a young Vietnamese woman on his list. The people surrounding the bus looked menacing, and some were armed. After the young woman boarded, Kieff shouted for the driver to slam the door and accelerate. She screamed, "My brother!" and Kieff looked back to see a young man running after the bus, frantically waving his arms and shouting. He had to make a split-second decision. Fearing that armed deserters might hijack the bus, he told the driver not to stop. While recounting this story four decades later, he began to cry, saying through his tears, "I thought I was doing the right thing. I didn't even know if he was on my list or not, and I don't know what happened to him, or to her."

It was late afternoon when the buses that had become separated from Moorefield parked near the embassy. A female Vietnamese passenger saw the crowd and despaired of getting over the wall. She told reporter Keyes Beech that the Communists would cut her throat, adding, "I've worked for the United States government for ten years, but you [Americans] do not trust me and I do not trust you." Even if she made it into Tan Son Nhut, she doubted that Americans would let her board a plane. "I'm going home to poison myself," she said.

The marines at the front gate told correspondent Ken Kashiwahara to go around to the back, where their comrades would let him in. He was worried about being mistaken for a Vietnamese and decided to shout, "The Dodgers won the National League pennant!" to prove his nationality. Luckily, a marine recognized him and hauled him over the wall. Keyes Beech tried entering through the rear gate. As he pushed through the crowd, his attaché case hit a baby, and its father punched him in the back. A teenager grabbed his arm and begged to be adopted. Beech yanked his arm away, and a marine pulled him inside. Beech reported, "Once we moved into that seething mass we ceased to be journalists. We were only men fighting for our lives, scratching, clawing, pushing ever closer to the wall. We were like animals."

Moorefield abandoned his sedan near the embassy. It was around five o'clock and the men on the outer fringes of the crowd were a volatile mixture of deserters, street toughs, and "Saigon Cowboys," young men whose wealthy families had bribed their way out of the draft. Some had come to steal or cannibalize the cars that evacuees had abandoned and to loot the embassy after the Americans left. Moorefield felt uneasy. He was wearing a blue jumpsuit and looked vaguely military, and his face was smudged with dirt that resembled smoke or gunpowder. Someone asked why he was not inside with the other Americans. Feeling vulnerable, he said he was a Canadian journalist. He felt ashamed of himself and thought, "I think I've played my hand." He pushed through the crowd and caught the attention of marines guarding the side gate. They opened it a crack, and he squeezed inside.

Joe McBride returned to the embassy about half an hour after Moorefield and found it even harder to get inside. He and Lacy Wright had been collecting people from safe houses in embassy vans and driving them to Khanh Hoi so they could board one of Ryder's barges. Most were U.S. mission employees and their families, relatives of State Department personnel, or members of the political class and intelligentsia. McBride and Wright had begun making runs to Khanh Hoi around noon. Wright was summoned back to the embassy, but McBride stayed out all afternoon. He crammed twenty-five people into a van seating twelve, bribed police, and siphoned gasoline from parked cars. Each time he returned to the safe house, he found more people waiting. He shouted, "Don't worry! We have room for everyone!" While he was loading people into his van, a well-dressed middle-aged man stepped forward and asked whom he wanted to take. "People who put themselves in harm's way," McBride said, "people who were courageous." The man helped him control the crowd and load the van but refused his offer to put him on a barge.

McBride was doing what he had promised all along—staying out in the street and evacuating "the right Vietnamese." Several days earlier Marvin Garrett, the U.S. mission security officer, had summoned him and other junior diplomats to another clandestine evacuation planning meeting. Garrett had told them, "Martin thinks there will be negotiations and an orderly departure, but most of us don't think it's going to work out that way. We have to be prepared to take care of ourselves." As he was assigning everyone a different stretch of the wall to guard, McBride told him, "I'm sorry but I won't do your wall thing, because I'll be out on the streets." When Garrett asked, "What are your priorities?" he said, "I think the Americans will get out, but I'd like to get the right Vietnamese out. I'm going to be out there."

By the time McBride returned to the embassy, it was dusk. The marines guarding the vehicle entrance told him that if they opened the gate, hundreds of people would try to storm inside, forcing them to shoot. McBride threw his Samsonite briefcase over the wall because it contained grenades and weapons that he wanted to keep away from the crowd. The marines suggested he go around to the consulate, where the gate was a sally port that made it easy to leave the compound but difficult for a large group to go in the other direction. He circulated through the crowd, gathering up stray Americans who had not yet made it inside with their Vietnamese families. Two huge marines, one black and the other white, came out of the sally port and stood on either side of McBride, blocking the crowd with their bodies as he fed his Americans and Vietnamese into the compound. He wrote them up for bravery, and they received awards.

As soon as McBride was inside, he stripped down to his underwear. Perspiration had drenched the seersucker suit that he had been wearing for the last five days. As he was wringing it out, a platoon of marines jogged out of the chancery. They crossed the compound and stood with their backs against the wall. Some held their M-16 rifles between them, turning them into steps so they could boost their comrades over the wall. Polgar had gathered several dozen friends and VIPs in a safe house across the street and wanted the marines to go over the wall and rescue them. At the last minute Wolfgang Lehmann dashed from the chancery shouting, "Get those men back in here, Lieutenant. No more Vietnamese get in here." Turning to McBride, who was still in his underwear, he said, "That goes for you, too!"

McBride dressed and went upstairs to his office. The entire floor was deserted. He saw smashed typewriters and vandalized furnishings and thought, "This is it. There's nothing more I can do." He stopped at Martin's outer office on his way to the roof and smelled whiskey. Martin grabbed him by the arm and pulled him aside. He said he had heard over the embassy radio what he had been doing, braving the streets to bring people to the docks, and wanted to thank him. McBride had never seen the ambassador so emotional, or for that matter emotional at all. McBride was one of the few Americans on the helicopter leaving from the roof. Martin had ordered that each flight include at least one U.S. citizen to counter any criticism that he was evacuating only Vietnamese; in other words, he was trickling out Americans to keep the airlift running.

CBS bureau chief Brian Ellis had a British passport and was considering staying to cover Hanoi's victory. He decided to consult friends at the embassy first. He stopped on the way at the Caravelle Hotel to collect his camera and passport and found that someone had locked his room from the inside. Mr. Ba, one of his Vietnamese drivers, shouted through the door that he was there with eleven family members and would let him in only if he promised to evacuate all of them. Ellis shouted back that the barrage had closed the airport. Ba repeated his demands, and Ellis abandoned his possessions. He arrived at the embassy to find a mob of desperate Mr. Bas surrounding its walls and blocking its main gate.

Press Secretary John Hogan saw him standing outside the gate and ordered it opened wide enough to let him slip inside. He told Hogan, "Look, I've decided it may be time for me to get out of here." Hogan replied (erroneously) that they were not evacuating journalists from the embassy, only from the DAO. Ellis climbed to Martin's office and told him that he wanted to leave. "Well, stick around," Martin said breezily. "We'll get you out of here." Ellis left as the sole American passenger on an Air America helicopter that had touched down briefly, leaving before the next group of evacuees could reach it. Its pilot said, "Welcome aboard flight 707 to Havana. I'm not sure where we're going, but these boys want to go to our ships." He explained that the three Vietnamese soldiers in the back had hijacked his helicopter at gunpoint. After landing on the *Hancock,* the helicopter was met by marines who made the Vietnamese and Ellis lie spread-eagled on the deck while searching for weapons.

Many of the Vietnamese outside the walls should have been inside. Among them were U.S. mission employees whose evacuation buses had either never arrived or been turned away from Tan Son Nhut, and KIP from Can Tho whom CIA agent Glenn Rounsevell had promised to evacuate. He and Polgar stood on the wall, searching for familiar faces and telling the marines whom to admit, like bouncers at a nightclub. John Bennett, the acting director of AID, called the

AID building and told his Vietnamese employees to rip off the covers of their copies of the U.S. mission phone directory, bring them to the embassy, and wave them in the air so that their American co-workers could identify them and pull them over the wall.

Women outside the walls wailed and wept. Men screamed, "I work for American ten years in Da Nang and I have letter. Look!" "Vietcong kill me!" "Please, sir, save my son!" and "American boss promise to take me!" Some rolled on the sidewalk in hysterics, crying out the names of the American servicemen, businessmen, and diplomats whom they had served as clerks, drivers, cooks, cleaners, bodyguards, and interpreters. Mothers tried to pass their babies to marines. Teenagers shouted that they had been separated from parents who were already inside. Some people waved expired U.S. government identity cards, letters of commendation from American friends and employers, and letters and telegrams from friends and relatives in the United States promising to support them and from former lovers promising to marry them. They had covered these precious documents in cellophane; the next day they would burn them. A reporter picked up a letter from the ground and read, "He is a person who believes firmly in the values of democracy and the free world. If he should fall into Communist hands his life would be in serious danger." Another letter commended a Mr. Nha, who had washed dishes at the air force officers' club in Pleiku in 1967, for having "faithfully served the cause of freedom in the Republic of Vietnam."

When the crowd was smaller, the marines had admitted Vietnamese with convincing stories and documents. Some softhearted marines admitted almost anyone. By late afternoon they had become less patient, firing volleys into the air and shouting, "Do not panic!" imagining this might calm people who expected a bloodbath. Because there was no comprehensive list to guide the marines, some tended to admit Americans and non-Asian third-country nationals, turning away people like Dr. Lem Truong, the highest-ranking woman in the South Vietnamese government.

Truong's odyssey had been as frantic and frustrating as Moorefield's, and they could easily have crossed paths. After rockets hit Tan

Son Nhut, she had telephoned her husband and teenage sons and begged them to leave with her. Her husband sounded uncertain and said that Communist sympathizers among his friends had promised that he would be safe because he was not in the military or government. Her thirteen-year-old son picked up the phone and said, "Mom, I want to come with you; take me with you if Dad does not want to leave." She promised to call him back. They spoke next in 1987.

Her friend Dr. John Evans called from the embassy at 10:00 a.m. and reported that Jacobson had agreed to include her staff in the evacuation but needed a list of their names. Evans was interrupted and said he had to hang up to attend to an important matter. She tried calling back, but the line was dead. After telling her teenage daughter that they were going to the United States, she sat on the couch with her rosary and prayed for divine guidance. Two senior officers from her ministry arrived with a list of evacuees, and after praying four fifty-bead rosaries, she asked her nephew to drive her to the embassy on the back of his motor scooter so she could hand the list to Jacobson.

A marine guard at the gate refused to admit her without a pass. As she was turning to leave, a retired Vietnamese colonel who worked at the embassy ran to the gate shouting her name. He was shocked that she was still in Saigon. She was a high-risk person, he said, and should have left weeks ago. She explained that she needed to get a list of her employees to Jacobson. The colonel dashed back into the chancery and returned ten minutes later to report that he had been unable to locate Jacobson or anyone in authority. In the meantime a large crowd had gathered behind her. People pushed toward the gate and the marines pushed back. She lost her footing and fell to the ground, breaking her glasses.

She jumped on the back of her nephew's scooter and told him to speed to the Grall Hospital. She hoped that a French institution might offer her some protection. As they were en route, she remembered that the Khmer Rouge had murdered patients at the French hospital in Phnom Penh and changed her mind. She noticed a group of Americans and Vietnamese standing in front of the USIA building and stopped to speak with Huynh Trien Vo, a former colleague at the

Ministry of Information. Vo said that a bus was coming to take them to the embassy and suggested she join them. She told her nephew to speed back to her house and bring back her mother and daughters in the family car. As she was worrying about how to contact her husband and sons, the bus arrived. It was already jammed, but Vo somehow squeezed aboard. She realized that getting her aged mother and infant daughter onto it would be impossible and waved good-bye to Vo when she saw her nephew approaching behind the wheel of her blue Datsun.

She sat in the passenger seat, while her mother, baby, sixteen-year-old daughter, and thirteen-year-old niece crammed into the rear. She asked her nephew to speed to city hall. The former head of her agency, Colonel Ha, had recently been promoted to mayor and might help her. He was out supervising rescue teams. After calling into his office, he told her that he and some friends had chartered a boat and that Truong and her family were welcome to join them. He also agreed that she could bring two other families who had no means of escape and that they should all wait for him at city hall. One of the other families met her there, but when Ha failed to return after an hour, she decided that something must have happened to him and decided to try her luck at Khanh Hoi. Soldiers and police refused to let her near the private vessels chartered by bigwigs and threatened to shoot out her tires. She raced back to city hall with ten people in her Datsun, sharing the passenger seat with two other adults and riding half out of the car, gripping its frame with one hand while holding her rosary in the other and praying. She saw the mayor's car going in the other direction and shouted for her nephew to follow him. When they arrived at a distant pier, more people joined them, and the men pulled a dilapidated wooden cargo ship from a shed and launched it. It had been built for inland waterways, not for a long voyage in open water.

Colonel Al Gray and Brigadier General Richard Carey arrived at the DAO by helicopter shortly after two o'clock from the navy task force. They were in no mood to have Graham Martin or anyone else micromanage their evacuation. Carey had already tangled with Martin during their meeting at the embassy on April 14, when Martin had made him feel, he remembered, "like an unwanted visitor." Hours before Gray flew to the DAO, Rear Admiral Donald Whitmire had summoned him to his quarters on the *Blue Ridge* to report having received a cable from the Pentagon ordering Gray's ground security force limited to a marine company of 150 men. Gray believed that a company was too small to protect Tan Son Nhut and told Whitmire, "Either we bring in a battalion or I don't go." Whitmire backed down.

Gray was as tough as that encounter made him sound. He was a tobacco-chewing, barrel-chested marine from the Jersey Shore who had received a battlefield commission during the Korean War, advised South Vietnamese troops in 1964, and returned to command American marines. In 1973, he had been sent to Okinawa to reform a troubled marine regiment. Racial tensions had led to fights and murders, and after examining the regimental records, he noticed that the men who lacked a high school diploma were responsible for most of the violence. He started an accredited high school on the base and wove its classes into his training schedule. Blacks and whites were soon helping one another with homework, and within four months most of the racial tension had evaporated. He was bringing that same common sense and humanity to the evacuation. He believed that leaving behind South Vietnamese who had been loyal to their country and to the United States was immoral. While briefing his officers before they flew to Tan Son Nhut, he said, "I'm not going to decide if a Vietnamese should go out or not, and I don't want my people doing it either." He repeated this admonition after landing at the DAO, circulating among his troops, and saying, "We're not going to play God. We're going to take out everyone who wants to go."

The first members of his ground security force landed in the DAO compound at 3:12 p.m. They ran down the ramps of three CH-53 Sea Stallion helicopters in full battle dress to cheers and applause from Americans and Vietnamese. Earlier that day, an air force colonel had told Foreign Service officer Don Hays that once the helicopters arrived, only Americans would be evacuated. In reply, Hays had gestured toward fifteen hundred Vietnamese evacuees sitting underneath the raised buildings of the DAO and asked, "What about them?" The colonel had replied, "They're your problem." After Gray arrived, Hays approached one of his marine officers and asked if they would be evacuating all the Vietnamese. The marine checked with Gray, who presumably repeated his admonition not to play God, and told Hays, "We're cleared to take everyone out."

Hays, an air force officer, and an American civilian organized the evacuees at one DAO landing zone into groups of seventy before escorting them to the helicopters. He sent the ill, the elderly, and family groups out first. Two women delivered babies while they were waiting. Fearing that they could not board with their infants, they left them on the tarmac. Hays scooped them up and put them and their mothers on a special flight. (One of the children became a U.S. Navy Seabee, and Hays ran into him in Albania years later.) Three ARVN troopers pointed their rifles at Hays and demanded evacuation. He promised to help them if they dropped their weapons. After they complied, he led them into an empty office and locked the door. A marine witnessing the incident said, "That took balls." Hays replied, "No. I've just had it up to here."

Between 3:15 and 5:30 p.m., a daisy chain of marine and air force helicopters evacuated almost five thousand Americans, Vietnamese, and third-country nationals from six landing zones scattered through the DAO compound, taking off from its tennis courts, baseball field, and parking lots. The helicopters were on the ground less than three minutes, and there was none of the chaos and mob rule that had marred the evacuations from Da Nang and Nha Trang. Air America and military helicopter pilots reported sporadic ground fire, but none of their passengers were wounded. The widespread attacks on Americans that Martin, Polgar, and others had predicted never materialized.

The same South Vietnamese MP lieutenant who had refused to allow Moorefield into Tan Son Nhut turned back evacuation buses throughout the afternoon, forcing their drivers to leave their passengers at the docks or outside the embassy. After becoming separated from Moorefield and Maloney, the SPG's heroic Captain Wood had assembled another convoy, collected more evacuees, and made several attempts to get through the gate. The MPs fired warning shots and shouted, "We want to go too!" He finally called Lieutenant General Carey at the Evacuation Control Center and explained the situation. Carey told him to have his buses fall back and ordered a Cobra gunship that was circling overhead to buzz the gate. Wood told the MPs that unless they let him through, the gunship would level their gate. They capitulated, and why Smith and Carey had not done this sooner, or simply taken control of the gate, has never been explained.

Instead of monitoring the evacuation from inside the DAO's Evacuation Control Center, Colonel Gray drove around Tan Son Nhut in a jeep, checking on his men and on the fighting at the northern end of the air base. Whenever he entered the ECC to transmit a report, Kissinger seemed to be on the radio, demanding to know how many more people were left and when the evacuation would end. Gray thought, "We'll be done when everyone's evacuated." He became so fed up that he unplugged Kissinger in mid-sentence and walked out.

When he and Carey landed, they had assumed that the embassy evacuees either had already been bused to Tan Son Nhut or were en route, except for a hard core of a hundred diplomats and marine guards who could be lifted off the embassy's rooftop helipad. They did not learn the truth until 4:00 p.m., when Major Kean notified Carey's deputy that three thousand Americans, Vietnamese, and third-country nationals remained in the embassy compound. They could not reach Tan Son Nhut by road, and would need to be airlifted to the fleet. Kean also requested a contingent of marines from the ground security force to control them and help manage the evacuation.

Some of these embassy evacuees had arrived on Air America helicopters whose pilots had dropped them off on the roof because they wanted to conserve fuel and the embassy was closer to the downtown helipads than Tan Son Nhut. Among these pilots was Marius Burke, who had been collecting people from the roof of 22 Gia Long Street before acting CIA operations officer O. B. Harnage relieved him. Burke then took a mid-afternoon break to return to Vung Tau and search for Jim Collins, the retired American who had come to evacuate orphans from the military academy. He failed to raise Collins on the radio but managed to fly fifteen orphans from the academy to the *Blue Ridge*. Most Air America pilots stood down at dusk, but Burke kept flying. He finally stopped at midnight after flying for fourteen hours, eating one sandwich, and evacuating over a hundred future American citizens.

Before Harnage began making pickups from 22 Gia Long Street, Polgar had asked him to go to the Lee Hotel at 6 Chien Si Circle and rescue a group of Polgar's South Vietnamese VIPs and friends. Harnage landed on the Lee helipad and went downstairs to collect them. His helicopter had attracted a crowd to the street outside the hotel. Desperate Vietnamese mobbed him, tearing his white shirt and begging to be evacuated. A policeman pulled him from the mob and escorted him back into the building. Two South Vietnamese soldiers rushed to the gate and demanded that he open it and fly them out. One pulled the pin from a grenade, pushed it through the gate's grille, and shouted, "We go with you or I drop the grenade." Harnage shoved the barrel of his Swedish machine gun into the soldier's face and said, "Go ahead, you'll never hear it go off." They locked eyes for several seconds before the soldier replaced the pin and melted back into the crowd.

Harnage decided that the crowd made it too dangerous to use the Lee Hotel. He returned to the embassy, and Polgar sent his VIPs to 22 Gia Long Street next. Harnage recruited Air America pilots Bob Caron and Jack Hunter and made four successful pickups from there, his last immortalized by Hubert Van Es's photograph. After almost being killed by a grenade at the Lee Hotel, Harnage had still ridden on the skids of Caron's helicopter so he could pack a few more Vietnamese aboard. He had acted instinctively, but upon reflection he believed he had taken those risks because after he had lived in South Vietnam for most of a decade, the country had become, he said, "part" of him. He had developed a father-son relationship with a Vietnamese teenager whom he was helping to earn a pilot's license, and he owed his life to a South Vietnamese soldier who had held his head above water to prevent him from drowning after a Vietcong assassination team blew his jeep into a drainage ditch. He had also heard about the Khmer

Rouge atrocities in Cambodia and expected the Communists would do the same thing in Saigon.

After Air America pilots Joe Weiss and George Taylor had made multiple pickups from Saigon rooftop helipads, their South Vietnamese assistant Cong said, "Would it be OK if we picked up my family?" Cong had been helping them evacuate people for the last two days, and Weiss and Taylor were stunned that he had never mentioned his family. "You're damned right we can pick up your family," Taylor said. The pickup proved to be among their trickiest and most dangerous. Cong's house was three stories high and surrounded by high buildings. The family saw them approach and began waving from a third-floor balcony. Vehicles and people filled the surrounding streets, making a landing impossible. Instead, Taylor and Weiss put the left skid of their helicopter against the side of the steeply pitched red tile roof while suspending the right skid over the balcony where the family was standing. One by one Cong's family members grabbed the skid so that Cong could lean down and pull them aboard. His mother nearly fell to her death. After everyone was safely aboard, there were smiles and tears. Taylor and Weiss needed to refuel, so they flew everyone out to the fleet. Cong insisted on returning with them to help evacuate more of his countrymen.

Air America helicopters landed on the roof of Walter Martindale's apartment building throughout the afternoon. He and his Montagnard guards Kulie Kasor and Nay Ri had counted off twenty-person loads, confiscated large bags, and hoisted women and children into the choppers. He promised two ARVN lieutenants who were brothers seats on the last helicopter in exchange for helping his Nung guards control the front gate and screen arrivals. Because his building was a designated embassy evacuation point, people continued arriving. By mid-afternoon the helicopters had attracted a mob to the surrounding streets, and Martindale looked down to see his cook Tua weaving through it while balancing a tray over his head containing Martindale's favorite lunch, a chicken sandwich and a glass of iced tea.

Two inebriated American contractors arrived, pushed everyone aside, and demanded to be admitted. After the guards pulled them over the fence, the crowd erupted in fury and tried to push down the front gate. Martindale had stashed the U.S. embassy's female telephone operators, Vietnamese employees of the neighboring Italian embassy, and some relations of his Franco-Vietnamese fiancée next door at the Italian embassy. When he realized that the crowd would keep them from entering his building, he told his guards to slide a ladder between the second-floor windows of his building and the embassy so they could crawl across it. One of the U.S. embassy's female telephone operators fell off and impaled herself on the metal spears of the fence separating the two buildings. As blood spread across the front of her *ao dai* dress, Kulie Kasor had to restrain Martindale from rushing into the yard and pulling her off. He shouted that if Martindale left the roof, they would lose control of the evacuation and no one would escape.

Moments later Martindale heard a crash. The mob had pushed down the front gate, and people were streaming into the building. He and the lieutenants rushed downstairs but arrived too late to lock the steel shutters separating the stairwell from the roof. The lieutenants drew their revolvers and backed up the stairs. The day before, Martindale had told pilots at Tan Son Nhut, "Boys, don't forget me!" They had not. Air America had ordered its pilots to fly to the fleet at sunset, but another helicopter dropped from the darkening sky. The pilot opened the door next to his seat and drew a finger across his throat, signaling that this would be his last flight. He pointed at Martindale and yelled, "YOU have to go!"

Martindale shook his head. He shouted at the lieutenants, "Start organizing another load. We'll put as many as we can aboard."

They led twenty more evacuees onto the roof. As Martindale was loading them, the pilot yelled, "We want you! No more Vietnamese!" Martindale ignored him and began marshaling another twenty for the next flight. After risking his life to evacuate his people from Quang Duc, Nha Trang, and Phu Quoc, he refused to abandon anyone. As the helicopter lifted off, more people burst from the stairway. He retreated to the edge of the roof as the lieutenants fired into the air to prevent the crowd from pushing him off.

Pilot Joe Weiss had volunteered to make a final attempt to rescue him. As he landed, Martindale could see him mouthing the words, "Come on! Come on!" Martindale decided there was nothing more he could do. He gestured for the two lieutenants to board the helicopter and turned to stare at the people he was leaving behind, searing their faces into his memory. As he took his final steps toward the helicopter, he became temporarily deaf and felt he was moving in slow motion. Once inside the chopper, his senses returned, and he heard the people he had abandoned swearing and screaming. He wept all the way to Tan Son Nhut.

By the time he arrived, the helicopter evacuation from the DAO to the fleet was winding down. Throughout the afternoon U.S. Marine and Air Force helicopter pilots had braved scattered small-arms fire while navigating through a lowering blanket of clouds. After 6:00 p.m., the Communists resumed their rocket and artillery attack, it began to rain, visibility deteriorated, and there were several near collisions. Don Hays was among the last American civilians to depart. After he had loaded people onto the helicopters all afternoon, the wind blast from the rotors had stripped off his shirt. He had also lost his shoes and arrived on a navy ship with only his revolver, a camera bag, and his State Department identification card.

Major General Smith and his staff left at 8:00 p.m. Brigadier General Carey departed around 11:00 p.m., and Colonel Gray followed a few minutes later. As one of the last CH-53s was about to lift off, forty Vietnamese broke a hole in the perimeter fence and charged onto the landing zone. Instead of making a quick takeoff or firing warning shots, the pilots and passengers, a mixture of U.S. military personnel and American civilians, encouraged them to sit on their laps or between their legs. By the end of the day, U.S. military helicopters had evacuated 4,829 people from the DAO. Aside from 395 Americans, most of the rest were Vietnamese. Except for the failure to seize control of the Tan Son Nhut gate from the Vietnamese MPs, the DAO evacuation had been almost flawless.

Military intelligence agent Nelson Kieff was among the last to leave. He had been destroying classified files when he looked out the window to see two army officers pouring gasoline into a steel drum and setting it alight. He decided to add his files to their fire, but by the time he got outside, they had left and their fire was out. He lifted the lid and saw bundles of U.S. currency. Most were charred, but some had survived. He returned inside and told his boss, Frank Aurelio, "The government has written it off. Let's help ourselves to a few hundred for spending money in Manila."

He went back, lifted the lid, stared at the money, and shoved his hands in his pockets to keep himself from impulsively grabbing a bundle of it. He walked around the barrel thinking, "What the hell do I need this money for anyway?" The life he had known in Vietnam was over, and many of his Vietnamese friends were dead. Did he want this to be the last thing he did here? He decided he did not. He burned the rest of the money and helped ignite the explosives that had been wired to destroy the DAO. The sprawling building burst into flames at 12:12 a.m. as he and Aurelio were leaving with Bill LeGro and Andy Gembara. As their helicopter rose over the burning building where American generals had managed this calamitous war, Gembara experienced "an overwhelming feeling of shame," as well as pride at having saved so many Vietnamese.

CHAPTER 20

Into the South China Sea

——|┝——

The CIA agents in Can Tho thought that the rockets the Communists fired into the city early on April 29 presaged an all-out assault. Consul General Terry McNamara thought they were a feint meant to discourage the ARVN high command from ordering General Nam to reinforce Saigon. Soon after 10:00 a.m., Jacobson called McNamara to report that Washington had ordered the evacuation of all U.S. personnel from South Vietnam and that McNamara and his staff should leave immediately.

"No other instructions, Jake?" McNamara asked, dreading his reply.

Jacobson sighed. "We want you to go out by Air America chopper," he said. "Americans only. When you've finished, Terry, send the choppers straight back to Saigon. We're going to need them desperately for our own evacuation."

"You know how I feel about taking the Vietnamese with me. If you're counting on our helicopters to help with the Saigon evacuation, you're not going to get them quickly if we use them to evacuate ourselves."

The line went dead before Jacobson could respond. Although McNamara was determined to evacuate everyone down the Bassac River, with or without Jacobson's approval, he decided to make a last attempt to secure it. He could not get a call through to the embassy via networks in Thailand and the Philippines but finally reached Jacobson on the civilian system. He argued that if the helicopters brought Americans out to the fleet from Can Tho, they would need to be refueled, and it could be hours before they reached Saigon. "We have the boats ready and waiting," he said. "The choppers can be dispatched directly to Saigon."

After a long silence Jacobson said, "Okay. Go by water. Send the helicopters to Saigon at once."

McNamara asked him to alert the navy that his convoy would be at the mouth of the Bassac by sunset.

CIA base chief Jim Delaney was in McNamara's office during this exchange. McNamara repeated Jacobson's approval of a river evacuation and said, "Jim, *all* personnel will evacuate by water. There are to be no exceptions. Send the choppers back to Saigon at once."

Delaney agreed to load his American agents onto the CIA's motor launch and its two armed Boston Whalers and meet McNamara's LCMs at the end of an island facing Can Tho.

It was just after eleven. McNamara ordered a noon departure and asked his staff to sweep through the consulate and urge everyone to hurry to their embarkation points. Departing at such short notice risked leaving people behind, but unless he left from the Delta Compound by noon, the ebbing tide could beach his LCM. Some Vietnamese working for the USIA would miss the evacuation because they had taken an early lunch. An American Catholic brother who delayed saying good-bye to his parishioners would spend a year in a Communist prison.

During a last sweep through the consulate Martin's deputy Hank Cushing found Sergeant Hasty, who commanded the marine guards, and CIA communications officer Walt Milford in the radio room destroying the CIA's decoding machinery and sensitive files. Both should have been hurrying to the Delta Compound. Milford's Vietnamese fiancée and her family were waiting for him there, as were Hasty's wife and her family. Milford and Hasty would reach the dock just minutes before noon.

Soon after Hasty arrived at the dock, his radio came alive, and he and McNamara heard the deputy CIA base chief saying, "Received permission from Saigon to use the helicopters as Air America choppers no longer needed in Saigon." McNamara was furious. Saigon was desperate for helicopters, and he doubted that the situation had changed within an hour. His aide Hank Cushing shouted that the CIA was to go by boat, adding, "The CG [consul general] orders this at once." The deputy CIA chief replied that Saigon had approved their helicopter evacuation but did not say who had approved it. McNamara heard a whomp-whomp and looked up to see an Air America Huey heading for the fleet. Years later he would call the CIA contingent "perfidious spooks" and write of watching them "abandon a battlefield, running for safe haven."

What really happened was more explicable and complicated. Before Jacobson called McNamara, two Air America helicopter pilots who had overnighted in Can Tho had flown the CIA's remaining KIP to the fleet. Shortly after Delaney and his officers left the consulate, one of the pilots had radioed the deputy CIA chief to report that both helicopters were returning to Can Tho to evacuate their CIA friends. The pilots had forged close friendships with the agents during the war in Laos and wanted to make sure they escaped. One pilot later admitted that Air America operations had ordered them to fly to Saigon to assist in the evacuation but added, "We said we had some good customers in Can Tho and had to return there for at least one trip before we headed in." Before the deputy chief could say that the CIA contingent had orders to join McNamara on his boats, he saw the helicopters approaching the Coconut Palms tennis courts and radioed back, "I wish I had as much money as I'm glad to see you." He and Delaney had not planned to disobey McNamara, and the helicopters had landed without their encouragement, but given the opportunity to escape by helicopter, they understandably took it.

By noon, 17 Americans, 3 Filipinos, and 294 Vietnamese had boarded the LCM and the rice barge at the Delta Compound. Most were on McNamara's A- and B-lists, but there were some last-minute additions. Can Tho's deputy air force commander arrived in uniform with his family before slipping into civilian clothes. The Vietnamese crew of McNamara's LCM never appeared, so he took the helm. As a joke, the marine guards presented him with a helmet liner saying, "Commodore. Can Tho Yacht Club." When Cary Kassebaum asked where he had learned to pilot a boat, he mentioned his World War II service in the navy. Kassebaum probed, and he admitted having been a cook on a submarine.

Mud began appearing along the shoreline, but whenever McNamara prepared to cast off, another evacuee arrived or another passenger begged him to wait for a relative. Milford, the CIA communicator, refused to leave without his fiancée, and Hank Cushing was about to drag him aboard when a shout came up from the LCM that she was already there. The mistress of a CIA officer arrived in tears, crying that her lover had disappeared. The others persuaded her to jump aboard, and she left with nothing but her *ao dai*. Hank Cushing's house overlooked the dock, and his cook ran outside at the last minute, weeping and begging to be included. She was on McNamara's C-list, but he agreed to take her anyway. She insisted on fetching her son from school. McNamara gave her five minutes, but at that moment the boy wandered into the compound carrying his book bag. The moment McNamara shouted "Cast off!" six of the CIA's Filipino employees arrived. By the time they boarded the LCM, it was stuck in the mud.

Richard Armitage drove between Tan Son Nhut and Newport several times that morning to smuggle some of his Vietnamese friends into Dodge City. During one of his trips a deserter outside the gate held a gun to his head and shouted, "You take me inside!" Armitage answered in Vietnamese that he was turning around and driving back into Saigon. The deserter muttered "motherfucker" and disappeared. At Newport, Armitage briefed Captain Kiem on the deteriorating situation at Tan Son Nhut and suggested advancing his departure from late afternoon to 2:00 p.m. Kiem summoned his captains and told them they could take as many people as they could fit on their ships but must disarm any non-naval personnel. If the Communists attacked them from the shoreline, they should go full steam ahead because a disabled ship could block the channel. He summoned his headquarters staff and, shouting to be heard over the helicopters and artillery, yelled, "It's time to go! The enemy is closing in. You have two hours to bring your families to the ships. Don't panic, there's room for everyone." Some officers fell to the ground and rocked back and forth, holding their heads and weeping because they had lost the war and would become exiles.

Terry McNamara gunned the engines of his LCM and jerked its rudder from side to side. He freed the ship from the mud just as a mob of civilians rushed into the Delta Compound. The rice barge broke its propeller getting free from the mud, and he took it under tow. At 12:30 p.m., he met the LCM from the Shell Oil dock. An ARVN translator who was familiar with the channels was at the helm, so he decided to follow him down the river. Half an hour later, three Vietnamese Navy gunboats closed on his flotilla, firing their machine guns across the bow of the lead LCM. Their commanding officer, Lieutenant Quang, shouted that General Nam believed McNamara was evacuating soldiers and military-age men and had ordered him to escort his vessels back to Can Tho and screen their passengers. The sailors were upset that men their age were escaping and kept their guns trained on the LCMs.

McNamara persuaded Quang to contact his superior officer, Commodore Thang, and request instructions. The week before, McNamara had evacuated Thang's family through Tan Son Nhut, telling him, "If we do have to evacuate I'm intending to go down the river and we may need your help." After Quang disappeared into his cabin to radio Thang, McNamara asked Whitten, Sciacchitano, and his other Vietnamese speakers to circulate among the evacuees and confiscate their weapons. Many were armed and he feared a massacre if Quang ordered them back to Can Tho. He also used the time to transfer passengers from the damaged rice barge to the LCMs.

Commodore Thang arrived an hour later and remained in his launch. He knew that if he boarded McNamara's LCM, he would see military deserters and would have to arrest them and impound the boat. Speaking in a low voice, he told McNamara that General Nam believed that senior military officers were aboard his ships and had ordered them all back to Can Tho. Then he smiled and added, "Under the circumstances, I will not obey the general's order." Raising his voice so everyone could hear him, he shouted, "Do you have any military men, civil servants, or Vietnamese of military age in your boats?"

McNamara shouted back, "Of course not! The people in our boats are all my employees and their families."

"That being the case, I do not believe it is necessary to enforce General Nam's order."

Thang had purposely included in his crew a sailor whose father was aboard McNamara's LCM. Thang encouraged him to board the vessel and bid farewell to his father. They embraced and wept. Thang's crew looked down to hide their tears, and McNamara's eyes watered. The tension between the sailors and the evacuees evaporated. Thang and his men saluted as the LCMs pulled away. McNamara and his staff stood at attention.

Despite losing two hours, McNamara could still reach the South China Sea by nightfall. He had survived one of the CIA's objections to a river evacuation, interdiction by South Vietnam's navy. Thirty minutes later, he faced a second—a Communist attack. The channel wandered from side to side, so the LCMs seldom traveled in the middle. He was fifteen yards from the south bank when he heard a whoosh and saw a black rocket trailing fire and smoke heading for his boat. He pushed the levers to full speed, and the rocket passed six feet to his aft, exploding on the opposite bank. The LCMs were armored against small-arms fire, but a well-placed rocket-propelled grenade would have left scores of casualties. Sergeant Hasty likened the possible result to "tossing a grenade into a garbage can." His marines opened fire on a patch of tall grass and bamboo, becoming the last U.S. servicemen to fire hostile shots during the Vietnam War.

McNamara's greatest fear had been that the Communists would attack them when they reached a stretch of the river where the navigable channels wound through a maze of islands, forcing boats to hew close to the shoreline. As he was entering this treacherous area, the skies opened and a gray wall of water enveloped his boats. The wind and rain drowned out their engines, and his passengers emerged from the islands soaking wet but safe.

David Whitten, the former navy officer who spoke Vietnamese, had chosen to ride in the well of McNamara's LCM with the Vietnamese. The hurried departure from Can Tho, confrontation with the navy patrol boats, and rocket attack had distracted the passengers, but after the storm passed, Whitten noticed them becoming somber. As their country slipped past for the last time, some began weeping. Their grief was contagious, affecting even the children, even Whitten. He was twenty-eight and had spent most of his adult life in South Vietnam. As the familiar landscape passed, he realized that he would never see it again and wept along with them.

McNamara arrived at the mouth of the Bassac at sunset. As an orange sun set over the delta, he thought, "God, this is beautiful," and then, "This is probably the last time I will see this."

Despite Jacobson's promise to station a ship offshore, the sea was empty. The CIA communicator tried to raise the navy on his radio. No one answered because no one had provided him or McNamara with the password. There was no moon, and the LCMs had only dim running lights and kept losing sight of each other. Their compasses were broken, and their passengers had exhausted their food and water. McNamara had been standing at the helm for over eight hours without a break. Around 11:00 p.m., he steered toward a faint glow on the horizon. Three hours later he pulled alongside the *Pioneer Contender*.

The *Boo Heung Pioneer* reached international waters at sunset. Farther up the river North Vietnamese troops sprayed one of the MSC tugs with small-arms fire. Ryder's tug, the *Chitose Maru*, ran out of fuel and drifted toward the east bank of the river. Communist troops opened fire, but the barge's sandbag walls absorbed their bullets. Ryder radioed his boss, Dan Berney, on the *Blue Ridge* and asked if navy warplanes could buzz their attackers, saying it might persuade them "to put their damn heads down so they don't get serious and decide that they really want to blow us out of the water." Rear Admiral Whitmire relayed his request up the chain of command and called back to report that the Pentagon had denied it. He told Ryder, "Now, ain't that a shit?"

Ryder's tug had a pickup crew, and the chief engineer was an automobile mechanic. Ryder finally realized that neither he nor the mechanic had understood that you had to pump fuel from the ship's lower tanks into a main tank above the wheelhouse. Ryder did this, fired the engines, pushed off the bank, and reached the South China Sea that evening.

Captain Flink woke James Parker at midnight to complain that planes had just buzzed the *Pioneer Contender*. He wondered if they might be Communists sent to kill Parker and his Vietnamese refugees. A crewman interrupted to report that two small boats were approaching. Parker went to the bridge and recognized Terry McNamara's LCMs. "The consulate is coming," he told Flink. "You've got more guests."

"See, I told you that you were going to make my life miserable," Flink said.

Parker leaned over the side and shouted at McNamara, asking why he had taken so long and his passengers were so wet. McNamara was not amused.

After transferring his refugees to an MSC freighter, Bill Ryder collected Terry McNamara from the *Pioneer Contender* and brought him to the *Boo Heung Pioneer*. The captain was under Ryder's command and insisted that he take his cabin. Ryder offered it to McNamara, but he refused, saying that it was Ryder's "damned ship." They agreed to share it, and Ryder took an immediate shine to McNamara, calling him "quite a character." They stayed up late comparing notes and cursing the embassy.

Parker knew it was too late for him to rescue Loi, or Chau's children, but not too late to atone for abandoning them. He radioed MSC tugboat command and asked if they could use two landing craft. The reply came back that the vessels could mean life or death for refugees crowded onto Vung Tau's beaches and piers. The Filipino engineers and a Cambodian who had driven the LCMs from Can Tho volunteered to accompany Parker to Vung Tau. As they were leaving, the MSC command ordered Flink to proceed to Vung Tau and collect refugees. Flink followed Parker's LCMs to the mouth of the harbor, while Parker motored closer to shore.

Harnage had risked his life to rescue anyone on the Gia Long Street roof. Parker was braving Communist artillery fire to rescue refugees from Vung Tau. As he approached the harbor, he saw what he mistook for an island. He drew closer, and it became dozens of small boats packed with refugees. Men paddled toward him using pieces of wood and their bare hands. Women stood in boats holding out their children. Refugees scrambled aboard his LCM from junks, fishing boats, and rowboats. He brought them out to the *Pioneer Contender,* which was itself surrounded by barges and fishing boats. The first officer shouted down that the U.S. Navy was sending a tender to collect him. He pretended not to hear him and returned for more refugees.

After returning to the *Pioneer Contender* a second time, he climbed to the bridge and looked across a panorama of death and suffering. Communist gunners were firing shells into the harbor, sending up geysers and killing the unlucky. An ARVN helicopter exploded, raining down debris. He heard a familiar Vietnam War cacophony of explosions, helicopters, and screams and flashed back to slipping his friends into body bags, crawling through Vietcong tunnels, holding a dying comrade in his arms, and having Loi cover his body with his own. He snapped to attention, turned to the shore, and saluted Ayers and Castro-Carrosquillo and the rest of the American dead. Then he noticed riverboats loaded with food and furniture heading up the river to Saigon and realized that although his war was over, life in Vietnam would continue.

Some of the passengers on Lem Truong's cargo ship were military officers who had felt duty-bound to report back to their units on the evening of April 29. They returned the next morning after General Minh surrendered. Because Truong had not contributed to the cost of the boat, she and her family boarded last and slept in the hold. By the time the ship left the dock on May 1, it was carrying a hundred passengers, a number that would double during the next two days as it rescued refugees from barges, canoes, and a cargo ship that was floundering in rough seas.

No one knew how to steer the ship, repair its engines, or navigate. Once in open water, they tried heading for Singapore but traveled in circles, exhausting their fuel. Sharks shadowed them, and they debated whether it would be worse to live in a Communist Vietnam or be eaten by sharks. Other ships gave them a wide berth out of fear they might be pirates or armed deserters. Truong made an SOS banner from a white sheet and a piece of red ribbon. When the ribbon ran out, she used her lipstick to finish the second *S*. An American tanker saw it and drew alongside. She shouted to its crew in English, describing their predicament. The tanker alerted the U.S. Navy, and an LST took everyone aboard. A week later she and her family arrived in the Philippines.

Richard Armitage left on one of the last helicopters from Tan Son Nhut. He landed on the *Blue Ridge* wearing a filthy sport jacket and without identification or anything to persuade Rear Admiral Whitmire to give him a destroyer so he could meet Captain Kiem's fleet. He was saved by remembering that Whitmire had played on the U.S. Naval Academy football team several years before him and that his photograph had hung in the locker room above where he dressed. This was enough to persuade Whitmire to call Schlesinger, who ordered him to give Armitage whatever he needed. Armitage said he needed a destroyer to take him to Con Son Island and escort the South Vietnamese Navy to the Philippines. Whitmire called the commander of the destroyer escort *Kirk,* Commodore Donald Roane, and said, "We're going to have to send you back to rescue the Vietnamese navy. We forgot 'em. And if we don't get them or any part of them, they're probably all going to be killed."

When Armitage arrived, Roane groused that he was unaccustomed to taking orders from a strange civilian. "Sir, I am equally unaccustomed to coming aboard strange ships in the middle of the night and giving orders," Armitage said, "but steam to Con Son."

At dawn on May 1, the *Kirk* rendezvoused with thirty-four South Vietnamese Navy vessels that Captain Kiem had led down the Saigon River. Four were deemed unseaworthy and scuttled. The *Kirk* shepherded the others toward the Philippines and provided food and medical care to their thirty thousand sailors and civilian passengers. While they were at sea, the Philippine government announced that it would not permit them to dock at Subic Bay because they had become the property of North Vietnam following the surrender. Armitage suggested that because they had once belonged to the U.S. Navy and Coast Guard, Captain Kiem could simply return them. Kiem ordered their crews to disable their big guns and paint over their South Vietnamese identifying numbers, replacing them with American ones. Each ship held a changing of the colors ceremony. Their captains delivered speeches and ordered their South Vietnamese flags lowered. Voices cracked and tears ran down cheeks as crews and passengers sang their national anthem for the last time. As the Stars and Stripes went up, the sailors ripped the insignias from their uniforms and hurled them into the sea.

Erich von Marbod had left Tan Son Nhut on the afternoon of April 29 on one of the first Marine Corps helicopters to land on the *Blue Ridge*. Schlesinger had asked Whitmire to transfer him to the *Dubuque*, an amphibious transport ship with a large helicopter deck, and station it off Phu Quoc, where it could serve as a way station for VNAF helicopter pilots heading for Thailand. At first light on April 30, von Marbod asked the *Dubuque*'s captain to broadcast the coordinates for the route to Trat, Thailand, to the pilots. Some had overloaded their choppers with family and friends and needed to land on the *Dubuque* to refuel. By the time von Marbod had left the ship, he had, over the previous several days, played a pivotal role in sending 224 aircraft and two thousand South Vietnamese pilots and their families to Thailand. The Pentagon awarded him a medal, leading Martin to complain, "It [von Marbod's operation] wasn't worth . . . risking so much. But they finally gave him a medal for recovering the bloody planes."

The 420

Once Ken Moorefield got inside the embassy, he went to work. It was late afternoon, and the smaller CH-46 Sea Knight helicopters had started landing on the roof, and the larger CH-53 Sea Stallions would soon be arriving in the parking lot. When the sky began darkening, Moorefield realized that the parking lot's lights would be too weak to illuminate a nighttime evacuation. He rummaged through the embassy and found a 35 mm slide projector. He installed it on the roof of the fire station and trained its bright rectangle of light on the parking lot. He warned the marines guarding the gates that they were sniper targets and should stand behind the concrete wall instead.

He went into the chancery and answered a telephone ringing on an empty desk. A woman cried, "My God! I'm Vietnamese but I got American citizenship in 1973. I've got three kids. What can I do?" He mumbled, "I don't know what you can do. I'm sorry." He joined a cocktail party of CIA agents and eavesdropped on their gloomy conversations until one of them begged him to leave them alone in their misery. He ran into Tom Polgar, who said, "If only we hadn't cut off their supplies. If only we'd continued to provide them with the support they needed." He was in no mood for Polgar's autopsy and continued down the corridor. He looked into offices whose former occupants had trashed them by smashing watercoolers, pouring liquor onto rugs, and sweeping papers onto the floor. Like the abandoned champagne, cars, and military equipment, the rooms showed how lavishly Americans had been outfitted and how little it had mattered. He picked up a tin of tobacco for his pipe and searched for a souvenir to replace the ones he had lost in his getaway bag. He settled on a copy of Clausewitz's *On War*.

After returning downstairs, he sat on the steps by the chancery's rear entrance and watched the Sea Stallions land in the parking lot. Their official capacity was thirty-five combat-loaded marines, but this evening they were lifting off with as many as seventy civilian refugees. Some pilots shouted, "Put on some more!" Others struggled to get airborne and had to off-load passengers. As the clouds lowered and the rain increased, so did the danger. The helicopters had to fly straight up for two hundred feet to clear the surrounding buildings. If a pilot clipped a wall or collided with another helicopter and fell back into the landing zone, the evacuation would end.

Moorefield joined an impromptu party in Martin's outer office. Journalist George McArthur, Eva Kim, and others were drinking from paper cups. Martin emerged from his inner office and asked McArthur to join him. McArthur noticed that Nit Noy was tied to a chair leg and offered to take the poodle out with him. Martin thanked him effusively before launching into a bitter attack on Polgar. If newspaper articles are history's first draft, then Martin wanted the draft appearing under McArthur's byline to pin the evacuation's shortcomings on Polgar. He blamed him for using *New York Times* reporter Malcolm Browne as an intermediary for his own private negotiations with the Communists, charging that his shenanigans "might have cost us an extra day"—a day he had been counting on to complete the fixed-wing evacuation. He blamed Polgar for monopolizing the Air America helicopters to rescue his VIPs, arguing that otherwise one could have flown him to Tan Son Nhut that morning to make an earlier and more convincing case for continuing the fixed-wing evacuation. Finally, he blamed Polgar for undermining morale by sending his personal goods out of the country, remarking caustically, "Well, the smart ones like Polgar got their stuff out early."

Polgar walked in as Martin was excoriating him for shipping out his furniture, and McArthur left them alone. Their conversation could not have been pleasant. Several days earlier, after learning of Polgar's back-channel negotiations with the Communists, Martin had delivered his favorite threat, promising to cut off his balls and stuff one in each ear unless he stopped. Earlier that evening he had been overheard telling Polgar, "If I ever hear you say anything like that again you're going to spend the rest of your career in Antarctica."

While Martin was blaming Polgar for everything that had gone wrong with the evacuation, Kissinger was becoming increasingly impatient and testy. Head of the Joint Chiefs of Staff General George Brown had promised him that the helicopters would arrive within an hour of being ordered in, but that had not happened. The Pentagon had assured him that the evacuation from the embassy would be confined to a hundred American marines and diplomats, but at a WSAG meeting that had ended at 9:20 that morning (9:20 p.m. Saigon time), Brown had admitted that between five and six hundred Americans still awaited evacuation from the embassy and that Vietnamese were coming "over the wall and through the gates."

Brown accused Martin of putting only a few Americans on every helicopter while holding back others to keep the Pentagon from ending the airlift and asked Kissinger, "Can't you tell him to get them [the Americans] out of there?"

"Those are his bloody orders, goddamnit!" Kissinger exclaimed, adding, "Yes, I'll instruct the Ambassador to get those people out, but he's been ordered to get those people out a hundred times."

Kissinger later said that he and Ford had been "spectators of the final act," staffing "a command post with essentially nothing to do." He spent several hours in his West Wing corner office, enveloped by "the eerie silence that sometimes attends momentous events," while Ford watched updates on television, later remarking that it had been "the first time since the Civil War that an American President could see the immediate consequences of war."

Kissinger strolled into White House chief of staff Donald Rumsfeld's office and indulged in some black humor. Referring to Cambodia and South Vietnam, he said, "I'm the only Secretary of State who has ever lost two countries in three weeks." He had lost one in his capacity as secretary of state, he explained, and another as national security adviser.

Ron Nessen asked, "If we give you another title, will you lose another country?"

David Kennerly, who was photographing the fall of Saigon vigil, joked, "The good news is that the war is over. The bad news is that we lost."

Twenty-six members of the congressional leadership arrived at the White House for a briefing at 11:50 a.m., almost midnight in Saigon. Schlesinger boasted that the Pentagon (thanks to von Marbod) had flown $300 to $400 million in equipment out of South Vietnam, including many Vietnamese Air Force planes, and had arranged (thanks to Armitage) for a number of naval vessels to escape. Kissinger reported that among the administration's accomplishments was having "moved out over 45,000 high risk Vietnamese nationals," people "to whom we owed an obligation for their association with the United States." Although the administration had asked numerous countries to accept some of these Vietnamese, he predicted that 90 percent would come to the United States. The president had granted parole authority for 130,000, but he assured the congressmen that "it now looks like 50,000 will be the top number." One of them remarked, "Fifty thousand is all this country can absorb at any rate."

Kissinger did not know that the South Vietnamese Navy ships that Schlesinger had boasted of saving had thirty thousand refugees on board, or that the planes that von Marbod had rescued were bringing out the families and friends of the pilots, or that Ryder's tugs and barges were carrying over twenty-five thousand new American citizens, or that during the next several days the U.S. Navy would pick up another twenty thousand or so self-evacuated refugees in the waters off South Vietnam. He told these congressmen, who had made no secret of their opposition to accepting Vietnamese refugees, "There is no way the total number can go much beyond 50,000."

At 9:00 p.m., Rear Admiral Whitmire suspended the evacuation until dawn and ordered the helicopter pilots back to their ships for servicing and rest. He had navy regulations and common sense on his side. The weather had deteriorated, and his pilots had exceeded the flight hours permitted in a twenty-four-hour period and were complaining of hostile fire, a small landing zone, and a gimcrack lighting system. A CH-46 Sea Knight that had been flying over the task force on a search-and-rescue patrol had crashed into the sea, killing both pilots.

At 9:41 p.m., Martin received a cable from Scowcroft that put him in full honey-badger, go-for-the-balls mode. Scowcroft berated him for not evacuating the remaining Americans fast enough, cabling, "Understand there are still about 400 Americans in embassy compound. You should ensure that all, repeat all, Americans are evacuated in this operation ASAP. Warm Regards."

Martin knew that many of these Americans had Vietnamese wives and children whom they refused to abandon, and he knew that in his April 25 cable Kissinger had encouraged him to "trickle" the remaining Americans out with the endangered Vietnamese. This was precisely what he was doing—holding some Americans back and sprinkling them in among the Vietnamese to keep the airlift going. He cabled Scowcroft back at 10:00 p.m., asking, "Perhaps you can tell me how to make some of these Americans abandon their half-Vietnamese children, or how the President would look if he ordered this?" He complained that during the previous fifty minutes only one CH-46 had landed on the roof and not a single CH-53 had set down in the parking lot and that Whitmire had informed him that he wanted to suspend the operation until 8:00 a.m. He continued, "I need 30 CH-53 sorties damned quick and I have received nothing but silence since I asked for them. . . . Do you think you can get the President to order CINCPAC [Admiral Noel Gayler] to finish the job quickly[?] I repeat I need 30 CH-53s and I need them now."

Fifteen minutes later he sent a similar message to Admiral Gayler, repeating that he needed thirty CH-53 sorties, adding, "I can't come out until the 29th or 30th sortie, so please get them moving," a statement making it clear that he planned to leave on the last or second-to-last helicopter, thus confirming Kissinger's fears.

Gayler replied that more helicopters should already be arriving. They were not, and at 10:20 p.m. Martin fired off another cable to Scowcroft in the White House Situation Room. He warned that evacuating only Americans and leaving the Vietnamese behind would be a public relations catastrophe. "Among Americans here is Father McVeigh, head of Catholic Relief Services [CRS], who will not leave without his Vietnamese staff," he cabled. "How will President explain to Bishop Swanstrom, US head of CRS, or Fr. McVeigh's great and good friend Cardinal Cooke, why I left him? I repeat I need 30 sorties tonight. Please get them for me."

Scowcroft replied at 10:40 p.m., "Defense promises 30 CH-53s on their way." But instead of thirty sorties, Martin received a browbeating over his failure to evacuate IBM's Vietnamese employees. Ambassador Dean Brown, who headed the government task force managing the evacuation and resettlement of Vietnamese, cabled, "IBM headquarters reports its personnel still in Saigon and is most disturbed." At 11:06 p.m., Ford's chief of staff, Donald Rumsfeld, badgered Martin to evacuate the IBM employees, cabling, "I understand that 154 IBM employees, including their families, are still awaiting removal from Saigon." He added that they were "now standing in front of the IBM building" and asked Martin to "do your utmost to see that they were evacuated with the current helicopter lift." Martin read Rumsfeld's cable and said, "Shit!"

He cabled Gayler at 11:45 p.m. to report that although the CH-46s were again landing on the roof, "they carry about two-fifths of CH-53 capacity. I needed thirty CH-53 sorties capacity. I still do. Can't you get someone to tell us what is going on?" Fifteen minutes later he complained to Scowcroft and Gayler that even the CH-46s had ceased arriving, and said, "We need the capacity, repeat capacity, of 30 CH-53 sorties to get us out of here."

Martin was exhausted and gravely ill. He could easily have obeyed the White House and evacuated the remaining Americans and left with them. Earlier that day he had contemplated moving into the

French embassy and remaining until all the Vietnamese who had sought refuge in his embassy had left, and now he was attempting to blackmail the White House into continuing the evacuation by warning that prominent Catholic clerics in the United States would be outraged if any Vietnamese were left behind.

But it would not be Martin's bitter, threatening cables that would bring back the CH-53s. Instead, they returned because Lieutenant General Carey and other Marine Corps officers insisted on an honorable exit. Carey flew back to the fleet at 10:50 p.m., leaving Colonel Gray in command of the marines who remained at the DAO. After learning that the helicopters had stopped arriving at the embassy, Carey went up the chain of command, searching for an explanation. His attempts to contact Whitmire were stymied by a temporary glitch in radio communications, and it was not until 1:30 a.m. that he stormed into the combat operations center on the *Blue Ridge* shouting, "Who in the hell stopped my helicopters?"

Whitmire said he had.

"You don't have the authority to stop my helicopters!" Carey thundered. He demanded to know why Whitmire had done it.

"For safety purposes. The pilots have been flying too long."

"Marines don't get tired when it comes to something like this."

Whitmire, who was Carey's superior, was taken aback by his defiant tone. Carey pressed his argument, saying that suspending the flights until first light was unacceptable because by then Saigon might have fallen. Vice Admiral George Steele, who commanded the Seventh Fleet and was in the operations center, agreed with Carey.

A similar drama was unfolding at the CINCPAC command center in Honolulu, where Lieutenant General Louis Wilson, who commanded the Marine Fleet Force in the Pacific, was discussing the sudden halt in flight operations with Admiral Gayler. When Wilson heard that the pilots had stood down because of administrative restrictions on the maximum allowable number of flight hours, he exploded, promising, "I will personally see that any Marine that doesn't fly to continue to finish this operation will be court-martialed."

Gayler sided with Wilson. He knew from flying World War II

combat missions that a pilot could always fly more hours if necessary. He also feared that if the helicopters paused until first light, the
operation might never restart. Whitmire reversed his decision, and
the marine pilots prepared to resume the airlift. (The air force, whose
pilots had also exceeded their twelve-hours-a-day limit, did not send
them back into the air.) The only unanswered question was how many
sorties they would make.

Only a single helicopter landed at the embassy between midnight
and 3:00 a.m. Stuart Herrington circulated among the evacuees,
shouting through a bullhorn in Vietnamese, "Ladies and gentlemen,
please be quiet. Don't worry! You will all be evacuated. You will all
be evacuated. I'm here with you and I'll be on the last helicopter. My
government will not leave me behind and no one is abandoning you,
so relax! In a little while the helicopters will resume arriving and you
can cooperate by getting into family groups and stop shoving. Throw
away your suitcases and form a double line. Back away from the gate
so we can open it."

The pushing and shoving continued. An American contractor collapsed from a heart attack, and people swarmed around Herrington,
battering his arms and legs with their suitcases while jockeying for
position near the gate. A Vietnamese man tugged at his sleeve and
explained that the Vietnamese wanted to cooperate but the South
Koreans were shoving everyone aside. Herrington was ashamed that
despite having spent years in Asia, he had failed to distinguish between
the two peoples. After he addressed the Koreans in English, a Korean
naval officer stepped forward and promised to keep order. Summers
and Herron linked arms with Herrington and helped him push people
back from the gate. The South Korean contingent, comprising military officers, intelligence agents, and diplomats, formed a double line
to one side. A Korean officer took Summers aside and said, "We'll go
out on one of the last helicopters so you can evacuate all these panicky
Vietnamese first."

Shortly after midnight Martin came downstairs and asked Colonel Madison how many evacuees remained. Relying on estimates from Summers and Herrington, Madison reported that there were 173 marines, 53 Americans, and about 500 Vietnamese and third-country nationals for a total of 726. In fact, there were around 1,100 people left. The JMT delegation had underestimated the number because it was dark and the evacuees were spread throughout the recreation area, making an accurate count difficult.

At 2:00 a.m., Madison decided to close off the recreation area and bring everyone into the parking lot so that the JMT could organize some of them into seventy-person loads for the CH-53s while sending others into the chancery to board the CH-46s landing on the roof. As the JMT began closing off the recreation area, some evacuees who had been near the gate were rerouted to the rear of another line. This happened to architecture student Binh Pho and his girlfriend. He recalled Herrington's promises and told himself, "That's fine. There's no need to worry, we're so close."

As the evacuees filed out of the recreation area, Herrington and others on the JMT made the first accurate count of the evening. They told Colonel Madison that about 1,100 people remained. It was too late. Martin had reported 726 evacuees, and that number had gone to Gayler and the White House Situation Room. Based on that figure, Kissinger and Schlesinger agreed to send nineteen more helicopters and to insist that Martin leave on one of the last ones. Kissinger told Schlesinger, "If you don't tell him [Martin] that this is a presidential order he won't come out."

They concluded their conversation with an elegiac appreciation of Martin.

Schlesinger called him "a man with a mission."

"Well, he lost a son there," Kissinger replied.

"Yes. You have got to admire the bugger."

"Look, his thoughts are in the right direction."

"That's right. Dedication and energy." Before Kissinger could respond, Schlesinger added, "You weep."

That night at least, there was no talk of "Madman Martin" or of Martin "losing his cool" or going out like Chinese Gordon. Instead, their remarks were a perceptive summary of his strengths, albeit ones ill-suited to his current role.

He was indeed "a man with a mission"—a dedicated cold warrior who had had the misfortune of being pressured by Nixon and Haig into presiding over Kissinger's decent interval. Despite a debilitating illness, he had exhibited "dedication and energy," and as for his thoughts being "in the right direction," his words and deeds had shown that he believed his country had a moral responsibility to evacuate South Vietnamese. Nevertheless, a Communist disinformation campaign, combined with his pride, stubbornness, errors of judgment, and belief in his own infallibility, had conspired to turn the embassy's evacuation into a debacle. Schlesinger was right. "You weep." What else could you do in the face of such tragic heroism?

At 2:30 a.m., Admiral Gayler cabled Martin. "I have been directed to send you the following message from [the] President: 'On the basis of the reported total of 726 evacuees CINCPAC is authorized to send 19 helicopters and no more. The President expects Ambassador Martin to be on the last helicopter.'" Gayler added that Secretary of Defense Schlesinger wanted the last chopper to depart by 3:45.

Just before 3:00 a.m., the helicopters began arriving again on the roof and in the parking lot in quick succession. The line of evacuees snaking up the stairwell to the helipad moved quickly upward as each CH-46 carried away forty passengers. Down below in the parking lot, the CH-53 Sea Stallions were boarding as many as ninety Vietnamese and third-country nationals at a time.

Ross Meador was one of the last American civilians to leave. He had driven from breakfast at the Duc Hotel to the embassy, waving his revolver in the air to clear a path to the front gate. As a favor to his friend Father McVeigh, he had agreed to accompany a Vietnamese family. Their turn did not come until the last nineteen helicopters began arriving. As they jogged toward a helicopter on the roof, the mother's suitcase burst open, spilling out money, photographs, and other family treasures. She dashed about, dragging a child by one hand while scooping up the remains of her former life. A marine threw her into the helicopter, and Meador watched the wash from its rotors blow her money and photographs into the night.

The Sea Stallions descended to the parking lot through clouds and smoke, red taillights winking and white headlights moving like spotlights across the compound. Marines ran the evacuees up their ramps, and the helicopters lifted off within three minutes. Martin appeared around 3:30 a.m. and asked Madison for a count of the people still in the compound. Before returning upstairs, he was heard telling a marine, "Everyone in that compound is leaving—everybody."

Madison called Lehmann on his walkie-talkie and reported that they had 420 people remaining and that six more sorties would clear the compound in a matter of minutes. Among the 420 were the embassy firemen, South Korean diplomats and military officers, a German priest, and Y. I. Ching, the Chinese American merchant seaman from Hawaii.

Lehmann said he had been listening to the marines' communication net and had just heard that the pilots had received orders to limit the evacuation to the CH-46s that could land on the roof and only to board Americans.

"*Jesus,*" Madison said. "I've been telling these people for *hours* that we'll get them out. Give the ambassador the numbers. Tell him who they are. Tell him this is the honest-to-God end of it." He reminded Lehmann that the six choppers could clear the landing zone within twenty minutes and said, "We're not going anywhere until all of those presently marshaled inside the compound are evacuated."

Lehmann called back minutes later to report that Martin believed that he could arrange for six more CH-53 sorties. Martin's special assistant Brunson McKinley came downstairs and repeated Lehmann's assurances. Madison and Summers walked through the six groups of seated evacuees, promising that their departure was imminent.

Martin's request for six more helicopters was met with suspicion and derision on the fleet, in the Pentagon, and at the White House Situation Room. Throughout the afternoon and evening, when asked how many evacuees were left at the embassy, Martin had reported two thousand remaining but had then offered the same number several hours and many helicopter sorties later. Vice Admiral Steele, who commanded the Seventh Fleet and was aboard the *Blue Ridge* with Whitmire and Carey, decided that Martin's embassy had become "a bottomless pit" and that "through loyalty to our Vietnamese colleagues he [Martin] was going to keep the evacuation going indefinitely and . . . force it to keep going by not coming out himself." In fact, the number had remained constant throughout the early evening because of the difficulty in estimating the size of the crowd in the recreation area and the sympathetic diplomats and marines who had allowed hundreds more South Vietnamese to come over the walls and through the gates.

Gayler forwarded Martin's request for additional helicopters to the National Military Command Center at the Pentagon. Schlesinger, who had never supported a large-scale evacuation of Vietnamese, believed that Martin was "busily engaged in holding back Americans and putting aboard Vietnamese that he wanted to rescue" and "trying to evacuate all of the people of Southeast Asia." He called Deputy Secretary Paul Clements, who was representing the Pentagon in the White House Situation Room, and said that in his opinion the embassy was out of control and that even if they continued the evacuation for another twenty hours, it would still be full. He did not tell Clements, or Ford and Kissinger, that Martin was requesting only six more helicopters to make a clean sweep.

Why Martin had instructed Lehmann and McKinley to tell Madison that six more Sea Stallions were en route remains unexplained. Perhaps he misunderstood a radio message, an understandable mistake given the state of his health and the gimcrack nature of the communication network after the antenna at the DAO went down, or perhaps he assumed that the White House would accede to his demand, as it had to his other ones, or perhaps someone in the chain of command had promised him the phantom helicopters as a way to persuade him to leave.

At 4:30 a.m., after learning that the limit of nineteen helicopters had been reached, Lieutenant General Carey ordered Captain Gerry

Berry, the pilot of "Lady Ace 09," to evacuate only Americans and not to leave the roof without Ambassador Martin. He also gave Berry and Major Kean permission to use force to remove Martin from the embassy. When Vice Admiral Steele asked Carey what they should do if Martin refused to leave, Carey replied, "We put a Marine on either side of him and carry him out if we have to."

After Berry landed, a marine corporal at the helipad summoned Kean to the roof. Kean read Berry's orders and borrowed the corporal's headset so he could speak with Carey. Knowing that his transmission would be broadcast over the loudspeaker in the war room of the *Blue Ridge,* he told Carey that his marines were guarding the embassy walls and that between these walls and the chancery's front door "there are some four hundred people who are still waiting to be evacuated." Kean did not want their betrayal on his conscience, and so, speaking slowly and carefully, he told Carey, "I want you to understand clearly that when I pull the Marines back to the Embassy those people will be left behind."

Carey repeated that the order to remove Martin and restrict the airlift to Americans came directly from the president.

Kean walked downstairs to Martin's office and relayed the president's order, adding that a helicopter had landed on the roof and would not leave until he was on board. Martin stared back for several seconds, not saying anything or showing any emotion. He had already received a message from Kissinger informing him that President Ford wanted him on the next helicopter, and to that he had replied, "I don't take my orders from you, I only take my orders from the President." Now that Ford had given him a direct order, he would have to obey it.

Replying to Kean, Martin drawled in his southern accent, "Well there's a little more to be done, Major." He wrote a final message on a legal pad informing the White House that he would close the embassy at 4:30 and destroy its communications equipment. He concluded it, "This is the last message from embassy Saigon." Turning to Lehmann, he said, "Wolf, let's go upstairs."

The most dangerous place in the embassy had proved to be its helipad. There were no guardrails, and it was slippery from the rain, buffeted by the helicopters' propeller wash, and connected to the roof's lower level by an eighteen-step metal ladder. At 2:00 a.m., the marine ground controller had fallen from the helipad onto the lower roof and had to be medically evacuated. Moorefield volunteered to replace him and spent the next several hours guiding in the helicopters and loading them. Before Kean went downstairs to tell Martin that he had to leave, he informed Moorefield that no more CH-53s would be landing in the parking lot and that the remaining CH-46 sorties from the roof would be Americans only. Moorefield looked down at the 420 evacuees sitting on the ground, waiting for helicopters that would never arrive and thought, "Why isn't someone from the embassy saying, 'Hell no! We're not leaving until they go!'"

Martin appeared on the roof carrying a folded American flag under one arm. Shouting to be heard over the rotors, Moorefield said, "Mr. Ambassador, they say you have to take this helicopter. Presidential order." Martin looked spent, but his shoes were shined and his gray suit was pressed. Moorefield put a hand underneath his elbow, as he had while helping him down the metal stairs at Tan Son Nhut when they had arrived together in 1973. After walking him to Lady Ace 09, he put both hands underneath his armpits and gently lifted him into the helicopter. Polgar and Lehmann followed. Moorefield decided that there was, at last, nothing more he could do and joined the remaining American civilians on the next helicopter, leaving behind the marine guards, the 420 evacuees in the parking lot, and Colonel Madison and his JMT delegation.

It fell to Major Kean to tell Madison that during the last sixteen hours Madison and his men had been lying to the 420 people sitting on the ground in front of them.

Madison swore and said, "I'm not leaving until these people leave. We've been promising them they'd go all day. We have a firm number now and there's no reason we can't get them out."

"Presidential order," Kean said, "and I'm not going to risk my men any longer."

"Those helicopters were promised to us. We were promised six lifts to get these people out. I'm going to take this up with the ambassador or his deputy."

"You can't!" Kean pointed to the sky and said that Martin and Lehmann were aboard the helicopter that had just departed.

Herrington, Bell, Summers, and others on the JMT had been sitting on the hoods of cars that had been positioned so that their headlights illuminated the landing zone. Herrington saw Madison throwing up his arms in frustration as Kean walked back into the chancery.

Madison went from one man to the next, explaining the situation and saying they had no choice and should drift into the chancery one by one. He asked Herrington to leave last because he spoke Vietnamese, meaning he would be the last American to tell the last lie to a Vietnamese.

Herrington briefly considered staying and making himself a hostage but decided it would be a pointless gesture. The marines would never land helicopters in an unsecured area, and the North Vietnamese would take him prisoner. "Don't be a fool," he told himself. "You'll never get these people out. You have a wife and kids, and an army career. You won't get these people out so what good would it do?"

He spent several minutes on his walkie-talkie pretending to talk with the helicopters. He finally turned to a Vietnamese man and said, "I've got to take a leak." The man laughed as Herrington disappeared into the bushes.

A plaque in the lobby commemorated the embassy personnel who had lost their lives when the Vietcong stormed the building during the Tet Offensive. Herrington had asked an embassy engineer to crowbar it off the wall so he could take it with him. He thought, "Those guys would roll over in their graves if they could see what was happening now," and decided to leave it behind.

Summers and Madison had already left by the time Herrington arrived on the roof. He, Bell, Pace, and a single marine were the only passengers on a helicopter that could have brought out dozens of Vietnamese. Bell was so tired that he crawled aboard. He had accomplished what he had promised himself: see the war through to its end and rescue as many people as he could as a tribute to Nova and Michael. No one in the helicopter spoke. Bell and Herrington were so embarrassed that they avoided each other's eyes.

The sky was lightening, but the lights remained on in the parking lot. Herrington saw the abandoned evacuees staring up at his helicopter. The firemen stood out in their yellow slickers and helmets. Their families were already on the ships and would be watching as helicopters landed with evacuees, hoping to see their husbands and fathers. Herrington could not pick out the German priest, or the Vietnamese nuns, or the Korean diplomats and intelligence agents, but he knew they were there. Also there, although he did not know their names, was Rhee Dai Yong, who headed the South Korean intelligence agency in South Vietnam and would spend five years in Communist prisons, and Dr. Huynh Trien Vo, the assistant minister of information whom Lem Truong had seen boarding one of the embassy buses that afternoon and who would spend ten years in concentration camps. There was cabinet minister N. D. Xuan, who would die in one of the camps, and Minister of Finance Chau Kim Nhan, who would escape on a boat, and Y. I. Ching, the Chinese American seaman whom the marines would teargas in a few minutes when he tried to follow them as they withdrew into the chancery and who would spend six months in a Communist internment camp. There was architecture student Binh Pho, who for years would wake in a cold sweat, his heart racing, from nightmares featuring helicopters, and there was Thu Minh Nguyen, the wife of a U.S. mission employee, and her six children. She had been at the top of the stairs when a marine told her that the helicopter currently on the roof had room for only two of her six children. She decided to keep her family together and leave on the next helicopter, so she offered their places in line to the two people behind her. The next helicopter was Lady Ace 09. After Martin left, a marine told Nguyen to go downstairs and join the others in the parking lot. Her husband would spend twelve years in a concentration camp, and in 1978 she and her oldest son and daughter would escape on a fishing boat. Also left behind was twelve-year-old Carina Hoang and her mother, who had bought the fake papers claiming that their father worked for the embassy. Carina and her older siblings would be barred from attending school because her father had been an ARVN officer, and he would be incarcerated for fourteen years. Like Nguyen's children, Carina became a boat person, escaping in 1979. A decade later, her family was reunited.

The abandoned 420 were a fraction of the South Vietnamese who should have been evacuated. These included Alan Carter's USIA employees and their families, the people at Shep Lowman's villa, 9 justices of South Vietnam's Supreme Court, the 250 Vietnamese CIA employees marooned at a distant supply depot, the 70 CIA translators who never made it over the embassy wall, the people gathered at the Brink Hotel whom Moorefield had told to "stand fast," the 150 senior policemen whom Martin had promised to evacuate from police headquarters and who had waited there all day before giving up and fleeing, leaving behind files identifying their double agents.

Luck, contacts, perseverance, courage, and the bravery and resolve of their American and Vietnamese friends and employers played a part in determining who escaped. And so the Vietnamese working for Pan Am and the Military Sealift Command got out, while those working for IBM and the USIA did not. The 150 Vietnamese employed by the CIA's propaganda radio station escaped with their families because their American supervisors had moved the entire station to Phu Quoc on April 20 and had arranged to evacuate them on an MSC freighter, while the 150 Vietnamese CIA agents and employees who had been told to assemble at the Duc Hotel were abandoned.

Still, it is difficult to imagine how an evacuation that until its final days and hours was conceived and executed largely in secrecy and in defiance of senior U.S. and Vietnamese officials, and was managed by people who were sleepless, hungry, and fearing for their lives and careers, could have been perfectly equitable. Considering what was accomplished, and against what odds, and how quickly South Vietnam and its armed forces collapsed, evacuating so many Vietnamese in such a short period of time was a significant achievement. Nevertheless, many Americans left South Vietnam burdened by guilt.

Sensing this, a Vietnamese man who had come to say good-bye to an American friend who was waiting to board an evacuation bus told a group of Americans gathered on the street, "You may hear after you leave that some here have died, perhaps even at their own hand. You must not spend the rest of your lives with that guilt. It is just part of Vietnam's black fate, in which you, all of you, became ensnared for a time."

Stuart Herrington struggled to find words to describe the "sense of shame" that had swept over him as he flew away that morning. On reflection, however, he decided that it was astonishing how many Vietnamese had escaped and that the evacuation had in fact "exceeded any reasonable expectation of what should have been accomplished." But like many serving out the final days of Kissinger's decent interval, he could still see, years later, "the faces of those I knew we were leaving behind" while finding it more difficult to recall those of the Vietnamese he had sent to the United States to begin new lives as American citizens.

Epilogue

———｜├———

Six hours after Graham Martin left Saigon, President Minh surrendered unconditionally. He spent the next eight years in his villa cultivating orchids before leaving for exile in France and California.

After Jack Madison, Stuart Herrington, Bill Bell, and Harry Summers landed on the *Okinawa*, Summers asked a journalist, "Do you know what you just saw?" When the journalist answered, "The fall of Saigon," Summers said, "You saw betrayal of the first order." Herrington was weeping as he told a reporter, "They lied to us at the very end. . . . They promised. They promised. . . . I have never received an order in my life to do something I was ashamed of."

Madison and Summers told Lieutenant Colonel Jim Bolton, who commanded the helicopter unit based on the *Okinawa*, that six more sorties could have evacuated the 420 people left behind. Bolton was appalled and said, "If I had known that, there wouldn't have been any problem getting those people out." Colonel Summers said later about the 420, "The fleet thought they were operating with a bottomless pit and that they had to cut it off someplace, because the pilots were dead on their feet. . . . They didn't know that all that was left was six loads; if they had, they would have pulled them out. I thought it was sort of the Vietnam War in microcosm—great intentions and everybody trying to do the right thing, but managing to screw it up at the end."

Madison told Summers and Herrington, "We've got to get this betrayal down on paper while it's fresh in our minds." They wrote up a report and transmitted it under the guise of their weekly JMT report so it would be routed to the White House, Pentagon, and all commands and embassies around the world. Soon after returning to Washington, Madison resigned from the army. After Herrington retired, he became a military intelligence consultant. The Pentagon hired him to train military interrogators for the Iraq War. In a 2003 report commissioned by the army, he criticized the abuse of Iraqi prisoners as "counterproductive" and "technically illegal" and castigated the CIA for holding "ghost detainees." In 1996, Henry Kissinger watched a documentary about the fall of Saigon during which Herrington blamed him for betraying the 420 evacuees. Kissinger claimed to be "stunned." He called Herrington to apologize and insisted that no one had told him that anyone had been left at the embassy.

Summers retired in 1985 and had a distinguished career as an academic and commentator on military affairs. He later offered a compassionate evaluation of Martin's dilemma, saying that Martin had to maintain U.S. support for Thieu's government while not raising suspicions that America was abandoning Thieu, yet also plan how to evacuate Americans and Vietnamese. Summers concluded that Martin had erred on the side of ignoring evacuation planning because he believed that negotiations would make it unnecessary.

Bill Bell was posted to the Vietnamese refugee processing center at Fort Chaffee, Arkansas, where he debriefed former South Vietnamese officials. He ran into Lieutenant Colonel Pham Xuan Huy, the officer he had seen lurking outside the JMT offices. Soon afterward he married one of Huy's daughters. His own daughter, Andrea, survived the injuries she had suffered on the Babylift crash. During the next ten years Bell interviewed hundreds of Vietnamese refugees in the United States and Southeast Asia while searching for information about American MIAs. In 1988 he was appointed senior field investigator for the Pentagon's first POW/MIA search-and-recovery efforts in postwar Vietnam. In 1991 he opened the U.S. office for POW/MIA affairs in Hanoi, becoming the first American official to be posted to Vietnam since the war ended.

Walter Martindale spent the next seven months in the Philippines,

Guam, and Hong Kong coordinating the transport, processing, and resettlement of Vietnamese refugees. He had flown his adopted four-year-old son, Luc, and three-year-old daughter, Van, to the United States before the fall of Saigon. Their documents and clothes were misplaced while they were in transit, and they were misidentified as orphans. He finally located them and placed them in the care of his family. Adoptions by single parents were uncommon then, and it took him over a year to complete the process and for his children to receive citizenship and diplomatic passports so they could accompany him on foreign assignments. Martindale says they became "typical suburban kids" during his postings to Washington, D.C. He never learned the fate of the young Vietnamese woman who had fallen onto the iron fence separating his building from the Italian embassy. Four decades later, he said, "I can't tell you the nights I have dreamed about her and wondered what happened to her."

Lionel Rosenblatt left the State Department in 1991 and founded Refugees International, a nongovernmental organization providing humanitarian assistance to displaced persons. Craig Johnstone, who had accompanied him to Saigon, would become United Nations deputy high commissioner for refugees.

Ken Quinn, Ken Moorefield, Don Hays, Terry McNamara, and Theresa Tull had successful diplomatic careers. Quinn became U.S. ambassador to Cambodia. Hays was appointed U.S. ambassador to the United Nations for United Nations reform. Tull served as U.S. ambassador to Guyana and then to Brunei. Her friend General Truong was reunited with his wife and children in the United States several months after the war and became a computer programmer. Tull retired to Northern Virginia and frequently sees his children, who consider her a close member of their family.

Ken Moorefield served as U.S. ambassador to Gabon. When asked to reflect on the evacuation a decade later, he said, "There was so much life lived during the final ten days, with the country literally crashing down around our ears. The speed, the rapidity of the events during that experience makes it, in retrospect, almost as if a movie was being run in front of me at a very fast speed."

Terry McNamara also concluded his career as ambassador to Gabon. He wrote an account of his experiences during the evacuation that he dedicated to his aide Hank Cushing and to Major General Nam, calling them "both now dead but not forgotten."

Bill Ryder remains haunted by the people he prevented from boarding his overloaded barge at gunpoint. Over the years he has asked himself, "You know, who the hell am I to play God?" He adds, "Of course Kissinger and Ford had also played God, but they didn't have to look into the faces of those people."

Glenn Rounsevell learned that only a few of the thirty-three CIA key indigenous personnel whom he had not pulled over the embassy wall on April 29 had escaped on ships and barges. He assumed that the rest would spend years in concentration camps. After returning to Washington "guilt-ridden and saddened," he resigned from the CIA and pursued a career in education.

Tom Polgar concluded his CIA career as head of personnel. After retiring, he was hired to investigate the Iran arms scandal. He later became more sympathetic to Martin's position, telling an interviewer, "The [Ford] administration used Graham Martin as the fall guy, directing him to pursue a policy that simply had no chance of succeeding and for which there was no domestic support." One of their last exchanges had occurred on the *Blue Ridge*. After overhearing Polgar tell a group of senior naval officers, "Well, we got our people out," Martin had interrupted and said, "The fuck you did."

Over the next thirty years Richard Armitage served in several senior foreign policy and military positions, including assistant secretary of defense for international security policy in the Reagan administration and deputy secretary of state under Secretary Colin Powell in the George W. Bush administration.

Erich von Marbod became the Pentagon representative to the Interagency Task Force for Indochina and traveled across the United States identifying sites for resettlement camps. He has had a long and storied career at the Pentagon. During a 1976 congressional hearing on the evacuation, Martin accused him of having precipitated the shelling of Tan Son Nhut on the morning of April 29 by persuading the VNAF high command to encourage its pilots to fly their air-craft to bases in Thailand following the attack on the airport the day before. Lee Hamilton (D-Ind.) offered von Marbod an opportunity to respond. He declined because he was on assignment in Iran for the Pentagon and believed that his testimony would destroy Martin's chances for a senior position in the State Department.

Martin told an oral historian that it was "pretty obvious" that von Marbod was responsible for North Vietnam shelling Tan Son Nhut. "Von Marbod was a wonderful guy. I like him very much, but he's a bloody disaster area," he said. "He had no authority but he finally persuaded Ky of all people to get the planes out." Von Marbod could have made a strong case in his defense. Only a small number of VNAF planes left after the April 28 bombing. Most departed the next morn-ing as a consequence of the early morning barrage. Furthermore, intercepts of North Vietnamese communications and General Dung's memoir showed that by April 19 the Communists had already decided to shell Tan Son Nhut.

Four months after leaving Saigon, Lacy Wright ran into Jackie Bong in a drugstore near the State Department. She had been spirited out of Vietnam with the assistance of Americans she would later com-pare to the Righteous Gentiles. They married in 1976 and she changed her name to Bong-Wright, joined the Foreign Service, and accompa-nied her husband to postings in Italy and Brazil. She blamed Kissinger for abandoning South Vietnam, writing in her memoir that when they crossed paths at the entrance to the State Department in 1980, "My heart beat so loudly that I was shaking. I stopped right behind him, tears running down my face, without the strength to say a word." They finally met when Kissinger traveled to Brazil in 1995 with a group of American executives. When she told him that she was Vietnamese, he said, "I feel sorry when I see a Vietnamese."

The Communists arrested Dr. Lem Truong's fifteen-year-old son for distributing antigovernment leaflets. He cut his wrists so he could make an escape attempt while being transferred to a hospital. He failed, and Truong sent him money to bribe his way to freedom. In 1987 she finally got him and her husband and youngest son out of Vietnam with the help of a French general who was in charge of France's Indochina refugee program. After years in Communist prisons her son could hardly walk and had become so sensitive to light that he had to wear dark glasses. Truong's infant daughter, who had escaped with her on the boat, became a graphic designer at Condé Nast publications.

The 150 people on Truong's boat were among the tens of thousands of Vietnamese refugees whom the U.S. Navy rescued in the days following the surrender. Most had no documents and were not related to U.S. citizens. After a reporter asked the navy to justify picking them up and bringing them to the United States, a navy spokesman said, "They were there. They were on the high seas. They were rescued."

Architecture student Binh Pho and his girlfriend, who had hung back to help their friends manage their children, were among the abandoned 420. Before leaving the compound, Pho collected the piastres that they had turned into paper airplanes. He and his girlfriend broke up soon afterward, and he made several escape attempts. He was arrested, interrogated, and imprisoned for a year. Following his release he escaped to a Malaysian island and spent months in a refugee camp before immigrating to the United States. According to a handsome coffee-table book celebrating his life and work, he has become "a leading figure in the new international movement in contemporary wood sculpture."

On the twenty-fifth anniversary of the fall of Saigon, former president Gerald Ford told historian Douglas Brinkley, "I still grieve over those we were unable to rescue. . . . Yet along with the pain there is pride. In the face of overwhelming pressure to shut our doors, we were able to resettle a first wave of more than 130,000 Vietnamese refugees. To have done anything less in my opinion would have only added moral shame to military humiliation."

Henry Kissinger held a press conference in Washington on the afternoon of April 29, just minutes after Graham Martin boarded Lady Ace 09. He said, "Until Sunday night [Monday morning, April 28, in Saigon] we believed there was some considerable hope that the North Vietnamese would not see a solution by purely military means." He explained that once General Minh assumed the presidency, "we thought that a negotiated solution in the next few days was highly probable." He called North Vietnam's shift to a military solution "sudden," implying that it had not been part of North Vietnam's long standing plan. When asked why he believed this, he said that "the battlefield situation suggested that there was a stand-down of significant military activity" and that the Communists' public statements had suggested that they would negotiate with Minh. Referring obliquely to the administration's communications with the Soviets, he said, "There were also other reasons which led us to believe that the possibility of a negotiation remained open."

In August 1975 the State Department reported that 130,810 refugees from Indochina, most of them Vietnamese, were in its resettlement program. By the end of the year, 120,000 had been resettled across the United States. During the next twenty-five years they were joined by another 1.3 million Vietnamese. Some were boat people; others left under the United Nations Orderly Departure Program, a plan instituted to alleviate the horrors experienced by the boat people.

A Gallup poll released in May 1975 showed that only 36 percent of Americans supported the admission of Vietnamese refugees. The hostility to the Vietnamese came from working-class Americans, who feared that they would take their jobs, and members of the antiwar movement whose members, according to the noted Harvard sociologist David Riesman, demonstrated "an extraordinary callousness toward the South Vietnamese." The Seattle City Council voted 7–1 against a resolution proposing that the city welcome Vietnamese refugees, and Governor Jerry Brown of California was critical of the Ford administration's open-door policy toward Vietnamese refugees. Several days after the fall of Saigon, Senator George McGovern (D-S.D.), who had run for president on an antiwar platform in 1972, told students at Eastern Illinois University, "Ninety percent of the Vietnamese refugees would be better going back to their own land." He added, "I have never thought that more than a handful of government leaders were in any real danger of reprisals." He advocated "steps to facilitate their return to Vietnam," saying that he was planning to introduce legislation to pay for ships and planes to take them home.

Washington Post writer William Greider called Americans' hostility to Vietnamese refugees "a last poisonous convulsion from the finished war in Vietnam—so ugly and out of character with an American past when refugees were welcome." Nathan Glazer, the co-author of *Beyond the Melting Pot,* a groundbreaking work about immigration, blamed some of the antipathy on American journalists who had portrayed the South Vietnamese as "corrupt" and "unable to defend themselves."

The Ford administration and the military refused to bow to public opinion and political pressure. Speaking of the seventy-five thousand or so "self-evacuated" Vietnamese refugees—a number including the passengers on the South Vietnamese naval vessels, Bill Ryder's MSC barges, the people Jim Parker had rescued at Vung Tau, and the tens of thousands of Vietnamese who put to sea in anything that (briefly) floated—a State Department spokesman said, "The administration believes it has a moral obligation to help these refugees who fled from the Communist takeover in Vietnam."

There was no Cambodian-style bloodbath in Vietnam, but there were summary executions. How many is disputed, but they were probably in the thousands. Hundreds of thousands of South Vietnamese, including military officers, government officials, intellectuals, journalists, and those supporting the Thieu government and allied with Americans, were incarcerated in so-called reeducation camps where they performed hard labor. Many were incarcerated for between three and ten years, with some spending seventeen years in the camps. Tens of thousands died of malnutrition, mistreatment, and disease. Several months after the war, a Frenchwoman visited a Vietnamese friend who reported that a mutual friend, a former official of the central bank, was in a reeducation camp. When the Frenchwoman asked, "What's he studying?" her friend shot back, "You idiot! He's in a concentration camp."

Martin gave an impromptu press conference on the *Blue Ridge*. A reporter described his eyes as "flat" and his skin as "chalky." He mumbled the answers to a few questions "in a dazed monotone" before bumming a cigarette from a journalist. He spent months in hospitals in Italy and Maryland being treated for congestion in his lungs, cancer, and other ailments. He saw Henry Kissinger for the last time when they spent half an hour together in Kissinger's office. According to Martin, "Henry spent twenty-five of those minutes talking on the phone with [*New York Times* columnist] James Reston."

Martin told a congressional committee in January 1976, "If I could relive that month [April 1975] I would change almost nothing in the way the Saigon Mission reacted to the realities of the unfolding situation." He spoke of "dispassionate historians" vindicating the embassy's performance, and speaking as much to these historians as to Congress, he testified that because he considered the Justice Department's April 25 decision to grant an emergency immigration parole to fifty thousand endangered South Vietnamese "clearly insufficient," he had "interpreted the number to mean heads of families and not the families too." He added, "I thought we had an obligation to these people and I was insisting to the bitter end that we continue the lift until we got out all of the people that we had there ready to go." Several years later he told an interviewer, "During the last couple of weeks I was doing things that were totally illegal and getting criticized for not doing more."

Twelve hours before Martin left the embassy on April 30, he had ordered four tightly sealed suitcase-sized boxes flown to the *Midway*. The State Department assumed they were his personal effects and forwarded them to his home in North Carolina. The boxes contained classified State Department and CIA documents spanning the period from 1963 to 1975, many of them stamped "Top Secret." They included "eyes only" communications between Martin and Kissinger that had not gone through regular State Department channels. In December 1977, four high school dropouts stole Martin's red Fiat sports car from his house in North Carolina and abandoned it in the woods. Martin had been storing the embassy documents in the trunk. State police found some of them in the car; others turned up by the side of a road and in an abandoned house. After selecting the most important ones, the thieves attempted to sell them. The Justice Department decided not to charge Martin with gross negligence because of his age and health.

Martin claimed that he had been planning to donate the papers to the Lyndon B. Johnson Presidential Library, although he did not contact the library until several weeks after the police recovered them. Sources at the State Department speculated that he had wanted to use the papers to write a historical account that would protect his reputation from criticisms that might be leveled by Henry Kissinger. An unnamed State Department official said, "Graham Martin expected to get into a pissing match with Kissinger after Saigon. He always suspected that Kissinger would try to screw him and blame the fall of Vietnam on him." Martin was said to have complained to friends that Kissinger had been spreading rumors to reporters that he was insane. A former member of his embassy staff said, "He [Martin] never trusted Kissinger and, I guess, he got a little paranoid toward the final days." According to Frank Snepp, "He [Martin] told me he kept them so he could have the last word on Kissinger."

Martin never received another posting and retired from the State Department in 1977. On his last day at work he shared an elevator at the State Department with Walter Martindale. After telling Martindale that after thirty years of service he was retiring that day, he said, "I'm not even being given a luncheon or official farewell. I guess they blame us rather than Congress and the White House for losing Vietnam—but we know better and are in good company."

Duc Van Mai was one of the news agency employees whom Brian Ellis evacuated. He settled in California with his wife and five children. After becoming an American citizen, he changed his name to Brian Duc Van Mai. He has called Ellis every Thanksgiving, and in 2002 his daughter Julie wrote to Ellis to thank him for "that role that you've had not only in my life and the life of every person in my immediate family, but also the lives of the hundreds that you helped to escape." She continued, "For as long as I can remember, I've heard your name—always spoken with an air of respect, the kind that you have for an old friend, and a sense of fondness, that which you have for a loved one, a brother." She wrote in a postscript that her father had cried when he read her letter. His tears had flowed, she said, "because I think I was able to express the gratitude and appreciation that my father has felt towards you for years but was unable to find words in English to tell you. Or, perhaps there are no words to express the gratitude that he feels. How do you thank someone for saving your family? . . . Quite simply, you're our hero."

Acknowledgments

I am indebted to the principal characters named in this narrative who spent hours with me sharing their stories and supplementing them with letters, emails, and diaries. I met with Walter Martindale on four occasions, and he followed up with long and informative emails. I spoke with Ken Moorefield multiple times over the course of a year during which he patiently and in great detail described his experiences during this period. Bill Bell kindly hosted me at his home in Fort Smith, Arkansas, and spoke movingly about the loss of his wife and son in the Babylift crash. Brian Ellis entrusted me with his thoughtful and comprehensive written account of his meetings with Graham Martin and his white-knuckle trips to Tan Son Nhut. Lem Truong permitted me to draw from her unpublished account of her thrilling escape from Saigon. Tom Glenn followed up our interview with several illuminating emails. I can recommend the gripping books and article that he has written about his experiences in Saigon to anyone seeking to learn more about him and the activities of the NSA in South Vietnam. Lionel Rosenblatt was generous with his time, spending most of an afternoon reliving the pop-up underground railway that he and Craig Johnstone cobbled together in Saigon. Bill Ryder gave me a copy of his final report on the Military Sealift Command's evacuation from Saigon. Jim Parker was one of my first interviewees, and he supplemented our long and pleasant interview in Las Vegas with a number of suggestions and clarifications.

I have also drawn extensively on my interviews and correspondence with Richard Baughn, Erich von Marbod, Ross Meador, Al Topping, Nelson Kieff, Don Kanes, David Whitten, Alan Carter, Jaime Sabater,

Richard Armitage, Al Gray, Don Hays, Joe McBride, Theresa Tull, Terry McNamara, Marius Burke, Glenn Rounsevell, Lacy Wright, Jackie Bong-Wright, Jack Madison, David Kennerly, Stuart Herrington, Andy Gembara, Cary Kassebaum, and John Sullivan. I am grateful to them for welcoming me into their homes and offices and reliving memories that for some remain painful. Graham Martin's daughter Janet shared with me some fascinating and little-known aspects of the life and character of her proud, accomplished, stubborn, and ultimately heroic father. Had I included the exploits of all the Americans, South Vietnamese, and others who evacuated endangered Vietnamese during the spring of 1975, *Honorable Exit* would have been several times longer. Some of those whom I interviewed will not find themselves in these pages, not because their stories were less courageous and compelling but because of space constraints. Please accept my apologies.

I have also drawn extensively on the Foreign Affairs Oral History Collection at the Association for Diplomatic Studies and Training, the Gerald R. Ford Library Oral History Projects, and the Oral History Collection at the Texas Tech University Vietnam Center and Archive. All three collections are of a uniformly high standard. David Butler, author of *The Fall of Saigon*, published in 1985, conducted lengthy interviews with many of the same individuals who I interviewed three decades later and with others who are no longer alive. His notes and transcripts, available at the Rauner Special Collections Library at Dartmouth College, were an important resource. Professor Larry Engelmann conducted hundreds of interviews for his magisterial oral history, *Tears Before the Rain*. After his book was published in 1990, the indefatigable Engelmann continued interviewing Americans and Vietnamese, posting the results on his website, *Pushing On*. His interviews with Graham Martin, Tom Polgar, and George McArthur were particularly illuminating, and I am deeply in his debt. I also drew on several published collections of oral histories, including Al Santoli's *To Bear Any Burden* and Kim Willenson's *The Bad War*.

Terry McNamara, Bill Bell, Theresa Tull, Stuart Herrington, O. B. Harnage, Tom Glenn, and Jim Parker have written accounts of their experiences during this period, in some instances as part of longer memoirs. Their books are listed in my bibliography, and I recommend them to anyone wishing to learn more about these remarkable people. No one can write about the final months of the Vietnam War without consulting, as I did, former CIA agent Frank Snepp's *Decent Interval*. It was published in

1977 and remains the longest and most detailed account of America's exit from South Vietnam. During the last four decades, some of my principal characters have recounted their experiences to other authors and oral history interviewers. I have found that in some instances and in some minor respects their stories changed slightly over the years. I have done my best to reconcile any discrepancies and apologize if I have fallen short.

My wife, Antonia, has been patient and supportive while I wrote yet another book that required more time than was initially anticipated. Her love has given me the energy and confidence to complete *Honorable Exit* and the other books that I have had published during forty years of joyful marriage. My daughters Phoebe, Edwina, and Sophie, are now out of the house, but their frequent emails and phone calls have buoyed my spirits. Joe and Pamela McCarthy have continued providing support and encouragement, not to mention a bed and working space in Brooklyn during my periodic visits to New York. Fellow author Stephen Fenichell has been a thoughtful sounding board and good company during our monthly luncheons. And many thanks again to Sandy and Stephanie Carden and to their daughters, Isabel and Lily, who have welcomed me to their home in Florida for several weeks every winter. Other authors have the McDowell Colony; I have the Cardens.

I am grateful to Melissa Danaczko and Bill Thomas at Doubleday for their enthusiasm and encouragement. After Melissa departed I had the great good fortune to be handed over to the energetic and indefatigable Kristine Puopolo. She has given this manuscript more perceptive reads than any author has a right to expect from an editor, and her suggestions and edits have improved it immeasurably. Her associate Dan Meyer has been unfailingly efficient, insightful, and helpful in moving the manuscript through the publishing pipeline. I have been represented by Kathy Robbins for twenty-seven successful and productive years. She and the indispensable David Halpern have given the proposal, research report, drafts, and final version of this book so many thoughtful readings that I would not be surprised if they had unwittingly committed some passages to memory. I am dedicating *Honorable Exit* to the newest member of our family, my accomplished and kind physician son-in-law, Tom Gilliland, and to Ben Weir, a good and loyal friend who has contributed his ideas and research skills to my last several books.

Notes

ABBREVIATIONS

ADST—Association for Diplomatic Studies and Training, Foreign Affairs Oral History Collection.

CIA—Center for the Study of Intelligence, Central Intelligence Agency. Thomas L. Ahern Jr. *CIA and the Generals: Covert Support to Military Government in South Vietnam.*

DBC—David Butler Collection. Papers of David Butler at Rauner Special Collections Library, Dartmouth College.

FLEAP—Ford Library, National Security Council, East Asia and Pacific Affairs.

FLMF—Ford Library Martin Files. Gerald R. Ford Presidential Library, Ann Arbor, Mich. Archives. National Security Adviser. Files kept by Ambassador Graham Martin. Boxes 1–10, includes copies of files removed without authorization by Graham Martin.

FLNSA-Meet—Ford Library, National Security Advisers, NSC Meetings File.

FLNSA-Mem—Ford Library, National Security Advisers, Memorandum of Conversations Collection.

FLOHP—Ford Library, Oral History Projects.

FRUS—U.S. Department of State: Office of the Historian. *Foreign Relations of the United States, 1969–1976, Volume X, Vietnam, January 1973–July 1975.*

LDE—Larry D. Engelmann, "Pushing On." Unpublished oral history interviews conducted by Engelmann. lde421.blogspot.com.

MSC—Military Sealift Command. "Activities of the MSCOV During the Vietnam Evacuation." Memorandum from Acting Chief, MSC Office Saigon Residual (Bill Ryder), to Commander, Military Sealift Command, Far East, June 27, 1975.

OFW—U.S. Marine Corps, Ninth Marine Amphibious Brigade, "Operation

Frequent Wind," Aug. 5, 1975. U.S. Marine Corps, History and Museums Division.

RSP—Report on the Situation in the Republic of Vietnam. Hearings before the House Committee on Foreign Affairs, Subcommittee on Asian and Pacific Affairs. Testimony of Ambassador Graham Martin, July 31, 1974.

SBE—Summers, Lieutenant Colonel Harry G. "The Bitter End," *Vietnam Magazine,* April 1975.

TTU/ARC—Texas Tech University, Vietnam Center and Archives, Archive.

TTU/OH—Texas Tech University, Vietnam Center and Archives, Oral History Collection.

USDAO—U.S. Defense Attaché Office, Saigon, Republic of Vietnam. *End of Tour Report.* Major General Homer Smith wrote three versions of his report in 1975, marked I, II, and III.

USMC—U.S. Marine Corps, History and Museums Division. *Frequent Wind.*

VCE—The Vietnam-Cambodia Emergency, 1975. Hearings before the House Committee on International Relations. Part I: *Vietnam Evacuation and Humanitarian Assistance.* April 9–18, 1975. Part II: *The Vietnam-Cambodian Emergency, 1975.* Hearings of March 6–13 and April 14, 1975. Part III: *Vietnam Evacuation: Testimony of Ambassador Graham A. Martin.* Hearing of Jan. 27, 1976.

PROLOGUE: THE MAN IN THE WHITE SHIRT

1   Dutch photojournalist: Hubert "Hugh" Van Es, "Thirty Years at 300 Millimeters," *New York Times,* April 29, 2005.

2   "makeshift wooden ladder": Ibid.

2   Zoom in: Harnage, *Thousand Faces,* 158; Leeker, *Air America,* 1, 31–32.

2   "a gregarious, macho good old boy": Sullivan, *Of Spies and Lies,* 186.

2   The cigar was one: Harnage, *Thousand Faces,* foreword, 121–29; Fred Bernstein, "This Week O. B. Harnage Remembers America's Last Day in Vietnam," *People,* April 8, 1975.

2   seven years in Laos: Harnage, *Thousand Faces,* 48.

2   Earlier that afternoon: Ibid., 158–60; Bernstein, "This Week O. B. Harnage Remembers America's Last Day in Vietnam."

3   Van Es photographed Harnage: Ralph Ellis, "Famous Saigon Photo Captured Doctor's Escape," *Atlanta Journal-Constitution,* April 28, 2010.

3   Next came Tuyet-Dong Bui: Tiet-Tong Bui, interview.

3   "In the coming hours": *Saigon Post,* April 16, 1975.

3   It was there because: Gray, interview.

3   Air America pilots: Burke, interview; Robbins, *Air America,* 283; TTU/OH: Fillipi, 32–34; Leeker, *Air America,* 16–17.

4   He refused Burke's request: Burke, interview.

4   Bob Caron and Jack Hunter: Caron, interview; Zac Anderson, "A View from the Roof: Fort Walton Beach Resident Piloted Huey Seen in Saigon Evacuation Photo," *Northwest Florida Daily News,* April 29, 2006.

5   To make more room: Harnage, *Thousand Faces*, 158.

5   As he lifted off: Caron, interview.

5   Harnage never forgot: Harnage, *Thousand Faces*, 164.

5   "Don't look in their eyes": Dennis Troute, "Last Days in Saigon," *Harper's Magazine*, July 1975, 60.

5   A reporter who had refused: Hoffmann, *On Their Own*, 372–73.

5   "the look in the eyes": Moorefield, interview.

6   "Oh my God": Bui, interview.

6   "I am opposed": United Press International, "McGovern Opposes Airlift," *New York Times*, April 30, 1975, 18.

6   "We have them": Hoffmann, *On Their Own*, 333.

7   Between noon and 5:00 a.m.: "Air America Played a Crucial Part of the Emergency Helicopter Evacuation of Saigon," *MHQ: The Quarterly Journal of Military History*, June 2006.

7   Add them to the 45,000: Tobin, Laehr, and Hilgenberg, *Last Flight from Saigon*, 45.

7   Jackie Bong, the widow: Bong-Wright, *Autumn Cloud*, 194–99.

8   Teenager Linh Duy Vo: Linh Duy Vo, "A Fateful Lottery Ticket," www .generalhomersmithprize.org; LDE, General Homer Smith.

8   Two decades earlier: Greene, *Ways of Escape*, 161.

8   General Marcel Bigeard: Swain, *River of Time*, 276.

8   "seductive about Vietnam": Nessen, *It Sure Looks Different from the Inside*, 95.

9   "any great attachment": Engelmann, *Tears Before the Rain*, 53–54.

9   "not one of the people": Ibid., 74.

10 An American who had served: Ogden Williams, "Last Trip to Vietnam, April 4–22, 1975," unpublished memorandum supplied to the author.

10 "We're not going": Santoli, *Everything We Had*, 91.

11 "Every one of you folks": Manyon, *Fall of Saigon*, 110.

11 A journalist who witnessed: Ibid.

CHAPTER 1: OMENS

13 It was said that swarms: LDE, "Nguyen Thi Kim-Anh Remembers the Fall of Saigon"; LDE, "Huyen Lac."

13 An American diplomat: LDE, "Vincible Ignorance: Doug Pike's Vietnam."

14 During a state dinner: Hung, *Palace File*, 261–62.

14 North Vietnam's chief of staff: Dung, *Our Great Spring Victory*, 22.

14 "first big step": Vien, *Final Collapse*, 68.

14 "Is the South Vietnamese Defense": Todd, *Cruel April*, 100.

14 Nelson Kieff, a military intelligence: Kieff, interview.

15 "Roll up your sleeves": Lee and Haynsworth, *White Christmas in April*, 119–20.

15 "The cuts they": FRUS, 156.

15 While author and Vietnam War critic: Isaacs, *Without Honor*, 333.

16 "We are ready to withdraw": Kimball, *Vietnam War Files*, 120, 187.

16   "If we can live": Calvin Woodward, "Kissinger Papers: U.S. OK with Takeover," *Washington Post,* May 26, 2006.

16   "If a year or two years": "Tape: Nixon Mulled Vietnam Exit in 1972," *USA Today,* Aug. 8, 2004.

19   "all the U.S. cared about": LDE, "Keyes Beech."

19   "I am returning": FLNSA, April 3, 1975.

19   During the next two years: FLMF, box 8.

20   By then, Saigon wags: Isaacs, *Without Honor,* 143.

21   "Of course we have information": Herrington, "Third Indochina War," 91.

21   Like many in his generation: Herrington, interview.

21   Soon after Phuoc Long fell: Herrington, "Third Indochina War," 90.

22   An American contractor: Ibid., 193.

22   One evening a posse: Herrington, *Peace with Honor?,* 124.

22   After Phuoc Long fell: Bell, interview; Bell, *Leave No Man Behind,* 18, 69–71.

23   After hearing Gembara's report: Bell, interview; Bell, *Leave No Man Behind,* 70–71.

23   Soon after Phuoc Long fell: Gembara, interview.

24   After he struggled: McBride, interview.

26   While McBride was revisiting: Moorefield, interviews; Santoli, *To Bear Any Burden,* 113–15, 189–92, 229–32.

26   He had recently sent: CIA, 155.

27   "I want you to know": DeForest and Chanoff, *Slow Burn,* 249.

27   "If you attend": Parker, *Last Man Out,* 253–54.

27   CIA agent James Parker: Parker, interview; Parker, *Last Man Out,* 252–53.

CHAPTER 2: WALTER MARTINDALE'S CONVOY

29   Consular officer Walter Martindale: Martindale material in this chapter from Martindale, interviews and email correspondence with the author.

30   Tom Glenn, who headed: Glenn, interview.

32   Thompson had just returned: FLEAP, box 12.

32   In his memoir: Dung, *Our Great Spring Victory,* 16–21.

32   U.S. secretary of defense: James Cannon Papers, box 4, Gerald R. Ford Presidential Library.

32   In September 1973: CIA, 141.

33   A March 12 memorandum: *FRUS,* 185.

33   On March 11, he summoned: Hung, *Palace File,* 264–65; Vien, *Final Collapse,* 77–78; Todd, *Cruel April,* 140; Veith, *Black April,* 172–73.

33   On March 14, Thieu flew: Snepp, *Decent Interval,* 194–95; Veith, *Black April,* 176–78; Butler, *Fall of Saigon,* 75–77; Isaacs, *Without Honor,* 348–49; Todd, *Cruel April,* 142–43.

34   During the flight back to Pleiku: Veith, *Black April,* 178.

34   The next day, March 15: Ibid., 184; FLMF, box 8.

34   General Vien also neglected: Butler, *Fall of Saigon,* 88.

34 Phu also followed Thieu's order: Ibid.
35 U.S. provincial representative: Snepp, *Decent Interval,* 199–203.
36 Reporter Nguyen Tu called: Veith, *Black April,* 211–12.
36 While this tragedy was unfolding: Erich von Marbod, interview.
38 According to a Vietnamese woman: Jackie Bong-Wright, interview.
41 American generals had praised: Veith, *Black April,* 92.
41 Norman Schwarzkopf: Norman Schwarzkopf, *It Doesn't Take a Hero* (New York: Bantam, 1992), 140.
41 She had grown up in New Jersey: Sources for Tull and Truong material in this chapter: Tull, interview; Tull, *Long Way from Runnemede,* 51–60, 96–102.

CHAPTER 3: WHO LOST VIETNAM?
46 "Between you and me": Kissinger, *Crisis,* 449.
47 The night before leaving: LDE, George McArthur.
47 "he's a patriot": DBC, box 3, folder 80.
47 Despite Ban Me Thuot: *FRUS,* 191.
48 On this day, he told Ford: FLNSA-Meet, March 25, 1975.
48 "This is one of the most": Ibid.
48 "If we are not legalistic": Ibid.
48 "Fred, be careful": Hung, *Palace File,* 302.
48 Kissinger would later claim: Kissinger, *Crisis,* 425.
49 Years later, Kissinger would write: Ibid.
49 "I'm glad you're going": FLNSA-Meet, March 25, 1975.
49 He considered Martin: ADST, Habib, 57; LDE, Habib.
49 "I've been in this business": LDE, Habib.
49 There had been a testy: *FRUS,* 191.
50 "Remember, the one thing": FLNSA-Meet, March 25, 1975.
50 Earlier that year: DBC, box 4, folder 8.
50 He also told friends: Ibid.
50 He told his daughter: Janet Martin, interview.
50 "If the President": Ibid.; *VCE,* Part III, 537.
51 He made the request: FLMF, box 8.
52 "For more than 40 years": *RSP,* 12.
52 "nothing happened in Vietnam": DBC, box 4, folder 8.
52 "The one asset": FLNSA-Meet, March 25, 1975.
52 "the familiar profile": Utley, *You Should Have Been Here Yesterday,* 165–66.
53 But instead of a silver spoon: Sources for Martin's early life and career: Janet Martin, interview; Butler, *Fall of Saigon,* 145–49; Snepp, *Decent Interval,* 67–72; DBC, box 4, folder 8.
54 "I felt then": *RSP,* 7.
54 It was believed in Vietnam: Hung, *Palace File,* 316.
55 Mann's death had been: Janet Martin, interview.
55 Martin would acknowledge: *VCE,* Part III, 536.

55   He told friends: Dawson, *55 Days,* 100.

55   As Humphrey was preparing: Janet Martin, interview; Butler, *Fall of Saigon,* 145–49; Snepp, *Decent Interval,* 67–72.

56   Without hesitation Martin said: Lacy Wright, interview.

56   During World War II: Janet Martin, interview.

56   In a letter: *RSP,* 21.

56   "the most Machiavellian mind": LDE, McArthur.

56   "tended to consider": Kissinger, *Crisis,* 441.

56   "a man with a mission": Dan Oberdorfer, "America's Man in Saigon," *Washington Post,* April 13, 1975, A1.

57   Martin compared himself: DBC, box 4, folder 8.

57   Still, he was the only one: FLNSA-Meet: March 25, 1975.

57   His concern might have been: Engelmann, *Tears Before the Rain,* 53–54.

57   "Mr. President, I really": Ford, *Time to Heal,* 251; Kennerly, interview.

58   "Sure, David, I understand": Kennerly, *Shooter,* 168.

58   Ford asked if he could: Ibid.; Ford, *Time to Heal,* 251; Kennerly, interview.

58   Kennerly's black-and-white photographs: Kennerly.com.

58   "worked in the deep": Ibid.

59   "You mean that division": Butler, *Fall of Saigon,* 143; CIA, 169–70.

60   They might have been: Lewis Sorley, *Westmoreland: The General Who Lost Vietnam* (New York: Houghton Mifflin Harcourt, 2011), 154.

60   "Unless a more positive": R. W. Apple, "Vietnam: The Signs of Stalemate," *New York Times,* Aug. 7, 1967, 1.

60   "deteriorated considerably in the past": *FRUS,* 194.

60   Ford and Kissinger received: Ibid., 195.

61   Three days before: Dung, *Palace File,* 120.

61   And while Weyand was: *FRUS,* 196.

61   Kissinger meanwhile told reporters: John W. Finney, "Kissinger Revives a Vietnam Aid Plan," *New York Times,* March 27, 1975, 1.

61   Quinn was currently serving: Sources for Quinn material: Quinn, interview; Quinn, "Integrity and Openness."

62   "He was a friend": Von Marbod, interview.

CHAPTER 4: DESIGNATED FALL GUY

63   As passengers lined up: Snepp, *Decent Interval,* 281.

63   The week before: CIA, 161–62.

63   Polgar pulled Quinn aside: Quinn, interview.

64   He told a CIA officer: CIA, 169–70.

64   Theresa Tull had been sleeping: Tull, interview; Tull, *Long Way from Runnemede,* 104.

64   NSA chief Tom Glenn: Source for Glenn material: Glenn, interview.

65   Fred Thomas was serving: ADST, Fred Charles Thomas.

66   During a meeting of the National Security Council: FLNSA-Meet: March 28, 1975.

66   That same afternoon: Sources for Hays material: Hays, interviews; DBC, box 3, folder 48.

68   Martin did not suspect: Hays, interviews.

68   He told chamber members: Brian Ellis, interview; Isaacs, *Without Honor*, 373; Dawson, *55 Days*, 171–73.

69   "I can get in": Engelmann, *Tears Before the Rain*, 13.

69   "Wyatt Earp with airplanes": LDE, "Homesick Angel."

70   "Give the gun": Sources for Martin-Daly exchange: Engelmann, *Tears Before the Rain*, 54; Butler, *Fall of Saigon*, 155; DBC, box 4, folders 7, 8; Dawson, *55 Days*, 156.

71   Jacobson would later condemn: LDE, Jacobson.

71   He joined the first flight: Sources for Daly flight to Da Nang: Butler, *Fall of Saigon*, 162–70; LDE, "Homesick Angel"; Isaacs, *Without Honor*, 360–71.

72   "That's it. It's time": Bissell, *Father of All Things*, 39.

72   While Daly was barely: Snepp, *Decent Interval*, 256.

73   UPI reporter Paul Vogle: Willenson, *Bad War*, 299.

73   "felt a specific obligation": CIA, 167.

74   "one of the most tragic": USMC., 128.

75   During a State Department staff: *FRUS*, 198.

76   They talked late: Kennerly, interview.

76   Kennerly's Vietnamese and American: Ibid.

76   After *New York Times* correspondent: Cong. Rec., March 21, 1974, S4187-94.

77   He suspected his secretary: Gembara, interview.

77   "You guys [the press]": Kennerly, interview.

78   Martin was more guarded: Sources for Quinn material: Quinn, interview; Wright, interview.

82   Martin's third houseguest: Von Marbod, interview.

82   On March 27, Hung: Hung, *Palace File*, 375.

83   Hung and Thieu hoped: Ibid.; von Marbod, interview.

CHAPTER 5: "I'D TELL THE PRESIDENT THAT!"

84   "What's he going to do": Martindale, interviews.

85   The highway from Nha Trang: Ibid.; Kennerly, interview.

85   Two barefoot girls: Martindale, interviews.

86   They flew over: Kennerly, interview.

86   Kennerly asked the Air America pilot: Ibid.

86   "You tell the president": Martindale, interviews.

87   General Weyand arrived: Dawson, *55 Days*, 191–92.

87   Despite Al Francis's warning: Maurer, *Strange Ground*, 590; LDE, "Moncrieff Spear's Vietnam."

88   Instead of leaving: Martindale, interviews.

88   Military intelligence agent: Kieff, interview.

89   Kieff and Martindale cut a hole: Ibid.; Martindale, interviews.

89 "Get the hell out": Sources for evacuation from Nha Trang: Snepp, *Decent Interval,* 267–72; Maurer, *Strange Ground,* 590–93; ADST, Moncrieff Spear, 20–21.

90 As Martindale disembarked: Martindale, interviews.

90 Spear then turned: Kieff, interview.

90 Spear would say that leaving: Maurer, *Strange Ground,* 593.

90 "I'm so ashamed": Isaacs, *Without Honor,* 381.

90 Air America had placed: Sources for Burke material: Burke, interview; Burke, "Vietnam Report, Part One."

91 After reaching Saigon: Maurer, *Strange Ground,* 593.

91 McNamara had been planning to send: Sources for McNamara's background and planning for the consulate's evacuation down the Bassac River: McNamara, interview; ADST, McNamara interview; McNamara, *Escape with Honor,* 28–76; ADST, Moments in U.S. Diplomatic History, "Apocalypse Not—the Evacuation from Can Tho—April 1975," adst.org.

91 Still, he argued: Kassebaum, interview; McNamara, interview; McNamara, *Escape with Honor,* 99–100; DBC, box 4, folder 3.

92 His staff was an unconventional bunch: Kassebaum and McNamara, interviews; Kassebaum, *I Never Pushed a Cookie,* 126.

92 They all knew that although McNamara: Kassebaum, interview; McNamara, interview; McNamara, *Escape with Honor,* 28–59, 71–76.

94 After his staff agreed: McNamara, interview; DBC, box 4, folder 3; McNamara, *Escape with Honor,* 101–2; ADST, McNamara interview.

95 Whereas McNamara's staff saw: Rounsevell, Parker, McNamara, and Kassebaum, interviews.

95 McNamara and his staff believed: McNamara, interview; McNamara, *Escape with Honor,* 48–49.

96 Their dispute escalated: McNamara, *Escape with Honor,* 106–8.

96 Following the shelling: McNamara, interview; McNamara, *Escape with Honor,* 119–21.

CHAPTER 6: "IN THE SHADOW OF A CORKSCREW"

97 At a State Department staff meeting: *FRUS,* 201.

97 Several hours later, Kissinger chaired: Ibid., 202.

99 According to the meeting's: Ibid.

99 Kissinger followed up with: Ibid., 203.

99 He responded to Kissinger's demands: Ibid., 204.

100 "for planning purposes": Ibid.

100 "I knew very well": Kissinger, *Crisis,* 441.

101 "What worries me": Ibid., 450.

101 Martin responded to the WSAG request: *FRUS,* 205.

102 "I am not at all pleased": Ibid., 206.

103 After reading the official: Richard Baughn, interview.

103 His deputy, air force: Ibid.; LDE, "And the Edsel Genius," General Richard Baughn, 1, 2.

103   In mid-March, Smith: Sources for SPG and ECC material: Sabater, interview; USMC, 155–59 USDAO, III 16-B9-11, 16-C-2.

103   Sabater considered Smith's assignment: Sabater, interview.

106   Hanoi was on a "blood scent": Corn, *Blond Ghost,* 285.

106   This contravened the immigration laws: USDAO, III, 16-B-12.

106   Baughn believed that Americans: Sources for Baughn material: Baughn, interview; LDE, "And the Edsel Genius," General Richard Baughn, 1, 2.

107   "I have now met": Baughn, interview.

CHAPTER 7: PALPABLE FEAR

108   Former Da Nang: Moorefield, interviews.

109   Moorefield's father had been: Sources for Moorefield's background: Ibid.; DBC, box 4, folders 7, 8.

112   Still, he wondered: DBC, box 4, folders 7, 8.

112   Moorefield spent a month: Moorefield, interviews.

113   Moorefield's two tours: Ibid.

114   Moorefield's dispiriting conversation: Ibid.

114   The day before he left: Hays, interviews.

114   Theresa Tull refused to leave: Tull, interview; Tull, *Long Way from Runnemede,* 104–7.

116   Stephen Hosmer, a Rand Corporation: Samuel Adams, "Signing 100,000 Death Warrants," *Wall Street Journal,* March 26, 1975, 1.

116   Secretary of Defense Schlesinger: Isaacs, *Without Honor,* 393.

116   Two days later: John W. Finney, "Humanitarian Aid to South Vietnam Gains in Senate," *New York Times,* April 18, 1975, 1.

116   Kissinger informed the House: United Press International, "Communists Accused of Atrocities in Vietnam," *New York Times,* April 19, 1975, 12.

117   A January 5, 1975, memorandum: Veith, *Black April,* 473.

117   Under the heading: FLNSA-Mem: April 9, 1975.

117   A Buddhist monk: Michael Getler and Marilyn Berger, "Bloodbath: A Theory Becomes a Fear," *Washington Post,* April 19, 1975, A1.

117   "too many honest people": Howard Langer, *The Vietnam War: An Encyclopedia of Quotations* (Westport, Conn.: Greenwood Press, 2005), 52.

117   They knew that mass graves: Oberdorfer, *Tet!,* 201.

118   when Colonel Tran Van Doc defected: William Tuohy, "Saigon Fears Blood Bath Under Reds," *Los Angeles Times,* April 18, 1975, 1.

118   "We will treat humanely": Peter Arnett, "After the Fall: Blood Bath or Love Bath?," *Los Angeles Times,* April 22, 1975, 9.

118   After a defector: Herrington, "Third Indochina War," 277.

118   After capturing Ban Me Thuot: The Reverend Tom Stebbins, interview.

119   In Hue, they had executed: Oberdorfer, *Tet!,* 211; Dawson, *55 Days,* 92; Stebbins, interview.

119   An order issued: TTU/ARC, Douglas Pike Collection, folder 14, box 13.

119   An American tugboat captain: Ryder, interview; Lee and Haynsworth, *White Christmas in April,* 179.

119   U.S. military intelligence intercepted: FLEAP, box 13.

119   A captured Khmer Rouge document: Lee and Haynsworth, *White Christmas in April,* 179.

119   A Khmer Rouge radio station: UPI, "Khmer Reds Start Killing Foes," *Saigon Post,* April 21, 1975.

119   In a *Wall Street Journal* essay: Adams, "Signing 100,000 Death Warrants."

120   USIA country directors: Sources for Alan Carter material: Carter, interview; Butler, *Fall of Saigon,* 216–18; DBC, box 3, folder 25; Maurer, *Strange Ground,* 594–606; Willenson, *Bad War,* 305–6.

121   The undercurrent of fear: Carter, interview.

121   He sensed the "suppressed hysteria": Carter, interview; Maurer, *Strange Ground,* 599; Willenson, *Bad War,* 306.

121   The "palpable fear": William Tuohy, "Saigon Swims on at Cercle Sportif but Gaiety's Gone," *Los Angeles Times,* April 16, 1975, 1.

122   "It's harder for a South Vietnamese": Malcolm W. Browne, "Tensions Grow in Saigon," *New York Times,* April 4, 1975, 1.

122   While flying home with the Weyand mission: FLEAP, box 13.

123   In a second memorandum: Ibid.

123   Weyand's written report: Butler, *Fall of Saigon,* 235; Snepp, *Decent Interval,* 306; Lou Cannon, "Ford Gets Pessimistic Report," *Washington Post,* April 6, 1975, A1.

124   His verbal report was more: *FRUS,* 208.

124   "Why don't these people": Nessen, *It Sure Looks Different from the Inside,* 98.

124   David Kennerly arrived: Kennerly, interview.

124   He struck Betty Ford's private secretary: Sheila Rabb Weidenfeld, *First Lady's Lady: With the Fords at the White House* (New York: G. P. Putnam's, 1979), 110.

124   "the worst thing": Kennerly, interview.

125   When he met with Ford: Ibid.

125   "This is what's going on": Ibid.

125   Ford ordered them reinstated: Ibid.

125   While flying back to Washington: Richard H. Growald, "Kennerly Says His Vietnamese Friends Are Terrified," *Washington Post,* April 8, 1975, A10; Nessen, *It Sure Looks Different from the Inside,* 98–99.

CHAPTER 8: OPERATION BABYLIFT

127   Major General Smith supported: Snepp, *Decent Interval,* 302.

127   Ambassador Martin called: Fox Butterfield, "Orphans of Vietnam: One Last Agonizing Issue," *New York Times,* April 13, 1975, 199.

128   Twenty-year-old Ross Meador: Sources for Meador material: Meador, interview; Cherie Clark, *After Sorrow Comes Joy,* 68–71; Peck-Barnes, *War Cradle,* 110–14.

128   On the morning of April 2: Meador, interview.

129 At 9:00 p.m., Tom Clark: Ibid.; Cherie Clark, *After Sorrow Comes Joy*, 130–35.

129 Ed Daly stood: Cherie Clark, *After Sorrow Comes Joy*, 130–35.

130 Daly ripped the bill in two: Bob Shane, "Courage Revisited," www.vietnam babylift.org.

130 An air traffic controller: "Orphans of the Storm," *Newsweek*, April 14, 1975, 14.

130 Meador thought he had demonstrated: Meador, Interview.

130 "Breathes there an American": George F. Will, "The New Angels of Mercy," *Washington Post*, April 7, 1975, A21.

130 Among these dependents: Bell, interview; Bell, *Leave No Man Behind*, 72–73.

131 Bell can remember: Bell, interview; Bell, *Leave No Man Behind*, 72–77.

133 He found the corpses: Herrington, interview.

133 Bell wandered through: Bell, interview; Bell, *Leave No Man Behind*, 77–78.

133 There had been his hardscrabble: Bell, interview; Bell, *Leave No Man Behind*, 1–6.

134 Bell's colleague Stuart Herrington: Herrington, interview.

135 Martin saw it: Carter, interview; Willenson, *Bad War*, 306.

135 After seeing his father's: "The Stories: Trung," www.pbs.org.

136 He promised a delegation: Butler, *Fall of Saigon*, 247.

136 President Thieu praised: Dawson, *55 Days*, 256–57.

137 Moments before the blast: Manyon, *Fall of Saigon*, 80–81.

137 It was the first time: Baughn, interview; LDE, General Richard Baughn, 2.

138 Like Baughn and Smith: Gray, interview.

138 After visiting the evacuation: Ibid.

138 Baughn wrote a memorandum: Baughn, interview; Isaacs, *Without Honor*, 400–401; LDE, General Richard Baughn, 2; Snepp, *Decent Interval*, 334.

138 The operator at the DAO message center: Baughn, interview.

139 The embassy claimed: George McArthur, "AF General Who Aided 'Refugee' Airlift Recalled," *Los Angeles Times*, April 15, 1975, 1.

139 The Marine Corps history notes: USMC, 157.

139 The day after Baughn left: Gray, interview.

139 In his written report: OFW, 18–20.

139 The SPG's preparations: TTU/OH, Lieutenant General Richard Carey, 490–91.

140 A week later, he wrote: Camp, *Assault from the Sky*, 191.

CHAPTER 9: "PEOPLE ARE GOING TO FEEL BADLY"

141 Press Secretary Ron Nessen: Nessen, *It Sure Looks Different from the Inside*, 101.

141 "Nobody thought we would get": Hung, *Palace File*, 311.

142 White House counselor: Hartmann, *Palace Politics*, 318.

142 "more a statement": Oberdorfer, "America's Man in Saigon."

142 An embassy source told: George McArthur, "U.S. Credibility Weak in Evacuation," *Washington Post,* April 13, 1975, 19.

142 Only half of Congress: Nessen, *It Sure Looks Different from the Inside,* 102–3.

143 Seventy-five percent: Martin Arnold, "Hawks and Doves Are Glad It's Ending," *New York Times,* April 20, 1975, 144.

143 After Ford's speech: Murrey Marder, "U.S. Trying to Get Cease-Fire," *Washington Post,* April 12, 1975, 1; John W. Finney, "Congress Resists U.S. Aid in Evacuating Vietnamese," *New York Times,* April 12, 1975, 1.

144 The senators had requested: *FRUS,* 232.

145 After the meeting ended: Nessen, *It Sure Looks Different from the Inside,* 106.

145 *The Washington Post* reported: Murrey Marder and Spencer Rich, "Vietnam Exit Plan Forms, Includes Arms Fund," *Washington Post,* April 15, 1975, 1.

146 Representative Don Riegle Jr.: *VCE,* Part I, 94.

146 Erich von Marbod told: Hung, *Palace File,* 306–9.

147 At a meeting: *FRUS,* 212.

147 "I think we ought to get out": Ibid., 236.

147 "The careful record": Kissinger, *Ending the Vietnam War,* 550.

147 "You should know": *FRUS,* 237.

147 "interagency pressure for immediate": Ibid., 238.

147 At a WSAG meeting: Ibid., 249.

148 The next day, April 22: FLEAP, box 1, April 22, 1975.

149 "But the U.S. is going to be": *FRUS,* 256.

149 "a collapse under controlled": Ibid., 243.

149 "We really owe it": Kissinger, *Crisis,* 486.

149 "How many Vietnamese": *FRUS,* 254.

150 After thanking Dean: Isaacs, *Without Honor,* 276.

150 "good evidence that": *FRUS,* 256.

150 Kissinger was probably thinking: Kissinger, *Ending the Vietnam War,* 539.

151 "Defense Department officials": John W. Finney, "Fear in Pentagon," *New York Times,* April 22, 1975, 1.

151 "Defense wishes total": Kissinger, *Crisis,* 488.

152 "We think you should": *FRUS,* 232.

152 "It was apparent": Ibid., 233n5.

152 "But I want you to know": Ibid., 218.

152 Martin replied the next day: FLMF, box 8.

152 "anticipate events with sufficient precision": Ibid.

153 "the U.S. political situation": Ibid., box 10.

153 "He always ends up": *FRUS,* 257.

153 "My situation reminds me": Ibid., 260.

153 "I have an exhausted staff": Ibid., 262.

154 "There are only two": Ibid., 233.

155 "We have two nutty ambassadors": Ibid., 211.

155 "Our problem is to prevent": Kissinger, *Crisis,* 485.

155 Among Martin's contributions: Stanley Karnow, "The Hasty Retreat from Saigon," *New Republic,* May 19, 1975, 15.

155 Also contributing to the impression: FLMF, box 8.

155 During a conversation with Ford: *FRUS,* 240.

155 He came to his defense: Ibid., 243.

156 "You may think I am": FLMF, box 8.

156 "I don't think": Ibid.

156 During Kissinger's congressional testimony: *VCE,* Part I, 142.

156 He praised Martin for handling: *FRUS,* 238.

157 "watching our friends in Hanoi": Ibid., 209.

157 He insisted that the South Vietnamese: Ibid.

157 "panic in Saigon": FLMF, box 8.

157 "We will have the appearance": *FRUS,* 259.

CHAPTER 10: "NO GUARANTEES!"

158 The circuitous journey: Sources for Ellis material in this chapter and for the Ellis-Martin meetings: Ellis, interview; unpublished Ellis manuscript, "Saigon Evacuation 1975."

160 Nessen sent a memorandum: FLEAP, box 13, April 12 and 14, 1975.

165 The next year, Martin would tell Congress: *VCE,* Part III, 548–49.

170 In Martin's 1976 congressional testimony: Ibid., 599.

171 Martin's first "Scarlet Pimpernel" operation: Butler, *Fall of Saigon,* 198–99.

172 When someone mentioned evacuating: TTU/OH, Carmody, 315.

172 Martin also broached the subject: *FRUS,* 209.

172 Four days later, on April 11: Ibid., 233.

173 In mid-April he summoned: TTU/OH, Carmody, 328–34.

174 The profile spoke: Oberdorfer, "America's Man in Saigon."

174 Two days before: Utley, *You Should Have Been Here Yesterday,* 165–66.

175 "We are already in business": FLMF, box 8.

175 "It is also beginning increasingly": *FRUS,* 238.

CHAPTER 11: PLAYING GOD

177 Martindale persuaded Jake Jacobson: Source for Martindale in Phu Quoc: Martindale, interviews.

179 He made mistakes: Ibid.

180 He accelerated the pace: Ibid.

181 He hired a Vietnamese forger: Source for Gembara material: Gembara, interview.

182 Like Walter Martindale: Bell, interview.

183 While he had been in California: Herrington, interview.

183 On the way home: Ibid.; Herrington, *Stalking the Vietcong,* 267.

184 He arrived in Hanoi: Herrington, interview.

184 A week later, on April 18: Bell, interview.

185 Since returning from California: Ibid.; Herrington, interview.

185   Colonel Madison asked Herrington: Source for Madison material: Madison, interview.

187   Herrington asked Andy Gembara: Herrington, interview; Gembara, interview.

187   On his first run: Herrington, interview.

188   Bill Bell also faced: Bell, interview.

188   Pace was also a Vietnamese linguist: Bell, *Leave No Man Behind,* 71.

188   They drove day and night: Sources for Bell material: Bell, interview; Bell, *Leave No Man Behind,* 96–100.

190   After Madison had flown: Madison, interview.

190   Herrington had the painful job: Herrington, interview; SBE; U.S. Army Military History Institute: Harry G. Summers, "Last Days in Vietnam," Oral History Project, 56–58.

190   The incident haunted both men: U.S. Army Military History Institute: Harry G. Summers, "Last Days in Vietnam," Oral History Project, 56–58.

191   As Herrington was escorting: Herrington, interview.

191   Herrington realized that: Ibid.

192   Although Martin had fired: Source for Hays material: Hays, interviews.

CHAPTER 12: "GODSPEED"

194   *The Washington Post* described: Oberdorfer, "America's Man in Saigon."

194   He strong-armed USIA head: Carter, interview; Todd, *Cruel April,* 279–80.

195   "a loose cannon": Gayler, *Reminiscences,* 292.

195   Like Martin, Madison, and Baughn: Ibid., 285–90.

195   He found Martin: Ibid., 298.

195   At a gathering of CIA agents: Sullivan, interview; Sullivan, *Of Spies and Lies,* 208.

196   Martin dismissed them: *FRUS,* 241; Herrington, interview.

196   Smith next summoned retired: Herrington, interview.

197   During the April 19 meeting: Snepp, *Decent Interval,* 384–86; Butler, *Fall of Saigon,* 279–80; USDAO I, 12; USDAO III, 16-B-12.

197   Before the meeting ended: Snepp, *Decent Interval,* 386; Butler, *Fall of Saigon,* 280.

198   On April 16, Ken Quinn: Quinn, interview.

198   David Kennerly also played: Kennerly, interview.

198   Scowcroft's first cable: FLMF, box 10.

198   His second cable expanded: Ibid.

200   As Ken Moorefield was casting: Sources for Moorefield and his processing center at the DAO: Moorefield, interviews; Butler, *Fall of Saigon,* 322–26, 369; DBC, box 4, folder 12; Snepp, *Decent Interval,* 388–89, 402–3, 412–13; Santoli, *To Bear Any Burden,* 232–34; LDE, "Ken Moorefield Remembers the Fall of Saigon."

201   On April 21, the air force: Tobin, Laehr, and Hilgenberg, *Last Flight from Saigon,* 45.

201 The Saigon press corps: Dan Oberdorfer, "Saigon Press Corps," *Washington Post,* April 19, 1975, A1.

202 Two days later, almost: George McArthur, "Hanoi's Jets, Artillery Closing In on Saigon," *Los Angeles Times,* April 21, 1975, A1.

202 "It is essential that we get": FLMF, box 10.

205 "Ah, Mr. Moorefield": Moorefield, interview.

206 Joe McBride, the Foreign Service officer: McBride, interview.

207 He had even intervened: Ky, *Twenty Years and Twenty Days,* 213–15.

208 Martin cabled Kissinger: *FRUS,* 244.

209 The next morning: Ibid., 89.

209 Optimists in Saigon: Manyon, *Fall of Saigon,* 88.

209 He had complained beforehand: Engelmann, *Tears Before the Rain,* 149; Hartmann, *Palace Politics,* 32.

210 "From my first day": Nessen, *It Sure Looks Different from the Inside,* 91.

210 During the flight back: Hartmann, *Palace Politics,* 322; Engelmann, *Tears Before the Rain,* 150–51.

210 He was right: Hartmann, *Palace Politics,* 323; Engelmann, *Tears Before the Rain,* 151.

210 He arrived at Tan Son Nhut: Snepp, *Decent Interval,* 435; Todd, *Cruel April,* 327–28.

211 Martin saw Thieu off: Snepp, *Decent Interval,* 435.

CHAPTER 13: "MAKE IT HAPPEN!"

212 Pan Am flight 841: Thomas Taylor, *Where the Orange Blooms,* 223–24.

213 Two of the diplomats: Sources for Rosenblatt and Johnstone material in this chapter: Rosenblatt, interview; Butler, *Fall of Saigon,* 269–73, 359–60; Willenson, *Bad War,* 326–27; DBC, box 3, folder 61, box 4, folder 49; Marilyn Berger, "2 Aides Go Underground, Rescue 200 in Saigon," *Washington Post,* May 5, 1975, 1.

214 "We do not believe": Butler, *Fall of Saigon,* 272.

214 After Pan Am flight 841 landed: Thomas Taylor, *Where the Orange Blooms,* 224–26.

215 One American remembered: Tom Glenn, interview.

220 Since graduating from Annapolis: Armitage, interview; Mann, *Rise of the Vulcans,* 37–49.

220 He had resigned: Mann, *Rise of the Vulcans,* 37–49.

221 He returned to Vietnam: Ibid.

221 "Ricky, we've been looking": Armitage, interview; Mann, *Rise of the Vulcans,* 49.

221 Von Marbod stopped: Trest, *Air Commando,* 251; Hung, *Palace File,* 339.

221 Pan Am station manager: Sources for Topping material in this chapter: Topping, interview; David Lamb, "Refugees Reach Guam on Cloak-Dagger Flight," *Los Angeles Times,* April 25, 1975, A1; Al Topping, "Scrambling to Get Out Before the Fall," *Miami Herald,* April 23, 2013.

226 After the plane had been: Todd, *Cruel April,* 320–21.

226 Ross Meador, the long-haired: Source for Meador material in this chapter: Meador, interview; Cherie Clark, *After Sorrow Comes Joy,* 68–78; Peck-Barnes, *War Cradle,* 185–94.

CHAPTER 14: "I WON'T GO FOR THAT"

234 During a staff meeting: Sources for McNamara's background and planning for the consulate's evacuation down the Bassac River in the remainder of this chapter: McNamara, interview; ADST, McNamara interview; McNamara, *Escape with Honor,* 119–28; ADST, Moments in U.S. Diplomatic History, "Apocalypse Not—the Evacuation from Can Tho—April 1975"; McNamara, *Escape with Honor,* 104–5; ADST, Ambassador Francis Terry McNamara, 127.

235 On April 22, McNamara sent: LDE, David Sciacchitano; McNamara, *Escape with Honor,* 122.

235 They complained about the situation: LDE, David Sciacchitano.

235 McNamara found their report: McNamara, interview; McNamara, *Escape with Honor,* 122–24; ADST, Ambassador Francis Terry McNamara, 126; Butler, 288–91; DBC, box 4, folder 3.

236 After returning to Can Tho: McNamara, interview; McNamara, *Escape with Honor,* 125–28; ADST, McNamara, 127–30.

237 Delaney and McNamara continued arguing: Parker, interview; Parker, *Last Man Out,* 286–87.

238 None of the CIA agents: Sources for Jim Parker material: Parker, interview; Parker, *Last Man Out,* 2–5, 64–66, 78–79, 163, 255–62, 267–70; Parker, *Vietnam War,* 465–67.

241 CIA station chief Tom Polgar chose: Parker, interview; Parker, *Last Man Out,* 280–82.

242 In mid-April, Jim Parker received: Parker, interview; Parker, *Vietnam War,* 463–64, 478–81.

244 "Is this the American way": Sources for Parker adoption story and Chau: Parker, interview; Parker, *Last Man Out,* 278–80, 290–91; Parker, *Vietnam War,* 475–76.

CHAPTER 15: KISSINGER'S CABLE

247 NBC Vietnam War correspondent: Butler, *Fall of Saigon,* 268.

247 "We have just received": FLMF, box 8.

247 It asked that the U.S.S.R.: FLNSA-Mem, April 24, 1975.

248 After delivering Ford's oral note: Ibid.

248 He did not cable the text: FLMF, box 8.

248 The Soviets answered: FLNSA-Mem, April 24, 1975.

248 Kissinger read the Soviet reply: FLNSA-Mem, April 24, 1975; *FRUS,* 258.

249 President Ford suggested: *FRUS,* 258.

249 "I want you to know": Butler, *Fall of Saigon,* 299; FLMF, box 8.

249 "There is a great deal": Butler, *Fall of Saigon,* 299.

250 He explained himself: Kissinger, *Ending the Vietnam War,* 535.

250   In his reply to Kissinger's cable: FLMF, box 8.

250   After telling Thurmond: Kissinger, *Crisis,* 492.

251   Another senator who *did* feel that way: Ibid., 485–86.

251   "the need for [an] emergency": FLMF, box 8.

251   "Do not worry": Ibid.

251   "cut off your balls": Willenson, *Bad War,* 314.

251   "No, you don't really": Todd, *Cruel April,* 324.

252   Martin smiled and said: Snepp, *Decent Interval,* 431.

252   Later that afternoon he told: Burke, interview; Camp, *Assault from the Sky,* 201.

252   "Through other channels": FLMF, box 8.

252   On April 28, with: Ibid.

252   After reading Kissinger's April 25: Sullivan, interview.

252   "Well, I guess you might as well": Kanes, interview.

252   "The fix is in": Ibid.

252   When they met at Polgar's villa: CIA, 201; Corn, *Blond Ghost,* 289.

253   He returned to the embassy: Snepp, *Decent Interval,* 431.

253   For several weeks *New York Times:* Browne, *Muddy Boots and Red Socks,* 357–58.

253   "Peter, there will be no final battle": Arnett, *Live from the Battlefield,* 296.

253   "Events have validated": *FRUS,* 259.

253   He dispatched a self-congratulatory cable: FLMF, box 8.

254   "waiting some possible moves": Kissinger, *Crisis,* 486.

254   Ford said it all sounded: FLNSA-Mem, April 25, 1975.

254   "My thinking regarding": FLMF, box 8.

255   During a White House meeting: Murrey Marder, "Hanoi Changed Signals," *Washington Post,* April 30, 1975, A1.

255   Years later, however: Kissinger, *Crisis,* 540.

256   They were encouraged: Leslie Gelb, "Hanoi Is Signaling U.S. on Take-Over," *New York Times,* April 24, 1975, 1.

256   "not to press an immediate": FLMF, box 8.

256   Mérillon was so confident: Snepp, *Decent Interval,* 420.

256   But on April 25: Bell, interview; Madison, interview.

256   It would later be revealed: Dung, *Our Great Spring Victory,* 215.

257   Before leaving, he asked Jim Devine: SBE.

257   After boarding the plane: Bell, interview; Bell, *Leave No Man Behind,* 90–96.

257   "You Americans should not": SBE; Bell, *Leave No Man Behind,* 91.

258   Bell noticed that sacks: Bell, interview; SBE.

258   After the plane reached: Bell, interview; Bell, *Leave No Man Behind,* 94–96; SBE.

258   To pass the time: Bell, interview; Bell, *Leave No Man Behind,* 95.

259   He told von Marbod: SBE.

259   "For God's sake, give me": Ibid.

CHAPTER 16: RICHARD ARMITAGE'S COURAGEOUS SILENCE

260   One rocket hit the top floor: Manyon, *Fall of Saigon,* 96.

260   His spokesman condemned: Keyes Beech, "Hotel Rocketed: Polish Reds Move," *Los Angeles Times,* April 29, 1975, 6.

261   Communist artillery spotters: Herrington, interview; Herrington, *Peace with Honor?,* 167.

261   JMT linguist Stuart Herrington: Herrington, interview.

262   He called Major General Smith: Snepp, *Decent Interval,* 448.

262   "It may also be possible": FLMF, box 4; Butler, *Fall of Saigon,* 262.

262   "It appears evident": George McArthur, "Reds Fire 4 Rockets into Central Saigon," *Los Angeles Times,* April 27, 1975, 1.

262   Tom Glenn, the young cryptologist: Glenn, interview; Tom Glenn, "Bitter Memories: The Fall of Saigon (Part 1)," *Baltimore Post-Examiner,* Aug. 18, 2013.

262   Two days before delivering his warning: Tom Glenn, "Bitter Memories: The Fall of Saigon (Part 1)," *Baltimore Post-Examiner,* Aug. 18, 2013.

263   Glenn told Martin: Ibid.

264   Glenn hurried to Tom Polgar's office: Ibid.

264   "I finally understood": Glenn, "Bitter Memories."

264   Polgar began hedging: Pilger, "The Last Day," 18.

264   "There is no way": Ibid.

265   The CIA's Can Tho base chief: Sources for Rounsevell material: Parker, *Vietnam War,* 488; Rounsevell, interview.

266   Back in Can Tho: Parker, interview; Parker, *Vietnam War,* 491–92; McNamara, *Escape with Honor,* 132–34.

267   Air America pilot Marius Burke: Source for Burke material: Burke, interview.

269   He suggested that Kiem: Sources for Armitage-Kiem meeting: Armitage, interview; Kane, "Secret Evacuation of the VNN Fleet," 32–33; Do and Kane, *Counterpart,* 194–98.

270   Erich von Marbod had stopped: Trest, *Air Commando,* 251; Hung, *Palace File,* 339.

270   The next day: Von Marbod, interview.

270   He expected a cease-fire: Ibid.; Hung, *Palace File,* 339.

271   Von Marbod persuaded: Von Marbod, interview.

271   During the next several days: Von Marbod, interview and correspondence.

272   Von Marbod saw Martin again: Von Marbod, interview; Snepp, *Decent Interval,* 458–59.

272   After lunch von Marbod: Von Marbod, interview.

272   Armitage persuaded four U.S. servicemen: Armitage, interview; Mann, *Rise of the Vulcans,* 50–51.

272   Back at Tan Son Nhut: Von Marbod, interview; Mann, *Rise of the Vulcans,* 50–51.

273   Von Marbod radioed Armitage: Von Marbod, interview; Mann, *Rise of the Vulcans,* 50–51.

273 "I've got a problem": Von Marbod, interview; Mann, *Rise of the Vulcans*, 50–51; Willenson, *Bad War*, 333.

273 Von Marbod called Seventh Air Force: Von Marbod, interview; Trest, *Air Commando*, 251–52.

273 When CIA agent Jim Parker: Sources for Parker material: Parker, interview; Parker, *Last Man Out*, 296–303; Parker, *Vietnam War*, 492–97.

275 While helicopters were collecting: McNamara, interview; McNamara, *Escape with Honor*, 135–36.

275 He asked his driver: McNamara, interview; McNamara, *Escape with Honor*, 136–37.

CHAPTER 17: EIGHTEEN OPTIMISTIC MINUTES

276 Minh had told: Engelmann, *Tears Before the Rain*, 161.

276 The inauguration was then postponed: Terzani, *Giai Phong!*, 35.

277 "as if delivering": Pilger, *Last Day*, 32.

278 Headlines in *The Saigon Post:* Terzani, *Giai Phong!*, 42.

278 But Radio Liberation: Todd, *Cruel April*, 342.

278 *New York Times* reporter: Snepp, *Decent Interval*, 466.

278 "I thought South Vietnamese": Von Marbod, interview.

278 Tom Glenn had been walking: Glenn, interview.

279 One slammed into Joe McBride's: McBride, interview; Moorefield, interview.

279 Ken Moorefield grabbed his revolver: Moorefield, interview.

279 Bell watched as the A-37s: Bell, interview; Bell, *Leave No Man Behind*, 99–100.

279 When Ross Meador left: Meador, interview.

280 Earlier that day: Martindale, interviews.

280 After Jacobson refused: Burke, interview; Burke, "Vietnam Report: Part Two—Saigon Evacuation," 7–8.

281 Don Hays was in the embassy: Sources for Hays material: Hays, interview; DBC, box 3, folder 48; Butler, *Fall of Saigon*, 294–95.

281 Dr. Lem Hoang Truong's position: Sources for Truong material: Truong, interview; unpublished memoir supplied to the author by Truong.

283 An hour after the attack: Pilger, *Last Day*, 44–46; Snepp, *Decent Interval*, 467.

283 Polgar, who believed that the attack: Pilger, *Last Day*, 46.

283 Minutes later he cabled: FLMF, box 8.

283 He went on to describe: Ibid.

284 Kissinger cabled back: Ibid.

285 Quinn ran into David Kennerly's office: Quinn, interview; Quinn, "From Whitehouse to the White House," 10–11.

285 Ford ordered the flights: Snepp, *Decent Interval*, 468.

286 "No. They hit": FLMF, box 8.

286 By April 28, according to U.S. Air Force: Tobin, Laehr, and Hilgenberg, *Last Flight from Saigon*, 45.

286   Ken Moorefield felt responsible: Moorefield, interviews.

287   Moorefield walked back: Ibid.

287   After the attack ended: Engelmann, *Tears Before the Rain,* 141–42.

288   Moorefield rounded up: Moorefield, interviews.

288   Jake Jacobson convened: Snepp, *Decent Interval,* 473–74.

CHAPTER 18: FREQUENT WIND

289   "How are things going, guys?": Moorefield, interviews.

289   Sergeant Maloney found them: Maloney, "Sgt. Kevin Maloney's Fall of Saigon."

289   Before the day ended: John W. Finney, "Viet Cong Attack on Airport," *New York Times,* April 29, 1975, 1.

290   "Call up the Communist": Madison, interview.

290   Stuart Herrington ran: Herrington, interview; Herrington, *Peace with Honor?,* 171.

290   One shell exploded so close: Ibid.

291   "If they refuse": Madison, interview.

291   As Ky was leaving: Butler, *Fall of Saigon,* 400; Ky, *Twenty Years and Twenty Days,* 229.

291   Ross Meador and the Vietnamese nurse: Meador, interview.

291   Jim Parker woke: Parker, interview; Parker, *Last Man Out,* 305–7.

292   Air America pilot Marius Burke: Burke, interview; Burke, "Vietnam Report: Part Two—Saigon Evacuation."

292   Don Hays, the young diplomat: Hays, interview.

293   NSA head of station: Glenn, interview; Glenn, "Bitter Memories," 17.

293   Tom Polgar, who had bet: Butler, *Fall of Saigon,* 384.

293   At 7:30 a.m., Martin received: Ibid., 385.

293   "In view of the above": FLMF, box 8.

293   The National Security Council convened: FLNSA-Meet, April 28, 1975.

294   Kissinger cabled Martin: *FRUS,* 271.

294   He met in his office: Snepp, *Decent Interval;* Todd, *Cruel April,* 349–50; Dawson, *55 Days,* 328–29.

296   Jacobson wanted Martin: Snepp, *Decent Interval,* 483.

296   Jacobson warned him that Vietcong: Butler, *Fall of Saigon,* 388; DBC, box 4, folders 7–8.

296   As columns of black smoke: DBC, box 4, folders 7–8.

296   Martin turned to Colonel: Butler, *Fall of Saigon,* 390; Hung, *Palace File,* 325.

297   Smith broke in: Pilger, *Last Day,* 72.

297   Martin asked to confer: DBC, box 4, folders 7–8; Butler, *Fall of Saigon,* 390.

297   "If we can't": DBC, box 4, folders 7–8; Butler, *Fall of Saigon,* 390.

297   Erich von Marbod had been sitting: Von Marbod, interview.

297   "You have friends": Ibid.; Snepp, *Decent Interval,* 489.

298   Colonel Madison thought: Madison, interview.

298 Sporadic Communist artillery shells: Herrington, *Peace with Honor?*, 173–74.
299 He called Smith to report: Butler, *Fall of Saigon,* 391.
299 Martin called Kissinger: *FRUS,* 270.
299 "I repeat my request": Kissinger, *Crisis,* 530–31.
300 "The President insists": FLMF, box 8.
300 Martin argued that he should remain: Dawson, *55 Days,* 344.
300 During the National Security Council. FLNSA-Meet, April 28, 1975.
300 After learning about the delay: Kissinger, *Crisis,* 532.
300 The JMT was unpacking: Madison, interview; Herrington, interview.
300 Herrington looked out a window: Herrington, interview.
301 Herrington, Bell, Madison, and Summers: Sources for JMT at the embassy: Herrington, Madison, and Bell, interviews; Bell, *Leave No Man Behind,* 104–5; Herrington, *Peace with Honor?,* 176–78; Summers, "Bitter End," 70.
301 "Every one of you folks": Pilger, *Last Day,* 88.
301 Herrington had written: Herrington, interview.
302 "There is plenty of time!": Wallace, *River of Destiny,* 29–30.
032 They were promising to evacuate Thu Minh Nguyen: Katie Baker, "Remembering the Fall of Saigon and Vietnam's Mass 'Boat People' Exodus," *Daily Beast,* April 30, 2014, thedailybeast.com.
303 They were promising to evacuate Y. I. Ching: Dawson, *55 Days,* 339.
303 They were promising to evacuate Binh Pho: Wallace, *River of Destiny,* 28–29.
304 "Hey everybody, stay in line": Ibid., 29.
304 Martin had ordered that the evacuation: Snepp, *Decent Interval,* 543.

CHAPTER 19: KEN MOOREFIELD'S ODYSSEY
305 When rockets began: Sources for Moorefield assembling convoy and making his first run: Moorefield, interviews; Santoli, *To Bear Any Burden,* 234–35; Butler, *Fall of Saigon,* 398–99; Maloney, "Sgt. Kevin Maloney's Fall of Saigon," 5; Engelmann, *Tears Before the Rain,* 143.
306 They returned to find: Moorefield, interviews; Butler, *Fall of Saigon,* 423–24; Santoli, *To Bear Any Burden,* 235.
306 The dispatcher radioed: Moorefield, interviews.
307 At Newport earlier that morning: Ryder, interview; MSC.
307 The LST cast off: Ryder, interview; MSC.
307 Martin and Jacobson feared: Moorefield, interviews; Snepp, *Decent Interval,* 504.
308 They never resurfaced: Ryder, interview.
308 His tug pulled its barge: Ibid.
308 AID officer Mel Chatman: Chatman, interview.
309 "Sir, with all due respect": Engelmann, *Tears Before the Rain,* 127.
309 After returning to the French embassy: Butler, *Fall of Saigon,* 407; DBC, box 4, file 7.

309 After leaving Martin's residence: Source for Moorefield in the streets: Moorefield, interviews.

310 One of these buses had collected: Engelmann, *Tears Before the Rain,* 163–64, 174–76, 189–96; Hoffmann, *On Their Own,* 373.

311 After becoming separated: Engelmann, *Tears Before the Rain,* 175.

311 Ed Bradley thought: Ibid.

311 Ken Kashiwahara noticed: Ibid., 163–65.

311 As they were leaving: Ibid., 175.

311 DAO intelligence operative: Kieff, interview.

312 A female Vietnamese passenger: Engelmann, *Tears Before the Rain,* 192–96.

312 "The Dodgers won": Ibid., 165.

312 Keyes Beech tried entering: Ibid., 192–96.

312 Moorefield abandoned his sedan: Moorefield, interviews.

313 Joe McBride returned: McBride, interview.

313 "Martin thinks there will be": Ibid.

313 By the time McBride returned: Source for McBride at embassy: Ibid.

315 CBS bureau chief Brian Ellis: Ellis, interview.

315 "Look, I've decided it may be time": Ibid.

315 Many of the Vietnamese: Manyon, *Fall of Saigon,* 110.

315 John Bennett, the acting director: ADST, John T. Bennett.

316 A reporter picked up: Pilger, *Last Day,* 86.

316 Truong's odyssey had been as frantic: Truong, interview.

318 Carey had already tangled: TTU/OH, Lieutenant General Richard E. Carey, 471.

319 Hours before Gray flew: Ibid.

319 Gray was as tough: Gray, interview; Santoli, *Everything We Had,* 14–16, 69–70.

319 While briefing his officers: Santoli, *Everything We Had,* 90.

319 He repeated this admonition: Gray, interview.

319 In reply, Hays had gestured: Sources for Hays at Tan Son Nhut: Hays, interview; Butler, *Fall of Saigon,* 396–97; DBC, box 3, folder 48.

321 The MPs fired warning shots: TTU/OH, Lieutenant General Richard E. Carey, 473–75; Dunham and Quinlan, *U.S. Marines in Vietnam,* 181; Snepp, *Decent Interval,* 511, 531.

321 Instead of monitoring: Gray, interview.

321 Among these pilots was Marius Burke: Burke, interview.

322 Before Harnage began making pickups: Harnage, *Thousand Faces,* 156–58.

322 He had acted instinctively: Ibid., 121–24; Bernstein, "This Week O. B. Harnage Remembers America's Last Day in Vietnam."

323 After Air America pilots: George Taylor, correspondence with author.

323 Air America helicopters landed on the roof: Source for Martindale on roof: Martindale, interviews.

325 Throughout the afternoon: Camp, *Assault from the Sky,* 221.

325 Military intelligence agent Nelson Kieff: Kieff, interview; Snepp, *Decent Interval,* 536–37.

326 As their helicopter rose over: Gembara, interview.

CHAPTER 20: INTO THE SOUTH CHINA SEA

327 Soon after 10:00 a.m.: McNamara, interview; ADST, McNamara, 138–40; Butler, *Fall of Saigon,* 394–95.

328 During a last sweep: McNamara, *Escape with Honor,* 142.

328 Soon after Hasty arrived: McNamara, interview.

329 Years later he would call: McNamara, *Escape with Honor,* 138.

329 What really happened: Parker, *Vietnam War,* 504–5; Parker, *Last Man Out,* 311–12.

329 The Vietnamese crew: Kassebaum, interview; ADST, McNamara, 143–44.

330 Mud began appearing: McNamara, *Escape with Honor,* 146–49; ADST, McNamara, 144–45; McNamara, interview.

330 Richard Armitage drove: Armitage, interview.

330 Kiem summoned his captains: Do and Kane, *Counterpart,* 204.

331 Terry McNamara gunned: Sources for McNamara heading down the Bassac: McNamara, Whitten, and Kassebaum, interviews; ADST, McNamara, 145–52; McNamara, *Escape with Honor,* 146–47.

333 The *Boo Heung Pioneer* reached: Ryder, interview; MSC; Lee and Haynsworth, *White Christmas in April,* 180–81.

334 Captain Flink woke: Parker, interview.

334 After transferring his refugees: Ryder, interview.

335 Parker knew it was too late: Sources for Parker's rescue mission at Vung Tau: Parker, interview; Parker, *Vietnam War,* 510–17; Parker, *Last Man Out,* 316–26.

336 Some of the passengers: Sources for Lem Truong's voyage: Truong, interview; Truong, unpublished memoir provided to the author.

336 Richard Armitage left on one of the last: Armitage, interview; Herman, *Lucky Few,* 54, 62.

337 At dawn on May 1: Mann, *Rise of the Vulcans,* 51–52; Herman, *Lucky Few,* 109–12.

337 Erich von Marbod had left: Von Marbod, interview.

338 The Pentagon awarded him: Willenson, *Bad War,* 334.

CHAPTER 21: THE 420

339 Once Ken Moorefield got inside: Sources for Moorefield at the embassy: Moorefield, interviews; Santoli, *To Bear Any Burden,* 236–37; Butler, *Fall of Saigon,* 428–29, 434–35, 440–41; DBC, box 4, folder 12.

339 "If only we hadn't cut off": Santoli, *To Bear Any Burden,* 237.

340 Martin emerged from his inner office: McArthur, "It Became Sinful."

340 "Well, the smart ones": LDE, "George McArthur's Vietnam."

341 Several days earlier, after learning: Willenson, *Bad War,* 314.

341 "If I ever hear you say": Engelmann, *Tears Before the Rain,* 130.

341 "Can't you tell him": *FRUS,* 273.

341 Kissinger later said that he and Ford: Ibid.

341 He spent several hours: Association of Former Intelligence Officers, *Periscope Newsletter,* April 2005, 29.

341 Ford watched updates: Cannon, *Time and Chance,* 372.

341 "I'm the only Secretary of State": Nessen, *It Sure Looks Different from the Inside,* 110.

342 "If we give you another": Ibid.

342 "The good news": Ibid.

342 Twenty-six members of the congressional leadership: *FRUS,* 276.

343 At 9:41 p.m., Martin received: FLMF, box 10.

343 "Perhaps you can tell me": *FRUS,* 275.

343 "I can't come out until": Butler, *Fall of Saigon,* 439.

344 "Among Americans here": FLMF, box 10.

344 "Defense promises 30 CH-53s": Ibid.

344 "IBM headquarters reports": Ibid.

344 "I understand that 154 IBM employees": Ibid.

344 Martin read Rumsfeld's cable: Butler, *Fall of Saigon,* 440.

344 "they carry about two-fifths": FLMF, box 10.

344 "We need the capacity": *FRUS,* 277.

345 "Who in the hell": TTU/OH, Richard Carey, 498.

345 A similar drama was unfolding: Ibid.

345 "I will personally see": Ibid.

346 "Ladies and gentlemen, please be quiet": SBE; Herrington, interview.

346 The pushing and shoving: Ibid.

347 Shortly after midnight Martin came: Madison, interview.

347 "That's fine. There's no need to worry": Wallace, *River of Destiny,* 31.

347 Kissinger told Schlesinger: Kissinger, *Crisis,* 538.

348 "I have been directed to send you": FLMF, box 10.

348 He had driven from breakfast: Meador, interview.

349 Martin appeared around 3:30 a.m.: Engelmann, *Tears,* 472; Madison, interview; Snepp, *Decent Interval,* 558.

349 Madison called Lehmann: Madison, interview.

349 "*Jesus,*" Madison said: Ibid.; Butler, *Fall of Saigon,* 445.

349 Lehmann called back: Madison, interview; Butler, *Fall of Saigon,* 445.

349 Martin's request for: Butler, *Fall of Saigon,* 444.

350 Vice Admiral Steele, who commanded: Dunham and Quinlan, *U.S. Marines in Vietnam,* 199.

350 "busily engaged in holding back": Willenson, *Bad War,* 344.

350 At 4:30 a.m., after learning: TTU/OH, Richard Carey, 500.

351 Knowing that his transmission: Engelmann, *Tears Before the Rain,* 131–32.

351 Kean walked downstairs: Butler, *Fall of Saigon,* 446.

351 He had already received: FLOHP, Nessen, 21.

351 Replying to Kean: Butler, *Fall of Saigon*, 446.

352 Moorefield volunteered to replace him: Moorefield, interviews.

352 "Mr. Ambassador, they say": Ibid.; Snepp, *Decent Interval*, 559.

352 "I'm not leaving": Madison, interview; Herrington, interview; Herrington, *Peace with Honor?*, 185–86.

353 Madison went from one man: Madison, interview; Herrington, interview; Herrington, *Peace with Honor?*, 185–86.

353 Herrington briefly considered: Herrington, interview; Herrington, *Peace with Honor?*, 186.

353 A plaque in the lobby: Herrington, *Peace with Honor?*, 186.

354 Herrington saw the abandoned: Herrington, interview; Herrington, *Peace with Honor?*, 187.

354 There was architecture student: Wallace, *River of Destiny*, 31.

354 She had been at the top: Baker, "Remembering the Fall of Saigon and Vietnam's Mass 'Boat People' Exodus."

354 Also left behind: Hoang, *Boat People*, 100–101.

356 "You may hear after you leave": *Reporting Vietnam*, 728.

356 Stuart Herrington struggled to find: Herrington, *Peace with Honor?*, 187.

356 "the faces of those": Herrington, interview.

EPILOGUE

357 "Do you know what": Engelmann, *Tears Before the Rain*, 103.

357 "They lied to us": *Reporting Vietnam*, 746.

357 "If I had known that": Madison, interview.

357 "The fleet thought": LDE, "Harry Summers Remembers the Fall of Saigon."

357 "We've got to get this betrayal": Madison, interview.

358 In a 2003 report commissioned: "The Fight for the High Ground: The U.S. Army and Interrogation During Operation Iraqi Freedom," May 2003–April 2004.

358 In 1996, Henry Kissinger watched: Kissinger, *Ending the Vietnam War*, 552–53.

358 Bill Bell was posted: Bell, interview.

358 Walter Martindale spent the next seven months: Martindale, interviews and email correspondence.

359 "There was so much life": Santoli, *To Bear Any Burden*, 334–35.

360 He wrote an account: McNamara, *Escape with Honor*, dedication page.

360 "You know, who the hell am I": Ryder, interview.

360 After returning to Washington: Rounsevell, interview.

360 Martin had interrupted and said: DBC, box 4, file 7–9.

360 During a 1976 congressional hearing: *VCE*, Part III, 610.

361 Martin told an oral historian: Willenson, *Bad War*, 334.

361 Four months after leaving: Bong-Wright, interview; Bong-Wright, *Autumn Cloud*, 230.

361 The Communists arrested: Truong, interview and unpublished memoir.

362 According to a handsome: Wallace, *River of Destiny,* flap copy.

362 "I still grieve over those": Douglas Brinkley, "Of Ladders and Letters," *Time,* April 24, 2000.

362 Henry Kissinger held a press conference: "Excerpts from News Briefing by Kissinger," *New York Times,* April 30, 1975, 17.

363 A Gallup poll released: William Greider, "Enmity to Refugees Puzzling," *Washington Post,* May 3, 1975, 1.

363 "an extraordinary callousness": Ibid.

363 Several days after the fall: Associated Press, "Refugee Return Urged by McGovern," *Washington Post,* May 4, 1975, A19.

364 "a last poisonous convulsion": Greider, "Enmity to Refugees Puzzling."

364 Nathan Glazer, the co-author: Ibid.

364 "The administration believes": Lawrence Meyer, "U.S. to Accept All 70,000 of Self-Evacuated Refugees," *Washington Post,* May 2, 1975, A1.

364 "What's he studying?": Jackie Bong-Wright, interview.

365 "Henry spent twenty-five of those minutes": DBC, box 4, files 7–9.

365 Martin told a congressional committee: *VCE,* Part III, 544.

365 "During the last couple of weeks": Willenson, *Bad War,* 325.

365 Twelve hours before Martin left: Sources for Martin and the Saigon embassy papers: Gregory F. Rose, "The Stolen Secrets of Vietnam," *New York,* Nov. 27, 1978, 73–79; George McArthur, "Bonanza of Secrets in Files on Saigon," *Los Angeles Times,* Sept. 17, 1978, 2; Charles R. Babcock, "Graham Martin Won't Be Prosecuted," *Washington Post,* March 31, 1979, A3.

366 Martin never received: Martindale, interviews and email correspondence with author.

366 Duc Van Mai was one of the news agency: Ellis, interview; Ellis, unpublished manuscript.

Bibliography

BOOKS

Appy, Christian G. *Patriots: The Vietnam War Remembered from All Sides.* New York: Viking Penguin, 2003.

Arnett, Peter. *Live from the Battlefield: From Vietnam to Baghdad—35 Years in the World's War Zones.* New York: Simon & Schuster, 1994.

Baker, Mark. *Nam: The Vietnam War in the Words of the Men and Women Who Fought There.* New York: Morrow, 1981.

Bamford, James. *Body of Secrets: Anatomy of the Ultra-secret NSA.* New York: Doubleday, 2001.

Bell, Garnett "Bill." *Leave No Man Behind: Bill Bell and the Search for American POW/MIAs from the Vietnam War.* With George J. Veith. Madison, Wis.: Goblin Fern Press, 2004.

Berman, Larry. *No Peace, No Honor: Nixon, Kissinger, and Betrayal in Vietnam.* New York: Free Press, 2001.

Bissell, Tom. *The Father of All Things: A Marine, His Son, and the Legacy of Vietnam.* New York: Pantheon Books, 2007.

Bong-Wright, Jackie. *Autumn Cloud: From Vietnamese War Widow to American Activist.* Sterling, Va.: Capital Books, 2001.

Brinkley, Douglas. *Gerald R. Ford.* New York: Times Books, 2007.

Browne, Malcolm W. *Muddy Boots and Red Socks: A Reporter's Life.* New York: Times Books, 1993.

Butler, David. *The Fall of Saigon.* New York: Simon & Schuster, 1985.

Camp, Dick. *Assault from the Sky.* Havertown, Pa.: Casemate, 2013.

Cannon, James. *Gerald R. Ford: An Honorable Life.* Ann Arbor: University of Michigan Press, 2013.

———. *Time and Chance: Gerald Ford's Appointment with History*. Ann Arbor: University of Michigan Press, 1998.

Caputo, Philip. *Means of Escape*. New York: HarperCollins, 1991.

Clark, Allen B. *Valor in Vietnam, 1963–1977: Chronicles of Honor, Courage, and Sacrifice*. Havertown, Pa.: Casemate, 2012.

Clark, Cherie. *After Sorrow Comes Joy: One Woman's Struggle to Bring Hope to Thousands of Children in Vietnam and India*. Westminster, Colo.: Lawrence and Thomas, 2000.

Colby, William. *Lost Victory: A Firsthand Account of America's Sixteen-Year Involvement in Vietnam*. With James McCargar. Chicago: Contemporary Books, 1989.

Corn, David. *Blond Ghost: Ted Shackley and the CIA's Crusades*. New York: Simon & Schuster, 1994.

Dawson, Alan. *55 Days: The Fall of South Vietnam*. Englewood Cliffs, N.J.: Prentice-Hall, 1977.

DeForest, Orrin, and David Chanoff. *Slow Burn: The Rise and Bitter Fall of American Intelligence in Vietnam*. New York: Simon & Schuster, 1990.

DeFrank, Thomas M. *Write It When I'm Gone: Remarkable Off-the-Record Conversations with Gerald R. Ford*. New York: Putnam, 2007.

Do, Kiem, and Julie Kane. *Counterpart: A South Vietnamese Naval Officer's War*. Annapolis, Md.: Naval Institute Press, 1998.

Doland, Gil. *Legacy of Discord: Voices of the Vietnam War Era*. Washington, D.C.: Potomac Books, 2001.

Dougan, Clark, and David Fulghum. *The Fall of the South*. Boston: Boston Publishing Group, 1985.

Drury, Bob, and Tom Clavin. *Last Men Out: The True Story of America's Heroic Final Hours in Vietnam*. New York: Free Press, 2011.

Dung, Van Tien. *Our Great Spring Victory: An Account of the Liberation of South Vietnam*. New York: Monthly Review Press, 1977.

Dunham, George R., and David A. Quinlan. *U.S. Marines in Vietnam: The Bitter End, 1973–1975*. CreateSpace Independent Publishing Platform, 2013.

Emerson, Gloria. Introduction to *War Torn: Stories of War from the Women Reporters Who Covered Vietnam*. New York: Random House, 2002.

Engelmann, Larry. *Tears Before the Rain: An Oral History of the Fall of South Vietnam*. New York: Oxford University Press, 1990.

Esper, George. *Eyewitness History of the Vietnam War, 1961–1975*. New York: Ballantine Books, 1986.

Feltham, Dan E. *When Big Blue Went to War: The History of the IBM Corporation's Mission in Southeast Asia During the Vietnam War (1965–1975)*. Bloomington, Ind.: Abbott Press, 2012.

Fenton, James. *All the Wrong Places: Adrift in the Politics of the Pacific Rim*. New York: Atlantic Monthly Press, 1988.

———. *The Fall of Saigon*. New York: Granta, 1985.

Ford, Gerald R. *A Time to Heal: The Autobiography of Gerald R. Ford*. New York: Harper & Row, 1979.

Gayler, Noel. *The Reminiscences of Admiral Noel A. M. Gayler, U.S. Navy (Retired)*. Annapolis, Md.: U.S. Naval Institute, 2012.

Greene, Graham. *The Quiet American*. New York: Viking Press, 1956.

———. *Ways of Escape: An Autobiography*. New York: Simon & Schuster, 1980.

Haley, P. Edward. *Congress and the Fall of South Vietnam and Cambodia*. Rutherford, N.J.: Fairleigh Dickinson University Press, 1982.

Harnage, Oren B. *A Thousand Faces*. Victoria, B.C.: Trafford, 2002.

Hartmann, Robert T. *Palace Politics: An Inside Account of the Ford Years*. New York: McGraw-Hill, 1980.

Henderson, Charles. *Goodnight Saigon: The True Story of the U.S. Marines' Last Days in Vietnam*. New York: Berkeley, 2005.

Herman, Jan K. *The Lucky Few: The Fall of Saigon and the Rescue Mission of the USS Kirk*. Annapolis, Md.: Naval Institute Press, 2013.

Herrington, Stuart. *Peace with Honor? An American Reports on Vietnam, 1973–75*. Novato, Calif.: Presidio, 1983.

———. *Stalking the Vietcong: Inside Operation Phoenix: A Personal Account*. New York: Ballantine Books, 1987.

Herschensohn, Bruce. *An America Amnesia: How the U.S. Congress Forced the Surrenders of South Vietnam and Cambodia*. New York: Beaufort Books, 2010.

Hoang, Carina, ed. *Boat People: Personal Stories from the Vietnamese Exodus, 1975–1996*. New York: Beaufort Books, 2013.

Hoffmann, Joyce. *On Their Own: Women Journalists and the American Experience in Vietnam*. New York: Da Capo Press, 2008.

Hosmer, Stephen T., Konrad Kellen, and Brian M. Jenkins. *The Fall of South Vietnam: Statements by Vietnamese Military and Civilian Leaders*. New York: Crane, Russak, 1980.

Hung, Nguyen Tien. *The Palace File*. New York: Harper & Row, 1986.

Isaacs, Arnold. *Without Honor: Defeat in Vietnam and Cambodia*. Baltimore: Johns Hopkins University Press, 1983.

Isaacson, Walter. *Kissinger: A Biography*. New York: Simon & Schuster, 1992.

Kassebaum, Cary. *I Never Pushed a Cookie: The Foreign Service You Never Knew*. CreateSpace Independent Publishing Platform, 1996.

Kennerly, David Hume. *Extraordinary Circumstances: The Presidency of Gerald R. Ford*. Austin: Center for American History, University of Texas at Austin, 2007.

————. *Photo Op: A Pulitzer Prize–Winning Photographer Covers Events That Shaped Our Times*. Austin: University of Texas Press, 1995.

————. *Shooter*. New York: Newsweek Books, 1979.

Kimball, Jeffrey. *The Vietnam War Files*. Lawrence: University Press of Kansas, 2004.

Kissinger, Henry. *Crisis: The Anatomy of Two Major Foreign Policy Crises*. New York: Simon & Schuster, 2003.

————. *Diplomacy*. New York: Simon & Schuster, 1994.

————. *Ending the Vietnam War: A History of America's Involvement in and Extrication from the Vietnam War*. New York: Simon & Schuster, 2003.

————. *Years of Renewal*. New York: Simon & Schuster, 1999.

Ky, Nguyen Cao. *Twenty Years and Twenty Days*. New York: Stein and Day, 1976.

Lee, J. Edward, and H. C. "Toby" Haynsworth. *Nixon, Ford, and the Abandonment of South Vietnam*. Jefferson, N.C.: McFarland, 2002.

————, eds. *White Christmas in April: The Collapse of South Vietnam, 1975*. New York: Peter Lang, 1999.

Leeker, Joe F. *Air America in South Vietnam III: The Collapse*. Dallas: University of Texas ebook, 2008.

LeGro, William E. *Vietnam from Cease-Fire to Capitulation*. Washington, D.C.: U.S. Army Center of Military History, 1981.

Loescher, Gil, and John A. Scanlan. *Calculated Kindness: Refugees and America's Half-Open Door, 1945–Present*. New York: Free Press, 1986.

Mann, James. *Rise of the Vulcans: The History of Bush's War Cabinet*. New York: Viking, 2004.

Manyon, Julian. *The Fall of Saigon*. London: Rex Collings, 1975.

Maurer, Harry. *Strange Ground: Americans in Vietnam, 1945–1975, an Oral History*. New York: Henry Holt, 1989.

McNamara, Francis Terry. *Escape with Honor: My Last Hours in Vietnam*. Washington, D.C.: Brassey's, 1997.

Nessen, Ron. *It Sure Looks Different from the Inside*. Chicago: Playboy Press, 1978.

Oberdorfer, Don. *Tet!* Garden City, N.Y.: Doubleday, 1971.

Parker, James E., Jr. *Last Man Out*. New York: Ballantine Books, 1996.

————. *The Vietnam War: Its Ownself*. N.p.: James E. Parker Jr., 2015.

Peck-Barnes, Shirley. *The War Cradle: Vietnam's Children of War: Operation Babylift—the Untold Story*. Denver: Vintage Pressworks, 2000.

Pilger, John. *The Last Day*. New York: Vintage Books, 1976.

Porter, D. Gareth. *A Peace Denied: The United States, Vietnam, and the Paris Agreement*. Bloomington: Indiana University Press, 1975.

Reporting Vietnam: American Journalism, 1959–1975. New York: Library of America, 1998.

Robbins, Christopher. *Air America.* New York: Putnam, 1979.

Santoli, Al. *Everything We Had: An Oral History of the Vietnam War by Thirty-Three American Soldiers Who Fought It.* New York: Random House, 1981.

———. *To Bear Any Burden: The Vietnam War and Its Aftermath in the Words of Americans and Southeast Asians.* New York: Dutton, 1985.

Schwarz, George W., Jr. *April Fools: An American Remembers South Viet Nam's Final Days.* Baltimore: AmErica House, 2001.

Snepp, Frank. *Decent Interval: An Insider's Account of Saigon's Indecent End Told by the CIA's Chief Strategy Analyst in Vietnam.* New York: Random House, 1977.

Stebbins, Tom. *Hand in Glove: Memoirs of How God's Hand in My Life Made a Difference.* Deland, Fla.: Winning, 2009.

Sullivan, John F. *Gatekeeper: Memoirs of a CIA Polygraph Examiner.* Washington, D.C.: Potomac Books, 2007.

———. *Of Spies and Lies: A CIA Lie Detector Remembers Vietnam.* Lawrence: University Press of Kansas, 2002.

Summers, Harry G. *On Strategy: A Critical Analysis of the Vietnam War.* Novato, Calif.: Presidio Press, 1982.

Swain, Jon. *Rivers of Time: A Memoir of Vietnam and Cambodia.* New York: St. Martin's Press, 1997.

Taylor, Liz. *Dust of Life: Children of the Saigon Streets.* London: Hamish Hamilton, 1977.

Taylor, Thomas. *Where the Orange Blooms: One Man's War and Escape in Vietnam.* New York: McGraw-Hill, 1989.

Terzani, Tiziano. *Giai Phong! The Fall and Liberation of Saigon.* New York: St. Martin's Press, 1976.

Toai, Doan Van, and David Chanoff. *The Vietnamese Gulag.* New York: Simon & Schuster, 1986.

Tobin, Thomas G., Arthur E. Laehr, and John F. Hilgenberg. *Last Flight from Saigon.* Washington, D.C.: U.S. Government Printing Office, 1978.

Todd, Olivier. *Cruel April: The Fall of Saigon.* New York: Norton, 1990.

Trest, Warren A. *Air Commando One: Heinie Aderholt and America's Secret Air Wars.* Washington, D.C.: Smithsonian Institute Press, 2000.

Tull, Theresa Anne. *A Long Way from Runnemede: One Woman's Foreign Service Journey.* Washington, D.C.: VELLUM/New Academia, 2012.

Turley, Gerald H. *The Journey of a Warrior: The Twenty-Ninth Commandant of the U.S. Marine Corps (1987–1991): General Alfred Mason Gray.* Bloomington, Ind.: iUniverse, 2012.

Utley, Garrick. *You Should Have Been Here Yesterday: A Life in Television News.* New York: PublicAffairs, 2000.

Veith, George J. *Black April: The Fall of South Vietnam, 1973–75*. New York: Encounter Books, 2012.

Verrone, Richard Burks, and Laura M. Calkins. *Voices from Vietnam: Eye-Witness Accounts of the War, 1954–1975*. Newton Abbot, U.K.: David & Charles, 2005.

Vien, Cao Van. *The Final Collapse*. Honolulu: University Press of the Pacific, 2005.

Vo, Linh Duy. *To America, Love and Gratitude*. Downey, Calif.: L. D. Vo, 2000.

Wallace, Kevin. *River of Destiny: The Life and Work of Binh Pho*. Long Beach Museum of Art, 2006.

Watts, Ralph S. *Escape from Saigon: How the Church Survived the Final Days of the Vietnam War*. Nampa, Idaho: Pacific Press, 2005.

Willbanks, James H. *Abandoning Vietnam: How America Left and South Vietnam Lost Its War*. Lawrence: University Press of Kansas, 2004.

Willenson, Kim. *The Bad War: An Oral History of the Vietnam War*. With the correspondents of *Newsweek*. New York: New American Library, 1987.

Zabecki, David, ed. *Vietnam: A Reader*. New York: ibooks, 2002.

ARTICLES

Burke, Marius. "Vietnam Report: Part Two—Saigon Evacuation." *Air America Log* 1, no. 1 (1996). www.air.america.org.

Butterfield, Fox. "How Vietnam Died—by the Stab in the Front." *New York Times Magazine*, May 25, 1975.

Carey, Richard E., and D. A. Quinlan. "Frequent Wind." *Marine Corps Gazette*, Feb.–April 1976.

Fitzgerald, Frances. "Journey to North Vietnam." *New Yorker*, April 28, 1979.

Glenn, Tom. "Bitter Memories: The Fall of Saigon, April 1975." *Studies in Intelligence* 59, no. 4 (Extracts, Dec. 2015).

Hale, Richard W. "A CIA Officer in Saigon." *Vietnam Magazine*, June 2003.

Kane, Julie. "Secret Evacuation of the VNN Fleet." *Vietnam Magazine*, April 1995.

Leepson, Marc. "Escape to the Sea." *VVA Veteran*, April/May 2000.

Maloney, Kevin. "Sgt. Kevin Maloney's Fall of Saigon." Saigon Marines Association Page. fallofsaigon.org.

McArthur, George. "It Became Sinful: A Reporter's Story." *Vietnam Magazine*, April 1995.

Pilger, John. "The Fall of Saigon 1975: An Eyewitness Report." www.lewrockwell.com.

Quinn, Ken. "Integrity and Openness: Requirements for an Effective Foreign Service." *Foreign Service Journal*, Sept. 2014.

———. "From Whitehouse to the White House." *Foreign Service Journal,* April 2015.

Shaplen, Robert. "Letter from Saigon." *New Yorker,* Jan. 6, 1975.

———. "Letter from Saigon." *New Yorker,* April 21, 1975.

Shawcross, William. "Shrugging Off Genocide." *Times* (London), Dec. 16, 1994.

Smith, Homer D. "The Final Forty-Five Days in Vietnam." *Vietnam Magazine,* April 1995.

Summers, Harry G., Jr. "The Bitter End." *Vietnam Magazine,* April 1995.

ARCHIVES, MANUSCRIPTS, ORAL HISTORY COLLECTIONS, PAPERS, THESES

Association for Diplomatic Studies and Training. Foreign Affairs Oral History Collection.

Butler, David. Papers of David Butler. Rauner Special Collections Library, Dartmouth College.

Engelmann, Larry D. "Pushing On." Unpublished oral history interviews conducted by Engelmann. lde421.blogspot.com.

Gerald R. Ford Presidential Library, Ann Arbor, Mich. Archives.

Herrington, Stuart A. "The Third Indochina War, 1973–1975: A Personal Perspective." Maxwell Air Force Base, Ala., Air University, May 1980.

Texas Tech University. The Vietnam Center and Archive.

U.S. Army Military History Institute. "Last Days in Vietnam" Oral History Project, 1982. Oral Histories of Alan Carter, Wolfgang J. Lehmann, and Colonel Harry G. Summers Jr.

OFFICIAL U.S. GOVERNMENT RECORDS AND DOCUMENTS

Ahern, Thomas L., Jr. *CIA and the Generals: Covert Support to Military Government in South Vietnam.* Center for the Study of Intelligence, Central Intelligence Agency, 2008.

Hanyok, Robert J. "Spartans in Darkness: American SIGINT and the Indochina War, 1945–1975." Center for Cryptologic History, National Security Agency, 2002.

Military Sealift Command. "Activities of MSCOV During the Vietnam Evacuation." Memorandum from Acting Chief, MSC Office Saigon Residual (Bill Ryder), to Commander, Military Sealift Command, Far East, June 27, 1975. (Copy provided to the author by Bill Ryder.)

National Security Agency. *Cryptology Magazine.* "Special Issue—Vietnam," Oct. 1975.

U.S. Defense Attaché Office, Saigon, Republic of Vietnam. *End of Tour Report.* Major General Homer Smith wrote three versions of his report in 1975, marked I, II, and III.

U.S. Delegation—Four-Party Joint Military Team. *History: 31 March 1973–30 April 1975.*

U.S. Department of State: Office of the Historian. *Foreign Relations of the United States, 1969–1976, Volume X, Vietnam, January 1973–July 1975.*

U.S. Marine Corps, History and Museums Division. *Frequent Wind.*

CONGRESSIONAL HEARINGS

Emergency Military Assistance and Economic and Humanitarian Aid to South Vietnam. Hearings before the Senate Appropriations Committee. April 15, 16, 1975.

Foreign Assistance Authorization. Hearings before the Senate Committee on Foreign Relations. Testimony of Ambassador Graham Martin, July 25, 1974.

Indochina Evacuation and Refugee Problems. Hearings before the Senate Judiciary Committee, Subcommittee on Refugees and Escapees. Part 1: *Operation Babylift and Humanitarian Needs.* April 8, 1975. Part 2: *The Evacuation.* April 15, 25, 30, 1975.

Report on the Situation in the Republic of Vietnam. Hearings before the House Committee on Foreign Affairs, Subcommittee on Asian and Pacific Affairs. Testimony of Ambassador Graham Martin, July 31, 1974.

The Vietnam-Cambodia Emergency, 1975. Hearings before the House Committee on International Relations. Part I: *Vietnam Evacuation and Humanitarian Assistance.* April 9–18, 1975. Part II: *The Vietnam-Cambodia Emergency, 1975.* Hearings of March 6–13, 1975. Hearing of April 14, 1975. Part III: *Vietnam Evacuation: Testimony of Ambassador Graham A. Martin.* Hearing of Jan. 27, 1976.

Index

Illustration Credits

Page 1
Top: Courtesy of Melissa Urreiztieta
Middle: Courtesy of the Gerald R. Ford Presidential Library
Bottom: Courtesy of Bill Bell

Page 2
Top: Courtesy of Walter Martindale
Middle: Courtesy of Tom Glenn
Bottom: Courtesy of James Parker

Page 3
Top: Courtesy of Theresa Tull
Bottom left: Courtesy of Marius Burke
Bottom right: Courtesy of Ken Moorefield

Page 4
Courtesy of the Gerald R. Ford Presidential Library

Page 5
Top: Courtesy of the Gerald R. Ford Presidential Library
Bottom: Matt Franjola (courtesy of the Kennerly Archive)

Page 6
Top: Courtesy of the Gerald R. Ford Presidential Library
Bottom: Photo by Jean-Claude FRANCOLON / Gamma-Rapho via
    Getty Images

Page 7
Top: Courtesy of Bill Bell
Middle: Courtesy of Ross Meador
Bottom: Courtesy of Allan Topping

Page 8
Top: Courtesy of Le Quang Luong, ARVN Airborne
Bottom: Courtesy of the author

Page 9
Courtesy of Brian Ellis

Page 10
Courtesy of John Madison

Page 11
Courtesy of John Madison

Page 12
Top and bottom: Courtesy of Cary Kassebaum
Middle: Photo by nik wheeler / Corbis via Getty Images

Page 13
Department of Defense

Page 14
Top and bottom: Photo by nik wheeler / Corbis via Getty Images
Middle: Courtesy of John Madison

Page 15
Courtesy of John Madison

Page 16
Top: © Bettmann
Bottom: Courtesy of Theresa Tull

About the Author

Thurston Clarke has written eleven widely acclaimed works of fiction and non-fiction, including three *New York Times* Notable Books and the *New York Times* bestseller *The Last Campaign*. His *Pearl Harbor Ghosts* was the basis of a CBS documentary, and his bestselling *Lost Hero,* a biography of Raoul Wallenberg, was made into an award-winning NBC miniseries. His articles have appeared in *Vanity Fair, The New York Times, The Washington Post,* and many other publications. He is the recipient of a Guggenheim Fellowship and other awards and lives in upstate New York.

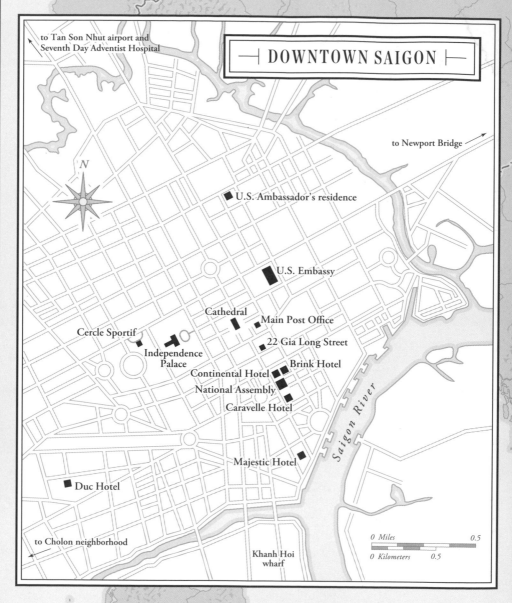

WITHDRAWN

BURMA

┤ DOWNTOWN SAIGON ├

to Tan Son Nhut airport and
Seventh Day Adventist Hospital

to Newport Bridge →

N

■ U.S. Ambassador's residence

■ U.S. Embassy

Cathedral

■ Main Post Office

Cercle Sportif

■ 22 Gia Long Street

Independence
Palace

Brink Hotel

Continental Hotel

National Assembly

Caravelle Hotel

Saigon River

Majestic Hotel ■

■ Duc Hotel

0 Miles   0.5

0 Kilometers   0.5

to Cholon neighborhood

Khanh Hoi
wharf

THAILAND   Gulf of Siam

© 2019 Jeffrey L. Ward